D1519581

MAGICAL MEDICINE

MAGICAL MEDICINE

The Folkloric Component of Medicine in the Folk Belief, Custom, and Ritual of the Peoples of Europe and America

SELECTED ESSAYS OF
WAYLAND D. HAND

FOREWORD
by LLOYD G. STEVENSON

University of California Press
Berkeley Los Angeles London

University of California Press
Berkeley and Los Angeles, California

University of California Press, Ltd.
London, England

Library of Congress Cataloging in Publication Data

Hand, Wayland Debs, 1907–
Magical medicine.

Includes index.
1. Folk medicine—Addresses, essays, lectures.
2. Medicine, Magic, mystic, and spagiric—
Addresses, essays, lectures. 3. Folk medicine—
United Staes—Addresses, essays, lectures.
4. Folk medicine—Europe—Addresses, essays,
lectures. I. Title. [DNLM: 1. Folklore—
Essays. 2. Medicine, Primitive—History—Essays.
WZ309 H236m]
GR880.H35 398'.353 80-51238
ISBN 0-520-04129-1

Printed in the United States of America

1 2 3 4 5 6 7 8 9

Dedicated to
Theodora
Alice
Paula
Esther Mae
and to the memory of
Margaret Anita
Lorraine
—nurses all

Contents

Foreword

This book puts in our hands a budget of real enchantment, and yet its rites are not for the most part subtle or complex. The union of anthropology, ethnography, and folklore in the study of medical belief and practice is devoutly to be wished, and with it, also, the history of *Schulmedizin,* which long kept, and has not altogether lost, elements of these other systems. Yet each of the cooperating endeavors must, of course, keep to its own business too. And the fascinating business of modern Western folklore, above all medical folklore, has found for itself few such numinous spots as the Center for the Study of Comparative Folklore and Mythology at the University of California at Los Angeles, where Wayland D. Hand has been serving it well for many years—in teaching, in writing, in compiling a great dictionary, and in other ways—and where many students have learned to share his zeal for its mysteries and its delights. *Magical Medicine* encompasses sacred and secular magic—major folkloric components of folk medicine—without any direct approach to primitive peoples and their beliefs and practices. This is not the desired unification; this is essentially straight folklore. And bewitching lore it is.

Now it is clear that in other hands the mingling of related themes has not always been a happy one; the genuine ethnologist has looked with some dismay, at least on occasion, at the fumblings of historians and others, whereas the professional folklorist has sometimes surveyed with lifted brows those who have wandered into his field and has found them lacking in more than diligence. In this book, however, we find diligence without dullness and professionalism without pretension in a broad and penetrating survey of folk belief, custom, and ritual. The range of source material and its critical but lively presentation and analysis will reward the folklorist, the ethnographer, and the medical historian. Professor Hand is not a healer but he has both the calling and the endowment of a born folklorist, so that we are fortunate indeed that his attention has been fixed for so many years on medical folklore. He brings to his varied tales a magic none too common in academia, and a scrupulous regard for truth and history by no means universal, of course, among magicians. Although he is fully aware of the ethnographers, aware of the medical historians, conscious of the work that is going on in fields related to his, he plows his own furrow and he obeys his own rituals. The rituals succeed: the crops flourish. Here is the harvest in a book that brings together good work heretofore widely scattered, the greater part of it not readily come by. Here we are admitted into the folklore of the Western world wherever it deals with disease, injury, and healing. Here, too, we come close to some of the unacknowledged sources of the ways that we ourselves often think, thought patterns that, although we do not share them, we recognize in the way we recognize kindred. These are ancestral voices, interpreted for us with knowledge and skill. *Magical Medicine* opens casements on another world, and yet a world that is not very far away.

Lloyd G. Stevenson

Preface

The series of articles on magical medicine drawn together in this volume grew directly out of long years of work on a standard Dictionary of American Popular Beliefs and Superstitions. *Magical Medicine* is intended to serve as a much needed counterbalance to the large body of folk medical scholarship that is largely concerned with the use of plants and other natural substances as curative agents of disease.

The essays in this volume appear just as they were written, footnotes and all. Stylistic variations, particularly in the notes, are explained by the differing editorial styles employed in various kinds of journals and *Festschriften* in which the articles were originally published.

This volume could not have been produced without the understanding of editors and publishers who have given me permission to reprint these papers. Specific bibliographical sources are given in connection with the articles themselves, but I should like to thank these keepers of the scholar's seal for realizing the advantages of making a scattered body of work available within the covers of a single volume. Some of the pieces, particularly articles appearing in European journals and memorial volumes, are not easily available in the American book trade.

For financial backing reaching back more than a decade, I am indebted to The National Endowment for the Humanities, The National Institutes of Health, and the National Library of Medicine. The Research Committee of the University of California at Los Angeles has backed my various research enterprises in the field of popular beliefs and superstitions since the 1940s, so it will come as no surprise that some of the most useful items in the present series of writings came to light in those early gleanings from the technical literature. My colleagues on this committee over many years' time know of my debt to the University of California for its loyal backing of my work throughout a long career.

To my colleagues in the field of folk medicine, Elizabeth Brandon, Austin E. Fife, Thomas R. Forbes, David Hufford, Joe S. Graham, Byrd Howell Granger, Douglas B. Price, Samuel X. Radbill, Charles H. Talbot, Don Yoder, and the late John Q. Anderson I wish to express my thanks for their help and encouragement; also to the participants in the historic UCLA Conference on American Folk Medicine in 1973.

Finally to my sternest critics, my research assistants and my students, I owe much for their support and devotion. Remembered with affection are Anna Casetta, Reba Bass, Sondra Thiederman, Linda Painter, and countless others over thirty years' time who searched laboriously for the research materials that found their way into these pages. Frances M. Tally and Jeannine E. Talley, working under a grant from The National Institutes of Health, compiled a bibliography of folk medicine from the earliest bibliography of the Surgeon-General's Office in 1880 through the volumes of the great multivolume *Index Medicus* for 1974. These researchers pursued references under a variety of headings: theurgic medicine, medical folklore, magic, primitive medicine, superstition, and so on, and later extracted folk medical entries from the most useful titles. This tremendous resource, coupled with deposits on folk medicine in the *Dictionary* files, gives UCLA's Center for the Study of Comparative Folklore and Mythology a collection of folk medicine from Europe and America that is unrivaled anywhere.

For her understanding of the importance of my research, and for needed forbearance during the many busy periods when these articles were being written, I should like to thank my wife Celeste. As is her wont, once again with this book she has done yeoman service with the proofs, using her considerable linguistic talents in foreign languages as well as in English to help me guard against errors and infelicities of style.

This volume goes forth with the hope that folk medical studies, whether carried on by medical practitioners, behavioral scientists of various kinds, and workers in the field of folklore, will help to make medical folklorists useful members of the scientific community.

Wayland D. Hand

Los Angeles
Epiphany, 1979

Selected Bibliography

Bibliographic references to articles in this volume have been drawn together from many sources. These individual entries come from books, monographs, articles, short notes, and single items gleaned from collections of folk beliefs large and small. It is obvious that the hundreds of sources in the footnotes cannot be gathered together into a bibliography of reasonable compass; hence the need for a selected bibliography of the principal works. Over and above this there are a few articles dealing with magical medicine itself. A list of abbreviations of journals and monographic series will make easier the handling of condensed references here and throughout the volume.

ABBREVIATIONS

ANQ *American Notes and Queries.* New York, 1941–1950.

Brown Coll. Brown, Frank C. *North Carolina Folklore,* ed. Paull Franklin Baum. 7 vols. Durham, N.C., 1952–1964. Hand, Wayland D., ed. *Popular Beliefs and Superstitions from North Carolina*, constituting vols. 6 and 7 (1961–1964).

CFQ *California Folklore Quarterly.* Berkeley and Los Angeles, 1942–1946. See *Western Folklore.*

FFC Folklore Fellows Communications. Helsinki, 1910 ff.

GB Frazer, James George. *The Golden Bough.* 3d ed., 12 vols. London, 1911–1915.

HDA *Handwörterbuch des deutschen Aberglaubens*, ed. Eduard von Hoffmann-Krayer and Hanns Bächtold-Stäubli. 10 vols. Berlin and Leipzig, 1927–1942.

HF *Hoosier Folklore.* Bloomington, Ind., 1946–1950. Continuation of *HFB.*

HFB *Hoosier Folklore Bulletin.* Bloomington, Ind., 1942–1945. See *HF.*

JAF *Journal of American Folklore.* Boston, 1888 ff.

KFG *Keystone Folklore Quarterly.* Lewisburg, Pa., 1956 ff.

KFR *Kentucky Folklore Record.* Bowling Green, Ky., 1955 ff.

MF *Midwest Folklore.* Bloomington, Ind., 1951 ff.

NCF *North Carolina Folklore.* Chapel Hill, N.C., 1948 ff.

NYFQ *New York Folklore Quarterly.* Ithaca, N.Y., 1945 ff.

PADS Publications of the American Dialect Society. Greensboro, N.C., 1944 ff.

PTFS Publications of the Texas Folklore Society. Austin, 1916 ff.

SFQ *Southern Folklore Quarterly.* Gainesville, Fla., 1937 ff.

TFSB *Tennessee Folklore Society Bulletin.* Maryville, Tenn., 1935 ff.

WF *Western Folklore.* Berkeley and Los Angeles, 1947 ff. (Succeeding the *California Folklore Quarterly* after Vol. 5.)

WVF *West Virginia Folklore,* Fairmont, W.Va., 1951 ff.

Allen, John W. *Legends and Lore of Southern Illinois.* Carbondale, Ill., 1963.

Anderson, John Q. "Magical Transference of Disease in Texas Folk Medicine," *WF*, 27 (1968), 191–199.

______. *Texas Folk Medicine: 1,333 Cures, Remedies, Preventives & Health Practices.* Austin, 1970.

Aurand, A. Monroe, Jr. *Popular Home Remedies and Superstitions of the Pennsylvania Germans.* Harrisburg, 1941.

______. *The Pow-Wow Book. A Treatise on the Art of "Healing by Prayer" and "Laying on of Hands," etc., Practiced by the Pennsylvania Germans and Others, etc.* Harrisburg, 1929.

Baker, Pearl and Ruth Wilcox. "Folk Remedies in Early Green River," *Utah Humanities Review*, 2 (1948), 191–192.

Bakker, C. *Volksgeneeskunde in Waterland: een Vergelijkende Studie met de Geneeskunde der Grieken en Romeinen.* Amsterdam, 1928.

Barriola, Ignacio Maria. *La Medicina popular en el pais vasco.* San Sebastian, 1952.

Bartels, Paul. "Durchziehkur in Winkel am Rhein," *Zeitschrift des Vereins für Volkskunde,* 23 (1913), 288–293.

Bayard, Samuel P. "Witchcraft Magic and Spirits on the Border of Pennsylvania and West Virginia," *JAF*, 51 (1938), 47–59.

Berdau, Emil. "Der Mond in Volksmedizin, Sitte und Gebräuchen der mexikanischen Grenzbewohnerschaft des südlichen Texas," *Globus*, 88 (1905), 381–384.

Bergen, Fanny D. *Animal and Plant Lore Collected from the Oral Tradition of English Speaking Folk.* MAFS, 7. Boston and New York, 1899.

______. *Current Superstitions Collected from the Oral Tradition of English Speaking Folk.* MAFS, 4. Boston and New York, 1896.

______. "Some Bits of Plant Lore," *JAF*, 5 (1892), 19–22.

______. "Some Saliva Charms," *JAF*, 3 (1890), 51–59.

Beveridge, J. M., M.D. "Survival of Superstition as Found in the Practice of Medicine," *Illinois Medical Journal*, 30 (1917), 267–270.

Black, G. F., and Northcote W. Thomas. *Examples of Printed Folklore Concerning Orkney and Shetland Islands.* Publications of the Folk-Lore Society, 49. London, 1903.

Black, Pauline Monette. *Nebraska Folk Cures.* University of Nebraska Studies in Language, Literature, and Criticism, 15. Lincoln, 1935.

Black, William George. *Folk-Medicine: A Chapter in the History of Culture.* Publications of the Folk-Lore Society, 12. London, 1883.

Bourke, John G. "Popular Medicine, Customs, and Superstitions of the Rio Grande," *JAF*, 7 (1894), 119–146.

Bouteiller, Marcelle. *Médecine populaire d'hier et d'aujourd'hui.* Paris, 1966.

Brandon, Elizabeth. "Les Moeurs de la Paroisse de Vermillion en Louisiane." Ph.D. dissertation, Université Laval, Quebec, 1955.

Brendle, Thomas R., and Claude W. Unger. *Folk Medicine of the Pennsylvania Germans. The Non-Occult Cures.* Proceedings of the Pennsylvania German Society, 45. Norristown, Pa., 1935.

Brewster, Paul G. "Folk Cures and Preventives from Southern Indiana," *SFQ*, 3 (1939), 33–43.

Browne, Ray B. *Popular Beliefs and Practices from Alabama.* University of California Publications: Folklore Studies, vol. 9. Berkeley and Los Angeles, 1958.

Bruton, Hoyle S. "Medicine," *NCF*, 1 (1948), 23–26.

Bushnell, John H. "Medical Folklore from California," *WF*, 6 (1947), 273–275.

Campbell, Marie. "Folk Remedies from South Georgia," TFSB, 19 (1953), 1-4.

______. *Folks Do Get Born.* New York, 1946.

Castillo de Lucas, Antonio. *Folkmedicina.* Madrid, 1958.

Clements, Forrest E. *Primitive Concepts of Disease.* University of California Publications in American Archaeology and Ethnology, 32 (1932), 185-252.

Cockayne, Oswald. *Leechdoms, Wortcunning, and Starcraft of Early England.* Chronicles and Memorials of Great Britain and Ireland During the Middle Ages, no. 35, 3 vols. London, 1864-1866.

Crandall, Mrs. F. W., and Lois E. Gannett. "Folk Cures of New York State," *NYFQ,* 1 (1945), 178-180.

Creighton, Helen. *Folklore of Lunenburg County, Nova Scotia.* National Museum of Canada, *Bulletin* no. 117, Anthropological Series no. 29. Ottawa, 1950.

______. *Bluenose Magic: Popular Beliefs and Superstitions in Nova Scotia*. Toronto, 1968.

Crosby, John R. "Modern Witches of Pennsylvania," *JAF*, 40 (1927), 304-309.

Cross, Tom Pete. "Witchcraft in North Carolina," *Studies in Philology*, 16, 3 (1919), 217-287.

Curtin, L. S. M. "Pioneer Medicine in New Mexico," *Folk-Say.* Norman, Okla., 1930, pp. 186-196.

Dalyell, John Graham. *The Darker Superstitions of Scotland.* Glasgow, 1835.

Dodson, Ruth. "Folk-Curing among the Mexicans," PTFS, 10 (1932), 82-98.

Doering, J. Frederick. "Folk Remedies for Diverse Allergies," *JAF*, 57 (1944), 140-141.

______. "Pennsylvania German Folk Medicine in Waterloo County, Ontario," *JAF*, 49 (1936), 194-198.

Dorson, Richard M. "Blood Stoppers," *SFQ,* 11 (1947), 105-118.

Elworthy, Frederick Thomas. *The Evil Eye, An Account of This Ancient and Widespread Superstition.* London, 1895.

Fauset, Arthur Huff. *Folklore from Nova Scotia,* MAFS, 24. New York, 1931.

Feilberg, H. F. Der böse Blick in nordischer Überlieferung," *Zeitschrift des Vereins für Volkskunde*, 11 (1901), 304-330, 420-430.

______. "Zwieselbäume nebst verwandtem Aberglauben in

Skandinavien,'' *Zeitschrift des Vereins für Volkskunde*, 7 (1897), 42–53.

Fentress, Elza W. ''Superstitions of Grayson County, Kentucky.'' Master's thesis, Western State Teachers College, 1934.

Fife, Austin E. ''Pioneer Mormon Remedies,'' *WF*, 16 (1957), 153–162.

Fogel, Edwin Miller. *Beliefs and Superstitions of the Pennsylvania Germans.* Americana Germanica, 18. Philadelphia, 1915.

Foster, George M. ''The Anatomy of Envy: A Study in Symbolic Behavior,'' *Current Anthropology*, 13 (1972), 165–202.

______. ''Relationships Between Spanish and Spanish American Folk Medicine,'' *JAF*, 66 (1953), 201–217.

Foster, Paul D. ''Warts and Witches,'' *Life and Health*, 66 (Oct. 1951).

Forsblom, Valter W. *Magisk Folkmedicin*. Finlands Svenska Folkdiktning 7, Folktro och Trolldom, no. 5, Helsingfors, 1927.

Fox, Dr. Ben. ''Folk Medicine in Southern Illinois,'' *Illinois Folklore*, 2 (1948), 3–7.

Funk, William D. ''Hiccup Cures,'' *WF*, 9 (1950), 66–67.

Gaidoz, Henri. *Un vieux rite médical*. Paris, 1892.

Gallop, Rodney, *Portugal. A Book of Folk-Ways.* Cambridge, 1936.

Gardner, Emelyn Elizabeth. *Folklore from the Schoharie Hills, New York.* Ann Arbor, 1937.

Gifford, Edward S., Jr. *The Evil Eye: Studies in the Folklore of Vision.* New York, 1958.

______. ''The Evil Eye in Pennsylvania Medical History,'' *KFQ*, 5, 3 (1960), 3–8.

Grabner, Elfriede. ''Verlorenes Mass und heilkräftiges Messen: Krankheitserforschung und Heilhandlung in der Volksmedizin.'' In Elfriede Grabner, ed., *Volksmedizin: Probleme und Forschungsgeschichte.* Wege der Forschung. vol. 63. Darmstadt, 1967, pp. 538–553.

Gregor, Walter. *Notes on the Folk-Lore of the North-East of Scotland.* Publications of the Folk-Lore Society, 7. London, 1881.

Grendon, Felix. ''The Anglo-Saxon Charms,'' *JAF*, 22 (1909), 105–237.

Guinn, Leon. ''Home Remedies from Scurry County,'' PFTS, 14 (1938), 268.

Gunda, Bela, ''Gypsy Medical Folklore in Hungary,'' *JAF*, 73 (1962), 131–146.

Halpert, Violetta. "Folk Cures from Indiana," *HF*, 9 (1950), 1-12.

______. "Indiana Wart Cures," *HF*, 8 (1949), 37-43.

Hand, Wayland D. "American Analogues of the Couvade," *Studies in Honor of Distinguished Service Professor Stith Thompson*. Ed. W. Edson Richmond. Indiana University Folklore Studies, No. 9. Bloomington, 1957. Pp. 213-229.

______, ed. *American Folk Medicine. A Symposium*. Berkeley, Los Angeles, London, 1976.

(See titles of articles in the present volume.)

______, and Marjorie Griffin. "Inhalants in Respiratory Disorders," *JAF*, 77 (1964), 258-261.

Harder, Kelsie B. "Home Remedies in Perry County, Tennessee," *TFSB*, 22 (1956), 97-98.

Hartland, E. Sidney. "Cleft Ashes for Infantile Hernia," *Folk-Lore*, 7 (1896), 303-306.

______. "Pin-Wells and Rag-Bushes," *Folk-Lore*, 4 (1893), 451-470.

Hastings, James, ed. *Encyclopaedia of Religion and Ethics,* 13 vols. Edinburgh, 1908-1926. (Reprint ed., New York, 1956-1960.)

Hellwig, Albert. "Das Einpflöcken von Krankheiten," *Globus*, 90, 16 (1906), 245-249.

Henderson, William. *Notes on the Folk-Lore of the Northern Counties of England and the Borders*. New ed. Publications of the Folk-Lore Society, 2. London, 1879.

Hendricks, G. D. "Don't Look Back," PTFS, 30 (1961), 69-75.

Herron, Miss, and Miss A. M. Bacon. "Conjuring and Conjure-Doctors in the Southern United States," *JAF*, 9 (1896), 143-147.

Hofschläger, R. "Über den Ursprung der Heilmethoden," *Festschrift zur Feier des 50jährigen Bestehens des Naturwissenschaftlichen Vereins zu Krefeld*. Krefeld, 1908.

Hohman, John George. *Long Lost Friend, or, Book of Pow-Wows*. Ed. A. Monroe Aurand, Jr. Harrisburg, Pennsylvania, 1930.

Holland, William R. "Mexican-American Medical Beliefs: Science or Magic," *Arizona Medicine*, 20, 5 (May 1963), 89-101.

Hovorka, O. v., and A. Kronfeld. *Vergleichende Volksmedizin: Eine Darstellung volksmedizinischer Sitten und Gebräuche, Anschauungen und Heilfaktoren, des Aberglaubens und der Zaubermedizin*. 2 vols. Stuttgart, 1908-1909.

Hurston, Zora. "Hoodoo in America," *JAFL*, 44 (1931), 317-417.

Hyatt, Harry Middleton. *Folk-Lore from Adams County, Illinois.* Memoirs of the Alma Egan Hyatt Foundation. New York, 1935. 2d ed. 1965.

______. *Hoodoo, Conjuration, Witchcraft, Rootwork.* 5 vols. New York and Quincy, Ill., 1970–1978.

Inman, W. S. "The Couvade in Modern England," *The British Journal of Medical Psychology*, 19 (1941), 37–55.

______. "Styes, Barley, and Wedding Rings," *The British Journal of Medical Psychology*, 20 (1946), 331–338.

Johnson, Clifton. *What They Say in New England: A Book of Signs, Sayings, and Superstitions.* Boston, 1896.

Jones, Louis C. "The Evil Eye among European-Americans," *WF*, 10 (1951), 11–25.

______. "Practitioners of Folk Medicine," *Bulletin of the History of Medicine*, 23 (1949), 480–493.

Jungbauer, Gustav. *Deutsche Volksmedizin: Ein Grundriss.* Berlin, 1934.

Kanner, Leo. "Superstitions Connected with Sneezing," *Medical Life*, 38 (1931), 549–575.

Kemp, P. *Healing Ritual. Studies in the Technique and Tradition of the Southern Slavs.* London, 1935.

Lathrop, Amy. "Pioneer Remedies from Western Kansas," *WF*, 20 (1961), 1-22.

Levine, Harold D. "Folk Medicine in New Hampshire," *New England Journal of Medicine*, 224, 12 (1941), 487–492.

Lewis, Gabe. "Old-Time Remedies from Madison County," PTFS, 14 (1938), 267–268.

Lick, David E., and Thomas R. Brendle. *Plant Names and Plant Lore Among the Pennsylvania Germans.* Proceedings and Addresses of the Pennsylvania German Society, vol. 33, 1923.

Martin, Roxie. "Old Remedies Collected in the Blue Ridge Mountains," *JAF*, 60 (1947), 184–185.

Morel, Robert, and Suzanne Walter. *Dictionnaire des superstitions.* Bibliothèque Marabout, n.d.

Moss, Leonard W., and Stephen C. Cappannari. "Folklore and Medicine in an Italian Village," *JAF*, 73 (1960), 95–102.

Moya, Benjamin S. "Superstitions and Beliefs among the Spanish-Speaking People of New Mexico." Master's thesis, University of New Mexico, 1940.

Naff, Alixa. "Belief in the Evil Eye among the Christian Syrian-Lebanese in America," *JAF*, 78 (1965), 46–51.

Neal, Janice C. "Grandad—Pioneer Medicine Man," *NYFQ*, 11 (1955), 277–291.

Nyrop, Kristoffer. "Kludertraeet. En sammelignende Undersøgelse," *Dania*, 1 (1900–1902), 1–31.

Peacock, Mabel. "Executed Criminals and Folk-Medicine," *Folk-Lore*, 7 (1896), 268–283.

Pettigrew, Thomas Joseph. *On Superstitions Connected With the History and Practice of Medicine and Surgery.* London, 1844.

Pickard, Madge E., and R. Carlyle Buley. *The Midwest Pioneer. His Ills, Cures, and Doctors.* Crawfordsville, Ind., 1945.

Puckett, Newbell Niles. *Folk Beliefs of the Southern Negro.* Chapel Hill, N.C., 1926.

Raaf, John E. "Hernia Healers," *Annals of Medical History*, n.s., 4 (1932), 377–389.

Radbill, Samuel X. "Whooping Cough in Fact and Fancy," *Bulletin of the History of Medicine*, 13 (1943), 33–55.

Radford, E., and M. A. Radford. *Encyclopaedia of Superstitions.* London, n.d. [1947].

Randolph, Vance. *Ozark Superstitions.* New York, 1947.

Reichborn-Kjennerud, I. *Vår gamle Trolldomsmedisin.* Skrifter uttgit av det Norske Videnskaps-Akademi i Oslo. 5 vols. Oslo, 1928–1947.

Relihan, Catherine M. "Farm Lore: Folk Remedies," *NYFQ*, 3 (1947), 81–84, 166–169.

______. "Farm Lore: Herb Remedies," *NYFQ*, 3 (1947), 81–84, 166–169.

Richmond, W. Edson, and Elva Van Winkle. "Is There a Doctor in the House?" *Indiana Historical Bulletin*, 35 (1958), 115–135.

Riddell, William Rensick. "Some Old Canadian Folk Medicine," *The Canada Lancet and Practitioner*, 83 (August 1934), 41–44.

Roberts, Hilda. "Louisiana Superstitions," *JAF*, 40 (1927), 144–208.

Rogers, E. G. *Early Folk Medical Practices in Tennessee.* Murfreesboro, Tenn., 1941.

Rolleston, J. D. "The Folklore of Children's Diseases," *Folk-Lore*, 54 (1943), 287–307.

______. "Ophthalmic Folk-Lore," *The British Journal of Ophthalmology*, 26 (1942), 481–502.

Sanders, Myra. "Some Medical Lore," *Kentucky Folk-Lore and Poetry Magazine*, 5, 2 (October 1930), 14–23.

Sartori, Paul. "Diebstahl als Zauber," *Schweizerisches Archiv für Volkskunde*, 20 (1916), 380–388.

Sébillot, Paul. *Le Folk-Lore de France.* 4 vols. Paris, 1904–1907.

Seligmann, S. *Der böse Blick und Verwandtes. Ein Beitrag zur Geschichte des Aberglaubens aller Zeiten und Völker.* 2 vols. Berlin, 1910.

______. *die Zauberkraft des Augens und das Berufen. Ein Kapitel aus der Geschichte des Aberglaubens.* Hamburg, 1922.

Seyfarth, Carly. *Aberglaube und Zauberei in der Volksmedizin Sachsens.* Leipzig, 1913.

Simmons, Frank. "The Wart Doctor," PTFS, 14 (1938), 192–194.

Simmons, Ozzie G. "Popular and Modern Medicine in Mestizo Communities of Coastal Peru and Chile," *JAF*, 68 (1955), 57–71.

Smith, Elmer L., and John Stewart. "The Mill as a Preventive and Cure of Whooping-Cough," *JAF*, 77 (1964), 76–77.

Smith, Lovisa V. "Folk Remedies in Andes," *NYFQ*, 7 (1951), 295–298.

Smith, Walter R. "Animals and Plants in Oklahoma Folk Cures," *Folk-Say: A Regional Miscellany.* Ed. B. A. Botkin. Norman, Okla., 1929. Pp. 69–78.

______. "Northwestern Oklahoma Folk Cures," PTFS, 8 (1930), 74–85.

Steiner, Roland. "The Practice of Conjuring in Georgia," *JAF*, 14 (1901), 173–180.

Storaker, Joh. Th. *Sygdom og Forgjørelse i den Norske Folketro.* Folkeminnelag, no. 28. Oslo, 1932.

Stout, Earl J. *Folklore from Iowa*, MAFS, 29. New York, 1936.

Stuart, Jesse. "The Yarb Doctor," *Kentucky Folk-Lore and Poetry Magazine*, 6, 1 (March 1931), 4–10.

Taboada, Jésus. "La medicina popular en el Valle de Monterrey (Orense)," *Revista de Dialectología y Tradiciones Populares*, 3 (1947), 31–57.

Temkin, Owsei. *The Falling Sickness: A History of Epilepsy from the Greeks to the Beginnings of Modern Neurology.* Baltimore, 1945.

Thomas, Daniel Lindsey, and Lucy Blayney Thomas. *Kentucky Superstitions.* Princeton, N.J., 1920.

Tillhagen, Carl-Herman. *Folklig Läkekonst.* Stockholm, 1958.

______. Papers on Folk-Medicine Given at an Inter-Nordic Symposium, May 1961, at Stockholm. *Arv. Journal of Scandinavian Folklore*, 18–19 (1962–1963), 159–362.

Van Andel, M. A. *Volksgeneeskunst en Nederland.* Utrecht, 1909.

Vicente Cifuentes, Julio. *Mitos y Supersticiones. Estudies del Folklore Chileno Recogidos de la Tradición Oral.* Tercera edición, 3d ed. Santiago de Chile, 1947.

Vuorela, Toivo. *Der böse Blick im Lichte der finnischen Überlieferung.* FFC, no. 201. Helsinki, 1967.

Webb, Wheaton Phillips. "The Wart," *NYFQ,* 2 (1946), 98–106.

Weiser-Aall, Lily. "Gelehrte Tradition über angeborene Fehler in der Volksmedizin, *Arv. Journal of Scandinavian Folklore,* 18–19 (1962–1963), 226–262.

Welsch, Roger L. *A Treasury of Nebraska Pioneer Folklore.* Lincoln, Neb., 1966.

White, Emma Gertrude. "Folk-Medicine Among Pennsylvania Germans," *JAF,* 10 (1897), 78–80.

Whitney, Annie Weston, and Caroline Canfield Bullock. *Folk-Lore from Maryland,* MAFS, 18. New York, 1925.

Whitten, Norman E., Jr. "Contemporary Patterns of Malign Occultism Among Negroes in North Carolina," *JAF,* 75 (1962), 311–325.

Woodhull, Frost. "Ranch Remedios," PTFS, 8 (1930). Austin, Tex., pp. 9–73.

Wuttke, Adolf. *Der deutsche Volksaberglaube der Gegenwart.* 3d ed. E. H. Meyer, ed. Berlin, 1900.

Yates, Irene. "Conjures and Cures in the Novels of Julia Peterkin," *SFQ,* 10 (1946), 137–149.

Introduction

The study of folk medicine during the past hundred years or more has recapitulated in many ways the study of medicine proper from the time of classical antiquity forward. As in the *Schulmedizin* of the earliest medical scholars, natural or botanic medicine was, and has remained pretty much from the beginning, the main interest of students working in the field of folk medicine. Not until the development of folklore as a science in the nineteenth century, however, were the magical components of folk medical practice gradually laid bare. It remained for William George Black in England as early as the 1880s to make certain formulations in the field of magical medicine, notably the transference of disease to other humans and animals, and the ritual consignment of human maladies to earth, air, and the watery element. In our own century Seyfarth in Germany, Hovorka and Kronfeld in Austria, Jungbauer in Bohemia, Castillo de Lucas in Spain, Reichborn-Kjennerud in Norway, Forsblom in the Swedish-speaking parts of Finland, and Araujo in Brazil have drawn upon the whole range of folklore to show the importance of magic, along with Christian miracle, in the diagnosis of disease and the healing of the sick. Reichborn-Kjennerud's *Våre gamle Trolldomsmedisin,* "Our Ancient Magical Medicine," in five small folio volumes published by the Norwegian Academy of Sciences, remains the classical statement in the field.

In my accumulation of materials for a Dictionary of American Popular Beliefs and Superstitions since 1944, a whole body of folk medicine has come to light. Much of this lore has been hitherto relatively unknown, particularly ritualistic and magical practices, and many of the components of faith healing as well. Over the past fifteen years or more in a series of writings, I have addressed myself to American magical medicine as a preliminary to a standard work for the entire field of folk medicine. The essays drawn together here in book form cover most of the general subject fields of magical medicine and, in one way or another, touch upon the individual magical motifs that give substance and cohesion to the whole field. The Index draws these widely ramifying motifs and elements together, as do also, of course, the copious footnotes to the individual articles.

The reader should be aware at the outset that materials have been drawn from European and American folk medicine, not from the medical magic of the so-called primitive cultures. Even though the magical medicine of primitives is rich in its way—particularly shamanism—the two medical systems are sufficiently different as not easily to be encompassed in any common study embracing the entire field. People knowledgeable in both traditions, however, will be surprised to learn, I am sure, that the magical medicine of modern Europe and America—despite the benefits of medical science, no less than of science in general and an advanced culture—has clung to an unusually rich and virginal body of magical lore that lies at the base of its folk medical thought. Actually, in its endless symbolism and imagery, and in its elemental magic and miracle, this corpus of modern Western folk medicine rivals the best exhibits of medical antiquity from China, India, Egypt, the Middle East, Greece, and Rome, and the earliest medical lore of Romance, Slavic, and Germanic Europe. In my view this folk medical legacy is not exceeded by comparable bodies of primitive medicine anywhere in the world. A possible exception, of course, is shamanism and various kinds of witch doctoring where resort is had to a whole congeries of magical practices that are themselves often an accepted part of a broader cultural substrate. Just as there are often parallels between different genres of folklore and their counterparts in primitive religion and tribal lore so also will correspondences be found between Western folk medicine and the medical practices of primitive peoples in various parts of the world. The founding of the journal *Ethnomedizin* in 1971, and *Medical Anthropology* six years later, will have, it is hoped, the effect of drawing a vast and sprawling field into a compass where its seemingly disparate components—primitive medicine and Western folk medicine—can be examined for their common elements. This process has already begun in the study of so-called ethnic medicine in many cities and rural areas of Europe, America, and elsewhere.

The magic of healing is twofold. In Christian communities religious miracle is the motive force. Faith healers draw their inspiration and power from God himself, or from the Virgin Mary and the saints. They regard themselves only as vessels through which the divine will is made manifest. The faith of the sick is joined with that of the healer, and this unified expression constitutes, in a sense, an act of worship, and often of sacrifice, by which the blessings of heaven are showered down. Secular magic usually draws on powers of nature and the universe, and often on nondivine agents and systems of power that can be manipulated by practitioners of the magic art. In many cases favorable auspices for healing may be sought in the natural order itself. Propitious times for healing can be observed; curative practice may be carried out at numinous spots; disease may be stripped away and dispersed to the four elements; and the ailing person restored and made whole. "Wholeness," as Yoder and others have shown, is the basic notion underlying healing, and being "made whole" is a well-known metaphor for being healed.

Although there is only one essay in this sheaf on folk healers, there are numerous references to faith healers. Most often, of course, these healers are engaged in magical acts. Even so the religious element is also often prevalent. In this general connection workers in the field have long since called attention to the fact that there is often an almost complete syncretism between sacred and secular magic, wherein Christian miracle is also often invoked to insure the success of a ritual that may otherwise be for the most part profane in character. Even the invocation of the Three Highest Names is often resorted to in ritualistic practices to which Christian people might normally take umbrage. These strange juxtapositions are countenanced, apparently, by the need and desperation of the moment. In sickness, more so than in any other vicissitude of life, people will throw all caution to the wind, as it were, and resort to trials and actions that they would not even consider under ordinary circumstances. It is on these human proclivities and on this crisis and despair that quacks and charlatans thrive. In ultimate ordeals where life itself hangs in the balance, resort to magic as well as to religion is commonplace, if not universal. It is for these best of reasons that Wundt, Freud, Rank, Jung, and other scholars since their time concerned with the mental and emotional life of man have found folklore such a valuable tool. Better than the doctor the folklorist is able to see the interplay of these religious and magical forces. It is baffling, but not hard to understand, that in times of crisis these almost antithetical belief systems are shared and invoked as much by the next of kin and by friends as they are by the sick and the dying. Together, at any rate, sacred rite and magic ritual conspire with the faith and devotion of the sick to bring about the miracle of healing.

A glance at the contents page will reveal the scope of magical medicine. Topics range from the magical and demonic causes of disease, including the evil eye and animals in the body, to disease viewed as divine retribution for sin and a misspent life. The somewhat humorous paper on styes deals with the taboos of seeing forbidden sights such as nakedness, deporting oneself in unseemly fashion around pregnant or lactating women, or relieving oneself in a public place. Styes and other ocular maladies, of course, result from breaking these age-old proscriptions. Themes also treat the riddance of disease by various means—transference, measuring, passing through, plugging, and other kinds of divestment, including a radical change of air—earth gases, the change of air at high altitudes, the biting air of lime kilns and gas works, the musty air of grist mills—and an exchange of air and froth, mouth-on-muzzle, with an overheated stallion. General treatises on the magical components of folk medicine and on the calling and endowment of healers round out the volume.

Taken together these essays constitute a primer, if not a handbook, of magical medicine, and pave the way for the further exploration of a badly neglected field. Not only is magical medicine in need of further study but the whole field of folk medicine requires such attention. The fieldwork of folklorists in our own day is valuable, but it does not go far enough; the sociopsychological analysis of the behavioral scientists adds to the picture, but it is proscribed by its limited time frame, just as primitive medicine for obvious reasons deals mostly with aboriginal peoples.

In consideration of the present status of studies, it is clear that more work in comparative folk medicine along the lines of Hovorka and Kronfeld in Austria at the beginning of the century is a development devoutly to be wished. In the effort to probe even further back historically, research efforts reinforcing the pioneer work of Bakker in Holland in 1928 are strongly indicated. Bakker's admirable book, *Volksgeneeskunde in Waterland: Een vergelijkende Studie met de Geneeskunde van de Grieken en Romeinen,* as the title says, is a comparative study of contemporary folk medicine in the Dutch town of Waterland near Amsterdam, with notes to medical analogues from the time of Hippocrates and Galen forward. Bakker's scholarly survey includes the work of medical scientists from early times to the present from all parts of Europe insofar as they undergird and illumine the work in folk medicine which he carried on as a sideline to his work as a general practitioner of medicine.

In efforts to trace out the roots of present-day folk medical practices, we shall do so at our own peril if we fail to enlist the help of medical historians in our common purpose. By general consent they are equipped better than any other kind of scholars to see the interplay of folk medicine with scientific medicine through the centuries and to see how folk medical ideas and theories have evolved. They are also in a position to show how certain kinds of folk medical knowledge found its way, piecemeal, into accepted medical practice, particularly in the area of herbal medicine. American medical historians have played an important role in fostering studies that involve lengthy time perspectives and broad geographical continua. A group of scholars at the Johns Hopkins University Medical School, headed by the noted medical historian, Henry E. Sigerist, spearheaded these efforts. Numbered among them are such well-known workers as Leo Kanner, Owsei Temkin, and Lloyd G. Stevenson. Genevieve Miller and Ilza Veith were also associated with the medical history work at the Hopkins, as was the celebrated Erwin H. Ackerknecht, who worked with Sigerist personally in his early Hopkins days. Ackerknecht, who later taught medical history at the University of Wisconsin, finished his teaching days in medical history at Zurich. Ackerknecht had an advantage over almost everyone else from the circumstance that he was, first of all, a medical doctor. Added to this was the fact that he possessed the credentials of an anthropologist, a medical ethnographer, and a medical historian.

In the light of these many equities that must be addressed, the author invites comment and help. He would be particularly grateful for analogues to matters raised in these papers from early *Schulmedizin* as well as from the still largely uncharted field of primitive medicine.

1
Folk Curing: The Magical Component*

The magical element in folk curing is a somewhat neglected field in folk medicine. Writers on the subject, particularly in America, have all too often been content to focus attention on treatments and therapeutic measures at the folk level that accord with many more or less standard medical categories of diagnosis and treatment. It is the purpose of this paper to fix attention on magical elements of folklore itself that have been taken over in folk curative practices. These magical acts, which serve as attendant circumstances to more routine, and often common kinds of doctoring, may rest either on a supernatural or sacral power, or they may derive from the common magic and marvel of folklore. In either case they bring an added measure of power and healing efficacy. In the hands of the devout believer, these magical procedures—and they alone—insure the success of the therapy.

Recently I have devoted myself to the writing of a few essays that treat specific kinds of folk medical magic, such as magical transference of disease,[1] 'plugging' and kindred practices,[2] and 'passing through'.[3] In the present paper I hope to give a brief summary of individual folk beliefs and customs that are so

*This article originally appeared in *Hereditas.* Essays and Studies Presented to Professor Séamus O'Duilearga, Former Honorary Director of the Irish Folklore Commission, Editor of *Bealoideas*, 1927–1973. Patron of the Folklore Society of Ireland. Dublin: Folklore Society of Ireland, 1975, pp. 140–156. Permission to reprint has been given by the editor of the Folklore of Ireland Society.

general that they may attach to a variety of diseases. In a sense, these magical acts may be thought of as being in the nature of attendant circumstances or states of being that promote the desired cures. Jungbauer, and before him, Seyfarth, have summarized these folkloric elements for the German-speaking areas.[4] An American example of the attendant circumstances of 'pulling through' will give in brief compass a summary of some of these important magical conditions that are still *de rigueur* in American folk medical practice.

> When a baby has an enlarged navel, wedge open a white oak tree and pull him through. . . . On putting the child through a tree, first observe that it must be early in the spring before the grass begins to vegetate; secondly, that it must be split as near east and west as it can. Thirdly, it must be done as the sun is rising. Fourthly, the child must be stripped quite naked; fifthly, it must be put through the tree feet foremost; sixthly, it must be turned around with the sun, and observe that it must be put through the tree three times. . . .[5]

This is almost a textbook case of the magical conditions of healing in folk medicine, and is rarely duplicated in the literature. In the treatment of individual magical elements, below, however, one should not fail to note the frequent multiple involvement of magical prescriptions.

Since we shall be talking entirely about conditions and circumstances that may enhance the folk medical act or insure its success, and since we must obviously begin somewhere, I propose to take up these acts according to the adverbs of time, manner, and place. Treatment according to other attendant circumstances will follow. Let us begin with the basic category of place. The crossroads, or merely a fork in the road, have always been considered among the most magical of places.[6] Here it is that spirits and supernatural creatures of all kinds congregate, here it is that the future is divined, and the sick healed,[7] including sick animals.[8] The notion is that diseases spread by spirits and other evil creatures can be left at the crossroads by the victim for his erstwhile tormenters to contract or he may leave the disease there for some other unwary person to pick up.[9] A good example of this latter kind of riddance is found in a prescription for the removal of warts in North Carolina:

> Take an Irish potato, cut it up, rub it on warts, put it in a sack and put it in a fork in the road. The first one who picks it up will have your warts; yours will disappear.[10]

Other kinds of *Zwischenträger,* i.e., intermediate agents of disposal, for example, are nine grains of salt rubbed on the wart and then disposed of at a crossroads by tossing the salt over one's left shoulder. This procedure is repeated for nine mornings, which itself involves a magic number and magical repetition.[11] Pieces of gravel tied in a cloth and thrown over the right shoulder at a crossroads is another means of disposal that involves a chance deposit at the magic area in question.[12] (We shall take up random tossing and disposal over the shoulder later.) Toothache is disposed of in Saxony by cutting one's nails at a crossroads on Friday, and burying them there.[13] In Pomerania, by symbolic magic rather than by contagious magic, gout is transferred to the first bird that flies over a crossroads.[14] For the highly elaborate ritual of pulling a person under an archway made of sods, the crossroads, once more, is the numinous spot at which such an involved ritual takes place.[15] In Denmark, sods cut from a point where three lanes meet are taken indoors, and fashioned into an arch over the rungs of an upturned stool. The child is then passed through the rungs to cure it of rickets. This was done on three successive Thursday nights, and strict silence was observed during the office.[16]

Like the crossroads, boundaries between property were thought to be especially efficacious. Near to Button Oak, in the forest of Bewdly, for example, grows a thorn in the form of an arch, one end in the county of Salop, the other in Stafford. This was visited by a number of people to make their children pass under it for the cure of whooping cough.[17] In a cure for measles, involving passing through a stone aperture rather than through the more common split in a tree, under a re-rooted bramble, etc., children suffering from measles were taken to a junction point of three parishes near Sligo, Ireland, to be passed through a large limestone flag set on edge with a more or less rectangular hole through it.[18] In Denmark, the only way to cure a child blighted by the glance of a whore, *skjörgesét,* was to cut sods at a place where four pieces of property abutted. The child was then passed through these sods.[19] *Jordskerva,* a sort of scurvy contracted by contact with the earth, was cured homeopathically by pulling the child through a hole at a field boundary three times before sunrise on a Thursday morning.[20] Solitary or out-of-the-way places, or even spots near a roadway, are favourable for the passing through of sods, or *jorddragning,* as this ritual medical act is called.[21] Meadowlands and other spots frequented only by wayfarers are spots sought out for the riddance and disposal of diseases of all kinds.[22] A wart cure from North Carolina, for example, emphasizes riddance at a place so remote as never again to be revisited:

> If you go to a place where you have never been and expect never to return to, rub an old bone over the warts, throw the bone over the left shoulder when finished, being sure not to look at it again.[23]

The relationship of curing rituals to directions, points of the compass, and the firmament, and their connections, in turn, with ancient cultic and mythological ideas is not easy to prove; however, healing of the sick, as an office of utmost gravity, was, under certain circumstances, carried out in the open air.[24] The ritual of 'passing through' seems to have been performed in both directional planes, north-south and east-west. In New Hampshire congenital 'fissure' (rupture?) in children was cured by passing the victim through a split ash sapling, with the gap running from north to south.[25] The observance of proper directions indoors as well as in the open is seen in an elaborate Devonshire ritual of curing fits, according to which the victim was made to go to the parish church at midnight on June 23, i.e., St. John's Eve, and walk three times through each aisle. Then he was supposed to crawl under the communion table three times from north to south as the clock struck midnight.[26] Movement from east to west, which is to be equated with 'sunwise', even though not specifically stated, is also encountered in cures for rickets, rupture, and other diseases by 'passing through' in the British Isles.[27] Passing through from east to west for an enlarged navel was seen in the first example (North Carolina) cited above. Disorders of the spleen, akin to a disease which the Pennsylvania Germans called *âgewachse,* were treated in Ohio by passing the child from east to west, as the sun goes, around the leg of a chair or table.[28]

Movement with the sun, i.e., sunwise or clockwise, is a magical prescription in many areas of folklore, but particularly in the field of custom and usage. In the British Isles this practice goes back to Druidic times.[29] Once more, examples may be taken from 'passing through' rituals. In Somerset the feature of 'sunwise' has been kept to the present day. The infirm child is passed through a tree sunwise three times, and then the tree is bound up with a hay band.[30] We have seen this same detail observed in the model, all-detail North Carolina example of magical circumstances cited at the beginning of this article. 'Withershins', i.e., against the sun, or counter-clockwise, has a special potency as reverse magic.[31] In parts of Cornwall, for example, it was the custom to pass rickety children through holed-stones nine times against the sun (withershins).[32] In Finland the same disease was combatted by passing the child through the reins of a bridle three times counter-clockwise.[33] In Scandinavia ailing children were handed out the window and taken around the house, *motsols* (Swed.), i.e., counter-sunwise, and then brought in again.[34] The notion of a reversal of things, and a return to the better, no doubt underlies this ritual.[35]

Other magical prescriptions having to do with direction are walking backwards, not looking back, and throwing things over the shoulder (and not observing where they fall).[36] An example of walking backward for the relief of a malady is seen in Simmenthal, Switzerland. To combat fever, one cuts fingernails and toenails on a Friday during the waning moon, and forces the parings under the shell of a crab. As the crab waddles away, backward, the fever departs.[37] In North Carolina it is believed that chicken pox can be got rid of by taking the patient to a hog barn, have him lie down there and then roll over three times. Finally he must walk backward thirty-three steps.[38] The taboo against looking back is as old as the injunction to Lot in the days of Sodom and Gomorrah, but it is still strictly observed in many magical rituals, including those having to do with folk curing. This taboo is often found, as we shall see, in connection with throwing things away that have been in contact with the patient.[39] Two North Carolina examples will illustrate:

> Cut a notch in a piece of wood for every chill that you have had, blow on it, and throw it into a running stream where you never expect to pass again. Go home without looking back, and you will never have any more chills.[40]

The second item reads:

> To cure a wart, pick up a rock in running water and rub your warts with it. Put it back in the same place, then go home without looking back.[41]

Whereas we have hitherto considered more or less specific directions, in considering divestment by throwing something away,[42] as, for example, over one's shoulder, the emphasis shifts to a random deposit. The whole point is that one does not know, and should not know, where the *Zwischenträger,* or intermediate agent, comes to rest. An excellent example is seen in a wart disposal cure from North Carolina:

> To make a wart go away, slice an Irish potato in half and rub the inside on the wart, then throw it over your shoulder and never look where it goes.[43]

Disposal over the left shoulder is the usual procedure, but occasionally the right shoulder is prescribed.[44] In the Pennsylvania German country sideache (side stitch) is treated by the victim's picking up a stone, spitting on it, and throwing it, not over the shoulders, but over the head, and without looking where it goes.[45]

Reverse magic seems to be at work in the turning of shoes upside down to stop the cramp, in a folk medical cure reported from North Carolina.[46] By turning the shoes, presumably, the victim reverses the pull on his muscles and thus relaxes the cramp. The turning of clothes wrong side out involves a slightly different kind of spatial orientation, in the sense that interior areas come to the surface, and vice versa. Just what this means, I do not know. However, the act of putting clothes wrong side out is generally thought in primitive magic to be a way of throwing harmful spirits off the track or deceiving them.[47] These ideas are not borne out, as far as I can see, in modern folk medicine, even though applications to witchcraft, magic, and ghostlore, would seem to confirm the older ideas. A single example of the magical efficacy of turning an item of clothing inside out will suffice to show how difficult it is, really, to read deeper magical meaning into what undoubtedly is an old folk medical practice:

> To cure sore throat, turn a stocking wrong side out and wear it tied around the throat at night.[48]

Having surveyed magical elements as they relate to place, direction, and related ideas, we can now turn our attention to considerations of time, i.e., times favourable to hasten the curative process. Let us begin with the time of day. Sunrise, or just before sunrise, is a highly favourable time for the gathering of sanative herbs, and for the carrying out of many kinds of cures.[49] To take the highly ritualized folk medical practice of 'passing through,' for example, one notes that this rite was performed at sunrise, or before sunrise, in such widely separated countries as the British Isles, France (seventeenth century), Poland, the United States, and Canada.[50] A recommended cure for warts in North Carolina is the washing of them in May dew, before breakfast, and 'just as the sun rises.'[51] Curing at sundown, or after sundown, is not so common,[52] but the whole period from sundown until sunrise, under certain circumstances, is efficacious for curing, just as it is a propitious time for the carrying out of most magical offices.[53] In parts of Denmark, for example, sods fetched for passing through ceremonies were often cut at sundown.[54] Midnight, of course, is a highly propitious time for curative practices of all kinds,[55] but especially for the fetching of water that is either blessed or resistant to deterioration, for the plucking of herbs,[56] or for the securing of graveyard dirt and other products from graveyards that are used in the folk materia medica.[57] In the familiar 'passing through' rituals, midnight is a favourite time for carrying out the office. In Jutland, for example, the victim's father cut a sod in a cemetery at midnight,[58] while the common pulling of a child through a split sapling was undertaken in Portugal at midnight on St. John's Eve by three men, each named John, and three women, each named Mary.[59] In Silesia, bread freshly baked at midnight was taken to a crossroads or boundary to be used against diseases that had failed to respond to less drastic measures.[60] The forging of chains at midnight for pregnant women to wear on their bodies to forestall stillbirth in Serbia,[61] and the forging of coffin nails into chains to be worn against gout in Saxony, attest the special favour of the midnight hour for folk medical activities involving blacksmiths. In the last-named instance, the act was best carried out at midnight on Good Friday by a smith in the naked state.[62] In Berry, France, peas were cast into a well at midnight to rid the officiant of warts.[63] I have not made a survey of days of the week favoured for healing in general, but both Thursday and Friday were used for 'passing through' rituals in Germanic Europe.[64] In Belgium and Luxembourg, further, a child slow in learning to walk was made to crawl through a re-rooted bramble, in silence, on Friday.[65] Sunday, of course, is a day favoured for curing in many countries.[66] Various saints' days are favoured for the curing of individual kinds of maladies, but St. John's Eve is perhaps more widely utilized for this purpose than any other time hallowed by association with saints.[67] For 'passing through' rituals, St. John's Eve was especially favoured in the Romance countries.[68] We have already noted the crawling under the communion table for fits at midnight on St. John's Eve in connection with our discussion of directions, i.e., north–south.[69] Before leaving the religious realm let us consider the church service itself as a favourable influence in healing. The detection of witches at certain points in the Mass is well known; so is the opening up of subterranean treasure troves during Divine Service on certain days during Holy Week. It comes as no surprise, therefore, to learn that peasants in Lower Bavaria crawled through a hole in a stone on which the altar rested. This was done to strengthen the back for work at harvest time. To heighten the flow of strength and health to their bodies, they performed the rite while the church service was in progress.[70] In another crawling-through ritual, children with rickets were forced, in western Finland, to crawl through a spill barrel whose bottom had been knocked out. This was done on a Sunday morning as the church bells rang out.[71] There is no room to take up here religious charms and incantations, including the simple recitation of the Lord's Prayer as a supernatural enhancement of the curative ritual. As is well known, such religious offices often constitute a crucial part of the folk curing process.

Of the non-religious holidays, May Day seems to have been more prominently identified with healing and fertility rites than other secular feast days.[72] Healing according to phases of the moon, the clipping of hair and the parting of fingernails, and the like, are so well known that I cannot devote space to the subject here. The long entry in *Handwörterbuch der deutschen Aberglaubens* will suggest the range of treatments and cures affected by the phases of the moon.[73]

As in other kinds of magical acts, repetition is an important part of many folk medical cures. The magic of threes for example, is resorted to in 'passing-through' rituals in most parts of Europe and in the United States, whether through trees, re-rooted brambles or berry canes, through a warm horse collar or under the belly of a donkey.[74] Involved is not only the common three-fold repetition of the act itself, but a repetition involving three successive Thursday nights, as in Scandinavia.[75] Already we have seen the magic of threes invoked in various connections in treatments of crossroads and boundaries, directions, sunwise, and withershins. The article on numeral magic, promised for the Appendix of the *Handwörterbuch des deutschen Aberglaubens,* was never written, so I cannot refer the reader to a convenient summary of the use of three, and the threefold application, as it applies to folk medicine. However, of the approximately 2,000 references to the number three in the general index, one may hazard the guess that a fair share of these entries would refer to folk medicine.[76] I must content myself here with giving a couple of random examples from North Carolina:

> To cure malaria, put a toad under a pot and walk around the pot three times.[77]

> If you will lie down and roll over on the ground three times the first time you hear a dove holler in the spring, you will not have backache all year.[78]

Seven, also a common magical number, is not widely encountered in folk medicine, although in Calabria, in a most unusual variation, children with hernia are pulled through a split oak seven times on St. John's Day.[79] For another example of the use of the number seven, see the treatment, below, of seven protective furrows gouged around Slavic villages as a means of warding off pestilence. The number nine, on the other hand, a multiple of three, is apparently more widely used in folk medicine than seven. In 'passing through' rituals, for example, it is found in the British Isles and the Romance countries as well as in the Germanic north.[80] We have already encountered this magic number in connection with treatments of crossroads and withershins, above, so I shall limit myself to but a single illustration, an item from North Carolina:

> Drink a teaspoon of flour and water for nine mornings as a cure for boils.[81]

We now come to some rather different kinds of magical elements in connection with folk medical practices. Because of their variety it is hard to summarize them under a convenient single heading. In the main they deal with states of being, attitudes, and subjective states on the part of the victim. However, certain desired effects can be produced only by an active pursuit of the magical object, the magical element, or the magical situation itself. Stealing and other furtive acts somehow convey a magical power on common objects that they otherwise would not have.[82] Thus it is, for example, that a child will learn to speak sooner, according to a belief current in the Erzgebirge, if it can get some bread to eat which has been stolen from a beggar or gypsy.[83] In Germany—place not stated—sore throat and hoarseness can be combatted by wrapping around the ailing part a cloth made from a portion of a flour sack stolen from the miller.[84] The most common kinds of stealing in America for folk medical purposes involve stolen washrags, stolen bacon, stolen potatoes, and the like. These objects are mostly used for the riddance of warts and other excrescences, including boils.[85] Boils are cured, it is thought, simply by the patient's carrying a stolen potato in his pocket.[86] A North Carolina item stressing a furtive act on the part of the patient reads as follows:

> When the blacksmith is not looking, bathe your warts in the water in which he cools his tools.[87]

This example illustrates admirably, I think, the real point at issue, namely, doing something surreptitiously. No blacksmith would object, certainly, to anyone's using his slake-tub for so harmless a purpose. I once talked with an old Los Angeles blacksmith who said that well-dressed ladies frequently came to his shop to request such water for cosmetic purposes.

Doing things in silence is another common prescription for carrying out curative measures. 'Passing through' ceremonies were often carried out in silence, particularly those involving pulling underneath upturned sods.[88] We have already noted the curious way of curing 'whore blight' in Denmark by pulling the victim through sods at boundary lines. Silence was part of this stern office. In Belgium and Luxembourg children learning to walk were pulled through brambles amid silence.[89] American examples also follow a wide range of diseases and circumstances, but one is especially worthy of note, since it involves doing something early in the morning 'before you speak to anyone'. This has to do with the removal of a corn by rubbing saliva on it for nine mornings, as stated, 'before you speak to anyone'. The point here, of course, is that there is no one, really, with whom one could speak under the circumstances. Related to this is the notion that one should not return a greeting, even if spoken to, while engaged in performing a cure. In an example from Jutland, the father goes out early to cut the sod for pulling his child through, but he must take care not to greet anyone on his way home to perform the actual rite.[90] Another kind of silence, or avoidance of hearing noise, is seen in an extremely rare folk medical belief and practice in Saintongue, Touraine. After the victim has dropped the number of peas corresponding to the number of warts he has into a well, he leaves the well as fast as his legs will carry him so that he will not hear the peas hit the water.[91]

Related to silence, and taboos on speaking, greeting people, or hearing certain kinds of things, are analogous ideas having to do with sight and memory. These practices are rare. In the disposal of warts and other excrescences by dropping peas, pebbles, and other similar objects into wells and other kinds of watercourses, certain restrictions are imposed. In Haute

Bretagne, for example, peas cast into a well to rid oneself of warts must be dropped with closed eyes. Neither should anyone view the ritual.[92] In North Carolina warts should be washed for three mornings—unseen by anyone—in water standing in an old stump.[93] Forgetting about something one has done, like not looking back, not returning to a place, and the like, falls under this category of highly personal attitudes and actions with regard to the work in hand.[94] It is based on the common notion that things forgotten are soon lost or disposed of.

Most matters hitherto discussed deal with external circumstances, with things which the patient must do, or with attitudes of mind. Two physical states that are of great importance in curing are (1) entering upon medical administrations on a fasting stomach, and (2) performing ritual acts of various kinds in the nude. Practitioners, as well as patients, of course, subject themselves to these conditions. Sometimes these two prescriptions are combined in the selfsame treatment. Pliny contains an unusually fine prescription for treating abscesses. After telling about the preparation of certain plants, including heating them for application, he goes on:

> Those with experience have assured us that it makes all the difference if, while the patient is fasting, the poultice is laid upon him by a maiden, herself fasting and naked, who must touch him with the back of her hand and say: 'Apollo tells us that a plague cannot grow more fiery if a naked maiden quench the fire'; and with her hand so reversed she must repeat the formula three times, and both must spit on the ground three times.[95]

For a treatment of fasting in its general lineaments, one is forced to fall back on the reliable *Handwörterbuch des deutschen Aberglaubens.*[96] American material, though plentiful, has never been brought together for study. In America the religious and sacral aspects of fasting are most often forgotten, and the act is regarded more as a way of getting the body prepared for medical ministrations by internal cleansing. Nudity, as we have seen above, is often a prerequisite for healing.[97] Pulling patients through trees to cure them of hernia, rickets, and other diseases is known throughout Europe, and in America.[98] As a matter of fact, the great German comparativist, Karl Weinhold, remarks that the ritual was best undertaken with the patient in the naked state.[99] Unusual kinds of pulling through include a pregnant woman's crawling naked through the chorion of a foal to insure easy delivery. This is done in Denmark,[100] or, she may crawl naked through the skeleton of a horse for the same purpose.[101] To protect villages from pestilence in the South Slavic countries, furrows were plowed around the village seven times by twelve naked youths and maidens. This took place at midnight from Saturday to Sunday after a new moon. It was forbidden to speak, to cast lascivious glances, or to touch a fellow toiler at the plow.[102] In this general connection it will be remembered that the so-called temple sleep, or *incubatio,* for the purposes of healing, was often undertaken in the nude.[103]

Purity and innocence are important in healing rituals.[104] Notions range from virginity and sexual purity to faithfulness within the marital bond; also to the innocence of children, and to sequestered plants upon which human eyes have not fallen. In my collection are unpublished accounts of the use of yarn spun by a girl under seven years of age for the treatment of arthritis. Since the girl is still in the age of innocence, this virtue is passed on to the wool used in the cure. An unpublished California item prescribes the urine of a faithful wife for the cure of sore eyes. In 'passing through' rituals there has been reported from Poland an unusual case involving virgins as officiants at the 'pulling through' ceremony. Moonstruck children are drawn through an apple-tree by two virgins, each being the eldest child in her respective family.[105] The use of a so-called 'maiden ash' is used for 'pulling through' rituals in parts of England, particularly in Dorsetshire and Herefordshire. A 'maiden ash' is described as a tree grown from its own seed and never touched by a knife.[106] In Newfoundland a so-called 'maiden dogwood' is used. It is a species which 'grows alone and never blossoms.'[107] That trees which have grown and developed in out-of-the-way places and hence have pretentions to 'innocence' and inviolability, is seen in an excellent example from Yugoslavia. Here the cane of a wild rose bush is split open for the 'passing through' ceremony. The bush is located by a seeress on the eve of an appropriate feast day. The bush must have sprouted that year, and the eyes of no human being must have, as yet, fallen upon it. A highly involved religious ritual follows.[108]

The dead and the realm of the dead, are important in folk curing. To be reckoned in this complex of beliefs and customs is the use of the wood (splinters) and nails of coffins, and various things having to do with the cemetery, the grave itself, and its contents, including the bones of the defunct.[109] These are made into medicaments themselves, or the funeral paraphernalia are pressed into service in various kinds of magical cures. For the wealth of material to be found one should consult the *Handwörterbuch des deutschen Aberglaubens* under appropriate headings such as *Friedhof*[110] and *Grab.*[111] The magical transmission of diseases to the dead by placing into the coffin dressings, rags, and other *Zwischenträger* that have been in contact with the sick person, is an interesting phenomenon in the magical transference of disease, or the translocation of disease, as the early workers called it.[112] The use of a dead man's hand, or 'hand of glory', as it is called, for the treatment of the king's evil is a well-known magical cure in folklore.[113] The dead man's hand was sometimes gained from the corpses of criminals on the gibbet. This introduces us to another whole area of magical curing power, and I have treated this in a special paper.[114]

NOTES

1. W. D. Hand, 'The Magical Transference of Disease', *North Carolina Folklore* 13 (1965), 83–109.
2. W. D. Hand, 'Plugging, Nailing, Wedging and Kindred Folk Medical Practices', in *Folklore and Society. Essays in Honor of Benj. A. Botkin* ed. B. Jackson (Hatboro, Pennsylvania 1966), 63–75.
3. W. D. Hand, ' "Passing Through." Folk Medical Magic and Symbolism', *Proceedings of the American Philosophical Society* 102 (1968), 379–402.
4. G. Jungbauer, *Deutsche Volksmedizin. Ein Grundriss* (Berlin 1934); C. Seyfarth, *Aberglaube und Zauberei in der Volksmedizin Sachsens* (Leipzig 1913).
5. *Frank C. Brown Collection of North Carolina Folklore* 1–7 (Durham, North Carolina 1952–1961); Vols. 6–7 (1961–1964) contain *Popular Beliefs and Superstitions from North Carolina* ed. W. D. Hand. (Hereinafter cited: Brown Coll.).
6. For a long and detailed article on the subject, s.v. *Kreuzweg* in H. Bächtold-Stäubli and E. von Hoffmann-Krayer, *Handwörterbuch des deutschen Aberglaubens* 1–10 (Berlin and Leipzig 1927–1942); see Vol. 5, 516–529. (Hereinafter cited HDA.). Cf. E. Schneeweis, *Serbokroatische Volkskunde. 1. Volksglaube und Volksbrauch* (Berlin 1961), 29; Jungbauer, *op. cit.*, 97.
7. HDA 5, 525–527.
8. *Ibid.*, 527–529.
9. *Ibid.*, 525.
10. Brown Coll. 6, 330, No. 2549.
11. Brown Coll. 6, 332, No. 2566.
12. Brown Coll. 6, 342, No. 2635.
13. HDA 6, 526 (Seyfarth, *op. cit.*, 218).
14. HDA 5, 526.
15. H. F. Feilberg, 'Zwieselbäume nebst verwandtem Aberglauben in Skandinavien', *Zeitschrift des Vereins für Volkskunde* 7 (1897), 45 (more specifically, 'where three paths cross').
16. Feilberg, *op. cit.*, 44.
17. *Notes and Queries,* 4th Ser., Vol. 3 (March 6, 1869), 216.
18. W. G. Wood-Martin, *Traces of the Elder Faiths of Ireland* 1–2 (London 1902), see Vol. 2, 228–229.

19. Feilberg, *op. cit.*, 45.

20. O. v. Hovorka and A. Kronfeld, *Vergleichende Volksmedizin* 1–2 (Stuttgart 1908–1909), Vol. 2, 694–695.

21. V. W. Forsblom, *Magisk folkmedicin* (Finlands svenska folkdiktning. 7. *Folktro och trolldom.* No. 5; Helsingfors 1927), 541.

22. S. X. Radbill, 'Whooping Cough in Fact and Fancy', *Bulletin of the History of Medicine* 13 (1943), 48.

23. Brown Coll. 6, 316, No. 2449.

24. For a treatment of directions in ancient mythology and folklore, see HDA 4, 27–34.

25. H. D. Levine, 'Folk Medicine in New Hampshire', *New England Journal of Medicine* 224, No. 12 (1941), 488.

26. E. Radford and M. A. Radford, *Encyclopaedia of Superstitions* (London 1947), 123.

27. T. F. Thiselton Dyer, *English Folklore* (London 1878), 171–172; Eveline Camilla Gurdon, *County Folk-lore. Printed Extracts,* No. 2, *Suffolk* (Publications of the Folk-lore Society 38; London 1895), 26–27 (the tree must be split early in the spring, as near east and west as possible, and the child passed through naked as the sun is rising).

28. *Folk-Lore* 8 (1897), 187.

29. HDA 8, 35–36, s.v. *Sonne; ibid.*, 1329, s.v. *umkreisen; ibid.*, 1337, s.v. *umlaufen.*

30. R. L. Tongue and K. M. Briggs, *Somerset Folklore* (Publications of the Folklore Society 114; London 1965), 221.

31. For a discussion of *withershins (widdershins)* or *deiseil* and its historic associations, see the revised edition of the E. and M. A. Radford *Encyclopaedia of Superstitions* by Christina Hole (London 1961), 329–330, s.v. *sunwise turn.*

32. *Folk-Lore* 54 (1943), 298–299.

33. Forsblom, *op. cit.*, 539.

34. *Ibid.*

35. Jungbauer, *op. cit.*, 88.

36. For a notion of the range of folk beliefs and customs involving 'backwards', see HDA 10, 288, s.v. *rückwärts.* See also E. Weinkopf, 'Die Umkehrung in Glaube und Brauch', *Oberdeutsche Zeitschrift für Volkskunde* 2 (1928), 43–56.

37. Jungbauer, *op. cit.*, 87.

38. Brown Coll. 6, 142, No. 1026.

39. HDA 8, 1346–1350, s.v. *umsehen;* G. D. Hendricks, 'Don't Look Back', *Publications of the Texas Folklore Society* 30 (1961), 69–75.

40. Brown Coll. 6, 147, No. 1080. This item also illustrates remote and unknown areas as being propitious for riddance rituals where the basic notion of 'losing' a disease is at issue.

41. Brown Coll. 6, 343, No. 2647.

42. Jungbauer, *op. cit.*, 88.

43. Brown Coll. 6, 329, No. 2545.

44. Brown Coll. 6, 325, No. 2515: 'Pick the wart until it bleeds, rub some blood on a grain of corn and throw it over your right shoulder, and never look back. The warts will soon be carried away.'

45. *Pennsylvania Dutchman,* Vol. 5, No. 14 (March 15, 1954), 2.

46. Brown Coll. 6, 165, No. 1239.

47. HDA 4, 1489. Cf. Jungbauer, *op. cit.*, 88; Weinkopf, *op. cit.*, 45.

48. Brown Coll. 6, 287, No. 2212.
49. HDA 8, 76–82; Jungbauer, *op. cit.*, 97.
50. Hand, 'Passing Through', 382–383, *passim.*
51. Brown Coll. 6, 113.
52. Jungbauer, *op. cit.*, 97; HDA 8, 77–82, s.v. *Sonnenuntergang.*
53. HDA 8, 77, s.v. *Sonnenuntergang.*
54. Hand, 'Passing Through', 388.
55. HDA 6, 432–435, s.v. *Mitternacht.*
56. *Ibid.*, 432–433; P. Sébillot, *Le Folk-Lore de France* 1–4 (Paris 1904–1907), Vol. 2, 240; A. Wuttke, *Deutscher Aberglaube der Gegenwart* (3rd ed., Berlin 1900), 14. sec. 12; Jungbauer, *op. cit.*, 97.
57. HDA 6, 433, s.v. *Mitternacht.*
58. Feilberg, *op. cit.*, 44.
59. R. Gallop, *Portugal. A Book of Folk-Ways* (Cambridge 1936), 52.
60. HDA 6, 433–434.
61. S. Seligmann, *Der böse Blick und Verwandtes. Ein Beitrag zur Geschichte des Aberglaubens aller Zeiten und Völker.* 1–2 (Berlin 1910), Vol. 2, 8–9.
62. Seyfarth, *op. cit.*, 267, as reported in HDA 6, 433.
63. Sébillot, *op. cit.*, Vol. 2, 320.
64. Hand, 'Passing Through', 382, 385, 388, *passim.*
65. A. de Cock, 'Eene oude Geneeswijze', *Volkskunde* 7 (1894), 71.
66. Jungbauer, *op. cit.*, 97.
67. HDA 4, 712–713; Jungbuaer, *op. cit.*, 98.
68. Hand, 'Passing Through', 382–383.
69. Radford, *op. cit.*, 123.
70. J. Frazer, *The Golden Bough* 1–12 (London 1911–1915), Vol. 11, 188–189.
71. Forsblom, *op. cit.*, 539.
72. HDA 5, 1549, s.v. *Maitag.*
73. HDA 6, 495–502, s.v. *Mond.*
74. Hand, 'Passing Through', 382, 383, 386, 388, 393, 395.
75. Hovorka and Kronfeld, *op. cit.*, Vol. 2, 694. Feilberg, *op. cit.*, 44.
76. HDA 10, 64–67. See also 'drei'-compounds
77. Brown Coll. 6, 232, No. 1798.
78. Brown Coll. 6, 120, No. 831.
79. *Mélusine* 8 (1896–1897), 202.
80. Hand, 'Passing Through', 382, 384, 385, 393, 400.
81. Brown Coll. 6, 133, No. 946.
82. HDA 8, 365–369, s.v. *stehlen;* Jungbauer, *op. cit.*, 79. For a more basic treatment of the magic attached to stealing, see P. Sartori, 'Diebstahl als Zauber', *Schweizerisches Archiv für Volkskunde* 20 (1916), 380–388, who puts forward the idea, among other things, that the power of the real owner goes with the stolen object. Jacob Grimm argued that one of the principal values of the stolen object lay in the danger of obtaining it. (J. Grimm, *Deutsche Mythologie,* 4th ed. by E. H. Meyer, 1–2 Berlin 1875–1878, see Vol. 2, 952). For another interpretation see Helen Creighton, *Bluenose Magic* (Toronto 1968), 238, No. 414 (notes on page 245).
83. HDA 8, 267, s.v. *stehlen.*
84. HDA 8, 366, s.v. *stehlen.*
85. Cf. Brown Coll. 6, 335, Nos. 2587, 2591, *passim;* 318–319, Nos. 2469, 2471, 2473, *passim.*

86. Brown Coll. 6, 132, No. 937.

87. Brown Coll. 6, 334, No. 2580.

88. Hand, 'Passing Through', 382, 388, *passim.*

89. de Cock, *op. cit.,* 70.

90. Hand, 'Passing Through', 388.

91. Sébillot, *op. cit.,* Vol. 2, 320.

92. Sébillot, *op. cit.,* Vol. 2, 320.

93. Brown Coll. 6, 333, No. 2577.

94. Brown, Coll. 6, 313, No. 2437.

95. *Natural History,* Book 26, LX.

96. HDA 6, 1157–1161, s.v. *nüchtern.*

97. For a general treatise on nudity, including magical material of all kinds, as well as matters pertaining strictly to folk medicine, see HDA 6, 823–916, esp. 841–852, s.v. *nackt, Nacktheit.* Cf. Jungbauer, *op. cit.,* 96.

98. Hand, 'Passing Through', 382, *passim.*

99. HDA 6, 901, s.v. *nackt, Nacktheit.*

100. *Zeitschrift des Vereins für Volkskunde* 12 (1902), 112.

101. HDA 6, 902, s.v. *nackt, Nacktheit.*

102. HDA 6, 434, s.v. *Mitternacht;* 847 ff., s.v. *nackt, Nacktheit.*

103. HDA 6, 884, n. 576.

104. Jungbauer, *op. cit.,* 96.

105. *Mélusine* 8 (1896–1897), 170.

106. *Folk-Lore* 16 (1905), 65.

107. Fanny D. Bergen, *Animal and Plant Lore* (Memoirs of the American Folklore Society 7; Boston and New York 1899), 101–102, No. 1166.

108. Hand, 'Passing Through', 386. (This is summarized in some detail.)

109. Jungbauer, *op. cit.*, 79.

110. HDA 3, 93–94, *passim.*

111. HDA 3, 1080–1081.

112. For a good treatment of this, see HDA 3, 1098–1101, s.v. *Grabbeigaben.* A shorter summary is to be found in Hand, 'Transference', 90–91.

113. *Encyclopaedia of Superstitions* ed. Christina Hole, 124–127.

114. 'Hangmen, the Gallows, and the Dead Man's Hand in American Folk Medicine' in *Medieval Literature and Folklore Studies. Essays in Honor of Francis Lee Utley,* ed. J. Mandel and B. A. Rosenberg (New Brunswick, New Jersey 1970), 323-329, 381-387.

2

The Magical Transference of Disease*

The magical transference of disease is one of the most engaging subjects in the whole field of folk medicine. Whether found among primitive peoples in remote parts of the world, among our European ancestors, or in twentieth-century America, the practice of ridding a person of a disease by transferring the malady to another person, to animals, plants, and to various kinds of objects rests on sympathetic magic.[1] By these principles the disease is passed on by direct or indirect contact between the victim and the person, animal, plant or object to which the disease is communicated. The transfer may also take place symbolically. In honoring a man who has worked in American folk medicine as well as in the broader field of folk belief, I shall attempt in this paper to summarize the various ways, in the folk mind, that diseases are passed on. Since Arthur Palmer Hudson's distinguished career has been largely identified with the State of North Carolina, I shall cite North Carolina material wherever possible, and follow up with other American material —this against Old-World beliefs and practices in pertinent areas of folk medicine.

For the purposes of this chapter it should be pointed out at

*This article originally appeared in *Folklore Studies in Honor of Arthur Palmer Hudson.* Chapel Hill, North Carolina: The North Carolina Folklore Society, 1965, pp. 83–109, constituting Vol. XIII, Nos. 1-2 of North Carolina Folklore. Permission to reprint has been given by the North Carolina Folklore Society.

the outset that I am not interested in mere riddance or divestment of disease, whether by burial, stripping, casting off, floating away, or other means. These symbolic rituals are widely known and easily understood. To claim our attention here the disease must be communicated to second parties or things and it must be expressly stated, or clearly implied, that the disease is received by a new victim, or a new receiving agent that is itself affected by the transfer. Neither does communication to an intermediate agent, a *Zwischenträger,* suffice for this discussion. Ideally for the argument of this study, it should be shown that when the disease is communicated from the victim to other persons, or to animals, it will continue its ravages or induce disease or death in the new victim. By an extension of folk thought, the evil effect can be imagined as extending also to plants, and by further analogy, even to inanimate objects.[2] For Anglo-Saxon England, however, Grendon notes that diseases are rarely transferred to lifeless objects.[3]

The communication of disease to trees and shrubs by means of plugging, wedging, nailing, and similar means, is being taken up in a special paper,[4] and these means will be alluded to here only as they relate to matters in hand. In connection with what has been said above with respect to the transfer of disease, however, it should be pointed out that in the case of plugging and nailing into seasoned wood, stone, or other kinds of materials, the new medium may be more often thought of as a place of storage, or as a place where the infection is brought to a state of arrest. Such cases would differ in fundamental conception, of course, from cases where the tree itself is affected to a point where it withers and dies, or gives other evidence of "attack."

We shall begin our survey by considering the direct transfer of disease by magical or other inexplicable means from one person to another.[5] Here, as in other kinds of transfer discussed in this paper, the infection of the new agent is thought to free the victim himself. Direct infection of an innocent party with a venereal disease, for example, is considered in North Carolina as an "only" means of ridding oneself of the malady.[6] In writing of this notion in the Ozarks, Randolph observes that "the best way to cure a 'dose' of syphilis or gonorrhea is by communicating it to as many other persons as possible," noting with grim humor that the theory is responsible for untold misery in the Ozark country.[7] Italians in New York at the time of World War I believed that syphilis could be cured by intercourse with a girl sexually immature,[8] but the entry in question does not specify that the girl herself was infected. Presumably she was.

The transmission of non-infectious diseases by contagious magic from one human to another, direct, rather than by means of a *Zwischenträger,* i.e., an intermediate agent, is not widely encountered. Epilepsy, however, was thought to be contracted by mere touch.[9] In India the exfoliated skin of a person afflicted with smallpox was left at the crossroads for the first person passing by to touch and thus acquire the disease.[10]

The absorption of the strength of a child or of a young person by sleeping with an older person has been noted for North Carolina,[11] and elsewhere in the United States, with threatened shortened life (Pennsylvania; Illinois). Coupled with this is the notion (Pennsylvania) that a sickly person sleeping with a well person will get well at the latter's expense.[12] In Pennsylvania warts were believed to be "catching," and it was thus prudent to avoid shaking hands with a person who had them.[13] A not so clear example of person-to-person contact is seen in a Kentucky belief that if you kiss your wart and then kiss someone, your wart will come off.[14]

Far more common than direct person-to-person contact in the transmission of disease, according to folk medical belief, is the transference of various kinds of diseases—generally noninfectious—by intermediate agents. Communication is effected by making direct contact with the person to whom the disease is passed on, or by leaving the disease on his premises. Of the latter means there are good accounts of the transmittal of ague to a neighbor by placing parings of the victim's nails and clippings of his hair in a bag, and placing the contents under the neighbor's threshold.[15] Black cites a classic example of transference by means of physical residue—parings of the nails, hair from the eyebrows and from the crown of the head—bound up in a clout with a halfpenny and laid down in a certain place where whoever found the bundle would take up the convulsions and the diseased person would be set free (Scotland, 1695).[16]

In addition to being transferred by means of bags, cloth, and the like,[17] diseases may be passed on through pins, either directly, or by means of some sort of parcel or packing in which the pin is secreted. In Missouri, for example, one runs a pin through a wart, puts the pin in the road, and the finder gets the wart.[18] In Nebraska, the pin is stuck in the wart, and then wrapped in a corn shuck, which is put in the road and transferred to the first person who steps on the shuck.[19] In another fine example of contagious magic (Kansas, before the turn of the century), the wart is picked, and the blood collected in brown paper which is thrown into the road without looking where it falls, and destined to pass to the person finding the bundle. The pin itself, by way of variation, is not transferred.[20] A further variation is seen in an item from New York State, 1896, wherein as many pins as one has warts are stolen, wrapped in paper, and thrown into the road for a passerby to pick up. No contact between the pins and the warts is mentioned, however.[21]

Pebbles or rocks and stones of various kinds are used as disposal agents, whether by contagious magic, by counting, or other means.[22] Novelist Jesse Stuart in his early days as a folklore collector tells of a Kentucky custom of curing styes by placing as many gravels on the eyelids as one had styes, and then throwing them into the road for an unwary traveler to pick up and contract the styes.[23] In Georgia, boils were rubbed with pieces of flint which one chanced to find sticking in the ground, and then rubbed. However, instead of leaving the contaminated stone for someone to pick up, the flint was placed back in the same position as found, the practitioner turning around, and leaving backwards.[24] This would seem to be a variety of "plugging," in the sense that the disease is put into a hole, which is then stopped up.[25] The transference of warts by means of pebbles rubbed over warts, wrapped or rolled in paper, and then disposed of so as readily to be found, is seen in North Carolina entries in the Brown Collection.[26] Even more widespread in North Carolina and elsewhere is the practice of counting pebbles to correspond to the number of warts, and then placing them in a paper bag, purse, box, etc., for passersby to pick up. The circumstances of the transaction (crossroads, thrown backward over the right shoulder, tossed over the left shoulder, etc.) exhibit usual magical practice, but transference is noted in all cases.[27]

The communication of warts and other diseases to people by means of paper as a disposal agent is known in different parts of the United States and Canada.[28] This transfer is effected by contagious magic, also occasionally by counting.[29] In this ritual act, warts are picked, or otherwise made to bleed, drops of blood are caught on paper, folded, and disposed of by throwing the folded paper behind the victim.[30] The blood may also be placed in an envelope, and dropped in the road for a finder to pick up.[31] Disposal may occur at a crossroad where the paper has been left by having been thrown over the victim's left shoulder.[32] As part of the disposal ritual, strict secrecy is often enjoined.[33] In all examples of transfer by communication of blood from the wart to paper, and subsequent disposal, clear reference is made to the new victim, e.g., "the one who finds it will take your wart"; "if anyone picks up the paper, your wart will pass to him"; "whoever picks up your blood will take your wart," etc., etc.

Paper as a packaging material, rather than as an immediate *Zwischenträger,* as in the four examples above, is encountered in different kinds of situations where mysterious disposal is resorted to, the finder not knowing what he is about to pick up. An example from Lancashire will illustrate: "for warts rub them with a cinder, and this tied up in paper, and dropped where four roads meet (i.e., where the roads cross), will transfer the warts to whoever opens the parcel."[34] An even more tempting package is reported from the French-speaking parts of Switzerland, where as many hairs and as many peas as the person has warts are placed in a parcel with an address on it, and left in the road for an inquisitive person to pick up, and thus contract the warts.[35] Counting, and not contagious magic, it should be noted, is involved here. This same kind of procedure is seen in an American example from Illinois, for instance, where anything at hand is rubbed on warts, and then is placed in a paper sack and thrown away for some person to pick up and take the warts.[36] The most common way of all in the United States and Canada for the riddance of warts, however, is the packaging of such common vegetables as beans, peas, potatoes, and, among the cereals, corn. Barley is used in Scotland.[37] Vegetables are usually counted, to equal the number of warts. They are then packaged and placed conveniently for pickup, or thrown away, or they are first brought into contact with the warts by touching, rubbing, and other means. The use of corn and beans under varying circumstances may be found in the Brown Collection;[38] likewise potatoes.[39] In Ontario peas, to the exact number, are rubbed on warts, tied in a package, and tossed over the left shoulder while walking along the street, there to await a hapless finder.[40] Other examples of paper as a packaging material rather than as an intermediate agent of contagious magic will be noted in this paper as they occur. Bits of straw, made into a bundle of its own, are likewise disposed of in the street or in a path.[41]

More common than communication of the disease to paper by immediate contact—drops of blood, touching, rubbing, and the like—is the use of cloths or textile goods of various kinds. A dishrag, preferably a stolen one, is one of the best known agents for the disposal of warts. It is either impregnated with blood from the warts, or rubbed on them, then disposed of in some place where the rag is likely to be picked up by someone.[42] In Texas corns are disposed of in essentially the same way, i.e., blood from the corn, induced by the prick of a needle, is dropped onto a cotton cloth, the cloth thrown away, and then picked up by an unwary victim.[43] Handkerchiefs are used in much the same way as dishrags and other kinds of cloth for the riddance of warts.[44] A curious Spanish example from New Mexico involves, not the knotting of string, cord, ribbon, etc., as we shall see in the next paragraph, but the knotting of a rag, and disposal in the usual way.[45] Before leaving rags as agents of transfer, however, one should note a variation of "plugging" from the Ozark country. Randolph describes a practice in which a stolen dishrag is rubbed over a wart, and then hidden secretly under a flat rock, care being taken to replace the rock in exactly the same position as found.[46] Finally a curious German custom should be noted here that involves the use of rags for ridding oneself of pesky skin eruptions (*die blinden Dinger*). Matter from these sores is rubbed onto a clean rag, which is then wrapped to the axle of a wagon, thus communicating the sores to the first person riding in the vehicle.[47]

Another means of communicating disease to second parties, perhaps best known in connection with charming away warts, is the transfer of the disease to twine, string, yarn, ribbon, and other materials of animal and plant fibre, by means of knots. A typical example, current in Texas, will suffice: "To cure warts, make as many knots in a thread as you have warts; then throw the string away. Whoever picks up the thread will get the warts instead of you."[48] The element of counting, it should be noted, is especially resorted to where warts and other excrescences that are separate and countable are involved.[49] Counting may extend by analogy to other maladies not so readily countable. In Maryland, for example, chills are counted, transmitted to a string by means of knots, thrown away, "and whoever finds the string has the chills transferred to him or her, and you are rid of them."[50] Toothache is charmed away in Newfoundland by tying knots in a fishing line, but transfer to fish, or to persons or objects is not mentioned.[51]

The buying and selling of warts, of course, involves direct transfer by sale and purchase,[52] but the transaction is often more subtly carried out. At Delphos, Kansas, before the turn of the century, for example, a young man would gallantly procure his sweetheart's warts by purchase.[53] That the transfer is a symbolic affair is seen in the fact that pins, ancient folk symbols of value and worth, are used as well as money.[54] In the Kentucky mountains, warts will go away if you give a girl who is not related to you a pin or something like a pin.[55] In this item, and frequently in this kind of disposal, the victim himself pays the price of the sale, but this does not seem to affect the transfer to the "buyer." An unusual kind of purchase by pins is reported from the Cumberland Mountains, where a witch buys the excrescence with pins.[56]

Sale of warts for coin is common, but specific mention of the fact that the buyer gets the warts is not. Representative references from Massachusetts,[57] Illinois,[58] and the Ozark country[59] illustrate the transfer of warts by sale. More common, of course, is the transfer by means of contagious magic as part of the "sale." In such cases the penny or other coin is either anointed with the blood from the wart prior to sale, or the coin is rubbed on the wart or otherwise brought into contact with it. The coin is disposed of in the street, at the crossroads, or in some other place where it is likely to be found and picked up.[60] An item from Indiana exhibits an unusual twist.[61] The sale of warts to a tree will be taken up under transference of disease to trees. A multiple involvement of pebbles counted out to represent the number of warts and placed in a bag, along with a penny, is seen in a Maryland wart cure. The bag and contents are placed on the roadside, and the finder gets the warts.[62] Before passing to other ways of transferring disease, I must cite one final item dealing with contagious magic. It is a way of curing a person of fever, as practiced in Portugal. A person with fever mixes nail parings with a little tobacco into a cigarette, which he drops at a crossroads without looking up. The person picking up the cigarette acquires the fever with it.[63]

We have already seen warts counted for purposes of transfer to pebbles and to knots in string, twine, and other such filaments. Now we come face to face with the magic of counting as it affects transfer of disease from one person to another. All examples deal with warts, and are to the effect that a person counting another one's warts will get them himself. Bergen says this belief is general in the United States.[64] An item of German-Canadian folk belief from Ontario specifies quite logically that "if you have more than one wart on your hand, get some person to count them and he will get them."[65] Another folk medical practice from Ontario involves counting, but the number of warts is written on a piece of paper, which is then placed in a stolen dish-cloth, and thrown into the road without anyone's seeing the act. Whoever picks up the parcel gets the warts.[66] In the early 1890's in Georgia riddance of freckles was affected by counting them, putting an equal number of pebbles into a paper, and then leaving the package where someone could step on it, and thus get freckles.[67]

Akin to the transfer of warts and other diseases by the magic of counting is the wishing of maladies on other people. Warts are wished onto the body of someone else,[68] wished off on the living without their consent,[69] or wished on a friend.[70] A stye is ceremonially wished onto the first person who passes by.[71] In Michigan praying for the pain to pass from one person to another—rheumatism from son to father in this case—is reported from French-American tradition.[72] In related kinds of subtle transfer, a disease is thought in the Orkney and Shetland Islands to pass into the hearer by his merely listening to a description of the malady. This may be counteracted if he spits covertly.[73] Merely looking into an open kettle containing tasty food, which has been placed at the crossroads, is said to be enough to rid the sufferer of jaundice as the disease passes to the inquisitive "pot-looker."[74]

The transference of styes by verbal magic is well known. The attendant circumstances vary considerably, whether the transference is carried out at midnight, at the crossroads, the street corner, or whatever; a stable feature, however, is always the command of the stye to leave and to go to some passerby, "the next one that passes by,"[75] ". . . the next feller passin' by!"[76] or ". . . the fust-un that comes by."[77]

Until now we have been concerned with the magical transfer of disease from one person to another, either directly, or in various indirect ways. Now we shall consider the role of the dead in relieving the living of disease.[78] Principally involved in such transferals are boils, goiter, epilepsy, toothache, and warts, with the difference, however, that the corpse becomes a *Zwischenträger* in the burial of the disease, rather than a direct victim. The following cure for warts from Indiana comes as close to communicating a disease to the dead as anything I know: "If you know someone who died that had warts, touch the hands of the corpse with your hands and your warts will go with the dead,"[79] but one should not lose sight of the fact that the new bearer already had the malady! In other cases that have come to my attention contagious magic is usually involved. The means employed in the transfer are already familiar to us, as the following typical examples will show, but the effect and emphasis is never so much on the dead as it is, symbolically, on the burial and decay of the warts. Examples chosen deal only with touching the dead, not with things merely placed in the coffin. "If you have a goitre on your neck, rub a dead person's hand over it three times. As the body decays, the goitre will disappear."[80] "For boils, go to the house where there is a corpse which is to be buried the next day, and ask him to take the evil with him."[81] "To cure epilepsy, remove the sufferer's shirt wrongside out, and place it in the coffin under the head of a corpse."[82] The wishing off of warts onto the dead in Indiana has not been described in detail,[83] but perhaps "wishing" is used figuratively by the author. Likewise, little is known about the exact method by which the devil takes one's warts. According to a Kentucky account, one must wait until someone dies, then just at midnight go to the grave, and call to the devil. He will take away the warts.[84] Even more involved is a Tennessee folk medical practice described as follows: "To remove a wart, take a black cat to the cemetery at midnight; when the devil comes to get his people, command the cat to follow the devil, and command the warts to follow the cat."[85] This in reality constitutes a transfer of disease to an animal, and leads up to the subject of the communication of disease to animals.

The close relationship between man and the animals he has domesticated has presumably existed from earliest times. The care given to animals and the affection showered on them—not only on pets, but also on beasts of burden, and producers of meat and fibre—is to be explained in the close working relationship between the husbandman and his animals. Man's abuse of animals may likewise be accounted for in terms of this same intimacy, a fact which explains why society has no words harsh enough to describe the horsebeater and the tormenter of dogs and cats. That man has always taken his spite and frustration out on the dumb creation, however, must be assumed. Whether these practical considerations shed light on the underlying notions of the scapegoat is hard to say,[86] but these ideas at least afford some insight into the thinking which underlies the symbolic passing of disease from humans to animals. This whole question had its emotional and sympathetic aspects, we can safely believe, long before experimental animals were used in medical research. Even so, the real answer is perhaps best to be found in notions of sympathetic magic,[87] for we shall see here the same folk logic and symbolism that we have come to see throughout this paper, and will continue to see also in the transfer of disease to trees.

The transfer of disease to animals is ancient[88] and worldwide.[89] With material far too copious to cite in detail, I shall limit myself to discussing the direct transfer of disease to animals by contagious magic, direct and indirect, by symbolic magic, and by wishing and similar thought processes. The magical acquisition of disease from animals will be taken up in a separate paper.

We can begin this phase of the discussion by pointing out that there is a direct counterpart to the riddance of venereal disease through sexual intercourse with other human beings, especially virgins or immature children of both sexes, namely, the communication of such diseases to animals.[90] In Mohammedan countries mares are favorite partners for men seeking to rid themselves of social diseases.[91]

The keeping of animals in the room where the sick are to absorb disease, or perhaps even to prevent it in the first place, is encountered in many places. Among Slavic and Germanic peoples, for example, guinea pigs were kept as pets in the house for this purpose.[92] Oldenburg peasants kept goldfinches or turtle doves in the house to draw consumptive diseases to themselves.[93] More difficult to envision, what with problems of sanitation and all, was the keeping of goats in the nursery to attract the diseases of sick children.[94] Black reports the practice in Nebraska of keeping cats around for asthma. When nine cats have caught the asthma from you, the account says, you will be cured.[95] Riddance by remote control—though by some sort of absorption, if one tries to get at the root of the symbolism—is seen in a German belief that gout is communicated to the first bird that flies over a crossroads.[96] Sleeping with domestic animals—dogs, cats, and guinea pigs—appears to be widely known and practiced. Dogs as sleeping partners are treated in the *Brown Collection,*[97] with representative entries from many parts of the United States, and also from Europe. It is invariably stated that the dog gets the rheumatism; sometimes details are added. In an Illinois item,[98] for instance, the dog is said to absorb the disease and become crippled. The death of a pelon dog after absorbing rheumatism is reported from Texas.[99] The use of cats for the same purpose is taken up in the *Brown Collection,* but does not seem so well known.[100] Apropos of the supposed absorption of rheumatic and arthritic pains by cat fur, the writer was astonished to find in the best drug stores in Paris in 1961 tanned cat pelts for sale. The use of the guinea pig for rheumatism—being constantly near one, fondling it, or sleeping with it—is found primarily in the German tradition in the United States and Canada,[101] but it is known among the Slavs, Magyars, and Jews.[102] In different parts of the United States puppies are secured for children to play with and sleep with. Through this contact the dog is supposed to take on the fits, and the child will grow better. A complete cure will follow only when the dog dies.[103] Bergen gives insight into the degree with which even reasonably intelligent people viewed this kind of magical transfer: "A few years ago, a young man in Holyoke, Mass. (a common-sense person)," she writes, "had a child ill with dumb ague. By advice he got a pup and put it in the child's cradle. The dog broke out in sores, and the child got well."[104]

Mere contact with an animal is often sufficient for the disease to pass from the victim to the animal. In Ontario, for example, the mere touching of a live frog to a goiter is sufficient to make the malady pass into the frog; however, final curing depends upon burying the hapless critter head downwards in the ground until he decays. When this happens the goiter will disappear.[105] Tying or binding a live frog to the affected part will cure a felon,[106] will cause chills to go out of the patient into the frog,[107] will cure asthma,[108] and, in a North Carolina example, spells resembling the hard ague.[109] In the Blue Grass country a live toad is bound to the back to cure rheumatism, the pain passing from the back of the sufferer into the toad.[110] Dorson notes an early American example (ca. 1709) of distemper's being extracted from a man by placing a rattlesnake around the man's waist. The snake died as the cure was effected.[111] Convulsions are treated in West Virginia by plucking the feathers from the breast of a live pigeon, holding the pigeon's breast to the pit of the stomach until the person comes to. The convulsions are drawn from the person, and the bird is affected with the malady.[112] In a similar Yorkshire practice, a live duck is used for colic, the duck dying as it takes away the pain from the sufferer.[113] Grendon notes that in Anglo-Saxon times the mere sitting on the back of an ass, face to the tail, was sufficient to transfer the disease to the beast.[114]

The transmission of a disease to an animal by exhalation of breath, or by oral contact, constitutes perhaps the most intimate means by which diseases are passed on to animals, carrying almost "breath of life" implications. A Texas folk medical practice will illustrate this kind of a cure: "Go down to the river and catch a frog. Pry open the frog's mouth and blow your breath into it. This must be done before daylight in the morning. The frog will die before sundown, but the asthma will go into the frog and will never bother the sufferer again."[115] Thrush was cured in Cheshire by holding a young frog in the mouth of the sufferer a few moments as the frog took the malady to itself.[116] A similar procedure was used elsewhere in the British Isles for whooping cough, with toads as well as frogs figuring in the cure.[117] In Ireland a trout was put into the child's mouth, then put back in the stream, carrying with it the whooping cough.[118] A live fish was pressed into service for coughs in the Pennsylvania German country, either by the patient smelling the breath, letting the fish breathe over the patient (reversal) or, contrariwise, letting the patient inhale the fish's breath.[119] As a logical extension of breathing, one also encounters spitting into the mouth of a frog to cure disease.[120] In antiquity toothache was transferred to a frog by spitting on it, a procedure which lacked the intimacy of direct mouth-to-mouth contact.[121] Unique as it is nondescript, a treatment for tuberculosis among the Spanish people of New Mexico prescribes the swallowing of a live louse, which is supposed to eat the germ.[122]

Rubbing an animal on an afflicted part of the body constitutes perhaps the most thorough and conscious kind of contact and contamination which occur in the whole gamut of contagious magic. Frogs, toads, and snails are among the creatures most widely used in this kind of magical transfer of disease from humans to animals. An example from Illinois will illustrate the typical treatment: "Rub the belly of a live frog on your goitre three times and throw the frog over your left shoulder. Your goitre will disappear and the frog will die."[123] Live snails are used in similar fashion for the cure of warts. After being rubbed on the wart the snail is either freed to crawl away with the excrescence,[124] or it is impaled on a thorn to die.[125] Among the Spanish-speaking population of the Rio Grande, epilepsy in children is treated by rubbing the naked body from head to foot with a newly born pig. The baby will break out into a copious perspiration and the pig will die.[126] The same kind of cure is undertaken for the transfer of mumps in Ireland, where a child, wrapped in a blanket, is taken to a pigsty and its head rubbed against the back of a pig. It is supposed that the mumps thereby pass from the child to the pig.[127]

The application of the warm viscera of chickens that have been killed, or of other animals, is credited with the drawing poison and other maladies from the sufferer. The animal is already dead—an apparent sacrifice—but the peristaltic action of the viscera is still able to draw out the impurities from the afflicted parts. Snakebite is frequently treated this way.[128] An illustration of the contagious principles is seen in a cure for rheumatism reported from Illinois: "Take a chicken and cut it in two and leave all the entrails in, and put your right foot in the chicken, and it will take all the rheumatism you have in your body. The poison will go into the chicken."[129] A child with fits is treated much the same way in Oklahoma, the best results being achieved by putting the child's bare feet into the entrails before the chicken is dead.[130] Diphtheria is treated in Louisiana by the application of the warm entrails of the cat to the child's throat.[131] The use of larger animals is not widespread, but in Pennsylvania it is believed among the people of German extraction that the sufferer of croup should stand in the warm spleen of a freshly slaughtered steer, and remain standing in it until the spleen grows cold.[132] Contact between the living creature and the patient by means of a bag or other container represents perhaps more of a convenience than any conscious effort to diminish the force or the immediacy of the contact. In such practices, the eel, frog, caterpillar, wood louse, or whatever, is applied to the afflicted part by means of a bag or other container. Whooping cough, for example, is prevented or combatted by placing a hairy caterpillar in a little bag affixed to the child's breast and left there for nine days to die.[133] A thimble hung around the neck is also used for the purpose,[134] or a caterpillar in a thimble inside a bag.[135] In all cases the whooping cough leaves when the caterpillar is dead and dries up. Live fishing baits tied up in a bag are placed around the neck of the sufferer, and the whooping cough leaves when the baits die.[136] A spider or a wood louse is sewed up in a bag, placed in a thimble or nut, and worn around the neck. As the insect dies the cough passes away.[137] In Kentucky a toad frog is bound around the neck in a velvet cloth and left on the goiter until it dies, at which time the goiter leaves.[138] Ague is cured in a similar fashion, a live snail being placed in a bag and worn about the neck for nine days. The snail is then thrown in the fire.[139]

The symbolic transfer of disease without direct contact between the carrier and its host follows the same general pattern as we have just seen, namely, the incarceration of the creature in a piece of muslin, a nutshell, a thimble, a box, a bottle, etc. The only difference is that no attempt is made to infect the carrier by direct contact with the host. Most of the examples of this folk medical regimen come from the British Isles, but I shall cite as typical two items from New York State: "Catch a grasshopper and put it in a thimble. Turn the thimble upside down and leave it there until the grasshopper dies. This will stop the fits."[140] The same authority reports a procedure by which two cockroaches are put in a jar and allowed to die. When they die the measles are over.[141] In the British Isles whooping cough is treated by catching a spider in a nutshell,[142] tying a common house spider up in a piece of muslin and pinning it over the mantlepiece (for easier dessication?),[143] or by catching a flying beetle and corking it up in a bottle.[144] In a more elaborate ritual, and no less brutal, twelve snails are threaded to a piece of gray wool and suspended on a nail from as high up in the chimney as one can reach.[145] In Somerset spiders are shut up in a box to cure ague.[146] The impaling of a black snail on a thorn hedge is noted for the Midland counties, or it is put between two stones.[147] All of these treatments contain vestigial ideas of animal sacrifice, as indicated above in the discussion of the scapegoat.

The communication of disease to an animal by means of an intermediate agent is much the same as the transfer of disease from one human to another, but the range of possibilities is somewhat limited. "Sale" of the disease to all intents and purposes does not exist, nor is there a "pickup" where an unwary person yields to a natural curiosity. Even so, it must be remembered that animals and birds do pick up hair, nail parings, teeth, and the like that have not been properly disposed of, and visit trouble on the hapless donors.[148] Feeding disease to an animal is perhaps the most common means of transfer, and the exchange usually takes place indirectly, with matter from the diseased part being spread on the food for the animal or other matter ingested. Along with chickens and roosters, the common household and barnyard pet, the dog, is perhaps the most frequent victim. In the British Isles whooping cough is cured by feeding hair from the victim to a dog between slices of buttered bread, the dog coming down with the disease.[149] The same remedy obtains for measles.[150] Meat instead of bread is also used as the host for hair taken from the nape of a child's neck.[151] In an unusual treatment for fever in the Pennsylvania German country, a pound of beef is boiled in the patient's urine and then fed to a black dog while still warm.[152] In a Louisiana wart cure, a piece of meat is stolen, rubbed on the wart, and then thrown in a spot where a dog would find the meat and eat it.[153] The sweat of a seriously ill person, in Germany, is swabbed off on bread or bacon, and then fed to a dog.[154] Communication of the victim's blood to an animal, in this case to a dog, is seen in a wart cure from Maryland where the wart is made to bleed, the blood put on bread and fed to a dog, and the dog getting the warts.[155] Blood from a wart, obtained in various ways, is placed on kernels of corn and fed either to roosters or to chickens.[156] Red roosters are specified in collections from Kentucky and the Ozarks.[157] Counting of the warts, and the impregnating with blood of an equivalent number of kernels of corn is reported from Kentucky and Illinois, roosters being the receiver in both curative practices.[158] Bread is used instead of kernels of corn in Alabama and Illinois.[159] Hogs take away warts by eating an ear of corn impregnated with blood,[160] and "eat up chills" after the victim has cut out as many knots (eyes) from a potato as he has chills, and then fed the potato to the hog.[161] Potatoes rubbed on warts are likewise fed to cows in a practice already familiar to us.[162] Bahama Negroes combat a severe headache by tying two live frogs, one on each temple, with a cloth, and taking care not to let them die in the process. When finally released, the frogs will be weak and die, but the headache will be gone.[163] In the realm of water-dwelling creatures, just as we have already seen fish swim off with a disease, in a manner of speaking, so likewise in a curative practice from Maryland now instanced, we can see an eel as a carrier of a disease fastened upon it by the magic of a contact: "A cure for ague is to take the patient's nail parings, all you can obtain, put in a bag, and tie about the neck of a live eel, which you then put back in the water. The eel dies and the patient recovers."[164] In the airy element, birds in Norway are credited with ridding the sufferer of boils by picking at a cloth which has been placed over the boil, with the bird getting the boil.[165] Finally, creatures living in the ground also serve as hosts to diseases which are communicated to them in ways that we have already seen. A crawfish, for example, will take away one's warts by taking over ten grains of corn placed on an incised wart and then placed in the creature's hole.[166] The burying of various kinds of *Zwischenträger* in anthills, where they are taken over and consumed, is, of course, well known.[167] An instance of the communication of chills and fever to ants without contagious magic, is reported from Haute Bretagne by Sébillot.[168]

Like other forms of the transfer of disease, the communication of human ills to trees is both ancient and widespread,[169] as is the absorption of disease and miasmas by such common plants as potatoes, onions, and garlic. We can examine first the riddance of disease by absorption into plants. A single example, one from New England, will suffice: "When you have the rheumatism, carry a potato in your pocket. The potato will become hard after a time, and believers in its virtues affirm that this is because the rheumatism has been absorbed.[170] Similarly, from Maryland: A raw onion pinned to the wall of a room where there is a fever patient will absorb the fever. It will shrivel and prevent the fever from spreading.[171] Among trees, elder is said to draw palsy from the sufferer.[172]

The ways in which a transfer of disease to trees is made are many, and there is also a wide variety of trees pressed into service for an even wider range of diseases. In parts of Europe birch trees are a favorite for this practice,[173] but the elm, the linden, and the willow are also used.[174] Among fruit trees,[175] the apple tree is perhaps most widely sought.[176]

Apart from plugging, notching, and nailing of disease to trees, which cannot be taken up here,[177] the tying or fastening of maladies to trees by thread, string, yarn, ribbons, garters, and the like, constitutes one of the main ways in which disease is transmitted.[178] In France, even a violin string is used to connect the victim with the tree.[179] An example from Illinois will illustrate typical features of the cure in America: "Tie a black string around your wart, letting it remain for three days; then remove the string and wrap it about a cherry tree, leaving it there for the same period of time. This will kill the cherry tree, but you will lose the wart.[180] In a more elaborate kind of ritual, divestment of ague in Vermont was effected by a man's tying himself (and thus the disease) to an ash tree, and then crawling out and leaving the disease tied there.[181] Equally interesting is the Dutch custom of tying one's garter to a fever tree (*koortsboom,* i.e., some kind of tree used for absorbing fever), the sufferer running away without looking back.[182] String as a *Zwischenträger* is seen in the cure of toothache, whereby the blood from around an aching tooth is communicated to a piece of string and the latter bound around the root of an apple tree.[183]

The counting, tying up and knotting of chills and warts into string and then tying these onto trees is encountered with or without contact with the patient.[184] In Texas a chain or string of button willows and eight other kinds of tree limbs are bound together and placed in the fork of the largest tree one can find. This is done in secret, and the patient backs away nine steps, then turns around, walks away without looking back, and does not talk about it.[185] Hay, straw, and wood fibre are similarly wound or bound together and used in the various ways indicated.[186] As we have seen earlier, cloths are impregnated with germs and disease, and these cloths or rags are hung on trees.[187] In Germany such trees are called *Lappenbäume,* i.e., "cloth trees."[188]

The transfer of disease, or specifically, the transfer of warts to trees by sale is uncommon, and the following North Carolina entry is wanting in detail: "Some people can sell warts to trees. After yours are gone you can go and find them on that tree."[189] Communication of disease to trees by verbal charm is well known in Europe,[190] but I do not have ready examples at hand for America.

Personal transfer of disease by the sufferer through direct contact with trees, or by acts performed in the immediate vicinity of trees, is not common. In North Carolina one climbs a tree with his hands, and without using his feet. He then jumps out of the tree, leaving the fever there.[191] I can not find examples in this country of hugging trees for the purpose of transferring diseases to them,[192] nor of biting into trees,[193] but these practices, like about everything else, will one day be found in the literature, or collected in the field once we know what to look for. Circumambulation of trees seems also not to be known.[194]

Transference of disease to metal need not detain us long. It happens either by absorption in fever[195] and rheumatic diseases, or by swallowing the metal. In Oklahoma, for instance, boils may be prevented by swallowing lead shot, usually one shot for each boil the patient has ever had. The theory is that the lead of the shot takes up or absorbs the poison, thus preventing its escape from the system through a boil.[196]

The transfer of disease to sticks and stones,[197] and to other inanimate objects,[198] is a rarity in folk medical practices of civilized peoples. Where such transference does occur it is perhaps more properly for the purpose of burial and decay, and even of safe keeping, than for communication to the element that might itself be affected by the transfer, as in all other kinds of magical transfer. The closest thing I can find to the kind of transference that has occupied us in this paper is an item from Ray B. Browne's collection from Alabama: "If you have a pain in your side pick up a rock, spit under it, put the rock back, and the pain will live under the rock."[199] In all other examples of the use of rocks, stones, and bricks—covering a variety of ailments —one must conceive of the stone mainly as a covering for the disease which is either buried, or stopped up. If this is true, then the use of stones in this fashion, should more appropriately be taken up as a phase of plugging.[200]

We may conclude this discussion with a somewhat humorous item from New York State. It shows the ingenuity of the folk in its conceptions of how diseases may be passed off from the sufferer to someone else or something else: "One who is afflicted with chills and fever should wrap himself tightly in a sheet, run around the house three times and jump under the bed. Thus the chill jumps into the bed, and he misses it."[201]

NOTES

1. Although William George Black's *Folk-Medicine: A Chapter in the History of Culture* appeared over eighty years ago (London, 1883), it is still one of the great handbooks on the subject. Particularly good, though short, is the chapter on "Transference of Disease" (pp. 34–48). The student of comparative folk medicine should also consult Hovorka and Kronfeld, *Vergleichende Volksmedizin* (2 vols., Stuttgart, 1908–1909). Transference of disease is to be found in the index under "Übertragung von Krankheit." See also Carl-Herman Tillhagen, *Folklig Läkekonst* (Stockholm, 1958), pp. 109 ff., and numerous entries in the index under "sätta bort sjukdom." James George Frazer's book on *The Scapegoat*, being Part VI and Vol. IX of *The Golden Bough* (3rd ed., London, 1933), is an indispensable work on the transference, not only of disease, but of evil in general. Since much of the material for this paper has been drawn from the *Frank C. Brown Collection of North Carolina Folklore* (Durham, North Carolina: Duke University Press, 1952–1964), I have dispensed with citing a long bibliography here, and ask the reader to consult Vol. VI, pp. xlix–lxxi and Vol. VII, pp. xxiii–xxxiii, where he will find a key to the abbreviations and symbols used here. In preparing this paper I had the benefit of discussing many points with Thelma James, who has been a close student of American folk medicine for many years.

2. Frazer devotes some thirty pages to the transference of evil, and of disease, to inanimate objects, and especially to transference to sticks and stones, but most of the material is taken from the practices of primitives (*The Golden Bough,* IX, 1–30). Comparable curative practices from the United States and non-native North America are rare and have a different emphasis.

3. Grendon, p. 129. Cf. Sébillot, III, 497 ff.

4. "Plugging, Nailing, Wedging and Kindred Folk Medical Practices," scheduled for early publication. Frazer has a good survey of "The Nailing of Evils," *ibid.,* pp. 59–71.

5. See Frazer, *ibid.,* pp. 38–46.

6. Fox, p. 6. Cf. Hovorka-Kronfeld, I, 116, 254 f.; J. D. Rolleston, "The Folklore of Children's Diseases," *Folk-Lore,* LIV (1943), 298, 302. For a more extended statement see the same author's article in the *British Journal of Venereal Diseases,* XVIII (1942), 5.

7. *Ozark Superstitions,* p. 150.

8. Knortz, p. 52.

9. Hovorka-Kronfeld, II, 222. There is a tabu in Ruthenia both against touching an epileptic or looking at him, and in Bulgaria the disease may be contracted by touching the victim.

10. *Folk-Lore,* XX (1909), 89. A crossroads was selected rather than a neighbor's door, say, so that the transmittal would be by chance, rather than by malignity focused on a particular person.

11. *Brown Collection,* Nos. 274, 640; cf. Guichot y Sierra, p. 296 (Spain).

12. Phillips, p. 164, No. 17.

13. Brinton, p. 183.

14. Thomas, No. 1477 (not stated that the wart is transferred, though perhaps implied); cf. Webb, p. 258.

15. Radford, p. 179. A curious transference of one's ague to a neighbor by burying a dead man's hair under the neighbor's threshold is reported from Devonshire; Black, *Folk-Medicine,* p. 27; Radford, p. 14.

16. Black, *Folk-Medicine,* p. 41. In ancient Rome, nail parings were kneaded into wax, and the wax pressed into the door of a neighbor before sunup, thus transferring the disease to him (Soldan-Heppe, I, 68). Cf. Frazer, *The Golden Bough,* IX, 47.

17. Frazer, *ibid.,* pp. 48–49; *HDA,* VIII, 1180, s. v. "Tuch." See also E. Sidney Hartland, "Pin-Wells and Rag-Bushes," *Folk-Lore,* IV (1893), 451–470.

18. Bergen, *Current,* No. 915; *HDA,* VI, 935, s. v. *Nadel.*

19. Black, p. 28, No. 61 (Nebraska).

20. Davenport, p. 129. Thelma James has reminded me of the collateral notion that blood should not touch the ground.

21. Bergen, *Current,* No. 914; *Brown Collection,* No. 2667.

22. Cf. Frazer, *The Golden Bough,* IX, 48.

23. Stuart, p. 10.

24. Steiner, No. 80.

25. See my forthcoming article on "plugging."

26. Nos. 2638, 2644, *passim.* See an example from England in *Notes and Queries,* 1st Ser., Vol. 6 (1852), 409.

27. *Brown Collection,* Nos. 2634–2636, *passim.* Cf. also Black, p. 27, No. 58; Wintemberg, *Oxford,* No. 18; M. C. Balfour and Northcote W. Thomas, *Examples of the Printed Folk-Lore Concerning Northumberland* (Publications of the Folk-Lore Society), LIII (London, 1904), p. 49.

28. For a more general treatment, see Frazer, *The Golden Bough,* IX, 48.

29. See the Canadian examples (Waugh), treated under "counting," below; likewise, the disposal of freckles in paper, after counting, as seen in a suggested remedy from Georgia that also involves pebbles.

30. Rogers, p. 34; cf. *Brown Collection,* No. 2586.

31. Hyatt, No. 4136.

32. Thomas, No. 1491; Hyatt, No. 4185.

33. Thomas, No. 1491.

34. Black, *Folk-Medicine,* p. 41 Cf. *Folk-Lore,* XXXIX (1928), 174–175 (Wales).

35. Sébillot, III, 498.

36. Norlin, p. 205, No. 21.

37. Gregor, p. 49; Black, *Folk-Medicine,* pp. 41–42 (counting only).

38. Corn: Nos. 2494–2496, 2516, *passim*; beans: No. 2406. For both kinds of entries; contagious magic is noted where it occurs.

39. Nos. 2548–2549 (rubbing of potato on wart before disposal).

40. Waugh, No. 310. Bits of chewing tobacco taken from the mouth, counted, rubbed on the wart, etc., are wrapped up and thrown away in the same result. (*idem,* No. 297).

41. Davenport, p. 129 (contact with wart by measurement of the wart with straw); Thomas, No. 1525.

42. Cf. Stout, No. 717. In this example from Iowa, the stolen dishrag is rubbed on the warts, then placed in a paper sack, carried some distance, then thrown over the left shoulder without looking back. See also Black (Nebraska), p. 28, No. 75 (cotton bag used as a container for the top part of the wart which has been cleanly cut off with a sharp knife; it is noted that the wart will remain unless the bag into which the severed wart is placed is picked up by someone). In another example from Iowa, a cord is rubbed on the warts, thrown away, and then picked up by another person (Stout, No. 790).

43. Lake, p. 152.

44. Brewster, *Cures,* p. 40, No. 3 (handkerchief impregnated with blood of wart, dropped at crossroad for passerby; Stuart, p. 7.)

45. Espinosa, p. 410, No. 9 (the first person who happens to pass by the road-crossing where the rag has been thrown away, will grow a wart, and the other one loses it). Communication of the disease to the carrier (a small rag) is not by blood, or by other contact, but simply by symbolic knotting.

46. Randolph, p. 128; cf. *Brown Collection,* No. 2604. This Ozark item has some aspects of "safe-keeping" that are frequently associated with plugging, yet one should not overlook the primary aspects of burial and decay even though they are not mentioned. Odd varieties of "plugging," which involve burial under closely fitted stones and bricks, and under sods which have been removed and then exactly replaced, are treated in a forthcoming article.

47. *HDA,* IX, 45, s.v. *Wagenachse.*

48. Hendricks, p. 9, No. 189.

49. For a treatment of "knotting" in connection with warts, see the *Brown Collection,* Nos. 2437–2442. Cf. *HDA,* V, 17–18, Hovorka-Kronfeld, I, 214, II, 774. These writers tell of an unusual method of disposal after the knotting of strings. The string is placed in the pack of an itinerant Jewish peddler, presumably with the thought that he himself will get the warts, or pass them on to others (II, 773). Cf. Storaker, *Sygdom,* No. 386 (warts tied into a chain). Untying of the knots by the new victim is a rarity. Cf. the Swiss reference cited in Webb, p. 105.

50. Whitney-Bullock, No. 1816.

51. Patterson, pp. 286–287. Cf. Wilson, *Folk Beliefs,* p. 162.

52. Black (Nebraska), p. 27, No. 56; Doering-Doering, I, 63.

53. Davenport, p. 130. For other clever ways in which the transaction is made, see Randolph, p. 137 (payment by buttons in barter for the wart); Johnson, *What They Say,* p. 121 (barter for pencil and other trifles). An unusual purchase, by which the seller loses his wart, but the buyer does not actually get it, is treated in Webb, p. 101.

54. Hyatt, Nos. 4195–4196.

55. Thomas, No. 1502.

56. Shearin, p. 320. It is not stated that the witch gets the warts; they simply disappear.

57. Bergen, *Current,* No. 902. "Sell your warts for money, throw the money anywhere, but on your own land. Whoever picks up the money gets also the warts."

58. Hyatt, No. 4222. ". . . Mrs. H. gave her niece a penny for each wart she had, and in a week Mrs. H. had a handful of warts."

59. Randolph, p. 127. "Just give a boy a penny or a nickel for each wart, and they will pass from you to him as soon as he spends the money." Another item (pp. 127–128) specifically takes up the matter of transfer, but the question is unresolved.

60. Whitney-Bullock, No. 1817; Bergen, *Current,* No. 904; Knortz, pp. 49–50; *Hoosier Folklore,* VI (1947), 48–49 (West Virginia); Foster, p. 62.

61. Halpert, *Warts,* p. 40. "Warts: rub thirteen times with a penny bearing your birthdate, and throw the penny away. In thirteen days the wart will disappear and reappear on whoever finds the penny."

62. Whitney-Bullock, No. 1815.

63. Gallop, p. 69.

64. Bergen, *Current,* No. 874. Cf. Knortz, p. 49; Whitney-Bullock, No. 1814; Fogel, No. 1735.

65. Wintemberg, *German I,* p. 48.

66. Waugh, No. 300.

67. *Journal of American Folklore,* V (1892), 62.

68. Paul D. Foster, "Warts and Witches," *Life and Health,* LXVI (Oct. 1951), 8; Gardner, No. 64 (someone else whose name you know, but with whom you are not acquainted).

69. Halpert, *Warts,* p. 41.

70. Hyatt, No. 4262.

71. W. S. Inman, "Styes, Barley and Wedding Rings," *British Journal of Medical Psychology,* XX (1946), 333.

72. Richard M. Dorson, "Blood Stoppers," *Southern Folklore Quarterly,* XI (1947), 114.

73. G. F. Black and Northcote W. Thomas, *Examples of the Printed Folklore Concerning the Orkney & Shetland Islands* (Publications of the Folklore Society, XLIX, London, 1901), p. 159.

74. *HDA,* V. 526, s. v. *Kreuzweg.*

75. Allison, No. 120.

76. Randolph, p. 138.

77. *Brown Collection,* No. 2301: "Go to the forks of a road and say: 'Sty, sty, git out'n my eye / An' ketch the fust-un that comes by.' " For further examples, together with variants from elsewhere, see Nos. 2295–2302.

78. *HDA,* VIII, 455, s.v. "Sterbende." Cf. Grendon, p. 131.

79. Halpert, *Warts,* p. 41. Cf. Grendon, p. 131.

80. Thomas, No. 1218. In an Illinois item the victim of goiter kneels near the dead person and asks the corpse to take the goiter away. After burial, as the body decays, the goiter gradually fades away (Hyatt, No. 5280).

81. Storaker, *Sygdom,* No. 229.

82. Fogel, No. 1534.

83. Halpert, *Warts,* p. 41.

84. Thomas, No. 1461; *New York Folklore Quarterly,* III (1947), 257.

85. Farr, *Riddles,* No. 44. Cf. *Brown Collection,* No. 2451.

86. The best general discussion of the scapegoat is still that of Frazer, admirably set down in *The Golden Bough* (3rd ed., Vol. IX, 1933). In the strict discussion of transference in folk medicine, one should not lose sight of the general transfer of evil, of moral blemish, and of sin. To Frazer's own disquisitions on the Sin Eater (*ibid.,* pp. 43 ff.) should be added those of E. Sidney

Hartland, "The Sin-Eater," *Folk-Lore,* III (1892), 145–157. For the student interested in following up modern beliefs and practices that bear on the ancient idea of the scapegoat, I offer two simple references—one from each side of the Atlantic. These two items are a token of what I am sure is a considerable body of material. Georgia (Negro): A bullfrog squeezed to death in the hand cures the chills (Campbell, p. 2); North Riding of Yorkshire: In the summer of 1889 a child was in bed with whooping cough, and allowed to have a cat sleep with him, with the following result in his own words, "Ah smickled it, and ah mended, an' t' cat deed." By this he meant that he gave the cat the infection, and thus was enabled to recover while the cat died in his place ([Eliza] Gutch, *Examples of the Printed Folk-Lore Concerning the North Riding of Yorkshire, York and the Ainsty,* Publications of the Folk-Lore Society, XLV, London, 1899, pp. 179–180). In this connection see the Pennsylvania German item in note 124 for the rubbing of a toad on a wart until the toad dies, and the similar brutality in the treatment of goiter (note 106). The impaling of snails after they have been infected would also seem to have some underlying notion of sacrifice (note 145, *passim*). Further, see the whole section on the maltreatment of animal carriers who are not brought into contact with the host, yet who are mercilessly corked up, starved, or otherwise done in.

87. Cf. Frazer's classic statement in *The Golden Bough,* I, 52–219.

88. Grendon, p. 129.

89. Mrs. [Eliza] Gutch, p. 180; Sébillot, III, 243. Cf. *Motif-Index* D2161.4.1.

90. Hovorka-Kronfeld, I, 254.

91. Hovorka-Kronfeld, I, 255.

92. *HDA,* VI, 76, s. v. *Meerschweinchen.*

93. Radford, p. 86.

94. *HDA,* IX, 901, s. v. *Ziege.* This was also a preventive measure. The keeping of goats among flocks, and even in the stall among horses and cows to ward off disease, by the goat's attracting the disease himself, is, of course, well known (*ibid.*). Whether this is a carry-over from the old scapegoat idea is not indicated, but the practice does arouse speculation.

95. Black, p. 34, No. 3.

96. *HDA,* V, 526. It is not specifically mentioned that the bird contracts the disease.

97. No. 1975.

98. Hyatt, No. 5334.

99. Woodhull, p. 13.

100. No. 1973.

101. Waugh, No. 258; Wintemberg, *Waterloo,* 13; Wintemberg, *German II,* p. 87. Cf. *HDA,* VI, 76, s. v. *Meerschweinchen.*

102. Hovorka-Kronfeld, II, 43.

103. Johnson, *What They Say,* p. 75; Smith, *Animals,* p. 73; Smith, *Folk Cures,* p. 81.

104. Bergen, *Animal,* No. 885.

105. Waugh, No. 288. Grumbine, p. 278, notes the holding a common toad against the goiter until he dies. For a general discussion see *HDA,* III, 137–138, s. v. *Frosch.*

106. Hyatt, No. 4750 (leave the frog on the felon for several hours; the frog will die and the felon will become well).

107. Puckett, p. 365 (a live frog tied to the patient's big toe).

108. Randolph, p. 135. A live frog is tied to the patient's throat, completely absorbing the disease if left there until the frog dies.

109. *Brown Collection,* I, 649: "There was once an old man who lived in Wake county who had terrible spells. He shook like a man with a hard ague. He was said to have been conjured by a witch. An old Negro woman told him if he would catch a frog just before he felt a spell coming on, and tied it to the foot of the bed, the frog would have the spell instead of him, and he would never have another. He did that and the frog shook so that the breath was knocked out of him, and he was too weak to move for several hours. The man never had another spell." Note that the contact with the patient was indirect, even if it were clearly established that the man was in bed just before the attack came on.

110. Thomas, No. 1325. Cf. *Brown Collection,* No. 1993; also No. 1978. In Normandy it was believed that if a toad were caught before sunrise, and laid upon the pulse of a patient's right wrist, the person's fever would pass into the toad, causing it to die (Johnson, *Normandy,* pp. 191–192).

111. *American Folklore* (Chicago, 1959), 17–18. This reference came to me through the courtesy of Thelma James. Ancient Araucanian medical practice provided for the passing of snakes over the bodies of the sick so that the reptile would carry the sickness to the evil one (*Notes and Queries,* CLXXVII [1939], 481–482, citing Sadleir in *Man,* V [1905], 105).

112. Musick, p. 7, No. 32.

113. Gutch, p. 68.

114. Grendon, p. 129.

115. Woodhull, p. 50. Cf. Black, p. 34, No. 4 (Nebraska).

116. Radford, p. 127. In Belgium, a small frog, held by its hind legs, and suspended into the mouth of a victim of malignant sore throat, was supposed to suck out the poison (*Folk-Lore,* XL (1929), 85).

117. Radford, p. 259.

118. Radford, p. 259. An excellent instance of this selfsame practice is noted from Kansas, and its lineage can be traced through an Irish grandmother (*Western Folklore,* XXIII [1964], 22). It is clearly stated that the fish swims away with the disease [whooping cough]).

119. Brendle-Unger, p. 132. In all instances the fish was returned to the water alive. For a treatment of animal inhalants in the treatment of disease, see Wayland D. Hand and Marjorie Griffin, "Inhalants in Respiratory Disorders," *Journal of American Folklore,* LXXVII (1964), 259–260. In Maryland "the foam or saliva of a horse was believed to have strong curative powers, especially for consumptive cough, of which the patient is cured in three days, but the horse dies" (Whitney-Bullock, No. 1771).

120. *HDA,* III, 136, s. v. *Frosch.*

121. *HDA,* IX, 880, s. v. *Zahn.*

122. Moya, p. 73.

123. Hyatt, No. 5238. Cf. Wintemberg, *Waterloo,* p. 13. In the Pennsylvania German country warts were rubbed the same way as goiter with the first toad found in the spring. The rubbing continued until the toad died. (Brendle-Unger, p. 68).

124. Thomas, No. 1514 (added details). Cf. *Brown Collection,* No. 2477.

125. Napier, 97. The *Brown Collection* (No. 2477) contains references to the varied fate of the snail.

126. Bourke, p. 119.

127. *Folk-Lore*, LIV (1943), 298.

128. *Brown Collection,* Nos. 2130 ff.

129. Hyatt, No. 5328. Cf. *Brown Collection,* No. 974.

130. Smith, *Folk Cures,* p. 81; Smith, *Animals,* p. 73. In the latter account the author remarks that "the dying of the chicken . . . seems to have something to do with the cure."

131. Roberts, No. 393.

132. Fogel, No. 1757.

133. Wintemberg, *Waterloo,* p. 15. Cf. Radford, p. 257.

134. Relihan, *Remedies,* p. 169.

135. Marie-Ursule, p. 173.

136. Fitchett, p. 360.

137. Brendle-Unger, 133.

138. Stuart, p. 10.

139. Kittredge, *Witchcraft,* p. 94.

140. Relihan, *Remedies,* p. 84.

141. Relihan, *Remedies,* p. 166.

142. Addy, p. 91 (as the spider pines away the cough will die).

143. Black, *Folk-Medicine,* p. 61.

144. Black, *Folk-Medicine,* p. 61.

145. Radford, pp. 257–258.

146. Radford, pp. 14, 224.

147. Addy, p. 89, Cf. *Brown Collection,* No. 2477.

148. *Brown Collection,* Nos. 390 ff. (teeth); 493, 846, 1560, 1578, *passim* (hair). For an instance of meat's being placed where a dog will find it, see note 153, below.

149. Radford, p. 103; Black, *Folk-Medicine,* p. 35.

150. Radford, p. 103.

151. *Notes and Queries,* 1st Ser., Vol. 2 (1850), 37.

152. Brendle-Unger, p. 93.

153. Roberts, No. 509.

154. *HDA*, IV, 472, s. v. *Hund.*

155. Whitney-Bullock, No. 1735.

156. Various examples are listed under No. 2506 in the *Brown Collection.*

157. Thomas, No. 1451; Randolph, p. 129.

158. Thomas, No. 1454; Hyatt, No. 4169. Seven grains of corn fed to the neighbor's chickens is a cure reported from Illinois, Hyatt, No. 4097. Cf. *Brown Collection,* No. 2497.

159. Browne, No. 1953; Hyatt, No. 4081.

160. Stout, No. 751 (one must watch the hog eat the corn).

161. Puckett, p. 365.

162. Stout, No. 791.

163. Clavel, p. 37. Cf. *Brown Collection,* No. 1584.

164. Whitney-Bullock, No. 1761.

165. Storaker, *Sygdom,* No. 228.

166. Thomas, No. 1450.

167. *HDA,* I, 363, s. v. *Ameise.*

168. "Traditions et Superstitions de la Haute-Bretagne," p. 137.

169. Frazer, *The Golden Bough,* IX, 54–59; *HDA,* I, 957, f., s. v. *Baum*; Grendon, p. 129.

170. Johnson, *What They Say,* p. 75. Cf. *Brown Collection,* Nos. 2022–2023.

171. Whitney-Bullock, No. 1797. Cf. *Brown Collection,* Nos. 1437–1440, *passim.*

172. *HDA,* III, 840, s. v. *Gichter.*

173. *HDA,* I, 1337, s. v. *Birke.*

174. *HDA,* VIII, 1294, f., s. v. *Ulme*; *ibid.,* V, 1308, s. v. *Linde*; IX, 246, *Weide*; III, 837, s. v. *Gicht.*

175. *HDA,* VI, 1176, s. v. *Baum.*

176. *HDA,* I, 519, s. v. *Apfelbaum.*

177. As already stated, these procedures constitute the subject of a special article. The pulling of patients through natural holes in trees, or through holes in sapling trees made by splitting, together with other kinds of "pulling through," await treatment at a later date.

178. *HDA,* VIII, 1305–1306, s. v. *umbinden.* The knotting or binding symbolically ties up and binds the disease to the ribbon, string, or whatever (*HDA,* I, 864, s. v. *Band*).

179. Sébillot, III, 412 (the violin string is first time around the patient's sore throat, and then fastened to a tree).

180. Hyatt, No. 1230.

181. Bergen, *Animal*, No. 1155. Cf. a simpler cure from Pennsylvania, Owens, p. 124. See also, Black, *Folk-Medicine*, p. 38.

182. de Cock, II, 9, No. 254.

183. Brendle-Unger, p. 117 (somewhat more elaborate than indicated in the summary).

184. Measurement of the patient's girth at the chest, in the Ozarks, going alone to the woods, finding a tree of the same girth, and then tying as many knots in the string, attaching it to the tree at the same height as the patient's chest. A tabu against looking back is also part of this elaborate ritual of transference (Randolph, p. 134). In an example not involving contagious magic, Georgia folk tie as many knots as they have chills into a string, and then tie the string to a persimmon tree, with the same tabu against looking back (Steiner, No. 81). Tying, binding, and knotting in connection with witchcraft is treated in Seligmann, I, 328–333, *passim.*

185. Hatfield, pp. 157–158. Cf. *HDA,* IX, 247, s. v. *Weide.* Toothache is also "knotted" into willows (*HDA*, I, 1018, s. v. *beissen*).

186. Sébillot, III, 412; *HDA*, VIII, 1377, s. v. *umwinden.*

187. *HDA,* VIII, 1180, s. v. *Tuch*; IX, 98, s. v. *Wäsche.*

188. *HDA,* V, 908 ff., s. v. *Lappenbäume.*

189. *Brown Collection,* No. 2676.

190. *HDA,* VIII, 1294, s. v. *Ulme*; IX, 246 f., s. v. *Weide*; Suppl., 27, s. v. *Opfer.*

191. *Brown Collection,* No. 1465.

192. *HDA,* VIII, 1303, s. v. *umarmen.*

193. *HDA*, I, 1018, s. v. *beissen.*

194. *HDA*, I, 1337, s. v. *Birnbaum*; IX, 246, s. v. *Weide.*

195. Thomas, No. 1199 (steel placed under the bed for fever; it draws the electricity from the body).

196. Smith, *Folk Cures,* pp. 77–78.

197. Frazer, *The Golden Bough,* IX, 8–30; Grendon, p. 130.

198. One must view the tying of a wart with a string, and then tying the string to a rafter, in an Illinois practice, as an incomplete transfer, since the wart leaves when the string rots, not when anything happens to the rafter!

(Hyatt, No. 4236). Likewise, the curing of "go-backs" in children in Pennsylvania by measuring the disease and then hanging the strings on a gate that is in constant use, until the strings wear away, does not affect the gate so much as it does the well-known *Zwischenträger,* string (White, p. 79). On the face of things, it would seem that originally such a deposit would really be for the purpose of transmitting the disease to another person at a much travelled place.

199. Browne, No. 1426. In this connection one might also consider the following entry from Maryland: "To cure backache, pick up a stone, spit under it, lay it down, and walk away without looking back" (Bullock, p. 10).

200. This I propose to do in a later article. Likewise the passing of cripples and other sufferers through stones is a variety of magical divestment, i.e., "pulling through," and cannot be treated here.

201. Relihan, *Remedies,* p. 83. For the transfer of a chill to the bolster, by crawling under the bed, see the *Brown Collection,* No. 1079.

3

The Folk Healer: Calling and Endowment*

The fear of physical incapacitation and the dread of disease are so great in the human species that man, as part of the folklore with which he invests his life, has created a whole hierarchy of healers. These range in the so-called civilized segments of society from unassuming practitioners singled out by birth, physical characteristics, virtue, occupation, name, and other qualifications—often seemingly irrelevant to the healing function—to a more demonstrative professionalized healing caste in primitive societies. In this latter category, healers run the gamut from simple root and herb doctors and other medical practitioners, whose services are for hire, to shamans of great pretense and display.

The healer's art in primitive societies has been widely treated in the literature,[1] and shamanism itself boasts a rich bibliography.[2] This survey, therefore, will concentrate on certain more or less rare kinds of folk medical practitioners in Europe and America. These healers generally do not operate as a class, but more often as lone functionaries. Even so, as Mackensen observes,[3] there is some degree of confraternity, and there do exist ways and means of transmitting medical knowledge and trade secrets. This is true of herb doctors and dispensers of plant and

*This paper was read before the annual meeting of the American Folklore Society, Los Angeles, 13 November 1970. It originally appeared in the *Journal of the History of Medicine,* 26 (1971), 263-275. Permission to reprint has been given by the editors and the Yale University Press.

animal simples and other medicaments; it is also true of granny medicine, and particularly true of midwifery,[4] which, of course, has long been professionalized. It is generally not true of practitioners in the field of folk medical magic, where secrecy, mystery, and idiosyncrasy figure so importantly as part of the curing experience and the psychological processes that surround it.

The folk healer's art is acquired in several ways, but essentially the endowment falls into three main categories, namely, a gift specially conferred, one innate in the healer, or one resulting from some unique condition, a newly acquired status, or even happenstance. Religious healing of all kinds, which I am not considering in this paper, involves most often, in one way or another, the investiture of the healer with the divine gift, and is a benison either claimed by the ministrant himself, or imputed to him by his clients. In the case of many kinds of secular healers, particularly those whose services are openly for hire, the healing virtue is often self-proclaimed, and is usually backed up by enough loyal followers to constitute a kind of ongoing testimonial. The healers presented for review here, however, are reasonably free of outward show and ostentation; some may even be self-effacing. In their quiet way they, too, may claim a loyal following, though it is likely to be somewhat smaller and perhaps more select. In some cases, the virtues of the healer may be known to only a few. Details are often scanty, and actual cases of healing are rarely reported. Most often it is simply asserted that for this, that, and the other reason, such and such a person is a born healer, or that for a variety of reasons, likewise, he has become one.

The circumstances and accidents of birth continue a good point at which to begin. Widely known in this country as well as abroad is the supposed ability of posthumous children to cure diseases. Although they are regarded as 'born healers,' so-called posthumous children do not ordinarily cultivate this talent until adulthood,[5] and women as well as men are pressed into service for the healing office.[6] An item from Kentucky would indicate that occasionally youngsters themselves perform the cure. 'A baby strangled with thrash can be cured quickly by having the breath of a posthumous child blown down its throat. The orphan must not, however, accept pay for his services.'[7] Thrash [thrush] is most often involved in cures by those posthumously born, but they also treat hives and other diseases. In Ohio, for example, whooping cough is prevented by taking the hair of a girl who has never seen her father, putting it in a bag, and hanging it around the neck of a boy. In this unpublished item it is specifically stated that such a measure will prove ineffectual if performed on another girl.

Extensions are made from the true posthumous child to those who for one reason or another have not seen their fathers,[8] including those hapless children whose fathers have disappeared.[9] In an Indiana entry a person who has never seen his father after reaching maturity is represented as being able to blow into a child's mouth and cure the 'thrash.'[10] In North Carolina the circumstance of a child's not having seen his father is assignable, among other reasons, to the fact that he was an illegitimate child.[11] From these borderline cases involving thrush, the notion has been stretched even further to include any person who has never seen the baby's father,[12] and further still in Ohio, where anyone who has not seen the baby's parents may be called upon.[13] The healing power of a posthumous child in Scotland is thought to be so strong that such a person need only look at the patient.[14] This notion has evidently lingered on in some parts of America. In Kentucky, for instance, a posthumous child need not breathe or blow down the throat of a baby afflicted with thrush in the accepted way; he need only look down the throat to effect the cure,[15] or, according to some, simply touch the victim.[16]

The unusual curing power attributed to seventh sons, or to seventh sons of seventh sons is well known in European folk medical tradition.[17] As in other kinds of medical lore with which we are dealing, reasons are seldom stated. Liebrecht, however, has called attention to the magical qualities of the number seven in the context of healing,[18] and Seemann has made application to magical persons and creatures.[19] For the belief in the gift of healing of seventh sons in America, as summarized in the Brown Collection,[20] I can now multiply references manyfold. Because of the widespread belief in this endowment, I shall concentrate on less well known details. Henderson, writing in the 1860s, reported that this tradition was so strong that 'when seven sons were born in succession parents considered themselves bound, if possible, to bring up the seventh as a doctor.'[21] In the Ozark country, for example, a seventh son of a seventh son is thought to be a physician in spite of himself, endowed with healing powers which cannot be denied. Even if such a man does not study or practice medicine, he is very often called 'Doc' or 'Doctor' by common consent.[22] The well-known folk singer Doc Hopkins was a seventh son, and was, likely in accordance with this tradition, given the first name of Doctor. Old Doc Cassell, who lived in Somerset, Ohio, was the seventh son of a seventh son, and was supposed to have 'electricity in his hands' and to be able to cure scrofula.[23] In upper Michigan it was thought that the seventh son of a seventh son was able to draw the pain from his patient to his own body. In so doing he was said to perspire freely, his body was reported to quiver, and articles in the room to vibrate from his emotions.[24] In this connection Henderson in the 1860s, writing on the healing power of seventh sons, as well as twins and children born with a caul, reported that this power was 'held to be so much subtracted from their own vital energy,' that if much drawn upon 'they would pine away and die of exhaustion.'[25] Both the Micmac and Penobscot Indians believed in seventh sons as powerful healers by virtue of their birth, a notion probably borrowed from white settlers predominantly from parts of Europe where this belief was held.[26] In the curing of thrush, for example, seventh sons cured the disease in the traditional way, namely by blowing or breathing into the mouth of the victim, as in the case of healers posthumously born.[27] Likewise, seventh sons rub warts, one of the customary ways of ridding one of these excrescences.[28] In France, as well as in the British Isles, rubbing, stroking, or simply touching were curative means ascribed to seventh sons.[29]

Seventh daughters in an unbroken chain of female children were also thought of in many countries as endowed with the gift of healing,[30] and it is not surprising that there should also be variations to include a seventh daughter of a seventh daughter,[31] as well as the inevitable seventh daughter of a seventh son.[32] The importance of numerology in healing is seen in the attribution of healing power to children in an uninterrupted succession of male or female births in denominations other than seven. As early as the 1730s, the twenty-first son born in wedlock, without a daughter intervening, could perform prodigious cures of scrofula.[33] The fifth or sixth consecutive sons or daughters of the same mother, in the Spanish and Spanish-American tradition, often automatically become *saludadores.*[34] The special gift of blood stopping, in parts of Michigan, fell to a ninth consecutive son.[25]

Children born with a caul are supposed to have the gift of healing, as well as enjoying the gift of second sight and immunity to drowning, but the tradition is nowhere as widely believed as the two special benefits mentioned and several other beliefs associated with children born with the so-called veil. The healing gift is known, among other places, in parts of the British Isles and in France and Holland. The belief has been brought to America in the folklore of these countries but is apparently little known here.[36] The tradition persisted among the French in Louisiana,[37] where children born with a *gif,* or veil, were thought to be destined to become remède-workers.[38] In Michigan anyone born with a caul can stop bleeding.[39] The gift is innate but does not become operative until the holder attains a certain unstated age.[40]

Other unusual physical characteristics include the anomaly of a child born by breech birth. In the British Isles such individuals were reputed to have the gift of healing in their feet and were pressed into service to trample the trunks of those afflicted with rheumatism or lumbago and to tread upon sprained members.[41] In Scotland these healers also resorted to rubbing and were paid well for their services.[42] By way of extension upon the gift, rheumatism could also be treated by a woman newly delivered of a child by breech birth.[43] Although they doubtless exist, I can find no trace of these folk medical practices in America, except as they may be practiced by Americans of Japanese extraction who have brought the practice from their homeland where the procedure is said to be common. That lefthanded people possess a medical talent in rubbing is not well known. Since my files are not cross-referenced I can find only one instance of the massage by left-handers, namely, manipulation for the cure of stiff neck. This item is from Louisiana.[44] Children born with teeth, known as healers in Europe,[45] are unheard of as born healers in America, as nearly as I can discover, nor is the loss of teeth, apparently, thought to impede the healer's art, as in Norway.[46]

Relatively unknown in the Germanic and Anglo-Saxon folk medical traditions is the special marking of a healer which is found in the folklore of the Romance-language countries. In France, for example, the seventh son of a seventh son, with no female intervening, is a *marcou.* He has on his body the mark of the fleur-de-lis, and, like the King of France, he has the power to cure the king's evil.[47] In the Spanish and Basque tradition the healer was supposed to have a cross under the tongue or in the roof of the mouth.[48] This belief is also encountered in Latin-American folk tradition, where a St. Catherine's wheel, as well as a cross, is the distinguishing mark.[49] Foster says that the Chilean *perspicaz* is clearly a lineal descendant of the Spanish *saludador* because of this marking.[50] Henderson speaks of seventh sons being marked with seven stars as a badge of their healing office,[51] but I am unable to trace this belief to America.

Twins enjoy a reputation as healers in both the Germanic and Romance-language countries,[52] and this tradition has been carried to the Americas, where extensions have been made to the so-called 'left twin,' i.e., a surviving twin.[53] Such a twin, by the laws of sympathy, was thought to gain the vitality and other attributes of its dead sibling.[54] Cures were not limited to thrush, but involved other diseases also. The healing virtue of twins often extended to the mother of twins as well, and involved skill in curing sprains and strained ligaments.[55] A mother of twin boys in the Midwest, for example, was credited with being able to cure erysipelas, if she would 'strike fire' with flint and steel on the head of the afflicted one.[56] For the cure of rheumatism in New York state one was supposed to find a widow who had twins[57] and have her step on the back or the part affected. We have already come across this kind of manipulation in connection with healers who were breech born. In Germany twin brothers were favored for pulling sick children through a split in cherry trees.[58]

The time of birth, and unusual circumstances surrounding it, are thought to endow the child with special gifts of healing.[59] Children born on Christmas,[60] on Maundy Thursday,[61] Good Friday, and other religious holidays, are born healers.[62] This tradition seems strongly represented in the Romance-language countries.[63] Wholly without religious connection is a Utah tradition that a person born in October has the power to cure a headache by rubbing.[64] In the Midwest a so-called 'seven-months' baby' was credited with possessing the healer's gift.[65] Of children born with the congenital grace of healing in the Romance tradition,[66] no token was more certain of the gift than the crying of the child in the mother's womb.[67] The gift was vouchsafed only if the mother told no one. In Chile the *perspicaz* was said to lose his gift if the mother revealed the happening.[68]

States of innocence, either in children or young people, moral excellence, and continuing fidelity among married adults, or virtuous unmarried adults, are considered part of the moral and spiritual gift of the healer. In a beautifully symbolic way, a baby's first tear is thought to cure blindness, as is seen in entries from Nebraska and Utah.[69] One is immediately reminded of the curing of the prince's blindness by the tears of his faithful wife, and mother of twins, in the Grimm tale of 'Rapunzel' (Grimm,

No. 12). The range of healers on a scale of innocence and virtue is seen in Kentucky, where the saliva of a child under six months of age is used against the bite of the deadly copperhead, the saliva of a virgin for snakebite in general, and in Monroe county, the saliva of a minister for the same purpose.[70] In Germany, yarn spun by a girl under seven years of age is worn to prevent gout and arthritic diseases,[71] and sick children suffering from various kinds of ailments are wrapped in the apron of a virgin bride to cure them.[72] By the same token of innocence, in Utah, the urine of a faithful wife is used for the treatment of sore eyes.[73]

By the vagaries of folklore, healing may be accomplished by people of moral taint as well as by the innocent and virtuous. In Scotland, for example, warts were removed by the patient's rubbing the growth against the father of an adulterous child, but care had to be exercised that this contact be made without the offender's knowledge.[74] The situation is reversed in Portugal, where the victim rubs his warts against the ribs of a cuckolded husband without the latter's knowing it.[75] Curing of this kind is noted from Alabama around the 1880s, where the father of an illegitimate child was specified.[76] Less offensive than the word 'illegitimate,' perhaps, is the designation, in North Carolina, of an 'unmarried father.'[77] An illegitimate child itself as a healer is rare indeed, but mention is made in the unpublished Ohio Collection of having an illegitimate girl blow into a baby's mouth to cure the thrush.[78]

The love relationship, as well as the marital bond itself, figures in the kind of curing we have just discussed. In Kentucky, for example, a jilted lover is supposed to be able to cure the hives and thrush.[79] On the other hand, in ceremonies involving a child's parents working in concert, it is generally assumed that a close bond between the parents exists. In the Galician tradition in Spain, for example, it is expressly stated that the father and mother who pull a child through a split trunk of a young tree for the cure of hernia must 'get along well together.'[80]

That marital status is involved in healing in one way or another is seen in the power supposed to reside in the names of the spouses, but most commonly in the name, or new name, of the wife herself. As is very well known, women who marry without changing their surname are thought to become healers automatically.[81] Whether ideas of double potency are involved, as in the case of the so-called 'left,' or surviving, twin, I cannot say. The strange thing about this belief is the fact that there is never any mention of healing until the girl marries a man with the same family name as her own. The belief in healers by virtue of name magic is well known in the British Isles, especially for the treatment of whooping cough, and to the instances cited by Radbill,[82] many can be added for eastern Canada, New England, and the eastern seaboard. Generally the victim of whooping cough—often a child—is given bread to eat baked by a woman whose surname has not changed after marriage.[83] Interesting variations, involving well-known principles of magic, are seen in a North Carolina ritual, where the bread is not given to the victim directly by the baker, but by another person, or, preferably, the bread is left in a place where the child suffering from whooping cough can steal it.[84] In Maryland, the woman who baked the bread may spread it with butter. If the child takes it, without thanking her, there will be no more whoop to the cough.[85] In New York state, after the bread is secured, the child is taken to another county to consume the bread. He must remain there an hour.[86] The patient occasionally was supposed to secure various kinds of comestibles other than bread, ranging from raisin and currant cake in the British Isles,[87] to boiled eggs in the midwestern part of the United States.[88] Among the Pennsylvania Germans it was specified that the eggs must be gathered by a woman whose name had not been changed by marriage.[89] In Illinois eggs were bought from such a person.[90] In Indiana, by way of extension upon medical services, wet nursing was considered best if performed by a woman whose maiden and married names were the same.[91] In parts of Europe there was much greater latitude. Healing could be performed by anyone of the same surname as the patient.[92]

In other connections we have already discussed parents of healers of their own children. Now in consideration of name magic we must once more think of husband and wife as healers working together. Here again, the obtaining of food is part of the ritual. Bread and butter secured from a man named Joseph whose wife is named Mary was thought to be efficacious for various kinds of cures in parts of England.[93] In some places food was not sought, simply the prescription from such a couple as to what one should do for whooping cough.[94] The names of the Holy Couple immediately come to mind, and perhaps their merit and sanctity lie at the root of this supposed medical efficacy. However, the names of John and Joan in married couples are connected with folk medical healing in the British Isles.[95]

The Romance counterparts are Jean and Jeanne in France and Juan and Juanita in Spain and the Spanish-speaking countries. John need not necessarily work with his wife with a counterpart name. Three men named Johannes, for example, conduct the exacting ritual of passing victims through trees in northwestern Germany.[96] This ceremony was carried out in France by a man named Jean.[97] In Spain the name of Manuel is associated with healing as well as Juan.[98] In Chile even the hat of a man named Juan was thought to be efficacious if used to cover the head of a woman in difficult labor.[99]

Other than to clergymen, to whom the gift of healing would accrue as part of the sacred office, the healing art is little attached to people in specific trades and occupations not connected with the medical profession. Blacksmiths and shepherds, well known as healers in Europe,[100] are as a class little thought of as healers in America, although this tradition may have lingered on somewhat in the Pennsylvania German country. Here, for example, it was thought that a blacksmith had the ability to cure man and horse alike.[101] The elaborate rituals engaged in by blacksmiths of the seventh generation of a family of blacksmiths, known in the north of England, never found lodgement, apparently, on our shores.[102] Carpenters as hereditary healers are unknown to me except in the Romance tradition.[103]

Total strangers and transients as healers are little known in America, and I have not encountered them at all in European folk medical tradition. In a recent paper I called attention to the ritual of divestment in Hollywood, wherein an unknown itinerant counts the victim's warts, writes them (the number?) on the inside of the hatband, and then magically takes the warts with him as he leaves town.[104] In another case involving a total stranger, a lady with a goiter who had stopped for a red signal light in Canoga Park, California, was accosted by a total stranger who prescribed the touch of a dead man's hand.[105] These unusual kinds of curers strongly remind one, of course, of the stranger riding up on a white or piebald horse to inform a sufferer from whooping cough how to rid himself of the malady. This unusual kind of advice is well known in the British Isles,[106] and has also been tolerably well preserved in this country, as references from such widely scattered places as New Hampshire, Maryland, Indiana, and Utah attest.[107] Cures were also prescribed by riders of grey horses as well as white and piebald animals. The prescription for whooping cough, simply offered, usually involved no other ministrations on the part of the rider, but in the Midwest, an unknown rider on a grey horse was credited with being able to take warts away with him.[108] We have thus seen strangers, in both old-time and modern settings, serve as actual ministrants and curers as well as advisers.

Since the various kinds of healers discussed in this paper are healers by virtue of unusual physical endowments, strange traits and abnormalities, as well as by unusual relationships and circumstances of one kind or another, one can little hope to find in these discussions the usual references to ways and means of passing on the healing art. By the very fact that such healers are specially marked and derive their power and virtue as healers from the accidents of birth and station, it is clear that the usual means of perpetuating the gift are totally unavailing. The gift, in a sense, is automatic; hence it is that one hears nothing at all of the transmission of the gift within families, except as in the case of seventh sons. Nor does one hear of the conferral of the healer's gift from one sex to another, or of any kind of transmission, personal or otherwise.

It is likewise clear that there is little or no talk of rewards and other perquisites, as one is accustomed to find among a more or less professional caste of healers. The withdrawal of the gift for the acceptance of pay, accordingly, is completely unheard of in this connection. Despite my disclaimers, I am sure that there must be some grafting of accepted notions concerning various faith healers and other kinds of folk medical practitioners on some of the special kinds of folk healers discussed in this paper.

NOTES

1. Cf. 'Health and the gods of healing,' by various authors and in different parts of the world, in *Hastings encyclopaedia of religion and ethics* (Edinburgh, 1908–26), 13 vols., VI, 540–556. (Hereinafter cited *Hastings*.)

2. J. A. MacCulloch, 'Shamanism' in *Hastings,* XI, 441–446. Siberian shamanism is treated at some length in V. Diószegi, ed., *Glaubenswelt und Folklore der siberischen Völker* (Budapest, 1963).

3. Lutz Mackensen, 'Sitte und Brauch' in Adolph Spamer, ed., *Die deutsche Volkskunde* (Leipzig and Berlin, 1934–35), 2 vols., I, 110.

4. For a good historical account of midwifery in folkloristic terms, see T. R. Forbes, *The midwife and the witch* (New Haven, 1966), pp. 112–155. Marie Campbell, *Folks do get born* (New York and Toronto, 1946), is a vademecum of knowledge concerning midwifery in present-day America (Georgia principally).

5. See the *Frank C. Brown collection of North Carolina folklore* (Durham, 1952–64), 7 vols., VI–VII, *Popular beliefs and superstitions from North Carolina,* W. D. Hand, ed. [1961–64], VI, 66, Nos. 413–414. (Hereinafter cited Brown Coll.)

6. H. M. Hyatt, *Folk-lore from Adams County Illinois* (New York, 1935), p. 211, No. 4404; cf. also No. 4403. Cf. also T. J. Farr, 'Tennessee folk beliefs concerning children,' *J. Amer. Folklore*, 1939, *52*, 114, No. 65. Cf. C. M. Wilson, 'Folk beliefs in the Ozark hills,' *Folksay* (Norman, Okla., 1930), p. 162.

7. T. D. Clark, *The Kentucky*. The Rivers of America. (New York, 1942), p. 118.

8. J. Q. Anderson, *Texas folk medicine: 1,333 cures, remedies, preventives, & health practices* (Austin, Tex., 1970), p. 89; Hyatt (n. 6), p. 211, No. 4403; T. J. Farr, 'Riddles and superstitions of Middle Tennessee,' *J. Amer. Folklore,* 1935, *48,* 327, No. 30.

9. Gordon Wilson, *Folklore of the Mammoth Cave region* (Kentucky Folklore Series, No. 4, 1968), p. 64.

10. W. E. Richmond and Elva Van Winkle, 'Is there a doctor in the house?' *Indiana hist. Bull.*, 1958, *35,* 133, No. 267.

11. J. D. Clark, 'North Carolina popular beliefs and superstitions,' *N. Carolina Folklore,* 1970, *18,* 8.

12. N. N. Puckett, *Folk beliefs of the Southern Negro* (Chapel Hill, N.C., 1926), p. 341; Tressa Turner, 'The human comedy in folk superstitions,' *Pub. Texas Folklore Soc.*, 1937, *13,* 168; Grace Partridge Smith, 'Folklore from "Egypt," ' *J. Amer. Folklore,* 1941, *54,* 58.

13. Unpublished item in the Newbell Niles Puckett Collection of Popular Beliefs and Superstitions, Cleveland Public Library. [No. 2894].

14. Walter Gregor, *Notes on the folk-lore of the North-East of Scotland.* Publications of the Folk-Lore Society, VII (London, 1881), 37.

15. Sadie F. Price, 'Kentucky folk-lore,' *J. Amer. Folklore,* 1901, *14,* 32.

16. John Hawkins, 'An old Mauma's folk-lore,' *J. Amer. Folklore,* 1896, *9,* 130. A more elaborate description is to be found in Julia Peterkin's *Green Thursday,* p. 91 (as quoted in Irene Yates, 'Conjures and cures in the novels of Julia Peterkin,' *Southern Folklore Quart.*, 1946, *10,* 146).

17. See W. G. Black, *Folk-medicine: A chapter in the history of culture.* Publications of the Folk-Lore Society, XII (London, 1883), 136–137; O. v. Hovorka und A. Kronfeld, *Vergleichende Volksmedizin* (Stuttgart, 1908–09), 2 vols., I, 391; Adolf Wuttke, *Deutscher Volksaberglaube der Gegenwart,* 3rd ed., E. H. Meyer, ed. (Berlin, 1900), p. 323, par. 479; E. & M. A. Radford, *Encyclopaedia of superstitions,* ed. and rev. by Christina Hole (London, 1961), pp. 301–302; Antonio Castillo de Lucas, *Folkmedicina* (Madrid, 1958), p. 75; L. C. Jones, 'Practitioners of folk medicine,' *Bull. Hist. Med.*, 1949, *23,* 489; Madge E. Pickard and R. C. Buley, *The Midwest pioneer, his ills, cures, and doctors* (Crawfordsville, Ind., 1945), p. 75; Anderson (n. 8), pp. xiv, 88–89, *passim.*

18. Felix Liebrecht, *Zur Volkskunde: Alte und neue Aufsätze* (Heilbronn, 1879), pp. 346–347, No. 11.

19. Erich Seemann, ' "Die zehnte Tochter": Eine Studie zu einer Gottscheer Ballade,' in G. O. Arlt and W. D. Hand, eds., *Humaniora: Essays in literature, folklore, bibliography, honoring Archer Taylor on his seventieth birthday* (New York, 1960), pp. 106–109.

20. Brown Coll. (n. 5), VI, 38, Nos. 223–224.

21. William Henderson, *Notes on the folk-lore of the northern counties and the borders.* New ed., Publications of the Folk-Lore Society, II (London, 1879), 306.

22. Vance Randolph, *Ozark superstitions* (New York, 1947), p. 207.

23. Puckett Ohio Collection, unpublished (n. 13). [No. 11167].

24. R. M. Dorson, 'Blood stoppers,' *Southern Folklore Quart.*, 1947, *11*, 109–110.

25. Henderson (n. 21), p. 306. On the debilitating effect on the curer, Wintemberg reports hearing a female conjurer say that if the patient's illness was of a very serious nature and she attempted to cure it, it always had a debilitating effect upon her, even if she did not see or come into contact with the sick person (W. J. Wintemberg, *Folklore of Waterloo County, Ontario* [National Museum of Canada, Bull., No. 116, Ottawa, 1950]), p. 23.

26. *J. Amer. Folklore,* 1896, *9,* 174 (Micmac); F. G. Speck, 'Penobscot tales and religious beliefs,' *ibid.*, 1935, *48,* 31.

27. Brown Coll., (n. 5), VI, 66–67, No. 418.

28. *Ibid.*, VI, 311, Nos. 2420–2421; Anderson (n. 8), p. 89.

29. Henderson (n. 21), p. 305; Mrs. Gutch, *Examples of the printed folk-lore concerning the North Riding of Yorkshire, York, and the Ainsty.* Publications of the Folk-Lore Society, XLV (London, 1901 [1899]), 169; J. G. Dalyell, *The darker superstitions of Scotland* (Glasgow, 1835), p. 70.

30. Arnold Van Gennep, *Manuel de folklore français contemporain* (Paris, 1937–57), 9 parts in 3 vols., I, Pt. I, p. 124; I. M. Barriola, *La medicine popular en el pais vasco* (San Sebastian, 1952), p. 127; Jeanne (Cooper) Foster, *Ulster folklore* (Belfast, 1951), p. 64.

31. *Superstitions. A catalogue of make-believe* (Tacoma, Wash., n.d.), p. 30.

32. F. W. Waugh, 'Canadian folk-lore from Ontario,' *J. Amer. Folklore,* 1918, *31,* 39, No. 581.

33. Dalyell (n. 29), p. 396.

34. G. M. Foster, 'Relationships between Spanish and Spanish-American folk medicine,' *J. Amer. Folklore*, 1953, *66*, 213.

35. Dorson (n. 24), p. 115.

36. Henderson (n. 21), p. 306; Jones (n. 17), p. 489; Hyatt (n. 6), p. 127, No. 2611.

37. Elisabeth Brandon, 'Les moeurs de la Paroisse de Vermillion en Louisiane (unpub. diss., Laval University, Quebec, 1955), p. 92.

38. H. T. Kane, *Deep Delta country* (New York, 1944), p. 227.

39. Dorson (n. 24), p. 108.

40. *Ibid.*, p. 109.

41. Black (n. 17), p. 137; Gregor (n. 14), pp. 45–46; E. & M. A. Radford, *Encyclopaedia of superstitions* (London, n.d. [1947]), p. 118.

42. Gregor (n. 14), pp. 45–46.

43. Radford (n. 41), p. 199.

44. Hilda Roberts, 'Louisiana superstitions,' *J. Amer. Folklore*, 1927, *40*, 168, No. 454.

45. Black (n. 17), p. 138; C. Bakker, *Volksgeneeskunde in Waterland. Een vergelijkende Studie met de Geneeskunde der Grieken en Romeinen* (Amsterdam, 1928), p. 4.

46. J. T. Storaker, *Sygdom og Forgjørelse in den Norske Folketro.* Norsk Folkeminnelag, No. 20 (Oslo, 1932), p. 9, No. 9.

47. Henderson (n. 21), p. 306. Liebrecht says that a person wishing to be healed need only touch the fleur-de-lis marking (n. 18), pp. 346–347, No. 11.

48. Castillo de Lucas (n. 17), p. 75; Barriola (n. 30), p. 128.

49. Foster (n. 34), p. 213.

50. *Ibid.*

51. Henderson (n. 21), p. 306.

52. *Revista de Dialectología y Tradiciones Populares,* 1947, *3,* 45; Foster (n. 34), p. 213.

53. P. G. Brewster, 'Folk cures and preventives from southern Indiana,' *Southern Folklore Quart.*, 1939, *3,* 40, No. 2. Cf. Henderson (n. 21), p. 307.

54. Radford and Hole (n. 17), p. 345.

55. *Revista* (n. 52), 1949, *5,* 309–310, 504.

56. Pickard and Buley (n. 17), p. 79.

57. Janice C. Neal, 'Grandad—pioneer medicine man,' *N. Y. Folklore Quart.*, 1955, *11,* 284.

58. Jacob Grimm, *Deutsche Mythologie.* 4. Ausg., E. H. Meyer, ed. (Berlin, 1875–78), n. 976. For a treatment of 'pulling through' see my article, ' "Passing through": folk medical magic and symbolism,' *Proc. Amer. phil. Soc.*, 1968, *112,* 379–402.

59. Foster (n. 34), p. 213.

60. *Ibid.*, A young woman in Los Angeles, of Italian parentage, claims that a child born on Christmas can cure headaches.

61. Foster (n. 34), p. 213.

62. *Ibid.*

63. Castillo de Lucas (n. 17), p. 75; Barriola (n. 30), p. 127.

64. Unpublished Utah Collection, UCLA.

65. Pickard and Buley (n. 17), p. 75.

66. Barriola (n. 30), p. 127.

67. Foster (n. 34), p. 213; Barriola (n. 30), p. 127.

68. Foster (n. 34), p. 213.

69. Paulette Monette Black, *Nebraska folk cures.* University of Nebraska Studies in Language, Literature, and Criticism, No. 15 (Lincoln, 1935), p. 16, No. 27; R. L. Welsch, *A treasury of Nebraska pioneer folk-lore* (Lincoln, 1966), p. 339. The Utah item, unpublished, was collected from an old Indian witch doctor in the vicinity of Layton.

70. L. C. Thompson, 'A vanishing science,' *Kentucky Folklore Rec.*, 1959, *5,* 101.

71. *Handwörterbuch des deutschen Aberglaubens* (Berlin and Leipzig, 1927–42), 10 vols., III, 838.

72. Wuttke (n. 17), p. 359.

73. Unpublished Utah Collection, UCLA.

74. Gregor (n. 14), p. 49. Cf. Black (n. 17), p. 138.

75. Rodney Gallop, *Portugal: A book of folk-ways* (Cambridge, 1936), p. 62.

76. Unpublished Alabama Collection, UCLA.

77. J. D. Clark (n. 11), *18,* 8, No. 77.

78. Puckett Ohio Collection, unpublished (n. 13). [No. 2897].

79. Wilson (n. 9), p. 64.

80. *Revista* (n. 52), 1944, *1,* 296; cf. Hand (n. 58), p. 382, *passim*; Paul Sébillot, *Le folklore de France* (Paris, 1904–07), 4 vols., III, 417.

81. Radford and Hole (n. 17), p. 245; Brown Coll. (n. 5), VI, 353, Nos. 2729–2730, *passim.* I do not find reference to this belief in Germany, although onomastic magic is otherwise widely known in German folk medicine.

82. S. X. Radbill, 'Whooping cough in fact and fancy,' *Bull. Hist. Med.*, 1943, *13,* 47.

83. Wintemberg (n. 25), p. 15; Annie Weston Whitney and Caroline Canfield Bullock, 'Folk-lore from Maryland,' *Mem. Amer. Folklore Soc.*, 1925,

18, 83, No. 1709; Brown Coll. (n. 5), VI, 353. No. 2729; Farr (n. 6), p. 114, No. 70; E. M. Fogel, 'Beliefs and superstitions of the Pennsylvania Germans,' *Americana Germanica,* 1915, *18,* 339, No. 1803.

84. Haywood Parker, 'Folk-lore of the North Carolina mountaineers,' *J. Amer. Folklore,* 1907, *20,* 249.

85. Whitney and Bullock (n. 83), p. 83, No. 1711.

86. C. M. Relihan, 'Folk remedies,' *New York Folklore Quart.,* 1947, *3,* 169.

87. *Notes and Queries,* 1852, *1st ser., 6,* 71.

88. Pickard and Buley (n. 17), p. 77.

89. T. R. Brendle and C. W. Unger, 'Folk medicine of the Pennsylvania Germans. The non-occult cures.' *Proc. Pennsylvania German Soc.,* 1935, *45,* 133. Cf. Radbill (n. 82), p. 47.

90. J. W. Allen, *Legends & lore of southern Illinois* (Carbondale, 1963), p. 84.

91. *Midwest Folklore,* 1955, *5,* 214.

92. Wuttke (n. 17), p. 323; Castillo de Lucas (n. 17), p. 466.

93. Black (n. 17), pp. 90–91; Radbill (n. 82), p. 47; *Folk-Lore,* 1943, *54,* 305–306.

94. Henderson (n. 21), p. 143.

95. *Notes and Queries,* 1852, *1st ser., 5,* 148.

96. J. G. Frazer, *The golden bough.* 3rd ed. (London, 1914–35), 12 vols., XI, 171–172.

97. Henri Gaidoz, *Un vieux rite médical* (Paris, 1892), p. 17.

98. Castillo de Lucas (n. 17), p. 51.

99. Julio Vicuña Cifuentes, *Mitos y supersticiones, estudios del folklore chileno recogidos de la tradición oral.* 3. ed. (Santiago, 1947), p. 170.

100. Grimm (n. 58), II, 963; *HDA,* Nachtrag, IX, 124, 257; M. A. van Andel, *Volksgeneeskunst in Nederland* (Utrecht, 1909), p. 94; Henderson (n. 21), p. 187; Gregor (n. 14), p. 45.

101. *Pennsylvania Dutchman,* 1951, *3,* 2.

102. Henderson (n. 21), p. 187; *J. Amer. Folklore,* 1905, *18,* 253.

103. *Revista* (n. 52), 1949, *5,* 503; Arnold Van Gennep, *Le folklore du Dauphiné* (Paris, 1932–33), 2 vols., I, 60. Because of the rarity of this kind of ascription, I am citing an item which I turned up after this article was submitted: 'A woman living near Clayton [Illinois] said that a house painter took her son's warts off merely by looking at them. This, she heard, was a special gift accorded to most members of the trade.' Hyatt (n. 6, 2 ed., New York, 1965), p. 290, No. 6336.

104. W. D. Hand, 'Folk medical magic and symbolism in the West,' in Austin Fife, Alta Fife, and Henry Glassie, eds., *Forms upon the frontier.* Utah State University, Monograph Series, XVI, No. 2 (Logan, 1969), p. 108.

105. *Ibid.*

106. T. J. Pettigrew, *On superstitions connected with the history and practice of medicine and surgery* (London, 1844), p. 73; Radbill (n. 82), p. 48; Henderson (n. 21), pp. 142–143.

107. Mrs. Moody P. Gore and Mrs. Guy E. Speare, *New Hampshire folk tales* (Plymouth, N.H., Federation of Women's Clubs, 1932), p. 216; Whitney and Bullock (n. 83), p. 83, No. 1712; Brown Coll. (n. 5), VI, 352, No. 2715. The Utah item is in the unpublished Utah Collection, UCLA.

108. Pickard and Buley (n. 17), pp. 79, 331.

4

Deformity, Disease, and Physical Ailment as Divine Retribution*

In the western world notions of crime and punishment and of sin and retribution are so deep and inveterate as to occupy the minds of people in most of their personal and social relationships. From earliest childhood, in the church, and in the school, youngsters are taught that disobedience does not go unpunished. Even when persons do embark upon lives of crime, they have not come to their low estate unknowingly; they have flouted the common law and the sense of decency that is born and bred to the bone. Their deeds at once are acts of personal shame and public disgrace.

These notions of personal accountability are by no means limited to the western world; they would appear to be universal in human experience. People are punished for their trespasses against their neighbors, for infractions of the mores of the group, or for impiety toward the gods and the ruling spirits. In addition to suffering material losses of various kinds, and to undergoing a wide range of penalties and punishments, transgressors are thought mysteriously to fall ill or to have diseases of one kind or another inflicted upon them. Sickness and disease as a punishment, in many societies, is thought to be inflicted by God or the ruling spirits and divinities, and most often such

*This article originally appeared in *Festschrift Matthias Zender. Studien zu Volkskultur, Sprache und Landesgeschichte.* Ed. Edith Ennen and Günter Wiegelmann. 2 vols. Bonn: Ludwig Röhrscheid Verlag, 1972, I, 519–525. Permission to reprint has been given by the editors and the publisher.

punishment is meted out for impious acts and infractions of the religious or moral code. Thus it is that in such widely separated parts of the primitive world as Polynesia and the Malay Peninsula,[1] Africa,[2] and primitive America, the gods mete out punishment in the form of physical malady.[3]

The seeking of the causes of disease is an almost universal human trait. In purely aetiological terms, an evil consequence, namely, disease, must have some evil cause. Where the malady can not be readily laid to some natural state, supernatural reasons are sought. This leads to speculation traversing the whole range of magic and religion. A notion of the cause of disease,[4] common to both the primitive and civilized community is the infraction of law, or the breaking of taboos.[5] Among the North American Indians the breaking of taboos is regarded as one of the principal causes of disease.[6]

The same notion of aggrieved gods and spirits among primitive peoples as we have seen above in the sending of disease to man is found in the high cultures from India,[7] through the Middle East,[8] to the classical lands.[9] Even as late as the time of Hippocrates, the gods were looked upon as the causers of disease, for which reason the practice of medicine had remained largely in the hands of priests.

In the Christian countries, where the conscience and one's innate sense of right and wrong are espoused as the highest of virtues, self-accusation often becomes the hardest taskmaster. In this preoccupation with sin and retribution, which is basic to the religious thought of both Catholics and Protestants, man has fashioned a whole system of divine justice, and everywhere sees the hand of God in his daily travail. It is for this reason that the confession of sin is considered precedent to healing, not only in Christian countries,[10] but in the ancient eastern religions[11] and among primitives.[12]

It is my purpose in this exploratory paper to fasten upon folk beliefs and notions that seek to connect physical infirmity and disease of all kinds with the pervasive notions of sin and transgression, and the hand of God himself in punishing sinners. In order to keep the paper within manageable limits, I shall consider only ''sinful'' acts that are punished by sickness, disability, and other untoward physical manifestations thought to be divinely imposed. In the popular mind these maladies are believed to be visited not only upon the sinner himself, but may likewise be extended to the next of kin, particularly to one's children. I shall return to this special aspect of divine punishment later in this paper.

In the main area of our survey, namely, Europe and America, it is transgression against the laws of God and the moral code that leads to sin and exposes the sinner, not only to sickness and disease,[13] but even to death, in accordance with biblical precept.[14]

In a field that is almost limitless, where I can not hope to do more than indicate the variety of these beliefs, I have drawn most heavily on superstitions, mainly because the vast resources to be found in folk legends are scattered and not accessible for study. To the small amount of material drawn from American folk legend, which is often nondescript and which, unfortunately, has not been indexed, I have drawn on the excellent collection of local legends from the West Eifel country, compiled by the man whom we are honoring in this Festschrift.[15] In the some eighty legends listed under "Gottes Strafe," and involving such unhappy endings as execution, hanging, suicide, drowning, lightning striking a house, and the like, only a handful of legends in Zender's collection involve the infliction of disease as a divine punishment. They are worth looking at as a group, for they represent a reasonable range of legends and local stories dealing with actual and supposed happenings. The largest number deals with the desecration of wayside crosses and other objects of religious veneration. A shepherd boy, for example, lost his hair for throwing rocks at a wayside cross (No. 437), and the same fate befell boys who used the head of Christ, severed from a toppled statue, as a bowling ball (No. 438). In another account people were afflicted with sores and boils (Geschwüre) for mocking a wayside cross that had been used for centuries in combatting this very malady (No. 514). Specific diseases include the following: lockjaw for a man who mistreated a clergyman (No. 674); a plague of cholera killing of all participants for their temerity in staging a Shrovetide procession on Ash Wednesday (No. 127); lameness for one who mocked St. Rockes (No. 517); blindness to a person who watched the daily progress of the demolition of a church sold at auction (No. 507). The severance of a foot by a train for a youth who kicked his father (No. 526), is reminiscent of the legend of "El mal Hijo," to which we shall return later.

Earlier in this paper I alluded to the inexorable nature of a person's sin or guilt, as extending even to one's children. These ideas, dating from the Old Testament times,[16] are still firmly fixed in people's minds today, as seen in various folk notions having to do with the connection between mother and child, birthmarks, and the whole process of "marking." One must distinguish, as Lily Weiser-Aall has done in an admirable paper,[17] between supernatural influcnces at work on the foetus of the unborn child, and the hundred and one kinds of things that happen in the prenatal period, either in the nursery itself or in things which the mother does, or fails to do, in and around the house. Many of these last named things have to do with happenings which have frightened the mother or overly engaged her attention; others deal with obsessions of various kinds and with yearnings for special kinds of foods and other kinds of longings. Birthmarks resulting from these kinds of prenatal happenings on the part of the mother rarely involve harm to the baby that could conceivably be thought of as stemming from God or other supernatural powers. A notable exception to the foregoing, however, is the mother's special preoccupation with cripples, with people beset by infirmities of various kinds, or with the unfortunate. This is especially the case if she mocks at them, is amused, or even smiles.[18] These folk notions of belittling the unfortunate are widely encountered in the United States and Canada. In Tennessee, for example, a pregnant mother took fiendish delight in imitating a clubfooted man, ignoring her neighbor's warnings. Her child, as it happened, was born so terribly club-footed that hope of its ever walking was almost abandoned.[19] In an account from Nova Scotia it was believed that making fun of another person's infirmity while a woman was carrying a child would unfailingly result in inflicting the same infirmity on the mother's own unborn child. A case is told of a woman in Seabright who was guilty of this sin, whose children were all born mentally deficient.[20] Other cases are noted from North Carolina,[21] Pennsylvania,[22] Alabama[23] and New York State:

> There are many other stories of monstrous births. One of the most striking is known in Troy where they tell of a rich, proud woman who in the days before her confinement used to ride with maid, coachman, and footman past miserable dwellings called the Barracks. One day, passing a poor woman and children, the rich lady observed to her maid, 'Doesn't she look like a sow with her five pigs?' When the little heir was born, he had instead of one hand a pig's foot, which was amputated and an artificial hand substituted.[24]

Crippling of children at birth and other forms of disfigurement are thought of as having been brought on by divine displeasure. Such unfortunate children are said to be "marked by

God'' (von Gott gezeichnet),[25] and their maladies are explained as resulting directly from the sins of their parents.[26] These notions are encountered in widely separated countries,[27] and they date from the times of ancient Israel, with the smiting of Bathsheba's first son,[28] and extend to the present day in areas as remote from the Holy Land as China, Hawaii,[29] and the United States.[30] In the folk mind, barrenness and stillbirth are also congenital conditions thought to be brought on by sin.[31] As late as 1890 in the Pennsylvania German country, for example, the hand of God was implied in the barrenness of one daughter and the stillbirth of the only child of another daughter for their worldliness and their refusal to join the church of their parents (Dunkard).[32] Congenital blindness, in the Scotch-Irish tradition of the same state of Pennsylvania, was laid to a mother's trying to get rid of an unborn child.[33] In the South Slavic countries blindness is supposed to result from intercourse with a *vile* or some other grave sin before the child is born.[34] In the Netherlands, Bakker says, monsters are believed to result from the wrath of God for copulation during the woman's period of menstruation.[35]

Certain diseases were believed in a bygone day to be sent by God, and some of them were supposed not to respond to ordinary medical treatment. Principal among these dreaded diseases was leprosy, with which Miriam of old was smitten.[36] Epilepsy, also known as the ''divine madness,''[37] syphilis, and other sexual diseases, were also often thought of as being sent by Providence and hence not susceptible to cure.[38] A physician of the fifteenth century, Pollich von Mellerstadt, had pondered the question whether diseases sent by God, such as syphilis, could be combatted by natural means,[39] and a French medical man by the name of Fernell (1497–1588) asked the same question.[40] The theory that diseases sent by heaven as a punishment for sin can be dealt with only by the church,[41] has found an echo in the American Midwest, where only God himself was supposed to be able to effect the cure.[42] In Yorkshire, St. Vitus dance was thought to be caused by the evil eye or by an evil wish or an evil prayer. If, however, it came as a direct visitation from God, the disease could not be cured by mortals.[43] Comparable beliefs are found in remote parts of the world. In Ceylon, for example, both Sinhalese and Tamil villagers believe that measles, chickenpox, mumps, smallpox, and all infectious diseases are sent by the gods, and, as a result, they take no medicine.[44]

Of all diseases that afflict man, blindness is regarded as one of the most grave and hopeless. Blindness very early took its place among physical maladies supposed to be inflicted by God himself, as witness the classic question posed in the Gospel according to St. John: "And as Jesus passed by, he saw a man which was blind from his birth. And his disciples asked him, saying, 'Master, who did sin, this man or his parents, that he was born blind'?"[45] In Old Testament times, the ancient Sodomites were struck with blindness as a punishment for the gross sins they committed.[46] The religious implications are clear, of course. In classical antiquity, where the whole system of values was different, the sun god Helios also meted out punishment by inflicting blindness.[47] In the more recent span of time covered by folklore, blindness has often been regarded as a mysterious or misunderstood punishment, even though the justice of such punishment as coming from God is perhaps more often hinted at than expressed.[48] Blasphemy is a stated cause, of course,[49] and so is the viewing of unseemly things such as persons or animals defecating, copulating, and the like.[50] The viewing of nakedness also belongs to this category of reprehensible acts which is punished with blindness.[51] Examples in legend extend from the striking blind of Tiresias for viewing Athene naked in the bath,[52] to the blindness that befell the hapless tailor, Peeping Tom, for peering out at Lady Godiva as she rode naked through the streets of Coventry, according to legend.[53] That notions of blindness as punishment still persist today is seen in an actual case reported from a well-known American city in the South. According to the story which circulates among folk song enthusiasts, a well-to-do musical impressario cheated a blind folk singer of royalties on his songs which appeared on phonograph records. Now in a mansion on a hill and without financial cares of any kind, the promoter himself is slowly going blind. People who know of the case say it is because of the man's sharp business dealing with the hapless blind singer.

Punishment affecting individual parts of the body for grave offenses is seen in a variety of folk beliefs and legends.[54] In France diseases localized in certain parts of the body are called "les maux de Saints," from the circumstance that certain saints are believed to preside over the areas of the body in question, not only in sending disease to these parts as punishment, but also healing these selfsame maladies.[55] Under this doctrine are explained such trifles as blisters on the tongue as a result of lying,[56] or styes from urinating or defecating in a public place, or watching someone do so.[57] Graver offenses involve the crippling or paralysis of fingers for swearing a false oath.[58] The abhorrence in which perjury was held is seen in the fact that crippling and paralysis of the fingers or hand might be passed on to the children of parents who had given false testimony.[59] The most heinous sin of all was that of a child striking its parents. Such a hand raised in anger against a parent was thought to become paralyzed and to wither.[60] In a Mexican legend from Colorado, a son struck his father, and from that moment his right arm began to wither, and his hand drew into knots. Year by year the hand grew more maimed and useless. This is what became of el mal hijo (the evil son), who now wanders around to warn others to avoid evil courses.[61] The notion that the hand of a child raised against its parents will grow out of the grave is well known in Germany and the Low Countries.[62]

The sins of pride are also punished by heaven in a physical way. In Old Testament times the daughters of Zion who went forth in worldly splendor and with wanton mien, according to the Scriptures, were cursed with baldness.[63] The so-called English Sweat (englischer Schweiß) which broke out in 1486 was later interpreted as the scourge of God to punish the sins of primping and lewdness.[64]

Mental ailments of all kinds were generally reckoned as being due to some sort of punishment,[65] and families burdened with these grievous afflictions often reflect on the possibility of some sort of divine intervention. Historically, madness, for instance, is one of several named diseases listed in Deuteronomy as being sent by God.[66] Well known in this same connection is the saying attributed to Euripides, "Whom God wishes to destroy, he first deprives of reason" *(Quos Deus vult perdere prius dementat)*. For reasons that are easy to understand, these ancient ideas have persisted to the present day. Many entries in my unpublished files bear on this subject, and, as recently as April 19, 1971, the Los Angeles Times carried a feature news account touching on the prevalence of this belief. In Hawaii, there is the same taboo against mistreating the feeble-minded, as we have seen in cases of mockery and belittlement, above. It is believed that if you do mistreat such an unfortunate person, someone in your own family will be afflicted by mental illness.[67]

It is difficult to account for the notion of the divine visitation of disease and physical infirmity of various kinds on humans as a punishment for their sins, as touched upon in this paper, unless one holds to a literal interpretation of scripture in both the Old and New Testament bearing on these ideas. The actual number of scriptural references, to be sure, is small and in comparison with references to God's displeasure with the wickedness of his children as expressed in terms of a much wider range of punishments: war, pestilence, earthquake, tempest, fire and brimstone, animal blight, etc., etc.[68] I can not, of course, assess the impact of these scriptural warnings on people of religious persuasion in Europe, and I have even less knowledge of the way preaching and revivalistic movements in Europe may have fastened upon these sensational scriptural and evangelistic warnings to win adherents and to keep the faithful in the fold. In America the sense of personal sin and of divine wrath has been deep from the earliest Puritan and Calvinistic teachings, through the development of religion on the frontier, to the revivalism and millenialism of the present day. A careful reading of this fundamentalist theology and of the pastoral writings to accompany it, would no doubt bring to light numerous accounts bearing out the belief held by religious people that God actually does punish sinners with bodily disease and suffering as well as with torment of soul as punishment for sin. These ideas have worked their way into folk medical lore to a greater degree than the written record shows at the present time. I trust that this introductory survey may serve to bring to light a fuller body of material for study than we now possess.

NOTES

1. C. S. Myers, Disease and Medicine (Introductory and Primitive). In: James Hastings, Encyclopaedia of Religion and Ethics. 13 vols., Edinburgh, 1908–1926. IV, pp. 726, 729. In the Malay Peninsula the thunder gods are thought to send disease on the winds because of the sins of the people.
2. Journal of American Folklore 68 (1955), p. 43.
3. A. F. Chamberlain, Disease and Medicine (American). In: Hastings, Encyclopaedia (see note 1), IV, pp. 732, 740.
4. For a treatment of the supernatural causes of disease, see Forrest E. Clements, Primitive Concepts of Disease, University of California Publications in American Archaeology and Ethnology 32 (1932), Berkeley, pp. 185–252.
5. Clements, Concepts (see note 4), pp. 187, 191; Spencer L. Rogers, Primitive Theories of Disease. In: Ciba Symposium, Vol. 4, No. 1 (April 1942), pp. 1192, 1200.
6. Chamberlain, American (see note 3), IV, p. 740.
7. G. M. Bolling, Disease and Medicine (Vedic), In: Hastings, Encyclopaedia (see note 1), IV, pp. 763, 769; J. Jolly, Disease and Medicine (Hindu), In: Hastings, Encyclopaedia (see note 1), IV, p. 754.
8. R. Campbell Thompson, Disease and Medicine (Assyro-Babylonian). In: Hastings, Encyclopaedia (see note 1), IV, p. 741; Herbert Loewe, Disease and Medicine (Jewish). In: Hastings, Encyclopaedia (see note 1), IV, pp. 755–756. Loewe cites copiously from the Old Testament.

9. E. Thraemer, Health and Gods of Healing (Greek). In: Hastings, Encyclopaedia (see note 1), VI, pp. 540, 545, 547 (including quotations from the Iliad and the Odyssey). References to Roman antiquity, Virgil and Ovid, mainly, are to be found in C. Bakker, Volksgeneeskunde in Waterland. Een vergelijkende Studie met de Geneeskunde der Grieken en Romeinen, Amsterdam 1928, pp. 377–378. See page 275 for an account of Apollo's causing an infectious disease to break out in the camp of Agamemnon because he had robbed the daughter of a priest (Iliad I–9).

10. Gustav Jungbauer, Deutsche Volksmedizin, Berlin 1934, p. 162.

11. Hastings, Encyclopaedia (see note 1), IV, pp. 757, 769.

12. Clements, Concepts (see note 4), p. 187; John G. Bourke, Medicine Men of the Apache, Ninth Annual Report of the Bureau of Ethnology, Washington 1892, p. 465; Journal of American Folklore 61 (1948), p. 348, n. 10.

13. Jungbauer, Volksmedizin (see note 10), pp. 35–38; A. de Cock, Volksgeneeskunde in Vlanderen, Gent 1891, pp. 24–25; Thomas R. Brendle and Claude W. Unger, Folk Medicine of the Pennsylvania Germans. The Non-Occult Cures, Proceedings of the Pennsylvania German Society 45 (1935), Norristown, Pennsylvania, p. 13.

14. Romans 6:23. "For the wages of sin is death. . . ."

15. Matthias Zender, Sagen und Geschichten aus der Westeifel, Bonn 1966.

16. The biblical warrant for this idea is found in Deuteronomy 5:9. "Thou shalt not bow down thyself unto them, nor serve them: for I the Lord thy God am a jealous God, visiting the iniquity of the fathers upon the children unto the third and fourth generation of them that hate me . . ." Cf. P. Kemp, Healing Ritual: Studies in the Technique and Tradition of the Southern Slavs, London, n. d., p. 42.

17. Lily Weiser-Aall, Gelehrte Tradition über angeborene Fehler in der Volksmedizin, Arv. Journal of Scandinavian Folklore 18–19 (1962–1963), pp. 226–262.

18. Bakker, Volksgeneeskunde (see note 9), p. 56; Schneeweis, Serbokroatische Volkskunde, Berlin 1961, p. 40.

19. William W. Bass, Birthmarks among the Folk, Tennessee Folklore Society Bulletin 25 (1959), p. 4.

20. Helen Creighton, Bluenose Magic. Popular Beliefs and Superstitions in Nova Scotia, Toronto 1968, p. 142, No. 246.

21. North Carolina Folklore 18 (1970), p. 119, No. 21. See also Wayland D. Hand, Popular Beliefs and Superstitions from North Carolina. In: The Frank C. Brown Collection of North Carolina Folklore. 7 vols., Durham, North Carolina, 1952–1964, VI, p. 23, Nos. 117–120.

22. Keystone Folklore Quarterly 7 (1962), p. 5.

23. Ray B. Browne, Popular Beliefs and Practices from Alabama, Folklore Studies IX (1958), Berkeley and Los Angeles, p. 119, No. 2066.

24. Harold W. Thompson, Body, Boots and Britches, Philadelphia 1940, pp. 114–115.

25. Adolf Wuttke, Der deutsche Volksaberglaube der Gegenwart. 3. Aufl. Berlin 1900, p. 218, paragr. 306.

26. Ibid., paragr. 307.

27. Bakker, Volksgeneeskunde (see note 9), p. 72; de Cock, Volksgeneeskunde (see note 13), p. 313; Kemp, Ritual (see note 16), p. 42; New York Folklore Quarterly 14 (1958), p. 233.

28. 2 Samuel 12:14.

29. News report in the Providence (Rhode Island) Evening-Bulletin, under date of Jan. 27, 1960, as reported in Western Folklore 20 (1961), p. 116.

30. Thompson, Body (see note 24), pp. 114–115.

31. Schneeweis, Volkskunde (see note 18), p. 39.

32. Pennsylvania Folklife 12 (Summer 1962), p. 42.

33. Henry W. Shoemaker, Scotch-Irish and English Proverbs and Sayings of the West Branch Valley of Central Pennsylvania, Reading Pennsylvania 1927, p. 12.

34. Kemp, Ritual (see note 16), p. 71.

35. Bakker, Volksgeneeskunde (see note 9), p. 69.

36. Numbers 12:10.

37. Owsei Temkin, The Falling Sickness. A History of Epilepsy from the Greeks to the Beginnings of Modern Neurology, Baltimore 1945.

38. Claudia de Lys, A Treasury of American Superstitions, New York 1948, p. 333; Bakker, Volksgeneeskunde (see note 9), p. 185.

39. Jungbauer, Volksmedizin (see note 10), p. 37.

40. Bakker, Volksgeneeskunde (see note 9), pp. 376–377.

41. Jungbauer, Volksmedizin (see note 10), p. 62.

42. Madge E. Pickard and R. Carlyle Buley, The Midwest Pioneer. His Ills, Cures, and Doctors, Crawfordsville, Indiana 1945, p. 102.

43. William Henderson, Notes on the Folklore of the Northern Counties of England and the Borders. 2 ed., London 1879, p. 152.

44. Gwladys Hughes Simon, Beliefs Common in Ceylon, Western Folklore 19 (1960), p. 126, No. 108.

45. John 9:1–2.

46. Loewe, Jewish (see note 8), IV, p. 756.

47. Thraemer, Greek (see note 9), VI, p. 546.

48. Handwörterbuch des deutschen Aberglaubens. 10 Bde., Berlin und Leipzig 1927–1942, I, p. 712, sec. 7, s. v. "Augenkrankheiten"; Kemp, Ritual (see note 16), p. 71.

49. HDA (see note 48), I, p. 712; Lutz Mackensen und Johannes Bolte, Handwörterbuch des deutschen Märchens. 2 Bde. Berlin und Leipzig 1930–1940, I, p. 275.

50. Jungbauer, Volksmedizin (see note 10), p. 36.

51. HDA, VI, pp. 836–839.

52. Ibid., p. 836.

53. E. Sidney Hartland, Peeping Tom and Lady Godiva, Folk-Lore 1 (1890), 207–226.

54. Jungbauer, Volksmedizin (see note 10), p. 35.

55. Marcelle Bouteiller, Médecine populaire d'hier et d'aujourd'hui, Paris 1966, p. 33.

56. Jungbauer, Volksmedizin (see note 10), p. 35; Hand, North Carolina (see note 21), VI, p. 487, Nos. 3668 ff.

57. Jungbauer, Volksmedizin (see note 10), p. 36.

58. Wuttke, Volksaberglaube (see note 25), p. 218, paragr. 307; Jungbauer, Volksmedizin (see note 10), pp. 35–36.

59. Jungbauer, Volksmedizin (see note 10), p. 36. Cf. Béla Gunda, Gypsy Medical Folklore in Hungary, Journal of American Folklore 75 (1962), p. 133.

60. Jungbauer, Volksmedizin (see note 10), pp. 35–36.

61. Publications of the Texas Folklore Society 9 (1931), p. 83. The legend cycle of the evil son has been treated by T. M. Pearce, The Bad Son *(El mal*

Hijo) in Southwestern Spanish Folklore, Western Folklore 9 (1950), pp. 295-301.

62. Wuttke, Volksaberglaube (see note 25), p. 218, paragr. 307; Bakker, Volksgeneeskunde (see note 9), p. 457.

63. Isaiah 3:16-24.

64. Jungbauer, Volksmedizin (see note 10), p. 37.

65. Kemp, Ritual (see note 16), p. 42.

66. Deuteronomy 28:21-28, especially 28.

67. Gwladys Hughes Simon, Folk Beliefs and Customs in an Hawaiin Community, Journal of American Folklore 62 (1949), p. 297.

68. Exodus 9:15; Deuteronomy 28:21-28; Bakker, Volksgeneeskunde (see note 9), p. 376; Jungbauer, Volksmedizin (see note 10), p. 201; Kemp, Ritual (see note 16), p. 42; Chamberlain, American (see note 3), p. 732.

5

Hangmen, the Gallows, and the Dead Man's Hand in American Folk Medicine*

The mystery that surrounds the life processes, including the inevitable cessation of life, has given rise to the rich and abundant folklore of the life cycle: birth, marriage, death.[1] Inextricably connected with the life cycle at all three main life crises, or rites of passage, as van Gennep denominated these changes,[2] are folk medical notions and practices appropriate to each new condition.

It is one of the ironies of folk medical practice that things connected with the realm of the dead should by some inexplicable logic be employed to combat sickness and sustain life. Perhaps this is part of the religious and philosophical dilemma expressed by a tenth-century theologian and philosopher in the famous dictum, *in medio vitae mortuus sum.* It is more likely, however, that the offices of hangmen, *Leichenwäscherinnen,* gravediggers, and even knackers, in caring for the sick, and the use of parts of the coffin, appurtenances of the gallows, graveyard earth, and even parts of the dead, rest on more primitive modes of thought than the theological aphorism stated by Notker of St. Gall. It is hard

*This article originally appeared in *Medieval Literature and Folklore Studies. Essays in Honor of Francis Lee Utley.* Ed. Jerome Mandell and Bruce A. Rosenberg. New Brunswick, N.J.: Rutgers University Press, 1970, pp. 323–329, 381–387.

to see, however, on what this special healing efficacy of agents and things connected with death is based, and why things that would normally be shunned are, by some mental quirk, especially sought out for curative practices. It is clear, of course, that the principles of decay and dissolution associated with death and the dead fit readily into frames of thought and logic looking to removal and dying off of warts, wens, moles, and other excrescences, as well as to the shrinking and disappearance of goiters, tumors, and other kinds of swellings. Accordingly, it would be more to the curing of such diseases as ague, convulsions, epilepsy, fits, fever, hiccoughs, and the like that the paradox really applies. At work, in any case, are principles of both homeopathic and contagious magic. Perhaps even more important in a strictly medical sense would be rudimentary notions of immunology and other considerations of antithetical vital forces summed up in the magico-medical prescription of *contraria contrariis.*

A possible resolution of this dilemma—the use of parts of the dead to cure the living—is seen in the case of people who have died violently, and ahead of their appointed time, or, better still, those whose lives have been forcibly taken. It has been argued, for example, that people hanged, or otherwise executed, continue to exert a vital force beyond the gallows or the executioner's block—a tenacious prolongation of life,[3] with the thought that this vital force and magical power continues to operate until their normal life span would have run out. Belief in the magical power of the bodily parts and products of executed criminals as remedies and amulets was known in classical antiquity, as attested by Pliny,[4] and these old superstitions, nurtured during the Middle Ages, have lived on until the present time. Important in these old beliefs and customs, of course, was the hangman himself. Some scholars believe that a sacral function attached to his office, holding, in a sense, that in taking a human life he represented deity in a sacrificial act.[5] The hangman's reputation as a healer, and as a trafficker in splinters from the gallows, as well as in pieces of the hangman's rope, the clothes and other chattels of the executed criminal, goes back many centuries.[6] In former times executioners openly advertised themselves as healers.[7] As payment, in part, for their grisly work went the clothes of the criminal,[8] which were disposed of without difficulty for medical as well as other magical purposes. It is interesting to follow in eighteenth-century England the transfer of the magical power of the hanged criminal to the hangman himself. This is seen in the curing of warts, wens, and other excrescences, in the first instance, merely by having the sufferer touch his afflicted part to the hand or other parts of the defunct.[9] As a result of his traffic with the dead, and by contagious magic, the hangman himself also rubbed people afflicted with warts, receiving at one time a fee of 2/6*d.* for his services.[10] Traffic in bodily parts of hanged criminals, particularly skulls, fingers, and the notorious dead man's hand, or "hand of glory,"[11] whether by sale or theft, continued unabated throughout the nineteenth century, and the practice has lived on pretty much to our own time.[12] A "collector," for example, is supposed to have offered £600 for the rope from which von Ribbentrop swung at the Nuremberg trials after World War II.[13] Unfortunately, little lore about hangmen has been reported in America, even though one may assume that dealings of the kind mentioned were resorted to in parts of the country where hanging was still practiced.[14] Executions in public, one of the main reasons for hanging when this method of execution was originally instituted, are now pretty much a thing of the past,[15] with the result that only a few people are ever allowed to witness such a spectacle. Under these circumstances active traffic in items of gallows magic is impossible, even though reports of the use, or the recommended use, of these products still continues today.

With the natural limitations of the subject—particularly in the matter of unrecorded and uncodified data—I shall nevertheless essay in these pages a sketch of folk medical curing in America by means of certain things connected with the dead, whether bodily parts of the dead or funerary objects of various kinds immediately connected with the dead and with death. Executed criminals constitute a special phase of this subject; and with this subject we shall begin, even though the data are scanty.[16] In Pennsylvania it is believed among people of German extraction that a wen will be carried away if it is passed across the head of a criminal just hanged.[17] Although the hand of a corpse, as we shall see later, has been used for a variety of ailments in America, the specific use of the hand of a dead criminal is apparently not reported in the literature I have examined.[18] Neither has there been reported the use of the powdered skull of criminals,[19] the rendered down fat of humans,[20] nor the drinking of fresh blood set free by the headman's axe.[21] The use of the hanged man's tooth for toothache is rare, even for Europe, but there is an instance of this unusual practice in Siena, Italy, in 1435.[22]

The use of the hangman's rope for medical and other purposes is well known in Europe.[23] In the United States its use seems limited to Pennsylvania, where it is encountered in both the Anglo-American and German-American traditions.[24] The North Carolina entry in the Brown Collection, submitted by a student from Indiana,[25] would seem to be a copying of a Pennsylvania text. The hangman's rope is also used for fits in Pennsylvania,[26] whereas people suffering from headache could be cured, it was believed, by tying around their head the halter wherewith a person had been hanged.[27] The King's Evil, or scrofula, was also treated with bits of the hangman's rope, but I do not find American examples.[28] Magical power was thought also to attach to the rope with which a person had committed suicide. The use of such a rope in the treatment of epilepsy is reported from Pennsylvania.[29] Convulsions in children are also treated in this way.[30]

Equally rare with the use of the hangman's rope in America for curing purposes, is the use of parts of the gallows or the gibbet. This is no doubt for the same reason—rarity of hanging at a time when folklorists, local historians, and other antiquarians came on the scene to report such happenings. Resort to contemporary police and warden's accounts of a former day, and particularly to diaries, family books of all kinds, and rare local histories, would perhaps add notably to our poor knowledge of American gallows lore.

Whether the reference to the use of a fragment of a gibbet or gallows on which people had been executed to cure ague, as reported in *The Casket* of Philadelphia for 1833 deals with American material earlier than the *Virginia Museum* from which it was taken,[31] or whether it rests on such earlier well-known sources as Aubrey's *Remaines of Gentilisme and Judaisme* (1686–1687),[32] cannot be learned. In a disease related to ague, namely, fever, the use of gallows wood goes back to the time of Pliny.[33]

The use of splinters from a gibbet as a sovereign remedy for toothache, whether carried in the pocket, or used to probe the aching tooth, is well known in England and elsewhere,[34] but I do not command instances from America.

If the use of the hand of an executed criminal is little known in American folk medicine, the custom of treating various kinds of ailments with the touch of an ordinary dead man's hand is much better known. There is an important reason for this over and above the sharp decline in hangings in America in recent times, as indicated above. In Europe, where the corpse was gibbeted, and left for birds to consume, folk medical practitioners could get at the corpse to sever the hand, as could thieves, who also appropriated the so-called "hand of glory," to make themselves invisible as they burglarized, and also to render the victims deaf to any possible noise.[35] Under less notorious conditions it was not difficult for sufferers to go to the house where the dead was laid out, or even to the undertaker's, when such mortuary establishments later came into general use. Examples of both circumstances, each involving the supposed cure of goiter, are seen in accounts from Ontario (1908) and from the Ozark country (1940's).[36] The practice of using a dead man's hand in the treatment of goiter is found not only in Pennsylvania (Anglo-American tradition as well as in the German tradition),[37] but also in New York State.[38] This cure is encountered in Ontario in both the Anglo-American and German-American traditions,[39] and also in the South.[40] Indiana entries run true to form,[41] as do two references from Illinois.[42] Two further accounts, both from Hyatt's great collection, add interesting details. The first tells of a fourteen-year-old girl going to the place where the dead person was laid out, taking the dead person's hand, and rubbing her goiter with it three times, after which she placed the hand back exactly as it was. Within a year her goiter was gone.[43] The second account is a *memorat,* telling of the use of the corpse's left hand for a goiter on the left side and the right hand for one on the right side, and the unsuccessful use of the left hand for a goiter on both sides of the neck: "and her goitre got well on the left side and never did get well on the right side."[44] This cure for goiter has not been reported west of Nebraska.[45] The use of a dead man's hand for goiter is, of course, well known in the British Isles and elsewhere in Europe.[46]

Similar procedures to those used for the cure of goiter were employed also for other kinds of tumors and swellings. Once more, the Pennsylvania German country is involved.[47] A variation on the treatment of tumors involved the use of a *Zwischenträger,* string or intermediate agent, namely, a string that had been tied around the finger of the dead man's hand was later tied around the tumor, and as the string rotted the tumor was supposed to disappear.[48] The method of curing swellings by the touch of a dead person's hand is as old as classical antiquity,[49] and as modern as the 1960's, as a recent report from Somerset shows.[50] Belief that a dead man's hand touched to a cancer will cure it was reported from Salt Lake City as recently as 1960.

The charming off of warts by means of touching or rubbing, a folk medical practice which is known in Europe,[51] is encountered not only in the Pennsylvania German country,[52] as one might suspect, but also in such widely separated places as Tennessee,[53] the Ozark country,[54] and Iowa.[55] The dispelling of wens, reported in *The Casket* of Philadelphia as early as 1833,[56] was, of course, known in England at a much earlier time.[57] In modern times this cure, among other places, has been reported from Suffolk (1895), Lincolnshire (1896), and Herefordshire (1912).[58] More recent American references to this practice, involving several southern states, as well as Pennsylvania, are to be found in the Brown Collection.[59] The removal of wens is also accomplished by Louisville Negroes who place a string around the neck of a deceased friend, and afterward wear it around their own necks with wens on them.[60]

"The touch of a dead man's hand," writes Randolph, "is popularly supposed to discourage moles, blackheads, enlarged pores, and other facial blemishes. I have seen a little girl, perhaps three years old, dragged into a village undertaking parlor and 'tetched,' in the belief that a large red birthmark on the child's face might thus be removed."[61]

Contact between the person seeking relief and the dead man is not limited to the latter's hand; it may extend to the fingers, to the face, and to other parts of the body; also it may involve the skull and the bones of the deceased, and even linen and cloths of various kinds that have been in contact with the dead person. The Alabama folk medical practice, around 1900, of putting the finger of a dead person in one's mouth for toothache,[62] is reported from Europe at an earlier day.[63] The application of the finger of a corpse to a wart, rather than the hand, as noticed above is reported from Norway.[64] Warts and moles are removed by rubbing the excrescences of the dead person's face, rather than bringing them into contact with his hand, according to an attestation from Illinois in 1935,[65] and a less certain report from California almost thirty years earlier.[66] In Illinois, likewise, the warts may be rubbed on the body of the corpse, the exact spot not being specified.[67] In other items from the same state interesting details are included, with a woman rubbing her wart on the corpse of a man three times, and vice versa.[68] The patient's own hand is rubbed over the corpse and then touched to the wart. This should be done as the full moon begins to decrease.[69] Tumors were treated in much the same way in Illinois: "If you have a tumor on the outside of your body, take it and rub it over a corpse of a dead person three times and it will go away. I know this is true, because when my father died, our neighbor had a tumor on her arm and she came and rubbed her tumor over my dead father three times, and in no time the tumor was gone.''[70]

The drying and powdering of moss found on human skulls, as reported in *The Casket* (Philadelphia, 1833),[71] and then taken as snuff to cure headaches, doubtless is a carry-over from European practices.[72] The grating of the skull itself, and administering it, with or without ginger, to infants and others suffering from fits, seems not to be known in America.[73] Drinking from a skull to prevent scrofula is reported in an American popular journal of 1869,[74] but I can find no ready parallels. In another unusual practice, reported from Norway, a bone is used in a curious way: ''For sudden gout or paralysis, which is called 'dead man's grasp,' stroke the sufferer with a bone from a corpse.''[75] Instructions are given to get the bone back to the graveyard before nightfall, and it is recommended that some one, who knows about these matters, and not a relative, be entrusted with the job.

Contact with the corpse by means of bed linen, shrouds, washrags, and the like, rather than by direct touching or rubbing, is noted for warts, as one might expect. Disposing of the washrag which has been used to wash a corpse by placing it under the eaves is noted from Pennsylvania.[76] A more involved ritual is recorded from Illinois: ''If you have a wart, go where they are laying out someone that is dead and take that piece of cloth that is over the dead one's face and rub that piece of cloth over your wart. Then you must put that piece of cloth in the coffin with that dead one and let it be buried with the dead, and your wart will go away.''[77] Toothache cures of this sort are reported from Norway, where a cloth that has been in contact with a corpse, is placed over the mouth;[78] or the gum over the tooth is probed with a pin which has been fastened to the sheet in which the corpse has been wrapped. Similarly, in Norway, a cloth which has been used around the jaw of the corpse to keep the mouth closed, is tied around the head of a sufferer from headache.[79] In Portugal, scrofula is cured by scratching the affected part until it bleeds with a toenail from the left foot of a corpse and wiping away the blood with a cloth which is then placed in the coffin.[80]

Even though material introduced in this short discussion is little more than an adumbration of the scope and variety of material which exists, I trust that it will stimulate workers in the field to dredge up data for a fuller account at some later date.

Since completing this paper, I have been able to turn up additional data in the Newbell Niles Puckett Collection of Ohio Popular Beliefs and Superstitions, which has come to me for editing. A cursory search of the folk medical holdings shows that the touch of a dead man's hand was recommended not only for the cure of goiter, but also for the removal of birthmarks and warts. Recommended cures for epilepsy include the use of rope with which a person has committed suicide and a broth made from the skull of a dead person. Headache was to be treated by hanging around the forehead a piece of rope with which a criminal had been hanged. These dozen items were collected from different parts of Ohio between 1929 and 1962 and stem from people of continental as well as British ancestry.

NOTES

1. Well-known folkloristic approaches to the life cycle, or life crises, have been made by Paul Sartori in his standard work, *Sitte und Brauch* (Handbücher zur Volkskunde, V–VIII, Leipzig, 1910–1914) under the rubric "Hauptstufen des Menschendaseins," and by Arnold van Gennep in his *Manuel de folklore français contemporain,* 9 vols. in 4 (Vol. II never appeared) (Paris, 1937–1958), and in his various collections of provincial French folklore under headings in most volumes, *du berceau à la tombe.*

2. Cf. Arnold van Gennep, *Les rites de passage* (Paris, 1909). This work is now available in English translation (*The Rites of Passage,* trans. Monika B. Vizedom and Gabrielle L. Caffee [Chicago: University of Chicago Press, 1960]).

3. *Handwörterbuch des deutschen Aberglaubens,* IV (Leipzig, 1927–1942), 39. (Hereinafter cited *HDA.*) Cf. also *HDA,* III, 1455. The reader will also find excellent material in the general area of this study in Mabel Peacock, "Executed Criminals and Folk-Medicine," *Folk-Lore,* VII (1896), 268–283. The British author has brought material together not only from the British Isles, but from other countries of Europe as well. For a general statement on the magical power of an executioner in medical matters, see O. v. Hovorka und A. Kronfeld, *Vergleichende Volksmedizin: Eine Darstellung volksmedizinischer Sitten und Gebräuche, Anschauungen und Heilfaktoren, des Aberglaubens und der Zaubermedizin,* I (Stuttgart, 1908–1909), 377–379.

4. *Natural History,* XXVIII, 2; cf. *HDA,* III, 1455.

5. *HDA,* III, 1439–1440, 1454–1455, *passim*; cf. Werner Danckert, *Unehrliche Leute: Die verfemten Berufe* (Bern und München: Francke, 1963), pp. 25, 30, 42, *passim.*

6. Danckert, *Unehrliche Leute,* p. 34.

7. Danckert, *Unehrliche Leute,* p. 43.

8. Ersch und Gruber, *Allgemeine Encyclopädie der Wissenschaften und Künste,* Zweite Section, H–N, Fünfter Theil, p. 321, s.v. "Henker." This custom is also alluded to in "Robin Hood Rescuing Three Squires" (Child Ballad, No. 140).

9. Alfred Marks, *Tyburn Tree: Its History and Annals* (London, n.d.), p. 48, as cited from the *Gentleman's Magazine,* XXXVII (1767), 276. "A man having been hanged at Tyburn on May 4, 1767, 'a young woman, with a wen upon

her neck, was lifted up while he was hanging, and had the wen rubbed with the dead man's hand, from a superstitious notion that it would effect a cure.' "

10. John Deane Potter, *The Fatal Gallows Tree* (London: Elek, 1965), p. 70.

11. E. and M. Radford, *Encyclopaedia of Superstitions,* edited and revised by Christina Hole (London: Hutchinson, 1961), pp. 179–180, s.v. "Hand of Glory"; cf. also "Dead Hand" (pp. 124–126). (This work is hereinafter cited as Radford-Hole.) T. F. Thiselton Dyer, *Strange Pages from Family Papers* (London, 1895), pp. 154–161.

12. For Germany, see *HDA,* IV, 46, *passim*; Potter, *The Fatal Gallows Tree,* pp. 70–71.

13. Potter, *The Fatal Gallows Tree,* p. 71.

14. As of fifteen or twenty years ago only six states prescribed hanging as a means of capital punishment, namely, Idaho, Iowa, Kansas, Montana, New Hampshire, and Washington; in Utah hanging is optional. *Encyclopaedia Britannica* (Chicago, London, etc., 1962), XI, 152, s.v. "Hanging."

15. The last "public" hanging in the United States took place in Kentucky in 1936. *Encyclopaedia Britannica*, XI, 152, s.v. "Hanging."

16. To stimulate further search, and to make available "jury texts," I shall cite references from the British Isles and the continent.

17. Thomas R. Brendle and Claude W. Unger, *Folk Medicine of the Pennsylvania Germans. The Non-Occult Cures,* Proceedings of the Pennsylvania German Society, XLV (Norristown, Pa., 1935), p. 68; John Graham Dalyell, *The Darker Superstitions of Scotland* (Glasgow, 1835), p. 129; E. and M. A. Radford, *Encyclopedia of Superstitions* (London, n.d. [1947], pp. 98, 256; William George Black, *Folk-Medicine: A Chapter in the History of Culture,* Publications of the Folk-Lore Society, XII (London, 1883), pp. 100–101.

18. European examples, of course, are numerous; a few references will suffice: Thiselton Dyer, pp. 157–158 (for smallpox); *HDA,* II, 1176 (epilepsy), 1455 (goiters, warts); IV, 44–45 (various); John Symonds Udal, *Dorsetshire Folk-Lore* (Hertford, 1922), p. 186 (skin complaints); Dalyell, *Darker Superstitions,* p. 129 (scrofula).

19. *Folk-Lore,* VII (1896), 270–271 (Denmark); *HDA,* III, 1455 (Amsterdam [1693]).

20. *Folk-Lore,* VII (1896), 269–270 (scrofula: France); *HDA,* III, 1455 (Bohemia [1613]).

21. *Folk-Lore,* VII (1896), 270–271 (epilepsy: Denmark; also wens: Denmark and Sweden); Danckert, *Unehrliche Leute,* pp. 42–43. In the Swedish-speaking part of western Finland an account is given of a woman who ran up with a little bit of bark when the head fell at an execution, and drank the blood to cure herself of epilepsy (V. E. V. Wessman, *Folktro och Trolldom.* 3. Människan och Djuren, Finlands Svenska Folkedigtning, VII [Helsingfors, 1952], 49–50). An instance from 1696 is also reported (p. 50). Cf. *HDA,* II, 1176, s.v. "Fallsucht." Epileptics are also reported to have drunk the blood of performers killed in the circus in ancient Rome (Danckert, *Unehrliche Leute*), p. 43.

22. *HDA,* III, 1455.

23. Radford-Hole, p. 181, s.v. "Hangman's rope"; *HDA,* III, 262ff., s.v. "Galgen"; cf. Index under "Galgenstrick," "Armsünderstrick," "Strick," etc.

24. Henry Phillips, Jr., "First Contribution to the Folk-Lore of Philadelphia and its Vicinity," Proceedings of the American Philosophical Society, XXV [1888], 164, No. 20 (epilepsy); *Folk-Lore,* VII (1896), 268 (epilepsy: Lincolnshire).

25. *Frank C. Brown Collection of North Carolina Folklore* (Durham, North Carolina: Duke University Press, 1952–1964; Vols. VI–VII, *Popular Beliefs and Superstitions from North Carolina,* ed. Wayland D. Hand, 1961–1964), VI, 179, No. 1348.

26. Phillips, p. 164, No. 20; cf. Brown Collection, VI, 193, No. 1478 (text possibly unreliable). Cf. *Folk-Lore,* XLIV (1933), 202 (fits: Lincolnshire—noose as well as rope).

27. *The Casket,* VI (Philadelphia, July, 1833), 264, No. 2. This reference was taken from the *Virginia Museum,* but without more precise details, and I am unfortunately unable to trace this publication, which appears to be a contemporary journal. Cf. Dalyell, *Darker Superstitions,* p. 128 (who says that the use of the noose dates from the time of Pliny); Black, *Folk-Medicine,* p. 100; George Lyman Kittredge, *Witchcraft in Old and New England* (Cambridge, Mass.: Harvard University Press, 1929), p. 142; Thomas Joseph Pettigrew, *On Superstitions Connected With the History and Practice of Medicine and Surgery* (London, 1844), p. 64; Radford, *Encyclopaedia of Superstitions*, pp. 141, 146; Ella M. Leather, *Folk-Lore of Herefordshire* (Hereford: Jakeman and Carver, and London: Sidgwick and Jackson, 1912), p. 79. Since writing this article I have come upon an entry containing a recommended cure for headache, employing the halter of a man who has been hanged. This is found in the *Farmer's Almanac* for 1832 (Boston: Willard Felt & Co.), p. 34. With the widespread failure in early days to credit sources in almanacs and other media of cheap print, it is not unlikely that the *Virginia Museum* may have copied the item which originally appeared in the *Farmer's Almanac.*

28. *Folk-Lore,* XI (1900), 217 (Devonshire); XXVII (1916), 415 (Herefordshire); Kittredge, *Witchcraft,* p. 142.

29. Brendle and Unger, *Folk Medicine,* p. 106; cf. Edwin Miller Fogel, *Beliefs and Superstitions of the Pennsylvania Germans,* Americana Germanica, XVIII (Philadelphia, 1915), No. 1548.

30. Fogel, *Beliefs and Superstitions,* No. 1772.

31. *The Casket,* No. 6 (June 1833), 264, No. 7.

32. Ed. James Britten, Publications of the Folk-Lore Society, IV (London, 1881), p. 118. This was repeated in the standard work on English folk medicine in the nineteenth century, Thomas Joseph Pettigrew, *On Superstitions Connected With the History and Practice of Medicine and Surgery* (London, 1844), p. 68. Cf. also Black, *Folk-Medicine,* p. 100; Kittredge, *Witchcraft,* p. 142.

33. *Natural History,* XXVIII, 30. (I have been unable to verify Professor Cyrus L. Day's reference, which he takes from Heckenbach [*Western Folklore,* IX (1950), 238, no. 31].)

34. Radford, *Encyclopedia of Superstitions,* p. 242; Kittredge, *Witchcraft,* p. 142.

35. Radford-Hole, pp. 179–180; cf. *HDA,* s.v. "Diebsdaumen," "Diebsfinger," etc. (Index).

36. *Journal of American Folklore,* XXXI (1918), 137, No. 23: "The cure by stroking or rubbing the goitre with a dead man's hand was tried quite recently in East Oxford township, the woman who had it coming from some distance to where the corpse lay"; Vance Randolph, *Ozark Superstitions* (New York: Columbia University Press, 1947), p. 148: "a small town undertaker tells me that an old woman in the neighborhood is always coming to his place, wanting to try this" [rubbing her goiter with a dead man's hand].

37. *Journal of American Folklore,* IV (1891), 124 (rubbing the neck three

times); II (1889), 31; Brendle and Unger, *Folk Medicine,* p. 79; E. Grumbine, *Folk-Lore and Superstitious Beliefs of Lebanon County* (Papers and Addresses of the Lebanon County Historical Society, III, 1905–1906), p. 278.

38. Emelyn E. Gardner, *Folklore from the Schoharie Hills New York* (Ann Arbor, Mich.: University of Michigan Press, 1937), p. 267, No. 27; *New York Folklore Quarterly,* VIII (1952), 89.

39. *Journal of American Folklore,* XXXI (1918), 22, No. 288; W. J. Wintemberg, *Folk-Lore of Waterloo County, Ontario,* National Museum of Canada, Bulletin, No. 116, Anthropological Series, No. 28 (Ottawa, 1950), p. 12.

40. Daniel Lindsey Thomas and Lucy Blayney Thomas, *Kentucky Superstitions* (Princeton, N.J.: Princeton University Press, 1920), No. 1218 (rub a dead person's hand over it [the goiter] three times; as the body decays the goitre will disappear [Louisville Negroes]); E. Horace Fitchett, "Superstition in South Carolina," *The Crisis,* XLIII (1936), 360.

41. *Hoosier Folklore,* IX (1950), 9; *Indiana History Bulletin,* XXV (1958), 126, No. 155 (Marion and Noble Counties); No. 156 (Clinton County).

42. *Journal of American Folklore,* XXXI (1918), 205; Harry Middleton Hyatt, *Folk-Lore from Adams County Illinois* (New York: Hyatt Foundation, 1935), No. 5277.

43. Hyatt, *Folk-Lore,* No. 5278.

44. Hyatt, *Folk-Lore,* No. 5279.

45. Pauline Monette Black, *Nebraska Folk Cures* (University of Nebraska Studies in Language, Literature, and Criticism, XV, Lincoln, 1935), p. 36, No. 42.

46. *Folk-Lore,* VII (1896), 268–269 (England and France); XL (1929), 119 (Norfolk); XLIV (1933), 203 (Lincolnshire); Black, *Folk-Medicine,* p. 101 (rubbed nine times from east to west and nine times from west to east); Radford, *Encyclopedia of Superstitions,* pp. 133, 142 (make a cross over the goiter with a dead man's hand); Hovorka und Kronfeld, II, 17–18; W. G. Soldan, *Soldan's Geschichte der Hexenprozesse.* Neu bearbeitet von Heinrich Heppe, I (Stuttgart, 1880), 68 (ancient Rome).

47. Fogel, *Beliefs and Superstitions*, No. 1566 (stroke the tumor with the hand of a corpse and it will disappear with the decomposition of the corpse); Brendle and Unger, *Folk Medicine,* p. 80; A. Monroe Aurand, Jr., *Popular Home Remedies and Superstitions of the Pennsylvania Germans* (Harrisburg, Pa.: Aurand Press, 1941), p. 13. European references: Black, *Folk-Medicine,* p. 101; Radford, *Encyclopedia of Superstitions,* p. 245 (placing the hand of a man who has committed suicide will cure tumors on the skin); James Napier, *Folk Lore: or, Superstitious Beliefs in the West of Scotland Within This Century* (Paisley, 1879), pp. 92–93; Kittredge, *Witchcraft,* p. 142 (especially if the person has been hanged).

48. Brendle and Unger, *Folk Medicine,* p. 80; Fogel, *Beliefs and Superstitions,* No. 1479.

49. Pliny, *Natural History,* XXVIII, 11.

50. R. L. Tongue and K. M. Briggs, *Somerset Folklore,* Publications of the Folklore Society, CXIV (London, 1965), p. 136 (a dead hand passed nine times over a swelling dispels it).

51. Radford, *Encyclopedia of Superstitions,* pp. 142, 249; *HDA,* III, 1393, s.v. "Hand"; VII, 621, s.v. "reiben."

52. Fogel, *Beliefs and Superstitions,* No. 1686; Aurand, *Remedies and Superstitions,* p. 13.

53. *Tennessee Folklore Society Bulletin,* XIX (1953), 54.

54. Randolph, *Ozark Superstitions,* p. 151.

55. Earl J. Stout, *Folklore from Iowa,* Memoirs of the American Folklore Society, XXIX (New York, 1936), No. 741.

56. No. VI (July 1833), 264, No. 4 as reported in *Western Folklore,* XII (1953), 29.

57. Cf. John Aubrey, *Remaines of Gentilisme and Judaisme,* Publications of the Folk-Lore Society, IV (London, 1881), p. 198; Kittredge, *Witchcraft,* p. 142.

58. *Folk-Lore,* VI (1895), 124–125; VII (1896), 268–269; Leather, *Folk-Lore of Herefordshire,* p. 84.

59. Vol. VI, No. 2703. An additional reference, one from Illinois, contains a first-person account of this curative procedure: "I had a wen on my hand. I tried several things and it would always come back. A negro man got burned in a fire and died. I went to see him and took his hand and rubbed it over my own, and it left and never came back" (Hyatt, *Folk-Lore,* No. 3964).

60. Thomas and Thomas, *Kentucky Superstitions,* No. 1546.

61. *Ozark Superstitions,* pp. 163–164. Cf. *HDA,* III, 1393 (rashes and sores).

62. *Southern Workman,* XXIX (1900), 443; cf. Joh. Th. Storaker, *Sygdom og Forgjørelse i den Norske Folketro,* Norsk Folkeminnelag, No. 41 (Oslo, 1938), No. 124.

63. Kittredge, *Witchcraft,* p. 142; cf. *Folk-Lore,* XXXIII (1922), 396.

64. Storaker, *Sygdom og Forgjorelse,* No. 377.

65. Hyatt, *Folk-Lore,* No. 4110.

66. Fletcher Bascom Dresslar, *Superstition and Education,* University of California Publications in Education, Vol. 5 (Berkeley, 1907), p. 111.

67. Hyatt, *Folk-Lore,* Nos. 4108, 4109 (rub it over the corpse three times). Also known in Nebraska; see Black, *Nebraska Folk Cures,* p. 28, No. 76.

68. Hyatt, *Folk-Lore,* Nos. 4111 (woman on man), 4112 (man on woman).

69. Hyatt, *Folk-Lore,* No. 4114.

70. Hyatt, *Folk-Lore,* No. 5661.

71. Vol. VI (1833), 264, No. 3, as reported in *Western Folklore,* XII (1953), 29.

72. Black, *Folk-Medicine,* p. 96; Radford, *Encyclopedia of Superstitions,* pp. 146, 220; Kittredge, *Witchcraft,* p. 142.

73. Cf. Black, *Folk-Medicine,* p. 97; Radford, *Encyclopedia of Superstitions,* pp. 123–124; Kittredge, *Witchcraft,* p. 142; *Journal of American Folklore,* XXII (1909), 123.

74. *Appleton's Journal of Literature, Science, and Art,* II (1869), 139.

75. Storaker, *Sygdom og Forgjørelse,* No. 261.

76. Fogel, *Beliefs and Superstitions,* Nos. 1699, 1737; Brendle and Unger, *Folk Medicine,* p. 65.

77. Hyatt, *Folk-Lore,* No. 4104. Disposal of disease by means of a *Zwischenträger* placed in a coffin is very common in Europe and is also somewhat known in America. Cf. *North Carolina Folklore* XIII (1965), 84–85, for a discussion of *Zwischenträger,* or intermediate agent.

78. Storaker, *Sygdom og Forgjørelse,* No. 125.

79. Storaker, *Sygdom og Forgjørelse,* No. 36.

80. Rodney, Gallop, *Portugal* (Cambridge: Cambridge University Press, 1936), p. 62; cf. Kittredge, *Witchcraft,* p. 142 (wear a napkin from the dead man's face around the neck and then drop it on his coffin in the grave).

6
Plugging, Nailing, Wedging, and Kindred Folk Medical Practices*

In an earlier paper I have taken up the general notion and practice of magical transference of disease.[1] Included in that discussion is the communication of disease from humans to trees by touching, rubbing, tying, braiding, and similar means, together with the sale of disease (warts) to trees. Reserved for the present paper, which includes European as well as American material, is a more intimate kind of transference, namely, the implantation of disease. Whereas in the methods named above the disease is outwardly fastened to the tree in a symbolic way, under "plugging" and its related forms, the disease is implanted or buried in the tree, whether deep or superficially, depending on how the transference is made. (Boring the hole into the roots of trees or into branches is little encountered in America.)[2]

Whether the tree itself is infected, exhibits outward signs of the implantation of disease,[3] or whether it actually may die as a result of the infection is rarely stated or implied. Even so, there can be no doubt as to the underlying belief in contagious magic, the transfer of disease, and the notion of a surrogate.[4] In addition to this, however, the reader should not be unaware of a competing idea, namely, the notion of the arrest of the disease

*This article was originally published in *Folklore & Society. Essays in Honor of Benj. A. Botkin.* Ed. Bruce Jackson. Hatboro, Pennsylvania: Folklore Associates, 1966, pp. 63–75. Permission to reprint has been given by the editor and Folklore Associates.

by finding a place of safekeeping outside the victim himself. Where either of these basic conceptions is present in the examples themselves, full details will be given. In other cases, it must be assumed that informants were unaware of the underlying folk medical principles and simply reported the practice as a general form of riddance or divestment, rather than as an active transfer of disease from a human being to a tree, or to other objects.

It is hard to generalize as to the kinds of trees selected, although hardwood trees seem to predominate: oak, beech, birch, maple, ash (rowan), ironwood, and the like. Pine, aspen, and woods of lesser hardness are pressed into service, too, but the willow, commonly employed for these purposes in Europe, is little used in America. Fruit trees (cherry, apple, peach, etc.) are sometimes made to serve, likewise mulberry.[5] Hickory and pine stobs—where such are mentioned at all—seem to be most favored.

The most frequent kind of "plugging" encountered in America involves the placing of a lock of the patient's hair into a hole bored into a tree, and then plugging the hole. Asthma, apparently, is more frequently treated this way in the United States than any other disease, and the practice seems widespread in the South and in adjoining states. A Tennessee practice is typical: "To cure asthma, someone went into the woods, bored a hole in a tree, put a lock of the patient's hair in the hole and stopped up the hole with a wooden peg driven in tightly."[6] In Pennsylvania a sugar maple is selected for the purpose, a lock of the patient's hair is plugged in, and then cut off.[7] More elaborate is a practice in the Ozark country, as described by Randolph: "To cure asthma, bore a hole in a black-oak tree, at the height of the patient's head. Drive a little wooden peg into the hole so as to hold the lock of hair. Cut the hair and peg off flush with the trunk. When the bark grows over the hole so that the peg is no longer visible, and the patient's hair grows out to replace the missing lock, the asthma will be gone forever."[8] In New York state, as a means of ridding a child of croup, a strand of the child's hair is placed into a hole bored in an apple tree.[9] Plugging with a rusty nail, rather than with a conventional wooden peg, is seen in a Texas cure for the nosebleed: "Stand with your back to a mulberry tree. Measure your height and then bore a hole in the tree. Cut a lock of your hair, put it in the hole, and drive a rusty nail in it. Your nose will never bleed again."[10] European examples of the use of hair in "plugging" are to be found, among other maladies, in treatments for ague[11] and whooping cough.[12]

A combination of hair and nail parings as the bodily offscourings are noted from Nova Scotia, with an apple tree indicated as the host for the toothache which is transferred.[13] A similar practice for the cure of asthma is found in Indiana.[14] A variation from hair is found in a Cape Breton practice of taking hair from the eyelashes or eyebrows, together with parings of the fingernails or toenails of the patient, boring a hole into a beech tree, and placing these shed bodily tissues into the hole.[15]

The use of nail parings only is not quite as widespread as the use of hair for communicating the disease to the tree by contagious magic, but the process is about the same.[16] These severed bits of corneous tissue are secured by pegs in holes bored into a tree. Asthma, for example, is transferred to an ash tree in Rhode Island: "Save all the nail parings of your hands and feet for a year. At the end of that time find an ash-tree of the same age as yourself, bore a hole in it, put in the parings, and plug up the hole."[17] Toothache is treated by "plugging" of nail parings in Newfoundland,[18] and also in New England, except, in the latter case, that the ritual is elaborated to include wrapping the parings in white paper, or in birch bark before insertion into the hole. For this operation a pine tree is favored.[19] Packaging of the parings is also practiced among the Pennsylvania Germans for the cure of epilepsy. The parings are wrapped in a bag before being placed in the hole.[20]

The expectoration of consumptives into holes bored in trees seems not to be known in America,[21] nor the "plugging" of excrement,[22] but close to the concept of the transfer of bodily essences is the implanting of breath itself. In a unique cure for chills recorded from a Negro informant in Maryland in 1913: "Ef youse goes to a oak-tree on de sunny side, en boe a hole in hit toward de north side dez bout to de h'art, en blow yo' bref in hit, en stop hit up tight, den de tre'll die, end yu's won't hab no mo' chills. Dat's sarta—in en sho, dat is, fo' I's dun been dun hit mise'f."[23] Notable here is the mention of the death of the new host, a basic notion often encountered in magical transference of disease to trees as well as to animals.[24]

As is to be expected in folk medical material of this kind, "plugging" also involves the transfer of disease to trees by *Zwischenträger,* or intermediate agents, as well as by direct contagious magic. These practices, which must be considered as lying somewhat outside of regular procedures, usually call for the introduction of kernels of corn that are rubbed on an excrescence, or similar kinds of things that are brought into direct contact with the disease before being plugged into a tree. An example from New England is typical of the process: "To cure a wart rub it with a corn, bore a hole in a tree, put the corn in the hole, and then plug it in. Your wart will make haste to leave when you have done this."[25] Strings that are used for counting, measuring, or circumscribing the ailment are likewise plugged, as the following practice from Nova Scotia will show. "Take a greasy string, tie a knot in it for every wart, bore a hole in the tree, and shove the string into the tree. When it moulders away, the warts will leave."[26] Decay of the implanted matter, of course, is not usually associated with "plugging."[27]

Plugging is often a part of rituals to "measure" the victim and to arrest the disease when the measurement is attained. Such practices are performed most often on children, and are all to the effect that when the child attains to such and such a height where the hole is bored, a door jamb or stick of some kind is notched, then the malady will cease. From a survey of the literature it is not clear whether measurement and circumscription was the original idea, or whether magical transference through notching, or plugging constituted the underlying *raison d'être.* The plugging of wisps of a child's hair into a hole bored slightly above the crown of his head would strongly suggest the very primitive notion of transference by contagious magic, yet in the scale of primitive thinking, the abatement of disease by marking an arbitrary limit likewise involves deep and inscrutable magical principles.

As noted above, plugging seems to have been used more in connection with asthma than any other disease. From a variety of entries for many parts of the country, a Louisiana variant will suffice: "To cure a child of asthma stand him up against a tree and bore a hole just above his head. Into this hole put some of the child's hair, and then stop it up. When the child grows above the hair he will no longer have the asthma."[28] In the Missouri Ozarks a black oak tree is specified, with the additional notion that the asthma will not leave until a new lock of hair has grown out to replace the wisp left in the tree.[29] In New York State a cherry tree is prescribed, and the plug must be of pine.[30] The blindfolding of the patient as he is led into the woods is noted for Nebraska.[31]

In the South, and elsewhere, croup, another predominantly children's disease, is dealt with in much the same way as asthma, as the following prescription shows: "If a child is subject to croup, measure its height on a good sized, live tree. Bore a hole in the tree at the point which marks the exact height of the child, take a lock of the little one's hair and put it into the hole, wedging it in tightly with a plug of wood. As soon as the child has grown a bit above the hole, it will cease to have croup, and never again will be troubled with it.''[32]

Combinations of hair and nail parings, as seen above, are likewise plugged into holes primarily bored at a given height in terms of measurement and ''outgrowing.'' Such a combination is presumably rare, for I can adduce but a single instance of the practice. This is from the white tradition of Nova Scotia: ''If a child has asthma, take and cut their finger nails, and then take their toe nails, lop off their hair near their temples, take them somewhere in the woods where they won't be often going. Take them to a tree, bore a hole, even with a child's head, put in the cuttings and stop up with a pine plug. When they grow above it, asthma will leave them.''[33]

In addition to using trees for plugging, folk medical practitioners also used door jambs, walls, posts, and pieces of wood.[34] As in other forms of the practice, tufts of hair were most commonly plugged, and measurement of the victim was frequently a part of the ceremony. Asthma, for example, was ''plugged'' into door jambs in Nova Scotia[35] and Illinois,[36] and croup was dealt with by boring holes into the door itself in Maryland.[37] A slightly more elaborate ritual was used to stop nosebleed in Nova Scotia, but we have already seen the use of hair and nail parings together, and the outgrowing of the disease when the hole is reached. In the entry under survey the hole is bored in the door itself.[38] The symbolism of the door as a place of egress may figure symbolically in the riddance of the disease, but this is a facet of the study that cannot be taken up here.

Plugging of disease in walls constitutes another variation of the basic practices seen in connection with trees. Once more asthma[39] and croup[40] are most often involved, and measuring and outgrowing are frequent features of the ritual. In the absence of more specific details, it is generally assumed that the holes are bored into wooden walls, for plugging and stopping up are generally indicated after the deposit of hair, not plastering over. Because of the vagueness in the matter of wooden walls as over against those of brick, the following reference from New York State is worth quoting in full: ''Let a croupy child stand beside the wall of a room in a house which is being plastered, rest an auger on his head, and drill a hole in the plaster. Cut a lock from the crown of the child's head, insert the lock in the drilled hole, and secure it with a peg. When the child grows above the peg, he will never have the croup.''[41] Convulsions are plugged in a board wall in Pennsylvania,[42] and whooping cough is disposed of in the same way in Louisiana.[43]

Spasms are plugged into posts in Iowa in a manner that we have come to view as the accepted way,[44] and whooping cough is transferred to a post in New York State, first by scratching a mark to indicate the height, then boring the hole, filling it with a lock of the patient's hair, and sealing the hole, as the entry reads. Furthermore, a cellar post is specified.[45] A plain board is made to suffice for the transfer of convulsions in Maryland.[46]

Closely related to plugging, in the sense that the disease is driven deep into a tree or other host, is the ''nailing'' of disease.[47] In most cases the nail becomes the immediate agent, or *Zwischenträger.* It is either used to probe a wound or an infected area, is anointed with blood, suppurating matter, or ''doctored'' with bodily tissue. It may also be laid on the affected area, or used to inscribe words, signs of the cross,[48] and the like, over the afflicted bodily part before being driven into a tree, a beam, or even into masonry.[49] In Europe, and in America, too, toothache appears to have been magically treated by ''nailing'' more than any other disease.[50] In this practice the tooth or gums are probed until blood comes, and the nail is then driven into a tree. Asthma and croup, by confusion with the practice of ''plugging,'' involve either nailing a lock of the patient's hair into the tree,[51] or measuring the victim as the hair is driven into the tree with the nail.[52] In New York State, measuring is part of the procedure noted: ''For asthma, take the patient into the woods, put his head against a beech tree, nail a lock of hair to the tree. Have the patient pull his head away, leaving the hair hanging in the tree. The asthma will disappear, but the tree will die.''[53] Three nails are driven into an oak tree in Illinois for asthma, but measuring figures just the same.[54] Measuring for toothache, an extension upon the more common practice of probing an aching tooth with a nail, and then driving it into a tree, is little encountered.[55]

The driving of nails into the roots of trees is apparently more common than plugging in the same rudimentary part of the tree.[56] The driving of nails into beams, posts, and, in restricted cases, plain boards, is also encountered.[57] The driving of a nail into dry or seasoned wood to avoid rusting of the nail following a puncture wound should not be confused with the practices under discussion. This was done to keep the nail from rusting or corroding as a symbolic means of keeping the wound itself clean and free from infection.[58]

The driving of nails into walls of wood is an extension of driving them into door jambs, beams, posts, boards, and the like, and need not concern us further.[59] Driving nails into walls of masonry is another matter, but once more variation of common principles seems to be operative, as the following Illinois practice attests: "If a child has asthma, stand him in the chimney corner and drive a nail into the masonry just the height of his head. When the child grows higher than the nail, he will be cured."[60]

The use of coffin nails[61] and horseshoe nails,[62] by way of substitution for regular nails, is largely a European development. The use of pins for "nailing," or "pinning," really is, however, known on both sides of the Atlantic.[63] From nails and pins to wooden pegs is an easy step, but the investigator should not confuse wooden pegs that are driven into the bark of trees, into stumps, or into the ground, with wooden corks or pegs that are used to stop up holes which have been bored into wood or stone. The routine probing of warts with a wooden peg, instead of a nail, and then driving the peg into a tree, is reported from Tennessee,[64] and the same practice is observed for the cure of corns in Illinois.[65] Randolph has a long and interesting account of the driving of a peg into an ironwood tree for the cure of *toothache.* These so-called "toothache pegs," he reports, are supposed to acquire a gummy substance while in the tree.[66] Lightning-struck wood is efficacious, in Europe at least, for these rituals.[67] The driving of wooden pegs into the earth for the curing of ague, chills and fever, and the like, is reported from the Ozark country.[68] This would appear to be an adaptation of a practice going back to classical times,[69] and it involves nails, of course, as well as wooden pegs.[70] The stanching of bleeding in a horse by touching a horse's wound with a wooden wedge and then driving it into a stump, is reported from Michigan by Dorson.[71]

Intermediate between the plugging and nailing of disease, is a folk medical practice which, for want of an established name in English, I have chosen to call "wedging."[72] This practice calls for the opening or slitting of bark, or other superficial parts of trees or wood, and the "placing" of disease in the hole. The opening is then either closed by pressing the slits back together again, or it is otherwise wedged tight. Incisions into which actual objects or substances of contagion may be placed qualify for discussion in this connection, as do notchings, if disease tokens from the patient, real or symbolic are communicated to the incision, and deposited there. The permanent transfer is definitely reinforced, as is often the case, when the incision is closed again and bound up in some way. This procedure has the effect almost of "plugging." (See the Pennsylvania item detailed in note 75, below.) A single example will differentiate attachment to a tree by incision rather than by the far more common way of simply tying a string to a tree, or wrapping a string around it, to establish contact and communicate the disease: From Kentucky: "For toothache, make the gums bleed, put the blood on a long cotton string, and tie the string around a dogwood tree at a place where an incision has been made in the bark."[73] Simple slitting or notching of the bark, as a means of measurement preliminary to "outgrowing" the disease, would not, I take it, qualify as "wedging" in the sense that I have outlined it.[74]

Because of their smallness, slits in the bark of trees are used more often to accommodate blood from the victim than hair, nail parings, or other bodily tissues. As the precious life fluid, on the one hand, or as the channel of pollution, on the other, blood figures ideally in all considerations of contagious magic. As we have seen many times in this paper, the treatment for toothache by a transfer of the blood from the aching tooth and gum to the tree once more predominates. A single example from Pennsylvania will suffice: "To cure toothache, take the patient to a sweet apple tree, peel back a little of the bark and cut a splinter out of the trunk. Make the patient pick his tooth with a splinter until the gum bleeds, then put the splinter back into the tree, and fasten the bark in place again, so that it will grow fast once more."[75] The natural healing over of a slit is also often a condition of healing or of the removal of a diseased condition, as the following wart cure from Kentucky shows: "Pick the wart until it bleeds. Split the bark of a persimmon tree and put the blood within. When the split grows up, the wart will leave."[76] Communication of the infected blood to the tree by the same knife that cut the incision in a wart is shown in a California example.[77]

Implantation of hair by a knife cut is an extension of the same process by either plugging or nailing, and its relationship to the two methods in question can be seen in the following Louisiana cure for croup: "To cure a child of croup, stand him up against a tree and run a knife through his hair into the tree burying some of his hair. When the child grows above the hair he will no longer have the croup.[78] Nail parings are similarly inserted into incisions in the bark of trees. In this practice toothache cures, once more, seem to predominate: Newfoundland: "For toothache, cut off part of the nails of the fingers and toes and insert them in the bark of a tree. This must be done secretly.''[79] Unique is the act of spitting into the bark of a tree which has been slit open and peeled back.[80]

We can end the main part of this paper by quoting a practice from Cheshire for the curing of warts. This example, by way of exception to most of the cures treated above, clearly shows that the malady has been transferred to the tree: ''Steal a piece of bacon and rub the warts with it, then cut a slit in the bark of an ash tree, and slip the bacon in under a piece of the bark. Speedily the warts will disappear from the hand, but will make their appearance on the bark of the tree.''[81]

Lack of space makes it impossible to treat aberrant forms of plugging, nailing, and wedging in detail, but some of them can be briefly suggested here. In such widely separated places as Louisiana and upstate New York, asthma is treated by taking tufts of hair from the victim and placing them either in a window casing or a crack in the door.[82]

Reserved for a further study are the related ideas and practices of banning and consignment of diseases under stones (covering, but not plugging), burial under sods, secretion into natural holes and crotches of trees, and the corking up of diseases in bottles. Verbal adjuration of disease in conjunction with the main practices treated above will likewise have to await treatment at a later time.

NOTES

1. ''The Magical Transference of Disease,'' *Folklore Studies in Honor of Arthur Palmer Hudson* (Chapel Hill, N. C.: North Carolina Folklore Society, 1965).

For a general treatise on the subject, see Albert Hellwig, ''Das Einpflöcken von Krankheiten,'' *Globus,* XC, No. 16 (1906), 245–249; Hovorka-Kronfeld, II, 874, 933; HDA, X, 367, 369; Carl-Herman Tillhagen, *Folklig Läkekonst* (Stockholm, 1958), 109–110, *passim.* (To conserve space, I am asking the reader to consult the bibliography to Vols. VI and VII of the *Frank C. Brown Collection of North Carolina Folklore* (Durham, N. C.: Duke University Press, 1961, 1964), VI, xlix-lxxi; VII, xxiii-xxxiii.)

2. Black, *Folk-Medicine,* 37; Hovorka-Kronfeld, II, 874 (both roots); HDA, I, 631, s.v. *Astloch* (branches). For the ''nailing'' of roots, see note 56, below.

3. See the second paragraph of the general paper alluded to in footnote 1, above, wherein it is stated that ''the disease must be communicated to second parties or things, and it must be expressly stated, or clearly implied, that the disease is received by a new victim, or a new receiving agent that is itself affected by the transfer.''

4. For a general discussion, see Hellwig, 247.

5. The general range of woods used for plugging comports pretty well with that given by Hellwig (246).

6. Rogers, 31. Other simple entries such as this include Whitney-Bullock, No. 1754 (Maryland); O'Dell, *Superstitions,* 3 (Tennessee); Puckett, 370 (Negro); Redfield, No. 41 (Tennessee). In this last item, the hole is plugged with a cork.

7. Bergen, *Animal,* No. 816.

8. *Ozark Superstitions,* 134–135.

9. Relihan, *Remedies,* 83. No mention is made of plugging up the hole afterward.

10. Woodhull, 61.

11. Black, *Folk-Medicine,* 39. Here specific mention is made of the transference of the disease to the tree. Cf. Radford, 139–140, Patten, 139.

12. Radford, 259. The vanishing of the cough was supposed to occur as the hair decayed in the rowan tree.

13. Bergen, *Animal,* No. 813. Cf. HDA, I, 113–114; III, 1286–1287.

14. W. Edson Richmond and Elva Van Winkle, "Is there a Doctor in the House?" *Indiana History Bulletin,* XXXV (1958), 122, No. 68.

15. Bergen, *Current,* No. 833. The sufferer must not see the tree, and it must not be cut down or burned.

16. HDA, II, 1505, s.v. *Fingernagel.* In the British Isles fever was placed in holes and plastered up so that the disease could not escape (Radford, 24, s.v. "Aspen Tree," and the same cure for fever is known in France, with birch trees being used as well as aspen (Sébillot, *Folklore de France,* III, 414). Plastering shut is not indicated, however.

17. Bergen, *Animal,* No. 815. Cf. Knortz, 52 (derivative from Bergen, apparently).

18. Bergen, *Animal,* No. 753; Cf. Brown Collection, No. 2341.

19. Johnson, *What They Say,* 164. Cf. Hellwig, 246–247.

20. Brendle-Unger, p. 108. Cherry trees are preferred for the ritual, with plugs made of young oak. Cf. HDA, II, 1175 s.v. *Fallsucht.*

21. HDA, I, 1341–1342, s.v. *Birnbaum.*

22. Hovorka-Kronfeld, I, 116.

23. *Journal of American Folklore,* XXVI (1913), 191. Cf. Puckett, 364.

24. Hellwig, 247. For further references to the death of the host tree see note 53, below.

25. Johnson, *What They Say,* 117. Cf. Puckett, 373.

26. Fauset, No. 330.

27. Cf., however, note 12, above.

28. Roberts, No. 381. Cf. Thomas, No. 1061; Rogers, 39, Brewster, *Specimens,* 362; Richmond and Van Winkle, 122, No. 67; Sanders, 18; Black, 34, No. 8; Wintemberg, *Waterloo,* p. 12; Farr, *Children,* No. 36.

29. McKinney, 107.

30. Gardner, No. 4.

31. Black, 34, No. 2.

32. Wiltse, *Folk-Lore,* 207. Cf. Brendle-Unger, 136; White, 79; Brown Collection, VI, 51, Nos. 303–304.

33. Fauset, No. 336.

34. As Frazer has observed in connection with his discussion of the transfer of evil and disease, "from knocking the mischief into a tree or log it is only a step to knocking it into a stone, a doorpost, a wall, or such like." (*The Golden Bough,* IX, 62).

35. Creighton, 86, No. 2 (hair wrapped in paper before plugging).

36. Hyatt, No. 4479. Cf. Richmond and Van Winkle, 122, No. 69 (hole above the door).

37. Whitney-Bullock, No. 1752; Bullock, 10. Cf. Brown Collection, VI, 51, No. 304.

38. Creighton, 94, No. 58.

39. Relihan, *Remedies,* 81; Stuart, 10; Davenport, 132.

40. Brendle-Unger, 136; No. 1762; Robert, No. 385.

41. Gardner, No. 16. A variant of this practice is to work some of the child's hair into the fresh plaster itself.

42. Fogel, No. 1777.

43. Roberts, No. 389.

44. Stout, No. 1035.

45. Augar, 168. When the lock of hair has dried up, the whooping cough will disappear.

46. Whitney-Bullock, No. 1755.

47. Frazer has a whole section on "The Nailing of Evils" (*The Golden Bough,* IX, 59–71), which includes material on pegging and wedging. Plugging, however, is treated as a part of a general chapter on the transference of evil disease (*ibid.,* 57–59). Also, whereas the editors of HDA treat *Verkeilen* (wedging) and *Verbohren* (boring) under *Verpflöcken* (plugging), *Vernageln* (nailing) has its own entry (X, 367, 369).

48. *Folk-Lore,* IV (1893), 454.

49. Hovorka-Kronfeld, II, 874.

50. *Brown Collection,* VI, 306, No. 2380 (and the old-world references given there). To these could be added important references from Sébillot (*Folklore de France,* III, 413–414), Storaker (*Sygdom,* Nos. 142–143, 149), *Notes and Queries* (1st Ser., Vol. 10 (1854), 505), and HDA, VI, 498, s.v. *Mond.*

51. Puckett, 370 (croup or asthma); Fogel, Nos. 1759–1761 (croup).

52. Brendle-Unger, 136. This is done for croup, and preferably by the victim's grandfather.

53. Crandall, 180. See also the entry from Neal, published ten years later, *New York Folklore Quarterly,* XI (1955), 283. For a discussion of the rare phenomenon of death to the host tree, see note 24, above.

54. Hyatt, No. 4488. Cf. also Turner, 169–170 (one nail only).

55. Kentucky: "If you stand a person against a tree and drive a nail into the tree just above his head, this process will cure toothache" (Thomas, No. 1408).

56. Newfoundland: "As a remedy for rheumatism, a galvanized iron nail is to be openly taken (not stolen or asked for). This is to be driven into the root of a red cedar-tree, taking pains not to crack the root. As the nail rusts, the rheumatism will disappear" (Bergen, *Animal,* No. 1172). For the removal of a wart by a rusty nail impregnated with blood from the wart, and driven into the roots of an oak tree, see Thomas, No. 1485. For plugging in the roots of trees, see note 2, above.

57. For the use of beams and posts in the "nailing" of toothache, see Brown Collection, I, 306, No. 2380, and the reference cited there. For unusual details, see the Indiana item in No. 2379. Cf. *Notes and Queries,* 1st Ser., Vol. 2 (1850), 130. Hernia is also cured this way in the Pennsylvania German country (Fogel, No. 1448).

58. For a discussion of this see Brown Collection, VI, xxviii and Nos. 1404, 1786–1787.

59. Brendle-Unger, 163 (inside wall, measuring, etc. for convulsions) with the following instructive note: "The 'evil thing' was nailed fast in the wall and

was drawn away from the child by being prevented from growing with the child.'' Cf. Dalyell, 134.

60. Hyatt, No. 4478. For the driving of nails into a boulder, *see Folk-Lore,* VI (1895), 157–158. Cf. HDA, I, 1388, s.v. *Blei.*

61. Radford, 207; HDA, II, 722, s.v. *Eisen;* VII, 955, s.v. *Sargnagel.*

62. *Zeitschrift für österreichische Volkskunde,* XXIII (1917), 121–122: HDA II, 722, s.v. *Eisen; Folk-Lore,* VI (1895), 157 (all for toothache). In 1788 at Sodersleben a boy had the smallpox. He was taken to the woods, and the horseshoe nail from the shoe of a black stallion was drawn through the pustules, and then driven into a tree (Hovorka-Kronfeld, I, 117).

63. Brown Collection, VI, 345, No. 2662; Hyatt, No. 4199; Richmond and Van Winkle, 133, No. 276 (more a place for a pickup of the warts than a direct transfer to the tree). Cf. Radford, 14, 242.

64. Farr, *Riddles,* No. 41; *idem, Superstitions,* No. 41.

65. Hyatt, No. 3988.

66. *Ozark Superstitions,* 143. An interesting detail involving ''measurement'' provides that the peg shall be driven into the tree at the exact height of the aching tooth.

67. HDA, I, 1420, s.v. *Blitzbaumholz*; Hellwig, 246.

68. Randolph, 133–134.

69. McCartney, 179, citing Pliny 28.63

70. Radford, 14, 114, 179–180.

71. *Southern Folklore Quarterly*, XI (1947), 106.

72. Hovorka and Kronfeld have suggested the term *Einkeilen,* (wedging) (II, 874).

73. Thomas, No. 1398; Price, 33.

74. Two examples from Tennessee and Kentucky, respectively, show cutting and notching, but lack the element of contagious magic: O'Dell, *Superstitions,* 33; Stuart, 10.

75. Bayard, 59; Wintemberg, *Waterloo,* 14 (splinter from a lightning-struck tree used to probe aching tooth; replaced exactly); Black, 22, No. 8 (toothpick used to probe the tooth is placed in the bark of a tree; not mentioned whether driven in (as a peg), placed in slit, or in the natural interstices of the bark; Radford, 243; Storaker, *Sygdom,* No. 147; HDA, IX, 247, s.v. *Weide.*

76. Thomas, No. 1496.

77. Dresslar, 108. Removal of the wart is conditioned on the healing of the cut in the tree.

78. Roberts, No. 382. Cf. Hyatt, No. 4487; Roberts, No. 379.

79. Bergen, *Animal,* No. 753; *Notes and Queries,* 3rd Ser., Vol. 7 (1865), 433.

80. Kentucky: ''To cure toothache, go to a wood, find a small hickory tree, take your knife, stand by the tree and mark the place even with your mouth; then move back, turn up the bark, spit into the place, and turn the bark down again. If it grows back, your tooth will not hurt any more (Thomas, No. 1414).

81. Black, *Folk-Medicine,* 38. Cf. Radford, 24–25.

82. Roberts, No. 380: ''Negroes cure asthma by taking some of the victim's hair, tying it up in a red flannel, and putting it in the crack of the door.'' In the New York item, part of the door casing, or the window casing was pried up and a lock of the child's hair inserted under it. When the child grew higher than the place where the hair was kept, he outgrew his asthma (Cutting, *Lore,* 41).

7

Measuring and Plugging: The Magical Containment and Transfer of Disease*

Measuring a patient in various ways as a means of either diagnosing his ailment or ridding him of the disease is a folk medical practice encountered on both sides of the Atlantic. In previous papers on the subject I have discussed measurement by means of string and other kinds of cordage and fibre and also the somewhat rarer method of outlining the ailing part of the body on the trunk of a tree, in the ground, or in the turf.[1] In this ritual of scoring, once the limits of the disease have been demarcated, it can be removed symbolically by hollowing out the contaminated part of the new host, be it wood or earth, and then treating the affected area in various ways. Implicit in this ritual, in addition to the measurement, of course, is the notion of the transference of the disease to the tree or to the earth by the simple process of contagious magic.

In the present paper I treat a kind of measurement that is more common than either of those just mentioned, particularly in the United States and Canada, namely, measuring with a stick or other lineal measuring devices by cutting and notching and then by nailing and plugging in trees and other vertical stationary objects. Common to these forms, as well as to certain other kinds of magical measurement for disease, is the notion that the unit of measure, the length marked, or the area circumscribed somehow prevents the ravage of the disease beyond the

*This article originally appeared in the *Bulletin of the History of Medicine*, 48 (1974), 221–233. Permission to reprint has been given by the editor and by the Johns Hopkins University Press.

confines measured. Perhaps in a more philosophical and symbolic sense, measurement, as Grabner has observed, constitutes a mysterious extension of oneself.[2]

First to be considered is the cutting of a stick, or occasionally a twig of some sort, to the exact length of the patient. The rationale behind this measurement is the belief that the ailment will be cast off when the child or young person outgrows the mark. Oddly enough, the stick, once measured, is never again put to the sufferer's back to see if the measuring device has really been outgrown. Actually, as things turn out, care is often taken that the stick never be found or that it never even be seen again. These taboos are a part of the ritualistic disposal of objects that have come in contact with the sick person and we shall consider this aspect of measuring later on.

In various parts of the South it was customary, for example, to cut a sourwood stick in a measuring ritual for the cure of asthma and phthisic, which are often regarded by common people of the area as the same ailment.[3] The stick was cut to the exact height of the sufferer. If a child or a young person was involved, he was measured in a standing position so that the stick, if bent at all, could be inclined to the patient's back.[4] In the case of babies, the measurement was undertaken in any way necessary to get the exact length of the infant.[5] In Kentucky when a small child was measured for asthma, it was believed that when he outgrew the sourwood stick the asthma would be gone,[6] but in the same state, and elsewhere, riddance of the disease often depended on what happened to the measuring stick itself.

I am not sure that other writers on measuring as a means of magical riddance have been willing to think of the unit of measure itself as a sort of intermediate agent, or *Zwischenträger,* to which the disease is communicated in the process of measurement. Since customs and rituals connected with measurement do conform in many ways to the patterns of storage, safekeeping, burial, casting off, floating away, and the like—processes so very common in magical disposal—I feel that we must consider the problem in this broader light. The full range of magical riddance by *Zwischenträger,* of course, cannot be treated in a paper of such restricted scope as this one, but we shall see enough examples to warrant the consideration of the unit of measure as a possible disposal agent of the disease as well as a mere marking device. Perhaps some of the means employed will become more apparent in other parts of this paper, but a few typical kinds of disposal are to be seen in connection with measuring sticks cut to length. In Kentucky, for example, the stick—kinds of wood not mentioned—was placed somewhere out of sight, such as in the loft or attic.[7] In Tennessee, if the sourwood limb were hidden so that no one could ever find it, it was thought that the baby would be cured.[8] Elsewhere in the Southern Mountains, just after the turn of the century, care was taken to hide the stick so that the child would never see it. If he ever did chance to see the stick, it was believed that the charm would be broken.[9] In Tennessee in the late 1930s the sourwood stick was cut to the length of the child and then laid in a dry place. The child then outgrew the phthisic just as it outgrew the stick.[10] Almost twenty-five years later, in the same state, one could still find the prescription about keeping the stick dry, but in this cure for asthma the taboo against seeing the measuring stick apparently no longer existed:

> Asthma. To cure the "tizzey," measure yourself, cut a dry stick of the same length, keep dry and in one corner of the sick person's room.[11]

Such developments over a period of time are, of course, common in folklore, but in an active tradition where enlargement, contraction, and substitution are common, even such reversals as the one we have just seen are not unexpected.

Disposal of the measuring stick by throwing it away is noted for both asthma and "tyzic" in Tennessee and North Carolina.[12] Croup in children was measured in the same way as asthma and phthisic. In the Great Smoky Mountains sourwood was used for this purpose, and the stick was hidden in the woods so that it could never be found.[13] In the Pennsylvania German country the elderberry wand, with which a child suffering from croup was measured, was placed where neither the sun nor moon would shine on it.[14] In North Carolina an ordinary stick was employed, and it was placed in the closet, not necessarily hidden, until the child grew past the mark.[15] Broomsticks, with which children suffering from asthma and phthisic were measured, were carried upstairs where they would never be seen again,[16] but in Illinois the broomstick was buried beneath the front doorstep, where it remained until the child had outgrown the asthma.[17]

The aspect of decay, which is often associated with the riddance of warts, applies to pieces of wood as well as to thread, beanstraw, and various other plant fibres. Usually the wart is circumscribed by these pliable fibres, and the measure is recorded by circumference. Measuring for warts by diameter is exceptional; however, in North Carolina and Kentucky we see a small stick utilized to measure the diameter of the wart.[18] In all of these entries we have the classical pattern of magical disposal. In the North Carolina example the stick is either thrown away or it is buried, and there is the additional prescription of measuring the wart without the sufferer's knowing it. Rotting of the stick in the first Kentucky entry is noted as a condition of the disappearance of the wart. The Fentress item involves burial at a secret place as well as the decaying of the measuring stick.

An unusual cure, one for hay fever, was practiced in parts of Alabama during the 1950s. A willow was cut to one's length, and then it was thrown into the loft of a barn to dry out. When it had dried out, it was believed that the hay fever would be gone.[19] This is strongly reminiscent of cures for rheumatism in which a small potato or a horse chestnut is carried in the pocket of the sufferer who finds relief when the potato or chestnut dries out and withers,[20] absorbing the disease, as it were, in the process.

Two unusual ways to measure a patient for the riddance of a disease are found in Illinois, an area far removed from the main part of the country where the custom of measuring is well known. The first one of these involves measurement in a more transitory way. An asthmatic child is taken to a tree and made to stand under a limb that just touches the top of its head. The limb is then cut off at the trunk and buried. When the child grows above the mark (which is to be seen by the cutting marks where the limb was), he will no longer suffer from asthma.[21] Far more unusual is another entry from Hyatt's standard collection:

> A baby was born with a rupture. Several years later a friend told his father to cut an elm tree down to the height of his son and split the tree down the center, and place the boy over this and say *In the Name of the Father, Son, and Holy Ghost* over him, and he should do this three times. The father did this and the boy was cured of rupture.[22]

Measurement against a tree, whether by a common marking of some sort, or by notching or nailing, almost invariably involved placing the mark at the exact height of the sufferer, or a trifle above, so that outgrowing the ailment could logically follow. Transference of the disease to the tree, if intended, is never mentioned. In any event, translocation is not as clearly indicated as in the case of plugging, where a sort of implantation takes place, occasionally followed by the withering or death of the tree. In cases of simple marking, notching, or nailing, interest centers on the kinds of trees sought for the purpose and on the details of the measuring ritual. In Indiana, for example, it was a Negro custom in Marion County to find a tree struck by lightning and to take the child's measure on it.[23] Sourwood trees were favored in Kentucky and were notched in the usual way, at the exact height of the asthma sufferer. It was believed that the disease would leave as the child outgrew the mark, or, according to some beliefs, two years afterward.[24] In the Vermillion parish of Louisiana, the French selected a smooth young growing tree and pricked a little hole in it with a quill. This was attended by the usual prognosis concerning the cure.[25] In places as remote from each other as North Carolina, Tennessee, and Texas, no special kinds of trees were mentioned for the affixing of the mark, whether by simple cutting at the proper height, or a more visible kind of notching.[26] Nailing represented a more permanent kind of marking. In Illinois a nail was driven just a bit above the head, so that the croup would leave when the child had grown as high as the nail.[27] The cure of a child suffering from croup, in parts of Texas, involved driving the nail at the exact height of the child, and in some cases on the north side of the tree.[28] As the bark grew over the nail, it was believed that the asthma would disappear. An oak tree was selected for this purpose in Illinois, and three nails were driven into the tree.[29] Croup was treated the same way in this state, except that the disease was not overcome until the child could "chin the nail," which apparently meant that the child would have to grow to a point where the chin reached the nail that had been driven into the tree earlier, level with the top of his head.[30] Placing the nail mark four inches above the head of a child suffering from rheumatism, draping some of the child's hair around the nail and nailing it fast, and then having the child return a year later when it grew up to the mark was a cure employed by an old Indian squaw in New York State in the 1940s. Returning the hair to the girl was supposed to bring about a remission of the disease.[31]

Measuring of children against doors and walls, either by marking, notching, or nailing, is encountered not only in the treatment of the common childhood diseases of asthma, croup, and phthisis, but also to combat convulsions and stuttering. As late as the 1930s in Indiana, a child suffering from phthisis was measured against three inner doors of a house. If he did not return to the house until after he had outgrown the marks, it was believed that the phthisis would be gone.[32] Measuring against the door sill—by which term the door jamb was most likely meant—was practiced in the Blue Ridge Mountain country for the cure of croup, and it was believed that the child would get well when he grew taller than the notch.[33] In Lane County, Oregon, far removed from parts of the country where ritual measuring for the cure of disease was common, people were treated for asthma and for stuttering by measurement against a wall.[34] This was before the turn of the century. Nailing into masonry was also practiced, as for example in Illinois, where a child was made to stand in the chimney corner and then measured for asthma.[35] In cases treated thus far where nailing is involved, I have purposely not discussed the deeper implications of nailing.

"Plugging," a well-known folk medical rite for the magical transference of disease, is also pressed into service in measuring rituals. When I mentioned this conjuncture of basic folklore ideas in an article on plugging, nailing, and kindred folk medical customs in 1966,[36] I had not yet made a formal study of measurement in connection with the magical riddance of disease. The present study has not only helped to clear up some of the questions and ambiguities encountered at that time, but has suggested new and fruitful lines of inquiry. In order to get the matter before us in a full folk medical text, it is well to let Brendle and Unger speak of this ritual as it was understood in the Pennsylvania German country, wherein not only measurement is taken up, but also magical arrest of the disease, and transference itself.

> Children are supposed to free themselves from chronic afflictions by outgrowing them. To outgrow means to overgrow. A child suffering from convulsions was placed against the inside wall of the house and a nail was driven into the wall at the exact height of the child. When the child grew beyond the mark, it freed itself from the affliction. This, of course, is a sympathetic cure. The "evil thing" was nailed fast in the wall and was drawn away from the child by being prevented from growing with the child.[37]

This ritual, as pregnant as it is concise, nevertheless does not get at the most basic notions of contagious magic, except in an indirect way. In subsequent parts of this paper we shall see numerous examples of the communication of human disease to a tree or to other hosts by means of plugging bits of hair and occasionally nail parings and the like in a hole measured at the sufferer's height and bored into a tree, a doorjamb or other vertical surfaces. Similarly, hair is held fast in the bark of a tree under the head of a nail driven at head level.

Transference of diseases to trees, as to animals, and even to humans, as I have shown in a study on the magical transference of disease,[38] often involves signs of disease and corruption in the new host. Although there are copious references in the literature to the withering and death of trees following the symbolic implantation of disease by means of *Zwischenträger,* these consequences must be considered somewhat exceptional as they relate to plugging as a part of the ritual of measuring for disease. In the Negro tradition of Maryland in 1913, however, one encountered the following cure for chills:

> Ef youse goes to a oak-tree on de sunny-side, en boe a hole in hit toward de north side dez bout to de h'art, en blow yo' bref in hit, en stop hit up tight, den de tree'll die, end yu's won't hab no mo' chills. Dat's sarta—in en sho, dat is, fo' I's dun been dun hit myse'f.[39]

Harm to the host tree after the implanting of asthma was still encountered in the folk medical traditions of New York state as late as the mid-forties, when a lock of the patient's hair was nailed to a beech tree.[40] According to the account, the patient was cured, but the tree died. Generally, however, the health of the tree is in no way affected. As a matter of fact, it is occasionally stated that the cure does not take effect until the bark has grown over the plugged hole, notably in cures for asthma.[41] Only a thrifty tree, of course, could experience such growth.

The classical forms of "plugging" involve boring a hole into a tree, stuffing the hole with hair, nail parings, and the like, and then plugging up the hole with a peg of some sort. In this treatise we are concerned mainly with the aspect of measuring the height of the sufferer by standing him or her against a tree, and then boring the hole at the level of the head. Asthma is the disease most often involved in these measuring and plugging cures, and the treatment for this malady alone can be traced in an unbroken chain of provinces, states, and regions between Nova Scotia and Missouri, Nebraska, and Texas.[42] Various species of oak trees, for example, are sought in Kentucky, Missouri, and Tennessee.[43] Although measurement is prescribed in the usual way in the last named state, emphasis seems to fall more on the element of plugging, where it is stressed that the hole must be bored to the heart of the tree, and that, after the hair has been placed in it, the hole must be surely plugged so that no air can penetrate the place of safe-keeping. The tree's growing over the plug is also made a condition of the cure. Cherry trees are specified in New York, the honey locust in Illinois, the sweet gum in Texas, and simply a green tree in Indiana.[44] Additional magical elements are seen in the Illinois entry, where the measurement takes place on the west side of the honey locust, and in the Texas ritual where the sufferer is forbidden to look back as he leaves the woods.

Implantation, in addition to measurement, is important in the plugging ritual as practiced in Nova Scotia. Here the fingernails and toenails, as well as the hair, of the sufferer from asthma are cut off before the trip is undertaken into a secluded spot in the woods "where they won't be often going." A tree is found, a hole is bored in it even with the child's head, and the cuttings are placed within. The hole is then stopped up with a pine plug and the time awaited until the child outgrows that point on the tree at which the plug was inserted.[45] In Georgia the asthmatic child coughs into the hole bored into a tree, symbolically leaving the malady deposited there. This part of the ritual outweighs, apparently, the measuring of the child before the hole is drilled.[46]

Measurement by plugging in a tree is ritually undertaken for the cure of such other diseases as croup,[47] phthisis,[48] fits,[49] tetter,[50] and nosebleed.[51] Short growth, so-called, most often measured with string by comparing the span of the outstretched arms with the height from the crown of the head to the soles of the feet,[52] is also occasionally measured by plugging, as entries from Maryland and Indiana attest.[53]

Before concluding the discussion of plugging as it relates to trees, notice should be given of variations on the notion of outgrowing the disease. We have already seen an example in Illinois of a child's outgrowing the mark of a nail driven in a tree by a far greater measure than was ordinarily envisioned. Croup would leave the child, it was claimed, only when he had "chinned the nail," i.e., had grown to a point where the chin reached the nail originally driven into the tree at the child's height.[54] Comparable to this is a curative ritual known in Pennsylvania and Indiana between 1870 and 1920, where a child suffering from "tissic" (asthma) was measured against a tree and a lock of his hair plugged into a hole bored at the height of his head. The delayed cure took effect when the child later grew to a point where his breastbone passed the plug in the tree.[55]

Nailing a mark on a tree as a means of indicating the height of a sufferer was discussed above. Now we can look at those aspects of nailing which involve plugging as well. In the Pennsylvania German country a child suffering from croup was placed against an oak tree and a nail driven into the tree at the level of the head in such a manner that some of the sufferer's hair was held fast under the head of the nail.[56] Even clearer notions of the close connection between nailing and plugging are seen in examples from Texas and Illinois. Nosebleed, for instance, is stanched in Texas by standing the sufferer up against a mulberry tree, measuring his height, and then boring a hole in the tree. A lock of hair is then cut and nailed fast into the hole with a rusty nail.[57] Even more unique is the ritual cure for asthma in Illinois:

> If a child has asthma—when the moon is first turning to dark, take the child and stand him up against a tree; then take a ten-penny nail and hammer that nail in the tree even with the child's top of the head, then pull that nail out, then cut a lock of the child's hair and put in that hole, then drive the nail back into the hole up to the head. When the child grows above the head on the nail, it will be cured. You must say *In the Name of the Father, Son and Holy Ghost* when driving the nail in that hole.[58]

Measurement by plugging was also carried out in seasoned wood of various kinds, as well as in trees. Posts were used for this purpose in Kentucky and Iowa, for example, and the plugging of hair into the hole was managed in the usual way.[59] Measurement by plugging into doors and doorjambs was relatively common, only slightly less favored, as a matter of fact, than in trees themselves. This tradition extends from French Canada and Nova Scotia through the Pennsylvania German country, into the Appalachians, into Ohio, and as far west as Illinois.[60] Almost all procedures involve the implanting of hair after the measurement was made, and the kinds of diseases treated range from cough and bronchitis to asthma, phthisic, undergrowth, hernia, and nosebleed. In the Adirondacks an ingenious kind of measurement was employed, whereby the child's hair was wedged into a window frame above the child's head so that he or she would lose the asthma when the mark was outgrown.[61] When measurement was made against walls, it was generally inside the house and in walls of wood and plaster, rather than those of masonry. Records of this practice are found from New York State to Alabama and Louisiana and as far west as Kansas.[62]

Measurement of patients in a recumbent position usually involves children too young to stand. In the Pennsylvania German country, for example, a liver-grown child was laid on a doorsill or threshold. Though this was manifestly not a vertical measurement, healing was predicated upon the child's outgrowing the measurement, in accordance with the general stipulations of "outgrowing."[63] Unique in horizontal measurement, and very rare, is the method of measuring an asthmatic child in Illinois. Here stakes were driven at the head and at the foot of the child lying on the ground under the eaves of the house, and it was believed that, as the child outgrew the distance between the stakes, he would outgrow his asthma.[64]

As the work of Grabner and others show, measuring is a form of curative magic that goes back to the Middle Ages in Europe, and perhaps back to Old Testament times.[65] Little is known historically, however, of the specific kinds of measurement treated in this paper or of the prevalence of these kinds of practices outside of Europe and America. It is my hope, therefore, that the examples offered here may serve as leads for others to follow in establishing larger patterns of belief, and perhaps in opening up speculations of the sort included in my opening remarks as to the symbolic extension of self. Finally, I hope that enough was said in the early paragraphs of the present paper to induce others to explore further the unit of measure itself as a possible intermediate agent in the magical transfer of disease. Most fruitful, it seems to me, would be the study not only of sticks and similar kinds of rigid and portable measuring units, but also of string and other kinds of lineal measure that are either symbolically disposed of or are rendered inert by storage or made permanently harmless by sequestering or by consignment to the realm of forgetfulness and oblivion. These are questions of considerable interest to scholars in the field of folk medicine where much basic work still remains to be done in philosophic and conceptual matters having to do with measuring, plugging, and the magical transfer of disease.

NOTES

1. Wayland D. Hand, "Measuring with string, thread and fibre: a practice in folk medical magic," in Walter Escher, Theo Ganter, and Hans Trümpy, eds., *Festschrift für Robert Wildhaber zum 70. Geburtstag am 3. August 1972* (Basel:

Verlag G. Krebs, 1973), pp. 240–251; Wayland D. Hand, "Magical treatment of disease by outlining the ailing part," *Bull. N.Y. Acad. Med.*, 1972, *48:* 951–954. (The first item is hereinafter cited: Hand. *Measuring.*)

2. Elfriede Grabner, "Verlorenes Mass und heilkräftiges Messen: Krankheitserforschung und Heilhandlung in der Volksmedizin," in Elfriede Grabner, ed., *Volksmedizin: Probleme und Forschungsgeschichte* (Wege der Forschung, vol. 63, Darmstadt: Wissenschaftliche Buchgemeinschaft, 1967), p. 549.

3. Wayland D. Hand, ed., *Popular Beliefs and Superstitions from North Carolina* (Durham, N.C.: Duke University Press, 1961–1964, constituting vols. VI–VII of the *Frank C. Brown Collection of North Carolina Folklore,* 7 vols., 1952–1964), VI, 120, no. 829 (hereinafter cited: *Brown Coll.*); Jerry S. Parr, "Folk cures of Middle Tennessee," *Tenn. Folklore Soc. Bull.*, 1962, *28:* 9.

4. Joseph H. Hall, *Smoky Mountain Folks and Their Lore* (Asheville, N.C.; Cataloochee Press, 1973), p. 50.

5. Mary E. Miller, "A folklore survey of Dickson County, Tennessee," *Tenn. Folklore Soc. Bull.*, 1958, *24:* 64.

6. Leonard W. Roberts, "Floyd County folklore," *Kentucky Folklore Record,* 1956, *2:* 54; William E. Barton, *Pine Knot* (New York, 1900), p. 154 (as cited in the *Kentucky Folklore Record,* 1956, *2:* 133).

7. Gordon Wilson, *Folklore of the Mammoth Cave Region* (Kentucky Folklore Series, no. 4, 1968), p. 61.

8. Miller, *op. cit.* (n. 5 above), p. 64.

9. Henry M. Wiltse, "In the field of southern folk-lore," *J. Amer. Folklore,* 1901, *14:* 207. Cf. Joseph D. Clark, "North Carolina popular beliefs and superstitions," *North Carolina Folklore,* 1970, *18:* 7, no. 36.

10. T. J. Farr, "Tennessee folk beliefs concerning children," *J. Amer. Folklore,* 1939, *52:* 114, no. 49.

11. Parr, *op. cit.* (n. 3 above), p. 9.

12. Cleo McGlasson, "Superstitions and beliefs of Overton County," *Tenn. Folklore Soc. Bull.*, 1941, *7*: 18, no. 13; *Brown Coll.*, VI, 120, no. 829.

13. Hall, *op. cit.* (n. 4 above), p. 50.

14. Edwin Miller Fogel, *Beliefs and Superstitions of the Pennsylvania Germans* (Americana Germanica, vol. 18, Philadelphia, 1915), p. 330, no. 1756.

15. *Brown Coll.,* VI, 51, no. 302.

16. Daniel Lindsey Thomas and Lucy Blayney Thomas, *Kentucky Superstitions* (Princeton University Press, 1920), p. 110, no. 1285; *Brown Coll.,* VI, 248, no. 1924; Lawrence S. Thompson, "The broom in the Ohio Valley," *Kentucky Folklore Record,* 1963, *9:* 92.

17. Harry Middleton Hyatt, *Folk-Lore from Adams County, Illinois,* 2nd ed. (New York: Alma Egan Hyatt Foundation, 1965), p. 253, no. 5642 (hereinafter cited: Hyatt, 2nd ed.).

18. *Brown Coll.,* VI, no. 2615; Thomas and Thomas, *op. cit.,* (n. 16 above), pp. 128–129, no. 1518; Elza E. Fentress, "Superstitions of Grayson County, Kentucky," M.A. thesis, Western State Teachers College, Bowling Green, Kentucky, 1934 (unpub.), p. 64, no. 61.

19. Ray B. Browne, *Popular Beliefs and Practices from Alabama* (Folklore Studies, vol. 9, Berkeley and Los Angeles: University of California Press, 1958), p. 70, no. 1148.

20. *Brown Coll.,* VI, 262–263, nos. 2022–2023; W. J. Wintemberg and Katherine H. Wintemberg, "Folk-Lore from Grey County, Ontario," *J. Amer. Folklore,* 1918. *31:* 93, no. 150.

21. Hyatt, 2nd ed., p. 254, no. 5660.

22. *Ibid.*, pp. 333–334, no. 7184.

23. W. Edson Richmond and Elva Van Winkle, "Is there a doctor in the house?" *Indiana History Bull.*, 1958, *35:* 122, no. 66.

24. Wilson, *op. cit.* (n. 7 above), p. 62, no. 5; Jesse Stuart, "The yarb doctor," *Kentucky Folk-Lore and Poetry Mag.*, 1931, *6,* no. 1: 10.

25. Elizabeth Brandon, *Les Moeurs de la Paroisse de Vermillion en Louisiane.* Ph.D. diss., Université Laval, Quebec, 1955, p. 270.

26. W. Adelbert Redfield, "Superstitions and folk beliefs," *Tenn. Folklore Soc. Bull.*, 1937, *3:* 15, no. 40; Ruth W. O'Dell, "Signs and superstitions," *Tenn. Folklore Soc. Bull.*, 1944, *10,* no. 4: 3; John Q. Anderson, "Magical transference of disease in Texas folk medicine," *Western Folklore,* 1968, *27:* 198; Joseph D. Clark, "North Carolina superstitions," *North Carolina Folklore,* 1966, *14:* 8, no. 168.

27. Harry Middleton Hyatt, *Folk-Lore from Adams County, Illinois,* 1st ed. (New York: Alma Egan Hyatt Foundation, 1935), p. 210, no. 4383 (hereinafter cited: Hyatt, 1st ed.).

28. Tressa Turner, "The human comedy in folk superstitions," *Pub. Texas Folklore Soc.*, 1937, *13:* 169–170; Anderson, *op. cit.* (n. 26 above), p. 198.

29. Hyatt, 2nd ed., p. 254; no. 5661.

30. *Ibid.*, p. 279, no. 6139.

31. *New York Folklore Q.*, 1955, *11:* 264.

32. Paul G. Brewster, "Folk cures and preventives from Southern Indiana."*Southern Folklore Q.*, 1939, *3:* 37, no. 3.

33. Roxie Martin, "Old remedies collected in the Blue Ridge Mountains," *J. Amer. Folklore*, 1947, *60*: 185, no. 25.

34. Donald M. Hines, "Superstitions from Oregon," *Western Folklore,* 1965, *24:* 11, no. 70.

35. Hyatt, 1st ed., p. 215, no. 4478.

36. Wayland D. Hand, "Plugging, nailing, wedging and kindred folk medical practices," in Bruce Jackson, ed., *Folklore and Society:* Essays in Honor of Benj. A. Botkin (Hatboro, Pa.: Folklore Associates, 1966), p. 66: "From a survey of the literature it is not clear whether measurement and circumscription was the original idea, or whether magical transference through notching, or plugging, constituted the underlying *raison d'être*."

37. Thomas R. Brendle and Claude W. Unger, *Folk Medicine of the Pennsylvania Germans. The Non-Occult Cures* (Proceedings of the Pennsylvania German Society, vol. 45, Norristown, Pa., 1935), p. 163.

38. Wayland D. Hand, "The magical transference of disease," *North Carolina Folklore,* 1965, *13:* 83–109. 1965. In order to demonstrate clearly that an actual transference of disease had taken place, as well as a symbolic one, I chose in that paper only examples that drew attention to the effect of the translocation of disease on the new host: "These symbolic rituals are widely known and easily understood. To claim our attention here the disease must be communicated to second parties or things, and it must be expressly stated, or clearly implied, that the disease is received by the new victim, or a new receiving agent which is itself affected by the transfer. Neither does communication to an intermediate agent, a *Zwischenträger,* suffice for this discussion. Ideally for the argument of this study, it should be shown that when the disease is communicated to other persons, or to animals, it will continue its ravages or induce disease or death in the new victim" (pp. 83–84).

39. *J. Amer. Folklore,* 1913, *26:* 191.

40. *N.Y. Folklore Q.*, 1945: *1:* 180.

41. Vance Randolph, *Ozark Superstitions* (New York: Columbia University Press, 1947), pp. 134–135; Grace Partridge Smith, "Folklore from Egypt," *Hoosier Folklore,* 1946, *5:* 69–70, no. 24; Wilson, *op. cit.* (n. 7 above), pp. 61–62.

42. Helen Creighton, *Bluenose Magic: Popular Beliefs and Superstitions in Nova Scotia* (Toronto: The Ryerson Press, 1968), p. 194, no. 7; Ruth Ann Musick, "Superstitions," *West Virginia Folklore*, 1964, *14*: 48, no. 5; Richmond and Van Winkle, *op. cit.* (n. 23 above), p. 122; no. 67; Pauline Monette Black, *Nebraska Folk Cures* (University of Nebraska Studies in Language, Literature, and Criticism, no. 15, Lincoln, 1935), p. 34, no. 2.

43. *Kentucky Folklore Record,* 1960, *6:* 63; Ida Mae McKinney, "Superstitions of the Missouri Ozarks," *Tenn. Folklore Soc. Bull.*, 1952, *18:* 107; *Tenn. Folklore Soc. Bull.*, 1950, *16:* 10.

44. Janice C. Neal, "Grandad—pioneer medicine man," *N.Y. Folklore Q.*, 1955, *11:* 283; Hyatt, 2nd ed., p. 255, no. 5669; George D. Hendricks, *Mirrors, Mice & Mustaches: A Sampling of Superstitions and Popular Beliefs in Texas* (Austin: Texas Folklore Society, 1966), p. 32; Richmond and Van Winkle, *op. cit.* (n. 23 above), p. 122, no. 68.

45. Arthur Huff Fauset, *Folklore from Nova Scotia* (Mem. Amer. Folklore Soc., vol. 24, New York, 1931), p. 197, no. 336.

46. *Foxfire,* 1968, *2,* no. 1: 10, no. 3.

47. Wiltse, *op. cit.* (n. 9 above), p. 207; Emma Gertrude White, "Folk-medicine among the Pennsylvania Germans," *J. Amer. Folklore,* 1897, *10,* 79.

48. *Brown Coll.*, VI, 55, no. 328: Brewster, *op. cit.* (n. 32 above), p. 37, no. 2 (notching, and replacing the chip rather than plugging *per se*).

49. Brewster, *op. cit.*, p. 36, no. 2.

50. Hyatt, 2nd ed., p. 269, no. 5895.

51. Black, *op. cit.* (n. 42 above), p. 30, no. 20 (mulberry tree); Hyatt, 2nd ed., p. 211, no. 4830.

52. Hand, *Measuring,* pp. 240–251, esp. pp. 243 ff.

53. Annie Weston Whitney and Caroline Canfield Bullock, *Folk-Lore from Maryland* (Mem. Amer. Folklore Soc., vol. 18, New York, 1925), p. 89, no. 1810.

54. Hyatt, 2nd ed., p. 279, no. 6139.

55. *Pennsylvania Folklife,* Oct. 1964, *14:* 37.

56. Fogel, *op. cit.* (n. 14 above), p. 330, no. 1759; Brendle and Unger, *op. cit.* (n. 37 above), p. 136.

57. Frost Woodhull, *Ranch Remedios: Man Bird, Beast* (Pub. Texas Folklore Soc., vol. 8, Austin, 1930), p. 61.

58. Hyatt, 2nd ed., pp. 254–255, no. 5667.

59. Thomas and Thomas, *op. cit.* (n. 16 above), p. 100, No. 1143; Earl J. Stout, *Folklore from Iowa* (Mem. Amer. Folklore Soc., vol. 29, New York, 1936), pp. 189–190, No. 1035.

60. William Rensick Riddell, "Some old Canadian folk medicine," *The Canada Lancet and Practitioner,* Aug. 1934, *83:* 42; Creighton, *op. cit.* (n. 42 above), pp. 194–195, nos. 6, 9; Brendle and Unger, *op. cit.* (n. 37 above), p. 140; *Brown Coll.*, VI, *32,* no. 176; VI, 55, no. 327; *West Virginia Folklore,* 1964, *14:* 60; *Folk-Lore,* 1897, *8:* 187; Hyatt, 2nd ed., p. 253, nos. 5643–5646.

61. Edith E. Cutting, *Lore of an Adirondack County* (Ithaca, N.Y.: Cornell University Press, 1944), p. 41.

62. Catherine M. Relihan, "Folk remedies," *N. Y. Folklore Q.*, 1947; *3:* 81; Brendle and Unger, *op. cit.* (n. 37 above), p. 136; Browne, *op. cit.* (n. 19 above), p. 24, no. 318; Hilda Roberts, "Louisiana superstitions," *J. Amer Folklore,* 1927: *40:*, 166, no. 385; Gertrude C. Davenport, "Folk-cures from Kansas," *J. Amer. Folklore,* 1898, *11:* 132.

63. Fogel, *op. cit.* (n. 14 above), p. 45, no. 98.

64. Hyatt, 2nd ed., p. 254, no. 5656.

65. Grabner, *op. cit.* (n. 2 above), pp. 539–540, *passim.*

8

"Measuring" with String, Thread, and Fibre: A Practice in Folk Medical Magic*

Several years ago Elfriede Grabner treated the subject of measuring people for diagnostic and curative folk medical purposes.[1] Her survey dealt principally with the German-speaking countries, but included several other European lands, as well as making mention of kindred practices among aboriginal peoples in various parts of the world. Having encountered several of these measuring practices in my study of American Folk Medicine over the last few years, I am placing them into the record herewith, for what light they will throw on the transmission of a magical practice in folk medicine from the Old World to the New. The measuring of people to learn, first of all, whether they are afflicted, and, secondly, to divest them of the disease if they have one, apparently is a practice going back to the time of Pliny the Elder, if not before.[2] The early accounts of measuring, from Hildegard, abbess of the Benedictine cloisters at Rupertsberg near Bingen on the Rhine, in the twelfth century, to numerous other writers up to the time of Martin Luther

*This article originally appeared in *Festschrift für Robert Wildhaber* zum 70. Geburtstag am 3. August 1972. Ed. Walter Escher, Theo Gantner, und Hans Trümpy. Basel: Schweizerische Gesellschaft für Volkskunde, 1973, pp. 240–251, constituting Vols. 68–69 of the *Schweizerisches Archiv für Volkskunde,* 1972 1973. Permission to reprint has been given by the editor and the publisher.

in the sixteenth, are sketched in the Grabner paper.[3] The same measuring practice was known in the Scandinavian north as early as the middle of the fourteenth century.[4] Most of the early writers cited depict what may still be regarded as perhaps the principal form of measuring. This constitutes taking the measure of the length of the body with string, thread, and the like, from extremity to extremity, and then comparing the length with its width, as measured from fingertip to fingertip of the outstretched arms. Since length and width are supposed to be equal, according to early ideas of body proportions,[5] any disparity as to length was thought to indicate an unhealthy state of some sort and the presence of disease itself. By this circumstance it was explained that the person had "lost his measure," as the saying went. This was tantamount to losing the vital force of life itself, and an early death was anticipated.[6] If the divergence was only minor, it was thought that the ministrations of the healer would still be availing. Notions of "lost measure," on the whole, seem not to be known in the United States, but this deficiency can likely be laid to insufficient collecting of data and the general lack of interest in the study of this phenomenon. Even so, an air of mystery hovers over measuring as a ritual act, as in Virginia, for example.[7] In the South Slavic countries, measuring is still resorted to in diseases thought to be inflicted by magical powers or demons.[8] Although these notions are not encountered in American folk medical tradition, resort is nevertheless had to special kinds of healers, such as wise women and cunning men, to deal with diseases by measuring that do not yield to common medical treatment. Even an element of fear seems to attach to the simplest kind of measuring. Such a routine and harmless thing as the measuring of children, particularly before they are a year old, is still frowned upon in many parts of the country out of feelings, perhaps, that the measure, after all, contains the real life essence of the child. This is the case in the South, and in parts of the Central States and the Southwest, where it is thought that the child would thereby be measured for a coffin.[9] These same notions are held in many parts of Europe, of course.[10] Along the Eastern Seaboard, and elsewhere in the country, measuring a child under one year of age is believed to stunt its growth.[11] On the positive side, measuring was believed to insure health and well being, particularly if the child were frail or sickly.[12] This notion echoes positive feelings about measuring in South Slavic lands as being healthy and stimulating.[13] It was customary there, for example, for a tailor to salute a person he was measuring for clothes with the greeting, "To your health!"[14] By way of contrast, in the mid-thirties in Illinois, it was believed that if you did so much as measure yourself, you would bring bad luck to your family.[15] Even measuring with a tape measure or yardstick was regarded as bad luck in the Scotch Irish and English tradition of Pennsylvania as late as the mid-twenties.[16]

Since measuring with string and other kinds of cordage appears to be one of the earliest and best known forms of ritual measurement for disease, we may begin with this phase of the subject. Specifically, it will be the purpose of this paper to point out extensions on the basic ideas set out in Grabner, and other writers,[17] to show the development of these curative notions and practices in America. So far as I know, no one has attempted to treat this folk medical prescription, although both Bourke and Knortz called attention to certain aspects of measuring in scholarly writings before the turn of the century,[18] and many collectors have since contributed items to what may now be regarded as a considerable body of evidence.

The classical measuring and comparing of length and width, as discussed by various writers,[19] seems not to have been well known in America, although this type of diagnostic test was practiced sporadically in Virginia, Pennsylvania, Maryland, and perhaps elsewhere, around the turn of the century.[20] Other kinds of equalizing measures, of course, have been employed in different parts of the country, as well as in Latin America.[21] A curious variation, involving a different principle of measurement, is seen in a measuring custom reported from Kentucky. "If a child is delicate, have an old woman measure it. If three times its diameter does not equal its height, it has decay."[22] It is not clear whether the diameter was calculated at the shoulders, the chest, the waist, or elsewhere on the torso.

Full-length measuring with string and other kinds of cordage is well known from the Eastern Seaboard to the Central States, and parts of the South, and is also encountered elsewhere.[23] Collectors are more at pains, however, to indicate the manner in which the string or yarn is disposed of than they are to give exact details as to how the measurement itself is made. In Illinois, three long strings, one white, one blue, and one red, were used until recently for the cure of erysipelas, and the measurement of the child was made by an old woman as the child lay on a board.[24] Generally, however, the measurement was taken with the child in an upright position. More precise measurements were possible when the patient, boy or girl, was nude, as seen in typical examples from Virginia and Indiana.[25] Not all measurements of the body were full length. In Louisiana in the mid-forties, for example, an undernourished child was measured only from the neck to the toes with a woolen string, not from the crown of the head to the feet, as was usually the case.[26]

Cross measuring from the left elbow to the right knee and vice versa, found in different parts of the Slavic countries,[27] in Hungary,[28], and in German speech islands in Southwest Europe,[29] has not been reported in America. In the Pennsylvania German country,[30] however, there is a measurement of the elbow, the wrist, and the foot that is reminiscent of a South Slavic cross-measurement, namely, from the right great toe to the middle finger of the left hand, and vice versa.[31]

Measuring of the head for headache, sometimes with cloth simulating a bandage, as described by Grabner,[32] is encountered in the British Isles,[33] but I am hard put to document this kind of craniometry in America. An example from Illinois is too vague to mean much.[34]

Perhaps the principal use of string measurement in a diagnostic way in this country is the measurement of the length of a person in terms of the length of his feet. This ritual is employed in tests for such childhood maladies as flesh decay, short growth, "go-backs," and the like, and is found throughout the Eastern, Southern, and Middle States.[35] The patient is first measured with a string in the usual way, namely, from head to toe. After this, the foot is measured from the heel to the tip of the toes, and then the body length is divided by this unitary measure. According to popular belief, the height should equal seven lengths of the foot, not six, as reckoned by Vitruvius,[36] the Roman architect and engineer, who was one of the first writers to occupy himself with bodily proportions. Discrepancies in measurement, where the length was supposed to equal the width for diagnostic purposes, indicated to the wise woman making the measurement that the child was suffering from the wasting sickness, "go-backs," or *abnemmes,* a Pennsylvania German term for a non-thrifty child, or other ailments equally mysterious. In Indiana, for example, if the seven lengths of the foot exceeded the patient's height, he was thought to suffer from "long growth," so called; if, however, seven lengths of the foot fell short of the length of the body, the malady was diagnosed as "short growth."[37] In other accounts from the same state, it is specified that the string used for measurement should pass down over the left hip to the heel.[38] Sometimes magic words are spoken, and the string is placed on the gate to be worn away, an interesting feature that we shall discuss later in connection with disposal of the *Zwischenträger,* or the agent of divestment.[39] Gore has pointed out the difficulty of precise measurement in these cases, what with the resiliency of yarn and other kinds of loose, fibrous cordage used in the calculations.[40] In rare cases an elastic cord was used that could be stretched, if necessary, to equal the child's length, for example, as among the whites in the Allegheny Mountains.[41]

There seems not to have been a well-defined category of "measurers" in the United States, say, that one could compare with the modern-day *Messerinnen* of Silesia and elsewhere in the German-speaking countries.[42] These healers were in the main elderly "wise women." In the United States this kind of healing office was not as well known, although in some parts of the country the practitioners were known as "string doctors," as, for example, in Illinois.[43] Whereas these magical healers were generally old women in Europe,[44] there appears to have been no such predilection for female functionaries in this country. Women, however, are specially noted as officiants in the measuring ritual in West Virginia,[45] although in the same account it is stated that only women can cure little boys and only men can cure girls.[46] A notable instance of an old crone's being summoned to measure a sickly child is seen in the case of Theodore Dreiser, in Indiana in 1871. An old German woman is reported to have measured the infant Dreiser from head to toe and from fingertip to fingertip of his outstretched arms in the approved classical fashion.[47]

Healers specializing in measuring apparently are viewed in the same light and fall under the same general prescriptions as apply to other kinds of healers. In Indiana, for example, the power to measure for short growth, a disease apparently related to *abnemmes,* "go-backs," and other maladies that befall infants and growing children, must be derived from someone else who has the power.[48] Posthumous children—sex not specified—are said to be especially endowed with this healing power.[49] As in the case of the other kinds of healers, those measuring children for short growth must never accept pay, or they will lose the gift.[50] The notion was once held in Virginia that the string used for measuring had to be made by a young child, a young girl, on a spinning wheel, but that practice stopped years ago, and any kind of thread is used nowadays. Borrowed into this tradition, no doubt, are ideas of innocence and pristine vigor that apply to healers generally where children under seven or eight are involved.[51]

Measuring is ordinarily only one part of the healing ritual, and is perhaps the least magical phase of the whole curative procedure. Disposal of the disease, once the limits of its possible ravages have been ascertained, through disposal of the *Zwischenträger* or through manipulations of the patient, lies at the heart of, and at core constitutes the magical efficacy of the healing office itself. As throughout folk medicine, and all of folklore, for that matter, there is constant adaptation of materials, ideas, and functions from one situation to another. It is not surprising, therefore, to find examples of "passing through," "plugging," magical incantations, and kindred magical practices in the various kinds of cures effected through bodily measurement or the circumscription and containment of disease by measuring its physical limits.

Two examples of passing through, one from West Virginia and one from Indiana, will indicate the range and complexity of these curative rituals, involving as they do, maintenance of the magical power resident in the thread by not allowing it to touch the floor, resort to repetition and numeral magic, observance of the fixed proportions of the measurement, verbal magic, and the ritualistic disposal of the strand used in the measurement. Here, then, is the magical procedure in the Pennsylvania German tradition of the neighboring state of West Virginia: "Measuring: You use a flax thread, start at the back of the head and measure to the heel. The thread shouldn't touch the floor. A loop is made and the child is passed through nine times.[52] If the feet measure more than a seventh of the length of the body, the child has undergrown. The thread must be placed somewhere so it will wear out fast, then the child will get better."[53] The Indiana variation on passing through is as follows: "If a child has short growth, take the string you measure him with, and make a loop out of it. Then you have the person step through it and bring it up over his head. While you are doing this, say, 'In the name of the Father, Son, and Holy Ghost, Amen'. Do this three times, one time each day. Each time you measure, use a different string, and hang it up some place where no one can reach it. After you have measured him three times (three succeeding days), then take all the strings and burn them together."[54] Passing a child three times through a warm horse collar in the

Pennsylvania German country, is another way in which a child was measured for short growth at the turn of the century.[55]

There seems not to have been over the years any uniform notion concerning the color of yarn, thread, string, or other fibres used in the measurement. Where colors are prescribed, however, red would appear to be favored.[56] We have already seen examples of color variation where more than one thread is used, as in the red-white-and-blue combination mentioned for the cure of erysipelas in Illinois. Tom Peete Cross has also noted color options.[57] American prescriptions ordinarily do not recommend raw or unbleached wool, flax, and the like, as seems to be the case in parts of Europe,[58] nor is silk recommended, as in so many other kinds of American cures where thread or string serves as the agent of disposal. It is understandable, of course, that red silk thread would, by the power of sympathetic magic, be thought to possess special efficacy for the curing of wild-fire or erysipelas, as in the Pennsylvania German country.[59]

Though it is nowhere expressed in so many words, the measuring of a disease itself, by the principles of contagious magic, is somehow thought to absorb the disease, or to subsume it magically within the physical limits of the measuring device. If there is a magical transference to the *Zwischenträger,* as all writers on the subject have shown,[60] then disposal of the agent is a logical necessity. This is done by burial or sequestering in a damp place so that the process of rotting and decay can be hastened.[61] Under the eaves, one of the most popular places to dispose of such carriers, was favored,[62] but many other places were utilized, including burial under the doorstep.[63] Disposal through wearing away rather than by decomposition is seen in a variety of methods whereby the agent is exposed to wear.[64] Most ingenious of all was the placing of the string or yarn on a gate, or even on the hinge of a gate, so that the wasting process could be accelerated.[65] Nowhere is there mention of the yarn's being carried away by some new host, as is often the case where items are disposed of near traveled places. In Indiana the string was wrapped around the door hinge,[66] or on the water pump cylinder rod within a few inches of the top,[67] while in some parts of the Midwest the string was twined around a grindstone.[68] In Pennsylvania the string was wrapped around a fencepost, which is logically associated with a gate,[69] but in Ohio the string is tied around a hot stove pipe, so as to be consumed almost immediately.[70]

Burying of the intermediate agent in measuring rituals is not as common as other methods listed here, but it is encountered in various places. In Louisiana an undernourished child is made to eat the ashes of the woolen string employed to determine his affliction.[71] In Maryland, to find out whether a child is suffering from marasmus, its body was measured with a string, legs and arms, and then the string was tied around an egg, and the egg was placed in a bed of hot coals. In this unusual kind of diagnosis, it was believed that, if the string burned with the egg, the child did not have marasmus, but, if it did not burn, the child had the disease.[72]

There is space only to mention the use of clothing instead of string or other kinds of materials as the medium of measure. The only references at my command come from the Italian tradition, and the practice seems not to have gained much of a foothold on our shores.[73]

Medidas, or measures of the body of saints and other holy personages, are utilized, or were until recently, in the Latin American tradition. In the early 1890s, Bourke called attention to the use of these more elaborate kinds of measurements, often simulating ribbons or broader pieces of cloth, supposed to be cut to the exact height of the saints in question, and containing prayers effective for ailments at different parts of the body, according to a vertical scale.[74] In sixteenth-century England one of these measuring cloths was known as "the length of our Lorde,"[75] and students of folklore can see actual fold-out prayers of this kind, on paper rather than on cloth, in the atlas volume of Spamer's standard work on German Folklore, where Lengths of Jesus and Lengths of Mary are shown, as well as similar measures of saintly persons.[76]

The use of straw, blades of grass, broom straw, and other plant fibres, as well as various kinds of yarn, thread, string, and similar manufactured products, for the measuring and magical riddance of corns, bunions, warts, wens, and other excrescences is fairly well known and can not claim space in this essay.[77]

It is hard to summarize a ritual of this complexity, and there is not space to do so. In describing how measuring works in the case of wasting sickness, or *abnemmes,* however, Brendle and Unger elucidate one important idea, even though it is but one of many. They write: "At the present time when we speak of taking a photograph we use the word *abnemme.* Similarly when a person was measured from the crown of his head to the sole of his foot and crosswise from tip to tip of his outstretched arms—the height is to be as great as the width—he is *abgenumme*, measured off or taken off. His correct likeness is taken. In that likeness his diseases are tied with knots. Symbolically a rebirth is represented."[78] This accords well with Grabner's observation that one's measure is a mysterious extension of oneself.[79]

NOTES

1. Elfriede Grabner, Verlorenes Mass und heilkräftiges Messen: Krankheitserforschung und Heilhandlung in der Volksmedizin, in: Elfriede Grabner, ed., Volksmedizin: Probleme und Forschungsgeschichte. Wege der Forschung. Bd. 63. Darmstadt: Wissenschaftliche Buchgemeinschaft 1967, 538–553. This had originally appeared in the Zeitschrift für Volkskunde 60 (1964) 23–34.

2. Historia Naturalis, Book 7, 17. I have used the Loeb Classical Library edition, tr. H. Rackham, W.H.S. Jones, and D. E. Eichholz, 10 vols. Cambridge, Mass. and London 1938–1962.

3. Grabner (see note 1 above) 538–541.

4. I. Reichborn-Kjennerud, Vår gamle Trolldomsmedisin. 5 vols. Skrifter utgitt av Det Norske Videnskaps-Akademi i Oslo. II. Hist.-Filos. Klasse, 1927, No. 6; 1933, No. 2; 1940, No. 1; 1942, No. 2; 1947, No. 1. Oslo 1927–1947. Vol. I, 103.

5. From the earliest history of lineal measure, the cubit, i.e., the distance from the elbow to the outstretched middle finger, has been used. It remained for the Roman architect and engineer Vitruvius to work out a system of measures that included the width of the fingers, the palm, and the length of the foot. Cf. J. Howard Gore's summary in Journal of American Folklore 5 (1892) 109 (Hereinafter cited: JAF.)

6. Grabner (see note 1 above), 538, 541, 553, *passim.*

7. JAF 5 (1892) 108 (with reference to "go-backs," a well-known but little understood wasting disease of children).

8. P(hyllis) Kemp, Healing Ritual. Studies in the Technique and Tradition of the Southern Slavs. London 1935, 122. Martin Luther was among the first to note the use of measuring against those maladies. Cf. Grabner (see note 1 above) 540.

9. Wayland D. Hand, ed., Popular Beliefs and Superstitions from North Carolina (constituting vols. 6 and 7 of the Frank C. Brown Collection of North Carolina Folklore. Durham, North Carolina 1952–1964). VII, 4, No. 4880, especially the notes.

10. William George Black, Folk-Medicine. A Chapter in the History of Culture. Publications of the Folk-Lore Society, 12. London 1883, 181: Kemp (see note 8 above) 123; Handwörterbuch des deutschen Aberglaubens, ed. Hanns Bächtold-Stäubli and Eduard Hoffmann-Krayer. 10 vols. Berlin and Leipzig 1927–1942. 5, 1855. (Hereinafter cited HDA.)

11. Edwin Miller Fogel, Beliefs and Superstitions of the Pennsylvania Germans. American Germanica, 18. Philadelphia 1915, 54–55, No. 154; Harry Emerson Wildes, Twin Rivers. Rivers of America. New York 1942, 313. Cf. HDA, 4, 1318; 5, 1855; Grabner (see note 1 above) 542.

12. Karl Knortz, Amerikanischer Aberglaube der Gegenwart. Ein Beitrag zur Volkskunde. Leipzig 1913, 9.

13. Kemp (see note 8 above) 123.

14. Ibid.

15. Harry Middleton Hyatt, Folk-Lore from Adams County Illinois. 1st ed. New York 1935, 140, No. 2880.

16. Henry W. Shoemaker, Scotch-Irish and English Proverbs and Sayings of the West Branch Valley of Central Pennsylvania. Reading, Pennsylvania 1927, 18.

17. Paul Sartori, Zählen, Messen, Wägen. Am Ur-Quell. 6 (1895) 87–88; Jacoby, Mass und Messen, HDA, 5, 1852–1861; Gustav Jungbauer, Deutsche Volksmedizin. Berlin 1934, 134, *passim.*

18. In his The Medicine-Men of the Apache. Ninth Annual Report of the Bureau of Ethnology, 1887–1888. Washington, D.C. 1892, 572–575, John G. Bourke briefly discussed "*Medidas,*" "Measuring Cords," "Wresting Threads," etc. Cf. also his shorter notices in JAF, 5 (1892) 241–242; 7 (1894) 135. J. Howard Gore wrote an insightful note on "The Go-Backs" in the same journal in 1892 (Vol. 5, 107–109), with special attention to proportional measurements in the cure of this little understood disease of infants. After this paper had been completed, I learned of the excellent treatment of "measuring" in Indiana from Professor Linda Dégh. See Barbara Ann Townsend and Donald Allport Bird, The Miracle of String Measurement. Indiana Folklore 3 (1970) 147–162. This study contains the largest body of texts in print for any area in this country, constituting the most complete survey we have of this magical practice. For technical reasons, I can utilize this material in the notes only, citing page references only, unless new facets of the subject are treated.

19. Grabner (see note 1 above) 538, 541, 544, 549, *passim*; Adolf Wuttke, Der deutsche Volksaberglaube der Gegenwart. 3rd ed. by Elard Hugo Meyer. Berlin 1900, 340; Gore (see note 5 above) 109. Many of these notions, perhaps most, are based on the observation of Pliny: "It has been noticed that a man's height from head to foot is equal to his full span measured from the tips of the middle fingers" (Natural History, 7, 17).

20. K. Knortz, Nachklänge germanischen Glaubens und Brauches in Amerika. Halle 1933, 113, as cited in Grabner (see note 1 above) 548.

21. George M. Foster, Relationship Between Spanish and Spanish-American Folk Medicine. JAF 66 (1953) 211.

22. Kentucky Folk-Lore and Poetry Magazine Vol. 3, No. 4 (January, 1929) 15. For entries dealing with measurement at the waist, see JAF 49 (1936) 196; Brown Coll., VI, 201, No. 1544; Folk-Lore 23 (1912) 474.

23. Ernest W. Baughman, Type and Motif-Index of the Folklore of England and North America. Indiana University Folklore Series, No. 20. The Hague 1966, F 950.3(a); Brown Coll., VI, 31, No. 175 (North Carolina); West Virginia Folklore 14 (1964) 49 (West Virginia); JAF 5 (1892) 108 (Virginia); ibid. 10 (1897) 79 (Pennsylvania); Publications of the Pennsylvania German Folklore Society 26 (1962) 136 (Pennsylvania); Indiana History Bulletin 35 (1958) 118, No. 1 (Indiana); Hoosier Folklore, 7 (1948) 17 (Indiana); Kentucky Folk-Lore and Poetry Magazine 6, No. 1 (March, 1931) 9 (Kentucky).

24. Harry Middleton Hyatt, Folk-Lore from Adams County Illinois. 2nd ed., Memoirs of the Alma Egan Hyatt Foundation. New York, 1965, 265–266, No. 5827. Cf. Indiana Folklore 3 (1970) 152 (naked on the floor); 149, 155 (naked on the stomach).

25. JAF 5 (1892) 108 (Virginia); Hoosier Folklore 7 (1948) 18 (Indiana); Indiana Folklore 3 (1970) 149–150, 152, 155.

26. Lyle Saxon, Gumbo Ya-Ya. Boston 1945, 531. Cf. Grabner (see note 1 above) 542.

27. Kemp (see note 8 above) 122.
28. JAF 75 (1962) 135.
29. Zeitschrift für österreichische Volkskunde 57 (1954) 141–143.
30. Publ. Penna. German Folklore Soc. 26 (1962) 136.
31. Kemp (see note 8 above) 122.
32. Grabner (see note 1 above) 544.
33. JAF 7 (1894) 226 (Ireland); Folk-Lore 33 (1922) 395–396 (Ireland).
34. Hyatt (see note 15 above) 2nd ed., 214. No. 4888.
35. JAF 5 (1892) 108 (Virginia); Southern Folklore Quarterly 8 (1944) 277 (Ohio) (Hereinafter: SFQ); Folk-Lore 8 (1897) 185–186 (Ohio); Hoosier Folklore 7 (1948) 19 (Indiana); Indiana Folklore 3 (1970) 149–150; Madge E. Pickard and R. Carlyle Buley, The Midwest Pioneer, His Ills, Cures and Doctors. Crawfordsville, Indiana 1945, 75 (Midwest).
36. JAF 5 (1892) 109.
37. Hoosier Folklore 7 (1948) 18. The three notes on measuring for short growth in this estimable state folklore journal (pp. 16–19) reveal the kind of detail that is so necessary for the appraisal of field data and theory based on such collectanea.
38. Ibid., 17; Indiana Folklore 3 (1970) 152.
39. Hoosier Folklore 7 (1948) 16.
40. JAF 5 (1892) 108.
41. JAF 7 (1894) 116.
42. Grabner (see note 1 above) 541 ff.; Black (see note 10 above) 114.
43. J. M. Beveridge, M.D., Survival of Superstition as Found in the Practice of Medicine. Illinois Medical Journal 31 (1917) 269; cf. Tom Peete Cross, Witchcraft in North Carolina. Studies in Philology 16, No. 3 (July, 1919) 263.
44. Grabner (see note 1 above) 541 ff.; Black (see note to above) 114.
45. West Virginia Folklore 14 (1964) 61. Female practitioners are favored in Indiana, too, as seen in the paper by Townsend and Bird (cf. note 18 above).
46. West Virginia Folklore 14 (1964) 61. Cf. Indiana Folklore 3 (1970) 149, 154, 160.
47. Theodore Dreiser, Dawn. Greenwich, Conn. 1965, 9–10; cf. W. A. Swanberg, Dreiser. Bantam Books No. Q 3345, New York 1967, 4.
48. Hoosier Folklore 7 (1948) 17.
49. Ibid.; Indiana Folklore 3 (1970) 159–160. For a treatment of posthumous children as healers, see Wayland D. Hand, The Folk Healer: Calling and Endowment. Journal of the History of Medicine and Allied Sciences 26 (1971) 264–265.
50. Hoosier Folklore 7 (1948) 17; Indiana Folklore 3 (1970) 150, 159.
51. See Hand (see note 49 above) 270–271.
52. For a broad general survey of passing through, see my article, "Passing Through": Folk Medical Magic and Symbolism. Proceedings of the American Philosophical Society 112 (1968) 379–402. For Indiana examples of "passing through," see Indiana Folklore 3 (1970) 150–151, 153.
53. Publ. Penna. German Folklore Soc. 26 (1962) 136.
54. Hoosier Folklore 7 (1948) 18.
55. JAF 10 (1897) 79. For European references to passing through in connection with measuring rituals, see Kemp (see note 8 above) 122–123; Wuttke (see note 19 above) 339.
56. JAF 10 (1897) 79 (Pennsylvania); Publ. Penna. German Folklore Soc. 26 (1962) 137. Cf. Kemp (see note 8 above) 121.
57. Cross (see note 43 above) 263.

58. Grabner (see note 1 above) 542–543, 550, *passim.*

59. A. Monroe Aurand, Jr., The Pow-Wow Book. A Treatise on the Art of "Healing by Prayer" and "Laying on of Hands," etc., Practiced by the Pennsylvania Germans and Others, etc. Harrisburg 1929, 53.

60. Grabner (see note 1 above) 544, 552; Kemp (see note 8 above) 121.

61. Indiana: A Guide to the Hoosier State. American Guide Series. New York 1941, 119; Indiana Folklore 3 (1970) 150, 161. Cf. Reichborn-Kjennerud (see note 4 above) vol. 1, 161.

62. Hoosier Folklore 7 (1948) 17; Indiana Folklore 3 (1970) 155; Publ. Penna. German Folklore Soc. 26 (1962) 136.

63. Brown Coll. vol. 6, 31, No. 175.

64. JAF 5 (1892) 108 (Virginia); Publ. Penna. German Folklore Soc. 26 (1962) 136.

65. JAF 5 (1892) 108 (Virginia); 10 (1897) 79 (Pennsylvania); Hoosier Folklore 7 (1948) 15 (Pennsylvania); SFQ (see note 35 above) 8 (1944) 277 (Ohio); Indiana History Bull. 35 (1958) 121, No. 52 (Indiana); Hoosier Folklore 7 (1948) 16 (Indiana); Indiana Folklore 3 (1970) 153, 161.

66. Hoosier Folklore 7 (1948) 19. Cf. Indiana Folklore 3 (1970) 154 (doorjamb).

67. Hoosier Folklore 7 (1948) 17.

68. Pickard and Buley (see note 35 above) 76; Indiana Folklore 3 (1970) 154, 161. The recent Indiana survey notes disposal on a buggy axle and the tying of the string around an automobile tire, revealing, as the authors say, an adaptability to modern living conditions. Indiana Folklore 3 (1970) 152 (buggy axle), 150 (auto tire). Cf. p. 161.

69. Wayland D. Hand, More Popular Beliefs and Superstitions from Pennsylvania, in: Two Penny Ballads and Four Dollar Whiskey, ed. Robert H. Byington and Kenneth S. Goldstein. Hatboro, Pennsylvania 1965, 145, No. 88.

70. SFQ 8 (1944) 277.

71. Saxon (see note 26 above) 531. Cf. Wuttke (see note 19 above) 340.

72. Annie Weston Whitney and Caroline Canfield Bullock, Folk-Lore from Maryland. Memoirs of the American Folklore Society 18. New York 1925, 92, No. 1852. Cf. Grabner (see note 1 above) 543, where the test involves jaundice. Cf. Indiana Folklore 3 (1970) 155.

73. JAF 7 (1894) 140 (Texas); California Folklore Quarterly 3 (1944) 213. Cf. Grabner (see note 1 above) 542.

74. JAF 5 (1892) 242; The Medicine-Men of the Apache, 572–573.

75. Bourke, Medicine Men (see note 18 above) 573.

76. Adolf Spamer, Die deutsche Volkskunde. 2nd ed., 2 vols. Leipzig and Berlin 1935, vol. 2, 9.

77. Cf. Brown Coll., vol. 6, 136, No. 974; 161, No. 1204; 339, Nos. 2613f.

78. Thomas R. Brendle and Claude W. Unger, Folk Medicine of the Pennsylvania Germans. The Non-Occult Cures. Proceedings of the Pennsylvania German Society, 45. Norristown, Pennsylvania 1935, 147.

79. Grabner (see note 1 above) 549.

9
Magical Treatment of Disease by Outlining the Ailing Part*

In my study of magical divestment of disease in the United States by measuring the focus of the ailment, by tracing the extent to which it has ravaged, or by other means used to circumscribe the spread of the malady, I have found few examples of outlining the ailing part and then scoring it with a cutting instrument.

I first heard of this practice while collecting folklore among a German-speaking population in southern Chile in 1967. It concerned tracing an ailing foot on the bark of a tree, then cutting out the bark within the outline of the foot—toes and all—which had been made. The notion was that once the bark had grown over the exposed surface of the tree, the malady would be gone. Since that time I have come upon enough references in the Hispanic and Latin-American tradition to indicate that this practice of folk medicine is tolerably well known in the Latin tradition.

Vicuña Cifuentes, the knowledgeable Chilean folklore scholar, notes its use for the cure of hernia.[1] A fig tree is selected for the operation, the bare foot placed against the trunk, and a cut made along the outline of the foot. It is not clear from his account whether the bark within the circumscribed area is removed; at any rate, Vicuña Cifuentes states that in the measure

*This article originally appeared in the *Bulletin of the New York Academy of Medicine*, 48 (1972), 951–954. Permission to reprint has been given by the editor and by the New York Academy of Medicine.

that the tree recovers its bark, the hernia will diminish in its own diameter, and that when the fusion of bark is complete, the hernia will disappear entirely. The healing over the incised part is also seen in cures involving "passing through" split saplings, which are later bound together,[2] and in some kinds of "plugging" where a cicatrix grows around the hole bored with an auger and then plugged up with a peg.[3]

The same procedure as noted in Chile is found in Colombia with regard to the scoring and removal of the bark within the area, but the manner of disposal differs somewhat. Here the removed portion is placed in the rear of a chimney to dry out.[4] Drying out, presumably, has the same magically therapeutic effect as the healing over of the area divested of bark, as we shall see in a practice reported from Pontevedra, Spain, for a mysterious disease known as *mal de aire*, i.e., a disease of the air. A child afflicted with the disease, who is often rickety, is taken up a hill within sight of the sea. A line is drawn around him as he lies on the ground, and the earth is dug out within the perimeter, taken home in a sack, and thrown in back of the fire. As the dirt finally burns and is consumed, the child is supposed to get better.[5] A somewhat modified form is reported from the province of Galicia. A patient suffering from tuberculosis of the lungs is made by a healer to lie on the ground over which sand had been spread. An outline is then drawn around the patient's body with the finger. After the patient is removed, the line is then erased with a knife. This is known as "cutting the evil or disease" (*cortar el mal*).[6]

The tradition of cutting into a live tree or plant is also known in the United States, but not widely, at least not so in published collections of folk medicine. In Brownsville and Austin, Texas, for example, student collectors reported some years ago the practice of the imprinting of a foot on a cactus for some unmentioned ailment. The circumscribed portion was then cut out and hung outside to dry. Healing took place when the excised part of the plant dried out.[7]

In the Pennsylvania German country, a practice of folkmedicine which lies somewhat between the cutting out of a portion of a live tree or plant and the removal of unproductive earth from within a circumscribed area is seen in the removal of a bit of "living earth," as it were. Here, a piece of turf in the meadow is cut out after the pattern of a foot with contusions, felons, and bunions. The sod is replaced upside down, with the roots presumably exposed and left to dry out.[8]

A Louisiana custom recorded 45 years ago shows a weakening of the tradition. A child suffering from croup was taken to the south side of a tree and a print was taken of its foot against the tree. When the child outgrew the footprint, he was supposed to recover from the croup.[9] Although there is no mention made of the manner in which the print was made, scoring may have been made with a sharp instrument. Outgrowing the circumscribed area is apparently the magical principle of the cure.

In these few examples of customs of folk medicine related to a single idea, it is difficult to determine any kind of common set of therapeutic principles. The Chilean cure exemplifies a sort of surgical treatment of the malady, followed by the healing over of the area operated on. The healing process, as noted, is encountered in the magical practices of passing through (for hernia, at least) and various kinds of plugging. In the cures from Colombia, Spain, and Texas, the main notion seems to be based upon the drying out, or killing off, perhaps, of the diseased part once it has been removed. The second Spanish example, the one from Galicia, definitely involved "cutting" the disease. The Pennsylvania cure involving the removal of the turf after the imprint was taken and then burying it wrongside up, involves, in the first instance, the magic of reversal. From a purely folk-medicine point of view, however, it seems more likely that the notion of divestment by implantation is the principal idea. In my article on plugging,[10] I allude to the burial of disease under sods and the consignment of diseases for safekeeping under stones and other objects as forms of implantation, if not directly of plugging itself. The item from Louisiana, different from all others in that the circumscribed area was not removed in any way, represents a well-known principle of folk-cure: namely, outgrowing, a subject on which I am now preparing a paper.

The excellent article on "*umkreisen*" in the *Handwörterbuch des deutschen Aberglaubens*, as it relates to folk medicine, suggests a variety of interpretations of these kinds of procedures, ranging from keeping the disease within prescribed limits, drying out the ailing part in the sun or burning it, keeping away evil influences by means of the magic circle, as when such a circle is placed around a woman in childbirth, and the like.[11] The operation of contagious magic and the transference of the disease directly to the tree, plant, or earth, rather than by transmitting it through a *Zwischenträger,* or intermediate agent, should be noted for all of the practices cited.[12]

It is my hope that this brief communication may be the means of bringing to light further examples, particularly for North America, of what I have reason to believe is a rather uncommon variety of "measuring" for disease.

NOTES

1. Cifuentes, V. J.: *Mitos y Supersticiones. Estudios del Folklore Chileno Recogidos de la Tradición Oral*, Tercera edición, 3d ed. Santiago de Chile, Editorial Nascimento, 1947, p. 316, No. 891.
2. Hand, W. D.: Passing through: Folk medical magic and symbolism. *Proc. Amer. Philos. Soc. 112:*379–402, 1968.
3. Hand, W. D.: Plugging, Nailing, Wedging, and Kindred Folk Medical Practices. In: *Folklore and Society. Essays in Honor of Benj. A. Botkin,* Jackson, B., editor. Hatboro, Pa., Folklore Ass., 1966, pp. 63–75.
4. Foster, G. M.: Relationship between Spanish and Spanish American folk medicine. *J. Amer. Folklore 66*:215, 1953.
5. Quibén, L. V.: Archivos: Medicina popular. *Rev. Trad. Pop. 1:*254, 1944.
6. Ibid., p. 322.
7. Hendricks, G. D.: *Mirrors, Mice & Mustaches. A Sampling of Superstitions & Popular Beliefs in Texas.* Austin, Texas, Texas Folklore Soc., 1966, p. 36.
8. Brendle, T. R. and Unger, C. W.: *Folk Medicine of the Pennsylvania Germans. The Non-Occult Cures.* Norristown, Pa., Pennsylvania German Soc., 1935, pp. 74–75.
9. Roberts, H.: Louisiana superstitions. *J. Amer. Folklore 40:*166, 1927.
10. Hand, W. D., op. cit.[3]
11. Bächtold-Stäubli, H., and Hoffmann-Krayer, E. von: *Handwörterbuch des deutschen Aberglaubens,* 10 vols. Berlin and Leipzig, de Gruyter, 1927–1942, vol. 8, pp. 1328–33, esp. 1331–33, s.v. "*umkreisen.*"
12. For a discussion of these matters, see Hand, W. D.: The magical transference of disease. *N. C. Folklore 13:*83–109, 1965.

10

''Over and Out'': Magical Divestment in Folk Belief and Custom*

Among the various ways in which diseases, evil forces, and annoyances of all kinds are either eradicated, or at least put out of mind, is a simple ritual of divestment, namely, the symbolical casting off of the oppressive agent or force. This is done by tossing something over one's head or shoulders, over a gate, over a wall, over a tree limb, over the roof, over the house, or simply off into space.

This kind of divestment is perhaps best seen in an act of folk medical magic, whereby the disease is ritually cast off. Magical riddance of this kind is most often performed on patients afflicted with warts, corns, felons and other excrescences. Involved is a simple form of contagious magic, whereby the malady is transferred to an intermediate agent, a so-called *Zwischenträger,* which is then disposed of by a simple toss over the shoulder, over one's head, or off into space. I cannot consider here other well-known forms of disposing of the intermediate agent such as burying, floating away, or sequestering. Of equal interest to tossing the malady free, are the various concomitant acts, many of which are themselves magical or symbolic.

Let us first consider how warts, corns, and other growths are tossed away, as it were. In American popular tradition, from

*This article originally appeared in *Miscellanea. Prof. Em. Dr. K. C. Peeters Door Vrienden en Collega's hem aangeboden ter Gelegenheid van zijn Emeritaat.* Ed. W. Van Nespen. Antwerpen: C. Govaerts, 1975, pp. 287–294. Permission to reprint has been given by the editor and the publisher.

which most of my examples come, warts are often rubbed with a dishrag and then the dishrag is thrown away. In Illinois, for example, a stolen dishrag is rubbed over the wart and then thrown over the eaves of the house.[1] Usually the toss is over the shoulder, and often the left one.[2] In another example from Illinois, however, an additional precaution is taken so that the disposal will be further insured. The patient walks to the crest of a small hill, with his back to the ridge. He then tosses the rag over the left shoulder so that it will fall on the opposite slope. Gravity, of course, is calculated to do the rest. He must then return home without looking back.[3] Picking warts until they bleed, and then impregnating the dishrag with the blood, i.e., with the substance of the wart itself, is practiced among the Negroes of Florida. Disposal of the rag over the shoulder is prescribed as well as the taboo of not looking back.[4] Impregnating a rag with the blood of a wart is a custom also observed among the whites of North Carolina. Disposal over the left shoulder in the customary way is observed, with the difference that the toss is made with the patient's back to the crossroads at the precise moment two people appear at the spot riding on one horse.[5] Transfer of the warts to the riders is not stated, but on the basis of similar rituals it may be assumed. Like dishrags and other fabrics, string may be used as the disposal agent. Where warts are involved knots are tied into the string—one knot for each wart—and the string disposed of by casting over the shoulder, as in Indiana and California.[6] In Illinois the string is thrown over the shoulder into a well, against which the sufferer had already backed up to position himself.[7]

Communication of the wart to various kinds of plants by rubbing the wart, and then disposing of the plant over the shoulder is a commonplace in all parts of the United States. Involved are potatoes, which are cut in half and rubbed on the wart. They are thrown over the shoulder in the usual way, as in Nova Scotia,[8] or they are tossed backwards into a pigsty, according to an Indiana account, without seeing which hog consumed the potato.[9] Beans, peas, and corn are commonly pressed into service, generally without impregnating them with blood. Other vegetables are also used. Once more, in rituals of this kind the attendant circumstances add to the magical character of the act. In New Hampshire, disposal of the bean over the shoulder is carried out on the full moon;[10] in Illinois a radish is bitten in half on the waning moon, rubbed on the wart and tossed over the shoulder;[11] and in Iowa a similar onion ritual is carried out at sunset.[12] Kernels of corn impregnated with blood which are tossed over the head or shoulder are often consumed by fowls in an obvious act of transference, as in North Carolina and Illinois.[13] A mole on the body is disposed of in the same way in Illinois by the patient's walking backward into a chicken yard, rubbing a kernel of corn on the mole and throwing it over the shoulder without looking back at the chickens in any way.[14] In the same state boils are pricked with a gooseberry thorn until the blood comes. The thorn is then tossed over the left shoulder.[15]

Notching sticks, or otherwise using them as measurements, involves more effort in the act of disposal. However, they are simply thrown over the shoulder, as in Alabama.[16] Throwing the limb over one's head at a crossroads and then walking away without looking back, as in North Carolina,[17] or throwing the stick over the left shoulder into the water from a bridge, as in Indiana,[18] are details that add unction and magical quality to disposal by the act of throwing. Disposal of the *Zwischenträger* into running water apparently goes back to Anglo-Saxon times.[19]

Animals and animal parts as well as plants are utilized in disposal rituals, and represent perhaps a deeper and more primitive level of thought. In North Carolina, for example, it was believed until the 1960's that if the first toad-frog that one saw in the spring were allowed to gaze upon a wart, and were then thrown over the sufferer's left shoulder, the creature would carry the wart with him as he hopped away.[20] Throwing a dead cat over a tree limb in the light of the full moon, as described in Texas, has sacrificial implications.[21] These notions of sacrifice come out more clearly in grisly rituals, reported from Maryland in 1925, and Illinois forty years later, whereby a chicken's head was cut off, the blood rubbed on the wart, and the head then tossed directly over the person's own head.[22] The rubbing of warts with beef,[23] and fat meat,[24] and then disposing of the intermediate agent by tossing it over the shoulder is well known; so is the use of bones for the same purpose. Noted in this latter connection are animal bones of various kinds.[25] In Illinois the ritual is carried out while eating at someone's place. The sufferer from warts steals the bone, goes to the door with his back to the yard, and then throws the bone over his shoulder as far as he can.[26] In a related cure two bones are rubbed together, and then disposed of in the usual way.[27] Chicken bones, including a so-called wishbone, are used in Illinois and Iowa.[28] The most unusual disposal agent connected with animals, perhaps, is a piece of dirt chipped away from the bottom of a horse's hoof. This is rubbed on the wart and tossed over the shoulder. When the first rain melted the dirt, it was believed that the wart would be gone.[29] The dry dung of a dog is used as a disposal agent in the same general way.[30]

Objects thrown over the shoulder include pebbles,[31] sometimes aggregating the number of warts one has, as in England.[32] In Illinois, for example, one stands with one's back to the water, and throws the pebble which has been rubbed on the wart into the water, and then returns home a different way.[33] In Utah a stone is used and tossed over the left shoulder, while in Texas a tiny white stone is found, kissed, then touched to the wart and discarded over the left shoulder without looking where the stone lands.[34] A piece of flint is used in North Carolina.[35] American Negroes in the South rub sand on the warts, and then toss the sand over the right shoulder.[36] Where employed as a disposal agent pins and needles are invariably used to prick the wart until it bleeds as a preliminary to being discarded.[37] A double transfer is seen in an Illinois entry where the pin is used to draw blood from the wart, which is then dripped on a white rock, which is then thrown over the shoulder.[38] Another double transfer involves pricking the wart, committing the blood to a piece of paper, and then running down the street at full speed. A wish is made while running, and the paper is thrown over the head while still running. You will lose the wart and gain your wish.[39] Stolen chalk,[40] a button,[41] and a match which has burned a wart are all discarded over the shoulder.[42] Miscellaneous objects pressed into service as disposal objects are often picked up at the time of the new moon. One looks at the new moon, stoops down and picks up whatever is underfoot. This is then rubbed on the wart and tossed over the left shoulder, as in Illinois.[43] In Kentucky, unknown material is simply picked up, rubbed on the wart nine times before being discarded over the right shoulder.[44] Secrecy is enjoined. Sometimes one walks backward ten steps before disposing of the object on which the foot rested.[45]

The disposal of coins—pennies usually—which have been rubbed on the wart takes place in prescribed fashion. The wart is either lost with the coin, as in examples from such widely separated places as New York, Iowa and Texas,[46] or it is transferred to the person who unwittingly picks up the penny, as in Nova Scotia, Maryland, and North Carolina, among other places.[47] In Pennsylvania less than twenty-five years ago a pow-wow doctor rubbed a penny on a corncob three times and threw the corncob over his shoulder, after which he mumbled some words while stroking the wart with the coin.[48]

Disposal over the head is much less common than over the shoulder. In Illinois the first tooth extracted is thrown over the head to guard against decayed teeth in the future.[49] Radbill, the authority on pediatric folklore, says that a common way to insure a good sound tooth to replace the one that had fallen out was to go behind the stove, throw the tooth over your head, and say, "mouse give me your iron tooth, I will give you my bone tooth," after which the teeth were to remain strong.[50] European disposal rituals likewise often look to the quality of the replacement tooth.[51] Styes were cast off, either by throwing a handful of sand over one's head, as in North Carolina,[52] or by throwing a pail of swill over your head without wetting yourself, as in Waterloo County, Ontario.[53] Magical transference of smallpox to a cat, by rubbing the tongue of a young heifer on the sores, and then throwing the tongue over one's head is reported from North Carolina.[54] A divestment ritual, totally unrelated to folk medicine, involves the youngest carpenter's apprentice throwing his axe over his head after having helped to construct a gallows. The axe was "retired" as it were, and could not be used henceforth.[55] The formal act of separation presumably releases the young artisan from blood guilt resulting from the use to which the gallows would be put.

Throwing objects over the roof or over the house required greater exertion of course and may therefore have involved somewhat heightened ritualistic importance. Once more, divestment is the principal idea, and the custom seems to be more prevalent in the areas of folk medicine than in other categories of folklore. In early Roman history, as Pliny reports, it was customary at the time of childbirth to throw a stone or a missile over the house to facilitate the delivery of the child. The implement, however, must have killed with one stroke, a human, a boar, and a bear. A light cavalry spear pulled from the human body would also suffice.[56] A positive effect is achieved, not divestment in the usual sense, but an act of separation, nevertheless, in which the mother is delivered of the child.

Other casting off rituals involving disposal by throwing the unwanted object, or a symbolic representation of it, over the roof of a house, or over a wall, are seen in a practice from Kentucky where a broken nail from a stumped toe is placed in a rag with two stones (to give weight for the toss?) and then thrown over the house.[57] A double transfer—three drops of blood on a brick, and then the throwing of the brick over the house—is reported for the cure of nosebleed in Illinois.[58] A cast tooth is not only tossed over the shoulder, as we have already seen, but in some places over the house as well. In Illinois a wish is made at the same time.[59] Essentially positive in character, and not involving divestment, are two Illinois practices having to do with moving from one house to another. The first prescribes throwing a broom over the house for luck before entering the new home for the first time.[60] The intent of the second custom is less clear: "A broom laid on the moving-van causes misfortune; let someone unrelated to the family carry the broom to the new house and throw it over the gate for luck."[61]

In the field of animal husbandry one notes a Tennessee practice with regard to the raising of baby chicks. To have good luck with them, the hatched eggshells are thrown over the housetop.[62] This can be viewed as a divestment ritual, I suppose, and may be construed as a way of progressing from one stage to another by removing impediments held over from the earlier stage of development. I have a feeling, however, that the explanation is not all that simple, as I shall set forth in the final three paragraphs of this short article reasons why one should search for deeper connections.

In German popular tradition a small egg contained in a membranous sack without a shell, and supposed to be the last egg to be produced by a hen in the laying season, is associated with the wind (hence the name *Windei*); it is also connected with witches and the nether powers.[63] So that it will not attract a flash of lightning to the house and otherwise cause misfortune such an egg is magically disposed of by throwing it over the roof of the house backwards.[64] In the South Slavic lands when a hen crows—itself a reversal of nature and a sign of great foreboding for the fowl's owner—the bird is thrown over the roof of the house. Sometimes it is tied up in a sack and buried (alive?) where it lands.[65]

The magical character of throwing an object over the roof on the house is perhaps best seen in Gypsy folk medical customs from Hungary. In Debrecen, for example, when a child suffers from "changing sickness" his clothing is torn off and cut with a scissors. It is then boiled in a new pot and thrown over the roof of the house. On a Tuesday, Friday, or Saturday, the clothing is buried at the crossroads, along with the pot and the water. A person removing this will, by way of warning, catch the disease.

In Panyola in the same country, the clothing is not only removed and thrown over the house, but the child is given a new name.[66] This is done, no doubt, to protect him from the pursuing forces that inflict disease. Finally, in Iran there is a ritual for the cure of croup and whooping cough, common childhood maladies. A black rag doll is taken and placed under the child's pillow, and a piece of black money placed under each corner of the mattress. After he has slept on these, money is given to the poor in order to attain merit. The doll is then thrown over a wall into the courtyard of an Armenian or a Jewish family. The whooping cough, which has gone into the doll, will go into the child that has picked it up, and the other child will recover.[67]

As we have seen, disposal and transference figure in many of the cures and other kinds of practices treated in this brief survey. Behind many of them are ideas associated with witchcraft and magic. The problem obviously is involved enough to invite a more detailed study of the subject than I have been able to engage in for the purposes of this paper. The difficulty with comparative studies of this kind is the fact that background information is lacking. Detailed studies of black dolls, of black money, of the utilization of eggs in witchcraft and other magical practices, of brooms and witchcraft—all these approaches would have to be employed to enable one to distinguish between a simple toss of something over the shoulder and a real ritual divestment of a besetting evil force. More taxonomic studies are needed to place vital information in the hand of the investigator for the endless correlations that would be necessary before one could establish convincing conjunctures and integral relationships. Better contextual data at every stage would be helpful, but these, unfortunately, are rarely available, and workers committed to the importance of contextual studies often lack the broad factual information to connect matters that at first blush appear to have only the most tenuous connections.

NOTES

1. Harry M. Hyatt, *Folk-Lore from Adams County, Illinois* (2nd ed., New York: *Memoirs of the Alma Egan Hyatt Foundation,* 1965), p. 305, No. 6642. (Unless otherwise stated, all references are to the 2nd edition of Hyatt.)

2. Fletcher Bascom Dresslar, *Superstition and Education* (Berkeley, California: *University of California Publications in Education*, Vol. 5, 1907), p. 109.

3. Hyatt, p. 306, No. 6648.

4. *Journal of American Folklore,* 44 (1931), 395, No. 12.

5. *Popular Beliefs and Superstitions from North Carolina,* ed. Wayland D. Hand, as Vols. VI–VII of the *Frank C. Brown Collection of North Carolina Folklore* (7 vols., Durham, North Carolina, 1952–1964), VI, 334, No. 2582. (Hereinafter cited: *Brown Coll.*)

6. W. Edson Richmond and Elva Van Winkle, *"Is There a Doctor in the House?" Indiana History Bulletin,* 35 (1958), p. 134, Nos. 302 (over the head), 305 (over the left shoulder); Dresslar, p. 110 (right shoulder).

7. Hyatt, p. 322, No. 6964.

8. Helen Creighton, *Bluenose Magic: Popular Beliefs and Superstitions in Nova Scotia* (Toronto, 1968), p. 236, No. 391.

9. Unpublished entry.

10. Mrs. M. P. Gore and Mrs. G. E. Speare, *New Hampshire Folk Tales* (Plymouth, New Hampshire, 1933), p. 216.

11. Hyatt, p. 309, No. 6713.

12. Earl J. Stout, *Folklore from Iowa* (*Memoirs of the American Folklore Society,* No. 29, New York, 1936), p. 178, No. 782.

13. *Brown Coll.,* VI, 325, No. 2507 (cast over the right shoulder to a chicken); Hyatt, p. 300, No. 6548 (thrown over the head to a white rooster).

14. Hyatt, p. 332, No. 7163.

15. *Ibid.,* p. 287, No. 6278.

16. Ray B. Browne, *Popular Beliefs and Practices from Alabama* (*Folklore Studies,* Vol. 9, Berkeley and Los Angeles, 1958), p. 115, No. 2008.

17. *Brown Coll.,* VI, 340, No. 2619.

18. *Ibid.,* VI, 341, No. 2629.

19. Felix Grendon, *"The Anglo-Saxon Charms," Journal of American Folklore,* 22 (1909), 131.

20. *North Carolina Folklore,* 12: 1 (1964), 8.

21. John Q. Anderson, *"Magical Transference of Disease in Texas Folk Medicine," Western Folklore,* 27 (1968), 195.

22. Annie Weston Whitney and Caroline Canfield Bullock, *Folk-Lore from Maryland* (*Memoirs of the American Folklore Society,* Vol. 18, New York, 1927), p. 85, No. 1739; Hyatt, p. 297, No. 6488.

23. *Western Folklore,* 24 (1965), 34.

24. Pauline Monette Black, *Nebraska Folk Cures* (*University of Nebraska Studies in Language, Literature, and Criticism,* No. 15, Lincoln, Nebraska, 1935), p. 26, No. 23; Hyatt, p. 308, No. 6692.

25. *Brown Coll.,* VI, 315, No. 2444; Hyatt, p. 315, No. 6820; *Publications of the Texas Folklore Society,* Vol. 5 (1926), 125.

26. Hyatt, p. 296, No. 6462.

27. *Ibid.,* No. 6463.

28. Hyatt, p. 297, No. 6489; Stout, p. 177, No. 772.

29. Hyatt, p. 307, No. 6674.

30. *Ibid.,* p. 306, No. 6653.

31. Hyatt, p. 313, Nos. 6781–6783.

32. Ella Mary Leather, *Folk-Lore of Herefordshire* (Hereford and London, 1912), pp. 83–84 (thrown over the shoulder where four roads meet); Ruth L. Tongue, *Somerset Folklore* (*Publications of the Folklore Society*, Vol. 114 [1965]), p. 43.

33. Hyatt, p. 313, No. 6784.

34. John Q. Anderson, *Texas Folk Medicine: 1,333 Cures, Remedies, Preventives & Health Practices* (Austin, Texas, 1970), p. 81.

35. *Brown Coll.,* VI, 342, No. 2633.

36. Newbell Niles Puckett, *Folk Beliefs of the Southern Negro* (Chapel Hill, North Carolina, 1926), p. 381.

37. *Brown Coll.*, VI, 345, Nos. 2660–2661; Hyatt, p. 314, No. 6806.

38. Hyatt, p. 310, No. 6728.

39. Hyatt, p. 312, No. 6763.

40. Emelyn E. Gardner, *Folklore of the Schoharie Hills New York* (Ann Arbor, Michigan, 1937), p. 271, No. 59.

41. Hyatt, p. 297, No. 6475.

42. Stout, p. 178, No. 780.

43. Hyatt, p. 309, No. 6709.

44. Elza W. Fentress, *Superstitions of Grayson County, Kentucky* (M.A. Thesis, Western State Teachers College, Bowling Green, Kentucky, 1934, unpub.), p. 62.

45. Daniel Lindsey Thomas and Lucy Blaney Thomas, *Kentucky Superstitions* (Princeton, New Jersey, 1920), p. 125, No. 1481.

46. *New York Folklore Quarterly*, 3 (1947), 256; Stout, p. 177, No. 768; *Publications of the Texas Folklore Society,* Vol. 30 (1961), p. 70.

47. Richard S. Tallman, *Belief and Legend from Northern Kings County, Nova Scotia* (Canning, Kings County, Nova Scotia, 1969, unpub.), p. 41; George Carey, *An Introductory Guide to Maryland Folklore and Folklife* (Bethesda, Maryland, 1970), p. 27; *Brown Coll.*, VI, 348, No. 2685.

48. *Pennsylvania Dutchman,* Vol. 3, No. 2, May 15, 1951, p. 3.

49. Harry Middleton Hyatt, *Folk-Lore from Adams County, Illinois* (*Memoirs of the Alma Egan Hyatt Foundation,* New York, 1935), p. 146, No. 3049.

50. Samuel X. Radbill, *"The Folklore of Teething,"* *Keystone Folklore Quarterly,* 9 (1964), 137.

51. Adolf Wuttke, *Der deutsche Volksaberglaube der Gegenwart* (3 ed. Elard Hugo Meyer, Berlin, 1900), p. 351; Josef Cizmar, *Lidové lékarství v Ceskoslovensku* (2 vols., Brno, 1946), I, 61.

52. *Brown Coll.,* VI, 296, No. 2293.

53. W. J. Wintemberg, *Folk-Lore of Waterloo County, Ontario* (*National Museum of Canada, Bull.* No. 116, 1950), p. 14.

54. *Brown Coll.,* VI, 275, No. 2116.

55. Werner Danckert, *Unehrliche Leute: Die verfemten Berufe* (Bern und München, 1963), p. 44.

56. Pliny, *Natural History,* XXVIII, vi, 33–34.

57. Thomas and Thomas, p. 109, No. 1269.

58. Hyatt, p. 208, No. 4774.

59. Hyatt, 1 ed., p. 324, No. 6628.

60. Hyatt, p. 508, No. 11285.

61. *Ibid.,* No. 11273.

62. *Western Folklore,* 15 (1956), 133.

63. Eduard von Hoffmann-Krayer and Hanns Bächtold-Stäubli, *Handwörterbuch des deutschen Aberglaubens* (10 vols., Leipzig and Berlin, 1927–1942), IX, 658–659.

64. *Ibid.*, II, 601.

65. P. Kemp, *Healing Ritual: Studies in the Technique and Tradition of the Southern Slavs* (London, 1935), pp. 125–126.

66. Bela Gunda, *"Gypsy Medical Folklore in Hungary,"* *Journal of American Folklore,* 73 (1962), 133.

67. Bess Allen Donaldson, *Wild Rue* (London, 1938), p. 33.

11

"'Passing Through'': Folk Medical Magic and Symbolism*

I. TREES, BUSHES, VINES, EARTH

Folk medical magic often involves both pagan and Christian elements, and ancient medical beliefs and customs still have not wholly disappeared from the civilized community. Among the most tenacious early folk medical practices to have lived on into the twentieth century is the primitive custom of pulling patients through or passing them through holes in trees, stones, or in the earth, or moving them, or causing them to walk, crawl, or creep through a variety of natural or man-made apertures for the curing of disease.[1]

In the present paper I propose to sketch the main outlines of this curious folk medical ritual, and particularly to assemble for the first time American folk medical literature on a practice that is almost world-wide. First of all, I shall treat passing through clefts in trees, whether natural or man-made, and crawling beneath rerooted brambles and other kinds of bushes—folk medical procedures which are still carried out, or were, until recently, all over Europe and in America. Then we can examine perhaps an even more primitive kind of ritual, namely, the passing of patients beneath holes in the earth made with upturned sods—a curative ritual that has lingered on in Scandinavia and elsewhere. A third main category of magical divestment of

*This article originally appeared in the *Proceedings of the American Philosophical Society,* 112 (1968), 379-402. Permission to reprint has been given by the editors and by the American Philosophical Society.

diseases, namely, crawling through holes in stones is found from the Orient to the Middle East, and in scattered parts of Europe, mainly in France and Ireland. Neither of these last two practices seems to be known in the Americas.

However, the act of crawling under the bellies of animals, principally donkeys, is known in the United States, as is the passing under table legs, through the rungs of chairs, ladders, and other man-made objects. A common denominator running through all of these folk medical practices is the magical divestment of disease, and the securing of health. Theories of how these ends are accomplished will be taken up at the end of the paper after we have had opportunity to see a wide variety of examples and to gain some notion of the underlying ideas.

In view of an almost universal worship of trees,[2] it is not difficult to imagine the awe and wonderment which natural clefts in trees evoked among their votaries. The rarity of these trees added to their value and esteem, not only for curative measures, but also for fertility practices,[3] and for a variety of other magical offices. In France such a tree was known as an *arbre à trou* or an *arbre fourchu*;[4] in Germany, as a *Zwieselbaum,* i.e., a tree with two parts, or a tree with a hole in it;[5] in Sweden, a *smöjträ* (figs. 1, 2), a dialectal form which some authorities associate with a verb stem *smöj*—meaning "to adhere to, or to cuddle," as well as "to put into";[6] in Denmark, a *kludetræ.*[7] Where two saplings have sprouted together, separated, and then rejoined, one speaks in the Swedish-speaking part of Finland as a *vålbundet trä.*[8] Such an oak in the Ardennes forest of France is known as *le chéne à deux pattes,*[9] but there is, apparently, no special name for trees of this kind in Spain.[10] Such trees are known in England, and there was a locally famous Shrew Ash at Richmond, in Surrey, also known as the Sheen Tree, which was much used at the middle of the last century for the curing of infantile ailments.[11] Such trees are referred to in America, and there appears to have been a well-known one in Burlington County, New Jersey, at the end of the last century.[12] Because of the unusualness of natural clefts in tree trunks or interlaced branches (fig. 5) that fuse into natural loops and apertures they are thought to possess supernatural power,[13] among other things, from the fact that fairy folk were thought to pass through them, as Zachariae has pointed out.[14] Since these elfin creatures moved through these holes, and since the purloining of milk from cows in the field was often laid at their door, it becomes clear why cows were milked through these "elf-holes" (*Elfenlöcher*) in branches when their milk production fell off.[15] Natural loops, or other smaller holes formed by misshapen branches, were often removed from trees and used as portable hoops (figs. 6, 7).[16] Pulling through the fork of a tree, as in an Illinois cure for baby's colic,[17] though derivative of the older idea, does not fully come under our purview. Passing under windfallen trees, likewise, is only an extension of the original idea.[18]

Because of the rarity of trees with natural clefts, it was a natural step, apparently, to split saplings and use them for curative purposes.[19] In Vermont and New Hampshire, and elsewhere in New England, for example, a small child with hernia was drawn through a split in a small tree, after which the halves were brought together again. If the tree healed properly, so would the rupture.[20] Two other cures of hernia by pulling through trees of unspecified variety—both of them from Romance countries—add interesting details of the ritual, including the employment of name magic. In Portugal the child is passed three times through a reed or sapling split for the purpose. This rite must be performed at midnight on St. John's Eve, by three men named John, while three women, each named Mary, spin, each with her own spindle, on one and the same distaff. The dialogue runs: "What are ye spinning, o ye Marys? Silken thread / To heal the reed where passed the ruptured child." Thereafter, as the plant heals, so should the injury to the child.[21] In Galicia, congenital hernia, or hernia caused by a blow or too much crying, is cured by cutting a tree longitudinally, and passing the child through the fissure nine times. This must be done by a man named Juan and a woman named Maria. The trunk is bound with straws, and if it heals properly the rupture is cured.[22]

Ash trees and oak trees, however, are the principal species employed for the curing, not only of hernia and rickets, but of infantile ailments generally. Gilbert White, in his *Natural History of Selborne* (1853), describes very fully the passing of children through trees, and the post-operative treatment of the tree. He says (p. 144):

> In a farmyard near the middle of this village stands, at this day, a row of pollard ashes, which by the seams and long cicatrices down their sides, manifestly show that, in former times, they have been cleft asunder. These trees, when young and flexible were severed and held open by wedges, while ruptured children, stripped naked, were pushed through the apertures, under the persuasion that, by such a process, the poor babes would be cured of their infirmity. As

> soon as the operation was over, the tree, in the suffering part, was plastered with loam, and carefully swathed up. If the parts coalesced and soldered together, as usually fell out, where the feat was performed with any adroitness at all, the party was cured. But where the cleft continued to gape, the operation, it was supposed, would prove ineffectual. . . .[23]

In some places in England the so-called "maiden ash" was split and pressed into service for this exacting office. A "maiden ash" was a tree grown from its own seed and never touched with a knife.[24] In Herefordshire a maiden ash was split and a child with a rupture was passed through, from the father's hands, into another man's, nine times. The father said, "The Lord giveth," and the other man replied, "The Lord receiveth." The tree was then bound up, and if it grew together the patient would recover.[25]

Whereas the ash appears to have been the favorite tree in England for cures involving the ritual of passing through,[26] the oak was more sought after on the continent, particularly in Scandinavia, Germany, and France.[27] The procedures, of course, are the same, and many of the attendant circumstances as well, as the following examples will show: From a recipe book at the end of the seventeenth century in Montbeliard, France: For a child suffering with hernia, take it to a small oak before sunrise, split the tree, and pass the child through three times, saying every time, "In the name of the Father, Son, and Holy Ghost."[28] In the Basque country a child with hernia is passed nude through the opening of an oak split down the middle on the Eve of St. John. Two brothers pass the child back and forth as the chimes of midnight sound, one saying, "Take, brother," and the other saying, "Give him to me, brother." After he is passed back with the same words repeated, his shirt is left hanging in the tree. When it rots, the two portions of the tree are bound back together.[29] In Calabria the treatment for hernia involves passing the patient through a split oak on St. John's Day, three times or seven times.[30] In Galicia we encounter the use of the split oak tree for hernia, and the binding up of the split halves of the tree afterward, with the usual prognosis. The only difference in this Spanish version is that the godmother and godfather pass the child through, while reciting a verbal charm.[31] In Wehlau, Province of Prussia, boys with a swelling of the scrotum are pulled three times through an oak of an arm's thickness that has been split. The tree is then bound up.[32] A cure for an enlarged navel in North Carolina contains a wealth of detail: When a baby has an enlarged navel, wedge open a white oak tree and pull him through. If the tree goes back together and lives, the baby will live. If it doesn't, the baby will die, too. On putting a child through a tree, first observe that it must be early in the spring before the tree begins to vegetate; secondly, that the tree must be split as near east and west as it can. Thirdly, it must be done as the sun is rising. Fourthly, the child must be stripped quite naked; fifthly, it must be put through the tree feet foremost; sixthly, it must be turned around with the sun, and observe that it must be put through three times; and next that you must be careful to close the tree in a proper manner and bind it up close.[33] One final item, lacking in detail though it is, is cited from Nova Scotia: If a child has fits, we would split an oak tree and put the child in it. If the oak tree grew, the child would get better, but if not, the child would die.[34]

Other hardwood trees used include a "standing" shellbark hickory in Clark County, Indiana,[35] and a "maiden" dogwood in Newfoundland, a species which grows alone and never blossoms. In this latter case the operation must be performed before sunrise on May 1 in the presence of the parents of the ruptured child.[36] Elms are frequently used in Italy mainly because the species grows plentifully there.[37] Of soft woods, the willow is most often used, not so much for passing through a split in the sapling itself,[38] but for the fashioning of portable hoops. The use of holly is most unusual.[39] Along the Rhine, pitted fruit trees—plum, peach, apricot, cherry—are recommended.[40] The use of a cherry tree against fascination is reported from Galicia. The mother ties the thumbs and toes together with a ribbon, and then sets out after midnight to find a person on the road who will help her split a cherry tree at dawn and assist in passing the child through it.[41] Apple trees are used in Poland for the cure of moonstruck children, i.e., children who have slept so the moon could shine on their faces. The office must be performed by two virgins, the eldest children in their respective families.[42]

More basic and primitive perhaps than pulling through a tree, whether through natural or man-made clefts, is the pulling or creeping under the roots of trees for the curing of disease.[43] Contact with the earth itself, as we shall see later in the discussion of crawling through holes in the earth, adds a measure of cultic primitiveness in view of notions about Mother Earth and her life-giving and life-sustaining properties. In the latter half of the nineteenth century in Serbia, at times of epidemic, villagers at Setonje sought "to lock up misfortune" by extinguishing the fires, after which the old women circled the village three times, and two men dug a passage under the root of an oak tree. In the dead of night a fire was rekindled by rubbing lime sticks together, and then everyone crept through the tunnel one by one, being marked with a cross on the shoulder by a stick charred in the fire.[44] In Bulgaria children with whooping cough crawled beneath the roots of the willow tree, after the earth had been scraped away.[45] In Pontevedra, Spain, and in the Erzgebirge in Germany, children with rickets were passed under the roots of trees.[46] In France a child with a hernia was brought under an oak tree, while women with the secret of curing the ailment danced around the tree saying prayers.[47]

Curing by crawling under brambles, briars, and other kinds of bushes whose drooping canes reroot to form a natural arch is widespread in Europe, America, and elsewhere.[48] Stripping and scarification, common in the procedure where thorny bushes are involved, oddly enough, are rarely mentioned. Radbill, quoting an earlier authority, says that "crawling under a bramble bush will scrape off the demons of whooping cough, rheumatism, boils, and other diseases in several districts of England."[49] In this connection, also, one should not lose sight of the fact that the patient comes into contact with the earth, which may impart life, strength, and vitality, as well as absorb corruption. On this interesting aspect of creeping through, one should note the observation of Wilfrid Bonser that the purpose of the ritual was to transfer the malady to the earth, while the thorns were supposed to prevent the disease from following.[50]

Another odd fact in connection with crawling through and creeping through is the circumstance that hernia and rickets, the two most common ailments for which children and others were passed through trees, are little treated in curative processes involving bushes.[51] On second thought, one can see how stout young saplings, symbolically at least, would better serve for bone disorders of all kinds as well as for permanent rejoining of ruptured parts.

Whooping cough is, or was, widely treated by the aforesaid method in England,[52] but this cure seems little known in the United States, except where brambles are considered together with briars and berry fruit bushes. In Maryland patients with whooping cough were dragged through a gooseberry bush or a bramble, both ends of which were growing in the ground.[53] Before treating other diseases by crawling through brambles, let us consider a Devonshire custom, where the operators give a verbal adjuration as the child is passed through the bramble, namely, "In bramble, out cough, / Here I leave the whooping cough."[54]

In Belgium and Luxembourg a child that is slow in learning to walk is made to crawl under a rerooted bramble, in silence, on Friday.[55] Boils were cured by the patient's passing under a bramble nine times,[56] while other skin disorders, such as pimples and blackheads, or pinsoles, can be cured in the same way. It is more advantageous if the arched bramble extends into two proprietors' lands. As in cures involving split trees, movement is from east to west, i.e., sunwise.[57] This custom has been transplanted to Texas, where blackheads are made to disappear by the same method, except that there is no mention of brambles extending onto a neighbor's property.[58] In some parts of England rheumatism was treated by passing through brambles.[59] In the Pennsylvania German country, liver-grown children were passed underneath a bramble that had struck root at the tip.[60] Considerable theoretical interest attaches to a cure of epileptic children in Dorsetshire, where youngsters were pulled through a prickly bramble bush, in the thought that the evil spirit could not follow, as it was filtered out and left behind.[61] Just as natural loops of boughs were removed from the tree and used as a sort of portable *arbre à trou,* so likewise, rerooted brambles were removed from their original sites and put to use elsewhere. In Brittany, for example, rerooted brambles were placed above stable doors to protect the stock from fairy influences and witchcraft.[62]

Crawling through rerooted briars involves the same general procedures that we have seen above for brambles, but there is added detail and the range of diseases is somewhat broadened. As in the case of brambles, briars extending onto adjoining property are also regarded as being more efficacious for crawling through than otherwise.[63] In a whooping cough cure from Herefordshire, the Lord's Prayer is recited while the patient is passed under the briar nine times. The patient must meanwhile eat bread and butter, and then must give some to a bird. As the bird dies, the cough is cured.[64] In a North Carolina cure for whooping cough, the patient is placed under the briar, rather than passed through it.[65] Diseases other than whooping cough for which patients were made to crawl through briars, or were passed through, in the United States, include the common cough,[66] sore throat,[67] and a childhood disease known as *abnemmes,* a sort of wasting sickness.[68] The two Pennsylvania scholars saw a symbolic rebirth in this act. Other nonfruitbearing bushes mentioned in these crawling-through rituals include prickly gorse,[69] elder bush,[70] and white-thorn trees.[71]

Berry fruit bushes constitute a final category of rerooted brambles that claim our attention. Blackberry bushes are used for magical curative practices in Germanic, Gallic, and Celtic countries, and no doubt elsewhere.[72] As in the case of briars and non-fruitbearing brambles, blackberry bushes are much used for crawling through and passing under for the cure of whooping cough, particularly in the United States.[73] No new details are to be noted in the American examples, except that silence was enjoined in a prescription contained in John George Hohman's *Long Lost Friend* of 1820.[74] A North Carolina practice is regular in every way,[75] but the procedure is varied in Maryland to include crawling through three times in each direction. This is followed by a drink of tea made from the roots of the bush.[76] A common cough is treated in Germany by crawling through a blackberry bush.[77] In areas as widely separated as Spain and the middle of the United States (Illinois), passing a child through a rerooted blackberry bush was practiced for the related childhood diseases of croup and colic.[78] Children having a difficult time learning to walk were made to crawl through these bushes in Germany.[79] Passing through a blackberry bush was practiced for jaundice in Montenegro, following an elaborate measuring ritual.[80] Of great historical importance, is the noting of this custom for Anglo-Saxon England in the curing of diarrhea.[81] Crawling through blackberry bushes was indulged for magical ailments such as nightmare (Hungary),[82] and was efficacious in combating magic and conjury of other kinds (Germany).[83] In Germany, also, married couples, alienated through witchcraft, could repair their difficulty by crawling through a rerooted blackberry bush.[84] In northwestern Europe rerooted blackberry brambles were cut off and fashioned into amulets for affixing to the bridles of horses.[85]

Raspberry canes stand more erect than blackberry stalks; hence rerooting is not so often encountered. The three examples cited are all from the United States, and they all involve whooping cough. All are completely typical.[86]

The tying of loops within brambles and bushes, rather than by natural rerooting is little known. Separation in the branches or canes, bottom as well as top, is effected by tying in a convenient loop. In Bulgaria, for example, a person suffering from scrofula crawls through such a man-made aperture three times, hangs his clothes on the vines as a sacrifice after the ordeal, and then, on the way home, crawls through a plowshare held high enough to let him pass through.[87]

The splitting of a single stalk of a bush, in the manner of the splitting of a sapling, is apparently little known. However, in the Homoljski district of Yugoslavia a cane of a wild rose bush is split amid the most elaborate rituals by a seeress, who, on the eve of a feast day, locates the bush which must have sprouted that year, and upon which the eyes of no other human have as yet fallen. Scattering ashes and bread at the roots of the bush she returns before dawn the next morning with a "redeemer," and with the patient. After elaborate preparations involving a jar of water drawn at midnight, a bunch of basil, incense, a censer, chains, and two wax candles, the longest branch of the bush is chosen and split, being secured with red thread. The patient is bound with chains, and the redeemer, who is an adopted brother, responds to the seeress' demand, "Accept God and St. John and release the living slave from the dead grave," by unfettering the sick person. The healer holds the loop over the sick person and the redeemer, and then the redeemer draws the patient through the hoop with his right hand. For recovery, it is necessary that the patient come through the hoop without touching it with his head.[88]

The use of natural loops formed by the boughs of trees,[89] the intertwinings of more than one branch, and the fashioning of hoops, wreathes, or garlands of vines or branches, is an extension of the idea of a portable *smöjträ,* or *smöjning,* as discussed above. The simplest form of these loops is a branch pulled low from a tree to form a loop through which a sick child can be pulled.[90] The most elaborate involve misshapen and freakish growths, or tangles, known in Germany as a *Hexenschlinge,* "witch's loop."[91] In Scandinavia these intertwined boughs are called "elf-bores" (*Elfenlöcher*), and women in labor are forced through them, no doubt to help secure supernatural aid in the delivery.[92]

The simplest kind of hoop, of course, could be made from the boughs of a willow, and the use of this tree for the purpose mentioned is attested from such widely separated areas as Ireland, Spain (Galicia), and Bosnia.[93] In the last-named country, the willow hoop was employed to combat fever, and was pulled over the head of the victim and drawn off at his feet. Basically, this constitutes a sort of "stripping," for the loop traverses the whole length of the body, as in crawling through, or in passing through. Scottish Highlanders forced sheep and lambs through rowan hoops at Beltane (May 1) and All Saints (Nov. 1).[94]

Wreaths and garlands likely involved a hoop made up of multiple strands of vines or boughs, or even of less sturdy materials such as straw. Wreaths of woodbine, or "girths" of woodbine, as they were known, were used for various ailments in Scotland in the sixteenth century. These were drawn over the body and let down over the patient from head to feet.[95] In western Finland a child suffering from rickets is pulled through a stalk of straw bound into a wreath in the open field.[96] In Scotland, at Wigton, a sick child was passed through a flaming hoop held by two women, as the child's mother looked on.[97] The whole matter of accompanying lustrations, including the use of fire as well as water, should be studied in connection with passing-through ceremonies. Kemp emphasizes these elements in her study of South Slavic curative rituals, but other writers have only occasionally noted them. Use of wreaths and hoops by primitive peoples is noted in Hovorka and Kronfeld, and in the *Golden Bough.*[98] These practices involve both preventive measures, as well as symbolic separation rituals. The passing of the hoops and wreaths over the body, from head to feet, is in many cases identical with rituals described for nonprimitive cultures.

From some points of view, creeping through holes in the earth (fig. 8) represents the most primitive stage of the whole complex of rituals having to do with pulling through.[99] Just as the earth nurtures trees, and all manner of plant life, so also do stones rest in her bosom. Man himself, and the animal creation, too, derive their life and strength from the earthy element. This attachment to Mother Earth is strong among people the world over, as witness the almost universal cultic devotion to *Gaea mater,* not merely among primitives, but among many sophisticates in religion, philosophy, psychology, and historians of the mental and spiritual life of mankind. In a folk medical sense, this devotion simply meant go "under the earth" to be healed.[100] Pulling through holes in snowdrifts represents a related idea, but this practice is limited, so far as I know, to Finland, where a child creeps three times through a snowdrift to cure rickets.[101]

The earliest history in Europe of the ritual of creeping through a hole in the earth, *trou de la terra,* is not known, but by the seventh century, A.D., Theodore Archbishop of Canterbury, prescribed a penance of bread and water for eleven days, for a parent who had passed his child through a hole in the ground and closed it from behind with thorns.[102] That this custom was practiced on the continent, too, is seen from a later attempt on the part of the church to combat what it regarded as a heathen practice. Burchard, Bishop of Worms, who died in 1025, A.D., imposed a penance on women who pulled squalling babes through holes in the earth.[103] Prescriptions against passing the sick, particularly children, through trees by St. Eloi, Bishop of Noyon in the sixth century, also applied, we are told, to the practice of pulling them through holes in the ground.[104] Even though *per terram foratam* was perhaps widely known in the early centuries of the Christian era, or perhaps before, in more recent times it seems to have been mainly remembered as something that was once practiced.[105] In the British Isles, for example, where there was a belief in the translocation of disease from the victim to the ground, it was said that "they pull their children through the earth and thus commit themselves and their children to the devil."[106] Though pulling through stones is still known in Cornwall, pulling through the earth belongs to an earlier time and way of thought.[107] The ancient practice seems to have hung on tenaciously only in the Scandinavian north,[108] and in the Baltic States, where it is known as *jorddragning,* "drawing or pulling through the earth." As noted earlier, this ancient custom is not found in the Anglo-American tradition in the United States, nor in folk materials derived from Europe or parts of Africa and Asia where high cultures developed.

Passing-through rituals in the earth usually involved grassy terrain, where sod could be cut, piled, and arched to make a passageway. Natural apertures of the sort required for the ritual are difficult to conceive, and, if they existed at all, are not reported in the literature. (Natural arches in rock formations, of course, are a different matter, and they will be treated later.) In keeping with the supernatural character of the magico-religious office, such holes in the earth were usually made in cemeteries.[109] They were also carried out at other localities known for numinous or supernatural activity, such as forks in the road,[110] a crossroads, or at property boundaries.[111] Illustrative of a ritual carried out where fields abut is a Danish ritual to cure a child, blighted by the glance of a whore, *skjögesét,* as the saying goes. The only way to relieve such a child of the evil effects was to cut sods at a place where four pieces of property came together. The child was then passed through three times amid silence.[112] Holes dug by the roadside, also, had the mystical benefit of a solitary place visited only by wayfarers.[113] Meadowland was also chosen for much the same reason.[114]

Rickets was treated by the patient's crawling under the earth, or being pulled through it;[115] likewise rupture, malformation, and other maladies of childhood. Included were treatments for various kinds of scurvy or rachitic conditions, induced by seeing or touching a corpse (*likskerfva*), seeing or coming into contact with harlots (*horskerfva*), or a sort of scurvy connected somehow with the earth itself, *jordskerfva.* For this last-named condition a hole was dug under the grass, and a child was pulled through three times on a Thursday morning before sunrise at a field boundary.[116] A child or a person suffering from any one of these ailments, nothing else availing, should have his body linen drawn through the loop of a church key.[117]

Just as natural loops in trees were detached and made into portable hoops for curing the sick, so also were sods cut from greensward and moved into houses for curing rituals. In Denmark the curing of rickets was undertaken on three successive Thursday nights, wherein a sod was cut from the juncture of three lanes, and placed on the rungs of a stool which had been turned upside down. The child was then pulled under the rungs, and the sod taken back and planted at the spot from which it was cut.[118] Strict silence was observed throughout the ceremony. A variant from western Jutland involves the victim's father in the spading of a large sod from a cemetery at midnight on Thursday. Within the large sod a hole is then cut large enough to permit the child to pass through. This is thereupon taken home, with the father being careful not to greet anyone or to talk with anyone on the way. After the child is passed through the sod three times from right to left, the father returns the sod to the cemetery and replaces it exactly as taken. If the grass sprouted and throve, it was a sign that the child would get well; however, if it withered, it was up with the child, and there was no hope.[119] In another part of the country, the sod was to be fetched at sundown. In comparing this ritual with the use of a portable *smöjning,* it will be noted that no attempt is ever made to replace the wooden hoop. If a comparison needs to be made, it should rather be an equation of the replaced sod with the split tree which is bound up again. In either case, the prognosis for the child rests on what happens to the curative agent. Involved ultimately in this consideration, of course, is the mystical connection between the life of the child, and the soul of the child, with Mother Earth herself, or with a tree that is nurtured at her breast.

II. STONES, ANIMALS, VESTMENTS, SHRINES, OBJECTS. THEORIES OF "PASSING THROUGH"

Closely related to the practice of pulling through or creeping through holes in the earth, which we examined at the end of the first installment of this article, is the movement or passage through holes in stones, which Gaidoz has called *pierres et rochers à trou.*[120] Encountered from early times in many parts of Europe,[121] and throughout the Near East, these stone rituals date from Indic antiquity.[122] Known at one time over much of the British Isles, they are now found mainly in Ireland, parts of Scotland, and in Cornwall (figs. 9, 10).[123] Belief in holed-stones is entirely unknown in America, at least in the Anglo-American tradition and in folklore derived from Europe. Veneration of stones, and the ritual use of holed-stones was perhaps more widely known in France than elsewhere on the continent of Europe.[124] Near the little town of Dourgne in southern France, for example, there are famous holed-stones implanted in a table-land on the mountain. These holes are of different sizes and shapes to befit various parts of the body. On August 6, festival of St. Estapin, pilgrims used to come from far and wide to be cured of their ailments.[125]

As with natural clefts in trees as over against trees especially split for curative purposes, so also with stones. Photographs reveal stones with natural fissures, on the one hand, stones with irregularly shaped holes worn by the action of water, and stones or stone columns conjoined in such a way as to leave fissures. On the other hand, many holes seem symmetrical enough to have been bored or otherwise shaped to fit a specific purpose. The relative curative merits of different kinds of holes are not discussed in the literature.

The range of diseases for which people sought relief by creeping through holed-stones is not as wide as for passage through holes in trees, but considerably wider than for movement through holes in the earth. Notably missing, however, is the treatment of hernia, even though rachitic ailments, and other kinds of crippling conditions were dealt with by local healers. Holes in stones were not filled in, nor could they be bound up to symbolize the joining of ruptured parts. On the other hand, we encounter for the first time the treatment of backache and other ailments of the trunk.[126] At St. Declan's Sacred Stone at Ardmore, County Waterford, for example, people with back ailments crawled through a stone aperture in a partial state of undress (fig. 11).[127] Near an old church in the Mühl region of

Austria, too, people believed they would be free of back ailments and pains in the loins if they crawled through a narrow place in the rocks,[128] while peasants in Lower Bavaria made a custom of crawling through a hole in a stone on which an altar rested in the belief that this would keep them from suffering back pains at harvest time. To enhance the flow of supernatural power they carried out their purposes while the church service was in progress.[129]

Perhaps the most frequently treated ailment by passing through holed-stones is rickets. By this fact, this dreaded bone disease of former times is the one and only disease subjected to curative practice by passing through all three of the principal natural objects: trees, earth, stones.[130] In parts of Cornwall it was the custom to pass rickety children through holed-stones nine times against the sun (withershins).[131] Cripples crawled through the stones of Dourgne, France, as noted above, and patients with spinal diseases sought cures at some of the famous holed-stones of Cornwall.[132]

Of the unusual diseases, and those associated with magic, epilepsy commands our attention for two notable entries. In Dorsetshire, a sick or epileptic child is drawn through a so-called "druidical" stone, in the thought that the evil spirit could not follow, and would thus be thwarted and left behind.[133] In a Scottish ritual for the same disease a fire was lighted where the stones came together.[134] Sufferers from palsy, and those who wanted to avoid coming down with the disease in old age, joined hands through a stone with a round hole in it at Stenhouse in the Orkneys. A child passed through this hole, called the Promise of Odin, was supposed never to shake with palsy in old age.[135] Sufferers from scrofula sought relief by creeping through holed-stones in Cornwall.[136]

The common childhood ailments of whooping cough and measles were cured at the ancient Long Stone at Minchin Hampton in Gloucestershire,[137] while children suffering from measles were taken to the junction point of three parishes near Sligo, Ireland, to be passed through a large limestone flag set on edge with a more or less rectangular hole through it.[138]

Consumption and rheumatism, diseases more common to adults than children, both figure in curative practices involving holed-stones. In Highland Scotland there was a famous holed-stone in Coll called *Clach Thuill,* the Hole Stone. Sufferers from consumption were passed through it in the three highest names, and offers of meat were left on the stone. By the processes of contagious magic the bird that took the food had the consumption laid upon it.[139] Elsewhere in Scotland consumptives passed through water-worn holes in rocks after the tops of nine waves had been caught in a dish and thrown on the patient's head.[140] Prevention of disease by passing through seems more pronounced in passing through stones than in other kinds of rituals involving passing through, crawling through, etc. Rheumatism could be prevented, for example, if a person crawled through the holed-stone at Men-a-Toll in Cornwall while uttering an appropriate incantation.[141] In the Gironde in France, a person walked around a big stone with a hole in it nine times, and was then forced through it to rid himself of rheumatism. More curious was the crawling beneath a menhir for the same purpose at Ymare, near Rouen, in such a way that the back would not scrape it, nor one's knees touch the ground.[142] (This is true also of the famous Men-a-Toll stones in Cornwall.)

In cases of impotence in a man he was given wine to drink that had been qualified by an herb growing through a holed-stone,[143] while childbirth itself was facilitated at Falkenstein ob der Ens by passing the mother through a holed-stone.[144] Marriage itself, and particularly betrothal, was solemnized by the clasping of hands through holed-stones.[145] In the graveyard of Kilchouslan, on the northern shore of Campbelltown Bay, Kintyre, there was a flat circular-shaped stone, the center of which was pierced with a hole large enough to permit a hand's being passed through. According to local tradition, an eloping couple, joining hands through this hole, were regarded as lawfully married and beyond pursuit.[146] Stones with smaller holes of this kind, so-called "secondary holed-stones," were used also for various aphrodisiac purposes.[147]

From these betrothal and nuptial customs involving holed-stones, it is clear that these natural and man-made apertures were used for purposes going well beyond sickness and health to include other offices having to do with man's welfare. Just as betrothals were solemnized, so also were oaths sworn. A so-called "Swearing Stone" in the churchyard at Castledermot was locally famous.[148] Speaking of the use of holed-stones, and particularly of a famous stone near Kollegor, India, Wood-Martin says:

> In the original use of the large apertures they seem to have been a literal, as well as a symbolic means, whereby an ailment, disease, or sin, might be left behind, or got rid of; they were also symbols by which a compact could be ratified, or an oath taken, by a well-known and public act.[149]

He speculates that at first, perhaps, the postulant crawled through the hole, and that, later as the holes diminished in size for one reason or another, he stuck only his hand into the hole, or his head and his hand, or, in the end, only his hand (fig. 12).[150] The wedding ring, Wood-Martin speculates, may represent the ultimate reduction of the original idea, where finally only a finger is passed through.[151]

At Chela, near Rabat in Morocco, there is a large stone scroll with Arabic inscriptions that is emplaced in a wall of masonry about three feet from the ground and extending upward another four feet or more. Near the center of the scroll, or slightly above the head of a person of average height, there is a hole large enough to permit of the insertion of a hand for the forgiveness of sins (fig. 13).[152] These various uses which we look upon as secondary with regard to physical illness, may not be secondary at all, but primary functions, as Nyrop held. As we shall see later, they offer explanations for notions of stripping and divestment in the literal sense, and for cleansing and rebirth in a figurative way.[153] In the matter of betrothal and the swearing of oaths, furthermore, holed-stones represent so-called binding rituals.

Resort to holed-stones to protect oneself against witchcraft and magic and other evil forces is another purpose, secondary to healing itself, that must be considered. As in the case of certain phases of passing-through holes in trees, magical and fairy influences could be prevented or counteracted by appropriate measures carried out through holed-stones. In Switzerland, for example, cows giving bloody milk as the result of witchcraft were milked through a hole bored in a piece of flint.[154] Milking bewitched cows through a so-called *Kuhstein* (''cow stone'') in German-speaking countries, de Cock tells us, was a protective ritual also carried out in Scotland.[155] Returning to the human element once more, we can note in this general connection a custom among villagers in Saintongue, France, whereby mothers passed their newborn infants through holes in dolmens to guard them against evil, present and future.[156] Thus we have seen in ritual acts connected with holed-stones, not only the curing of disease, but other important private and public functions as well.

Having surveyed the dumb creation in connection with passing through holes in trees, the earth, and stones, we can now come to the animal creation as a preliminary to a discussion of man himself, and the things that man has wrought which

FIG. 1. Smöjträd, Nydala, Småland, Sweden. Courtesy Nordiska Museet.

Fig. 2. Smöjning, or passing through a tree, Uppland, Sweden. Courtesy Nordiska Museet.

FIG. 3. Locally famous holly tree of Pamlico county, North Carolina, once cleft, through which ruptured persons were passed. Courtesy Joseph D. Clark.

Fig. 4. Garvie Huffman, 58, pictured beside a white oak tree in 1974, which he was pulled through as a baby. The tree as a sapling was split for the purpose. Courtesy Joseph D. Clark.

FIG. 5. Självväxt Knut or natural looped-knot, Arnäs, Ångermanland, Sweden. Courtesy Nordiska Museet.

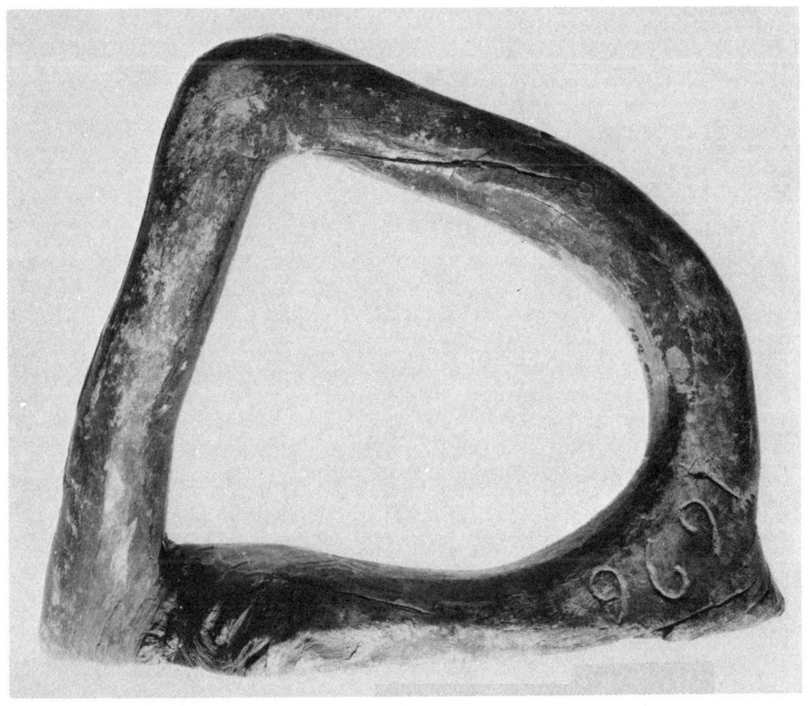

FIG. 6. Smöjträ with inscribed years "1696," Uppland, Sweden. Courtesy Nordiska Museet.

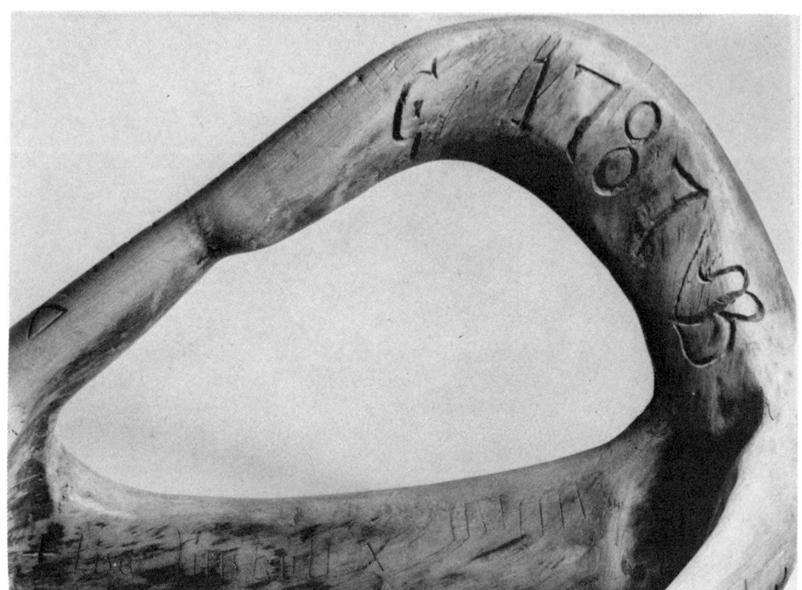

Fig. 7. Smöjträ of Lisa of Finshult, Småland, Sweden. Courtesy Nordiska Museet.

Fig. 8. Jorddragning, or pulling through the earth, Arnäs, Ångermanland, Sweden, 1933. Courtesy Nordiska Museet.

FIG. 9. Holed-stone, the Men-a-Tol, near Lanyon Quoist Cornwall. Locally called a "creeping stone" or "crickstone," and believed to cure rheumatism and other maladies. Courtesy Wellcome Historical Medical Museum and Library.

FIG. 10. Holed-stone, the Men-a-Tol, near Lanyon Quoist, Cornwall. "Go through the stone without touching it, and you will never have rheumatism." Courtesy Wellcome Historical Medical Museum and Library.

FIG. 11. St. Declan's Sacred Stone, Ardmore, County Waterford, Ireland. Pilgrims squeezed under this stone to cure pains in the back. Courtesy Wellcome Historical Medical Museum and Library.

FIG. 12. "Holed-stone" near Kollegor, India. Pilgrims seeking forgiveness and divine merit tried to squeeze through holes of this kind. Courtesy *Strand Magazine.*

FIG. 13. A Roman "secondary holed-stone." Chela, near Rabat, North Africa. The woman is inserting her hand in the hole to obtain forgiveness of her sins. Courtesy *The Graphic.*

are used in passing-through rituals. In folklore man's connection with animals often involves principles of imitative and contagious magic, in which man is able to appropriate to himself physical attributes and other animal traits that may prove of benefit. Primitive peoples were wont to gain the strength and swiftness of beasts, their virility, their ability to swim, etc., by consuming coveted parts of the animal in question. Civilized man, while to some extent marveling at the physical prowess of beasts, centered his attentions more on emulating their sagacity and other well-known mental and spiritual traits. These have been celebrated, not only in fabular literature, but also in beliefs, legends, and local stories and conceits connected with all creatures of the animal kingdom.

Thus it is, that even in the limited range of beliefs and customs concerning animals in the ritual act of passing through, or passing under, man seeks to gain the physical strength of the animal for his own ordeal. (This may not be fully true for the act of passing a child with whooping cough under the belly of an ass, as we shall see later.) In Denmark, for example, a girl who wants to assure herself of an easy delivery for the future, must crawl naked through the chorion (*Geburtshaut*) of a foal.[157] In this same connection an Italian traveler by the name of Pietro del Valle, tells of seeing a pregnant woman at a village in Persia in 1622 ask his camel driver to be allowed to crawl under his camel. Knowing that a female camel that has calved was best for this purpose, the driver made one such get up, and the woman then passed under the animal three times at the left.[158] Zachariae reports the prevalence of this custom in Abyssinia as well as in Armenia. In Rumania, children with stomach ailments were passed under and over bears that were led through the towns and villages by itinerant showmen.[159] Children were passed under the belly of a sow three times in different parts of Poland for unspecified ailments and for good health generally.[160]

The most commonly known curative ritual involving movement under animals is the passing of children under the bellies of donkeys for the prevention and cure of whooping cough. Whether this is from a sympathetic association of the beast with Jesus, in token of which the animal's hide bears the marking of a cross, or whether the whooping of the child resembles the wheezing and braying of the donkey, no one knows. The custom as related to whooping cough has been reported most widely in the British Isles, and appears to be not too well known elsewhere. From token representations, the use of the donkey for passing under in ailments other than whooping cough would suggest inadequate collecting and researching rather than the absence of a body of folk beliefs and customs bearing on the subject at hand. In the British Isles children are passed under the belly of a donkey;[161] this is more often done three times.[162] A court case in Belfast involving a child that had died following passing under a donkey three times, brought the prevalence of this custom to the attention of the general public as long ago as the 1890's.[163] (The owner of the donkey was free when it was ruled that the child died of bronchitis.) Black, the celebrated English authority on folk medicine, reports that the passing under and over of an ass should be followed up for nine successive mornings.[164] There are two cases of the threefold passage that involve a collateral interest, namely, inhalation as a treatment for whooping cough. The first has to do with the performance of the ritual on a high hill in the West Riding of Yorkshire, concerning which the correspondent to *Notes and Queries* expressed the view that the change of air was a factor in the cure.[165] More curious is a folk medical prescription from Scotland, in which the child was forced to inhale the breath of an ass before being passed three times under its belly and over its back.[166] The prescription of nine passages, a triply powerful extension of the magic number three, also is encountered in the literature,[167] as is the number seven, in France, but only in a single entry.[168] Black reports from Cornwall on a more elaborate ritual than is usual:

> The child is passed nine times under and over a donkey three years old. Then three spoonfuls of milk are drawn from the teats of the animal, and three hairs cut from the belly placed in it. After the milk has stood for three hours it should be drunk by the child in three doses, the whole ceremony being repeated three successive mornings.[169]

Feeding of the child with the milk of a female donkey, or from bread which a donkey has partly eaten, is often part of the passing-under ritual, and must be included in the discussion.[170] A North Carolina curative ritual, for example, involves the child's eating, not only bread which the donkey has tasted, but hairs clipped from the animal itself:

> A father was observed passing his little son under a donkey and lifting him over its back a certain number of times, with as much solemnity and precision as if engaged in the performance of a sacred duty. This done, the father took a piece of bread cut from an

> untasted loaf which he offered the animal to bite at. The donkey took hold of the bread with his teeth, and the father severed the outer portion of the slice from that in the donkey's mouth. He next clipped some hairs from the neck of the animal and cut them up and mixed them with the bread, which he crumbled. He offered this food to the boy who had been passed around the donkey and he now ate it while the animal was removed.[171]

The process is varied somewhat in the British Isles, or actually reversed, by the fact that the donkey eats food from the child's lap after the passing-under ritual.[172] As in other rituals having to do with passing through, prayers and incantations of various kinds were uttered during the passing-under ceremony.[173] Usually it was an invocation of the Trinity.[174] The sex of the donkey was important where milk from the animal was to be fed to the patient, as in the example from Cornwall cited by Black.[175] Female donkeys were generally preferred,[176] but by some accounts one should choose a donkey of the opposite sex, a mare for a boy, and a jack for a girl.[177] Passing the child under the legs of a donkey is exceptional, but this variation is reported from Northumberland, where the child is placed under the belly of the animal and between its forelegs.[178]

Just as hernia and rickets were mainly treated by passing through holes in trees, rickets largely by passing through or under the earth, backache and rachitic conditions by passage through holes in stones, so also does whooping cough appear to be the principal disease for which patients were pulled under the belly of a donkey. That a measure of consistency should prevail, and does, is seen from the fact that rupture was treated in Newfoundland by passing the patient under the belly of an ass, as was shingles, a disease not yet encountered in our discussion.[179] Croup and measles, both childhood diseases, were treated by passing the victim under a donkey. In Spain it was prescribed that a child with croup should mount a burro nine times, and then pass under it as many times.[180] (This appears to be a variation of the over-under procedure which we have seen, with the exception that the child mounts the animal rather than being passed over its back.) In Germany slobbering children, or those with an excessive flow of saliva, were forced to make contact with the mouth of the donkey, then be passed under it, and finally made to ride the animal.[181] This regimen is reminiscent of the case reported upon for the North Riding of Yorkshire, where a child suffering from whooping cough was made to inhale the donkey's breath before being passed under its body.

In the "Little Egypt" part of southern Illinois a patient suffering from whooping cough was advised less than twenty-five years ago to crawl under a mule,[182] while in the British Isles as well as on the continent horses were pressed into service in the same way as donkeys, but not exclusively for whooping cough. In Scandinavia, for example, a child suffering from a cough, or from congestion in the chest, was pulled under the belly of a stallion, or even a buck sheep.[183] In Scotland, and elsewhere in the British Isles, the ritual was performed with a piebald horse or pony.[184] As an appendage to our discussion of passing under animals, one should not fail to report on the passage under the body of a crude stone statue of a lion. This statue was located near Upper Elam, in Luristan, Persia, and was placed over the grave of a brave soldier. Soldiers given to cowardice were forced, on the night of a full moon, to pass beneath the body of the lion seven times.[185] It is fitting to end the discussion of passing under animals with this example, for it bears out admirably the thesis set forth at the beginning of the treatment concerned with animals as part of the whole complex of passing-through.

Before treating the passing through the legs of humans, and other parts of the human body, we shall treat the appurtenances immediately connected with horses, namely, the horse collar and other parts of the harness, leaving for later a discussion of wagons. From this point forward we shall increasingly be concerned with manufactured and fabricated items, rather than with natural objects, as heretofore. (Many holed stones, it should be stated once more, were of human manufacture, and even trees and sods in the earth were shaped to the needs of the votaries and practitioners.)

Pulling through the collars of horses or oxen is encountered in folklore, and especially in folk medicine, where it is a fitting corollary to creeping under horses themselves.[186] Most of the entries at my command are from the United States. Among childhood ailments, one may list the following: the treatment of fits and the "go-backs" in Maryland, where a child is drawn through an old horse collar, with the assurance that the disease will not return once his clothes have been burned.[187] In Pennsylvania a child with wind colic, or gripes, was put three times through a warm horse collar.[188] The same procedure was followed in West Virginia.[189] Passage through a warm horse collar three times was also prescribed for whooping cough in Illinois.[190] "Livergrown" children in the Pennsylvania German country, suffering from an ailment for which it was thought the liver grew fast to the backbone,[191] were treated by being passed three times through a warm horse collar.[192] Two essentially adult diseases, rheumatism and lumbago, were treated in the Pennsylvania German country by having the patient crawl through a warm horse collar three times in succession towards the sun.[193] Pulling through a horse collar was practiced for various kinds of magical ailments in Europe, such as the effects of being moonstruck as a result of having slept with the moon shining on one's face, as in Russia,[194] or being pinched or squeezed by trolls in Denmark.[195] Moreover, hysteria was treated by passing the victim through a horse collar in Russia.[196] Creeping through a horse collar as an ordeal to establish innocence in matters pertaining to witchcraft is likewise noted in Russian oral tradition. Persons suspected of having cast a horse collar over a bull, for example, i.e., having bewitched it, were forced one by one to crawl through a horse collar themselves to prove their innocence.[197] Passing through other parts of the harness was helpful for a variety of ailments.[198] Passing through a halter could facilitate childbirth (South Slavic countries),[199] cure rickets (western Finland),[200] or keep a child from crying (eastern Friesland).[201] For rickets a child in Finland was drawn through the harness just taken from a horse that had drawn a bridal carriage.[202]

Crawling under the human body, or parts of it, accords with the practice we have seen of passing under animals, and may actually precede it. In Hungary, for example, an expectant mother crawls under her husband three times in the hope of having an easy delivery.[203] Crawling through one's legs, particularly those of a woman, suggests a rebirth and the health and vitality that go with birth and life itself. Bartsch put forward the idea of rebirth in 1879, and it was later used to formulate theories of rebirth connected with passing through generally.[204] In northern Germany children passed through the legs of their fathers according to an old custom and in Mecklenburg sickly children were allowed to pass through the legs of their parents.[205] In a Finnish folk medical ritual carried out in a bathhouse, a child with rickets was handed through its father's legs by a medical practitioner known as an *Omlagaren* (Swed.). The child was handed through his father's legs from behind three times, and then consigned to some twigs, whereupon the father stepped on the child's mouth with his left foot and said, "Thou shalt cry no more, etc."[206] A *curandero* in Galicia stands with legs apart as a child suffering from *enganido,* general weakness in children, is passed in and around his legs nine times in a figure eight.[207] Sufferers from enchantment in Poland before the turn of the century were passed through a horse collar.[208] At Bassora on the Persian Gulf people were supposedly cured of mad-dog bite by passing between the legs of a mullah descended from the Prophet, a statue mounted on two pillars with legs astride.[209]

Passing through the empty legs of trousers, as distinct from legs with trousers on, is not always easy to identify, since precise details are often lacking.[210] Two items from Scandinavia, however, are fairly clear on this point. In western Finland for *krassa,* a rachitic condition in children, a child is drawn either through the left leg of his father's wedding trousers, or through his father's new underpants three days running at nine o'clock at night.[211] The only comparable American example at my command is from Mississippi, where it is prescribed that a child afflicted with whooping cough be passed through its father's trouser legs.[212]

Passing through a woman's underpants or bloomers, as an adoptive ritual is encountered among Bosnian Turks and elsewhere in the Near East, wherein the mother takes the child against her bare skin, and then brings it out from between her legs, as if she had given birth to it.[213] This same symbolic act takes place at the bosoms, as the child is passed under the shirt or chemise.[214] In Iran a newborn baby is passed three times into the neck and out of the skirt of the dress of a woman who has a healthy baby, so as to insure the health of the newcomer.[215] In Poland at the end of the last century a sufferer from rheumatism was passed through a shirt three times,[216] while as recently as 1930 a child suffering from rickets in western Finland was passed through his father's shirt.[217] During a cholera epidemic in Serbia in the nineteenth century, nine old women, naked, wove a shirt, sitting in silence by the light of a bonfire. A man and his family were made to crawl through the shirt; also his suite and all of the guard.[218] For the cure of rickets and other diseases, too, a father's marriage shirt was especially efficacious in western Finland;[219] likewise, a baby's swaddling clothes,[220] no less than the mother's body linen at time of lying-in. In Scotland if a child was enchanted, or in danger of being "forespoken," it could be cured by taking its own first shirt, or the petticoat the mother wore before confinement, or the linen she wore at the time of delivery, and passing the child through it three times, and then three times around the crook.[221] In

County Cork women approaching the time of their confinement pulled their clothes through "secondary holes" to facilitate childbirth.[222]

By way of extension on customs discussed above, it is easy to understand why the sick are pulled through clerical vestments in Norway, including the priest's collar.[223] Passing under the crypts of saints and other religious personages conferred special virtues, including the power of healing. Following up on his essay of 1892, to which he devoted a short chapter on "Passer sous la châsse du saint et sous le retable de l'autel,"[224] Gaidoz developed fully the theory of the impregnation of virtue in saints' tombs, relics, and the like, and the passing on of this power to the votaries who crawled beneath tombs, under altars, reliquaries, statues, and the Communion table itself.[225] Entries are mainly drawn from French sources but there are two fine items from Russia, including mention of the fact that Russian votaries passed beneath images of their saints while in procession.[226] In churches and other religious houses holes were found in stone work and masonry, through which votaries passed for various kinds of benefits, including deliverance from disease and sin. Space will not permit of more than the mention of one or two famous shrines. St. Wilfred's Needle in the crypt of Ripon Minster in England was the scene of passing hands through an aperture in connection with the betrothal and marriage rites.[227] At the church of St. Michael-la-Rivière in the diocese of Bordeaux the sick crawled through a hole at the end of the apse to cure themselves of disease. They then left gifts to the church as their worldly station permitted.[228] To be cured of fits, according to a Devonshire custom, one should go to the parish church at midnight on June 23, and walk three times through each aisle. Then he should crawl three times from north to south under the Communion table as the clock strikes twelve.[229] This Devonshire custom is typical of healing rituals elsewhere in the matter of detail, and for further examples the reader is referred to the bibliography contained in the present note.[230]

Passing under the crypts and tombs of saints and other holy personages does not constitute the only resort to the dead, or the realms of the dead in passing through ceremonies having to do with disease, health, and the well-being of man. From early times, barren women wanting children passed under the dead bodies of criminals on the gibbet.[231] In Norway the sick are pulled under a coffin with a corpse in it, probably in the thought that the dead person would take the sufferer's infirmities with him to the grave.[232] In the same country victims of epilepsy made a practice of running under the bier three times.[233] In Scandinavia, in a custom perhaps reminiscent of rituals of pulling the sick through the earth, sufferers were placed in open graves that were arched over and then removed in a ceremony approximating pulling through,[234] or they were pulled between two graves, as in Norway.[235]

Having treated the human estate, in which the passing of persons under the dead, as well as under the living, has been considered, we can now move to a rapid survey of passing-through rituals as they apply to things which man himself has made, and which surround him in the house, on his premises, or in the wider arena.

In the central provinces of India, for example, sufferers from fever walk through a narrow passage between houses, or under the eaves, to rid themselves of the complaint.[236] Rickets is treated in western Finland by shoving the patient three successive Thursday nights through a hole in a house which has been moved three times. Each time the child passes through the hole three times.[237] Within the house itself, the sick, usually children, are pulled through the rungs of chairs for various maladies.[238] Sometimes the chair is turned upside down.[239] (We have already noted instances of inverted chairs in connection with bringing sods into the house for rituals of pulling through the earth.) In the Pennsylvania German country children were pulled or passed under a chair, or through its rungs, for such assorted ailments as wasting sickness, *abnemmes* (where ideas of rebirth are suggested by the ritual), cough, and liver growth.[240] Disorders of the spleen, ailments perhaps akin to those which the Pennsylvania Germans called *âgewachse,* were treated in Ohio by passing the child from east to west, as the sun goes, around the leg of a chair or table.[241] The cure of liver growth, as noted above, could also be accomplished by passing a child under a table, around table legs, and the like, or have the child do so by crawling, either forwards, backwards, or both.[242] This same regimen was followed for pleurisy, which seems related in many ways.[243] Wasting sickness was also treated in the aforesaid manner, as was another common childhood complaint, colic.[244] The common cough, and hiccough, too, were dealt with by passing under the table.[245] There was also a taboo against young children's crawling under chairs or tables on the theory that their growth would be stunted, as seen in an entry from Illinois.[246]

Going around pothooks for whatever purpose does not qualify for discussion in a paper that deals primarily with passing through or under an aperture of some kind, but a South Slavic pot chain ritual does seem germane to our discussion. In brotherhood rituals, to symbolize the breaking of fetters, a ''brother'' is drawn through the pot chains, as well as through a hoop made of a branch of a wild rose-tree.[247]

Loops were even fashioned from bakery goods for sanative purposes or for other things having to do with human welfare, or for animals serviceable to man.[248] In Oxford it was the practice, for example, to cut the so-called ''groaning cheese'' in the middle, and then form it into a large ring, through which the child was passed on its day of christening.[249] In seventeenth-century Scotland three cakes were prepared of nine proportions of meal contributed by nine maidens and nine married women, and a hole was made in each for transmitting a child through it thrice in the name of the Father, Son, and Holy Ghost.[250] In the Beskide Mountains between Poland and Czechoslovakia, before the turn of the century, a cake made from flour kneaded in Holy Water was fashioned into a large ring, through which infants suffering from consumption were passed.[251] In former times bewitched cattle in Scotland were driven through oaten cake rings against bewitchment.[252]

Doors and windows, which constitute the only human portals in a house (fairy folk have numerous other ways of moving in and out), are natural sites for the enactment of passing-through rituals. For lack of space I cannot treat various betrothal and nuptial ceremonies that take place at the door or threshold, but refer the reader to the excellent treatment in *The Encyclopaedia of Religion and Ethics.*[253] Skin infections were treated in France by rubbing them with the peeled branch of a wild rose bush, and then placed over the door through which he passed an elder branch as long as the patient was tall.[254] Children were passed through windows in Scandinavia,[255] including a special window near the stove. The child was handed out this window to a receiver, who took it counter sunwise (*motsols* Swed.) around the house and then back inside. This routine was repeated three times.[256] Before the turn of the century in Greece a sick child was brought into the house by the door and passed out through a window three times, after which a rag connected with its sickness was hung on a tree.[257] A clear example of riddance, as exemplified in leaving a place, is seen in the Illinois prescription for the relief of toothache. Jumping through a window takes away the pain.[258]

The passing of the sick through hesps of yarn, particularly children, is widely known throughout Eurpoe,[259] but apparently is not met with in America. There are seventeenth-century attestations of this practice in Scotland in connection with the witch trials. After the passing-through ceremonies the yarn was burned, buried, or otherwise disposed of.[260] The origins of this custom lie in witchcraft, as most descriptions of the practice show. In Portugal, for example, a bewitched child is pulled through a hank of unbleached and unwashed yarn.[261] In Germany the attachment to witchcraft is so close that a child seized with a sudden fever and cramps in southern Saxony is thought to be bewitched, and is thereupon drawn through a skein of yarn known as a hangman's loop or noose (*Henkerschlinge*), which is kept at the end of the bench, near the stove.[262] The curing of rickets in Scandinavia, perhaps for want of details, does not seem immediately to be connected with witchcraft, although its magical connections, historically, cannot escape the attention of the scholar.[263] In this same general connection Scottish fishermen shoved fishing smacks through ropes to disenchant them, or to keep them free of magic.[264]

Baskets, barrel rungs, hoops of various kinds, and rings were portable items about the house and in the yard that could be utilized for curative rituals and other kinds of magical practices. Along the Lower Rhine, for example, a young man guilty of moral indiscretions, in consequence of which he was forced to break off a love affair, was forced to crawl through a bottomless basket. As he did it, he was pronounced pure and free as a child from its mother's womb, pure as the sun, pure as the moon, and pure as the light of day. This was done in the presence of his young friends in whose eyes he had been judged guilty of moral wrong.[265] To ease birth pains an expectant mother was supposed to slip through the hoop of a barrel that had sprung free of itself.[266] For rachitic diseases in western Finland a child was supposed to crawl through a spill barrel whose bottom had been knocked out. This was done on a Sunday morning as the bells rang to summon the faithful to church.[267] Frazer reports that people fleeing evil spirits in Asia Minor passed through a hot chain made into a loop. The underlying idea was that the pursuer was torn from his intended victim and thus left behind.[268] In the Basque country people suffering from rheumatism went on pilgrimages to the Cruz del Hernio, where the afflicted part was passed through an iron staple.[269] In Germany it was customary for children afflicted with bedwetting to urinate through some sort of a loop, including one on a harness,[270] while impotent men in the same country tried to regain their virility by urinating through a wedding ring.[271] In Swabia a man brought to this state by the magical tying of knots (*Nestelknüpfen*), and the ligation of his sexual apparatus, could gain release, supposedly, by urinating through a natural ring made by joining his thumb and little finger.[272]

Children were passed through the rungs of ladders for a variety of ailments,[273] including incessant crying in Germany,[274] and rickets in Denmark.[275] This Danish ritual was so secret in nature that a person stood guard as it was carried out. The practice is also found in America. In Nova Scotia, for example, hernia was treated by a midwife's passing the child through the father's legs as he and his wife stood by a ladder leaning against a house. The child was then passed through the rungs of the ladder, and into the hands of the mother. This operation was repeated three times, with a recitation of the names of the Trinity at each passing.[276] For the so-called "go-backs" in Maryland, the child was passed through the rungs of a ladder several times, or, as has already been noted, through a horse collar.[277] In North Carolina people suffering from spells worked by hair balls thrown by witches were treated by a witch doctor, who passed the victim through the rungs of a ladder, from bottom to top and then from top to bottom. After certain other administrations the patient was passed through a horse collar.[278]

In line with folk medical treatments we have already seen, victims of various diseases are pulled through staves in fences, or through other apertures.[279] In Sweden the passing through takes place at a gate through which a corpse has passed.[280]

Passing through wagons, or parts of wagons, goes back to antiquity, and is noted in the *Rig-Veda.*[281] This ancient custom was observed in Germany until recent times.[282] As late as the 1890's youngsters were pulled through the spokes of wagon wheels in Belgium to protect them against sorcery.[283] In western Finland rickety children were taken into a drying kiln by three people not related to the child, and then passed through and around holes of various kinds in the drying racks.[284]

The carrying out of passing-through rituals in public places is little encountered of course, but we can end this survey by mentioning at least two instances involving public transportation facilities. In Spain whooping cough was treated by passing a child nine times through the arches of a bridge.[285] The most curious example of passing through, in the sense that an ancient principle was given modern embodiment, is seen in an event that took place in 1898 near Khartoum in the Sudan. A woman wanting a child asked permission of a locomotive engineer to pass under the locomotive. When this was granted, her husband asked that she be allowed to crawl under a second time so that she might bear twins.[286]

Scholars have puzzled over the origin of passing through, and have sought in many ways, to explain the notions underlying this ancient custom. Perhaps the most obvious reason that suggests itself is divestment of the disease by stripping off or scraping off (*abstreifen* Ger.; *frottement* Fr.). These ideas were put forward by Busch in 1877,[287] and developed by Reinhard Hofschläger over thirty years later, when he sought to explain the practice in terms of animals ridding themselves of vermin by creeping through bushes.[288] Snakes crawling through narrow apertures to slough off their old skin would be another example of "stripping" from natural history.[289] Frazer has applied this principle to the human sphere with a cogent analysis of escape from ghosts of the dead. "To put it otherwise, they [the natives] conceive that the spirit of the dead is sticking to them like a burr, and that like a burr it may be rubbed or scraped off and left adhering to the sides of the opening through which they have squeezed themselves."[290] Present-day scholars have likewise addressed themselves to this general thesis.[291] Tillhagen and other workers apply it also to passing through the earth (*jorddragning*).[292] A principal difficulty with this simple explanation, as I see it, is the fact that in some cases passing through must be accomplished without touching, as we have seen above in connection with a South Slavic brotherhood ritual.[293] This case, and others like it that have been mentioned in this paper, would set at naught, seemingly, the basic notion of contact as a prime condition for the act of stripping off and scraping. In Sweden a woman suffering from an infirmity of some sort was advised by a wise woman to pass through a hoop made of stolen willow branches. She was supposed to crawl through silently, and without touching the hoop.[294] Crawling through the famous Men-a-Tol holed-stones in Cornwall, as pictured in figure 10 of the present article, was supposed to be accomplished without touching.

Closely connected with "stripping off" as a theory of the riddance of disease was Frazer's notion of the portal as constituting a barrier to further pursuit. In a series of striking examples taken from the customs of primitive peoples, Frazer sums up his views in the following statement.

> I cannot agree with him [Gaidoz] in thinking that the essence of the rite [of passing through] consists in the transference of the disease from the person to the tree; rather, it seems to me, the primary idea is that of interposing a barrier between a fugitive and his pursuing foe, though no doubt the enemy thus left behind is apparently supposed to adhere to the further side of the obstacle (whether tree, stone, or what not) through which he cannot pass.[295]

Frazer's examples all relate to pursuing spirits, demons, ghosts, and the dead themselves. To them must here be added instances of diseases unable to penetrate a barrier, as seen in the treatment of epilepsy in Dorsetshire described above.[296] One should note, however, that once more the escape is from a pursuing evil spirit that caused the epilepsy, not escape from an ordinary kind of ailment. The pursuers previously mentioned by Wood-Martin in an elopement ritual in Scotland, of course, are not demons or evil spirits at all, but most likely the parents of the couple or civil authorities.[297] One wonders whether the phrase "to pull through," and especially as it relates to overcoming an illness, may not be related to ideas of escaping from a pursuer or withstanding an assault, as expressed by Frazer.

Another basic notion associated with curative rituals of passing through is the doctrine of transference of disease to the object through which the victim passes.[298] This theory was enunciated by Jacob Grimm, with the view that the disease was communicated to the genius of the tree, stone, or earth.[299] Other scholars have shared or reiterated this view,[300] notably Gaidoz in his theory of *transplantio morbi.*[301] In this notion of the transfer of the disease, however, Gaidoz believed the patient also was thought to take unto himself the strength of the tree, the earth, or what not, through which he passed. In the case of passing under animals, the child, by a strange reciprocal process, took on the vitality of the beast, as his own infirmity passed into the animal.[302] This worked also in creeping under the earth (*jord-dragning*).[303] The connection between the patient and the tree, for example, is thought to be so vital on the Island of Rügen, that on the death of the patient, even many years later, his soul would pass into the tree.[304] By and large, however, and contrary to a pronounced tendency in magical transference of disease to living things such as trees and animals, the effects of the reception of the disease on the new host are never mentioned.[305]

The theory of rebirth and newness of life as resulting from passing through, and particularly through clefts in trees that resemble the female reproductive organ, was first set forth by

Felix Liebrecht.[306] Karl Weinhold, the learned editor of the *Zeitschrift des Vereins für Volkskunde,* regarded rebirth as a more plausible explanation for passing through than "stripping," but felt that Nyrop had gone too far in suggesting moral purification.[307] Nyrop and Gaidoz were also early adherents to Liebrecht's views.[308] Several more recent scholars have also addressed themselves to the subject.[309] Two examples of notions of rebirth, as expressed in the customs themselves, rather than in theories propounded by scholars, are seen in an ancient Greek custom reported by Plutarch, and a modern courtship custom, already reported on in connection with passing through a bottomless basket. This was done to obtain, not only moral regeneration, as expressed in the language itself, but represented, figuratively speaking, a rebirth from the mother's womb.[310] In ancient Greece a person pronounced dead, should he suddenly reappear, was obliged to go through a symbolic rebirth by emerging from the lap of a woman, and then be washed, diapered, and suckled.[311] Interpretations by the two Pennsylvania German scholars, Brendle and Unger, of a possible symbolic rebirth occurring by passing patients through rerooted brambles for wasting sickness were most likely arrived at without recourse to the writings of any of the scholars mentioned—at least these men appear to have made independent judgments.[312]

Since a rebirth implies, not merely a newness of physical life, but also moral regeneration in the Christian sense, it was not surprising that this latter interpretation should have been suggested in connection with passing-through rituals. Principal proponent of the theory was the Danish scholar Kristoffer Nyrop, who believed that purification from sin and notions of forgiveness were the original ideas, out of which notions of the curing of disease by crawling through (*Gennemkrybning*) were to develop.[313] In India sinners passed through holes for forgiveness of their sins,[314] and where the hole was too small for the suppliant to pass through, he stuck his hand through the hole to receive a benison.[315] Cleansing from sin and blood guilt on the part of soldiers returning to Rome from battle was effected by making them pass through a special gate known as the *Porta Triumphalis.*[316] Lustrations with fire as well as water, as we have seen in South Slavic crawling-through ceremonies, often were preliminary to the movement through the hole, or figured importantly otherwise in the ritual.[317] We have already considered the symbolic rebirth of a young man along the Lower Rhine by pulling him through a bottomless basket, but in the case in question the notion of purification seems even stronger in terms of the verbal part of the cleansing ceremony.[318] Likewise, a girl who had proved unfaithful had to undergo a similar ritual, the ordeal of a so-called "dry washing" (*Drüwäsch*), which culminated in her passing through a large handkerchief fashioned into a loop.[319] The leaving of gifts of money at the tree or at the shrine, usually in the form of token payments in small coins, suggests the idea of thank offerings. These offerings were for spiritual as well as physical renewal.[320] The leaving of clothing or rags associated with the disease, on the other hand, clearly suggests an emphasis on the bodily repair.[321]

Theoretical discussions on the origin and meaning of passing through will no doubt continue, and solutions will one day be forthcoming. For these deliberations additional data will be needed, particularly accounts of what the people themselves thought of phases of the ritual known to them, and what they said to explain the various ceremonies to which they themselves were a party. The detailed accounts of Kemp constitute a good beginning.

NOTES

1. Henri Gaidoz, *Un Vieux Rite Médical* (Paris, 1892); *Handwörterbuch des deutschen Aberglaubens* (10 vols., Berlin and Leipzig, 1927–1942) 9: p. 974 (hereinafter cited *HDA*); A. de Cock, "Eene oude Geneeswijze," *Volkskunde* 7 (1894); pp. 72–73; Carl-Herman Tillhagen, *Folklig Läkekonst* (Stockholm, 1958), pp. 116, 295; E. Radford and M. A. Radford, *Encyclopaedia of Superstitions* (London, [1947]), p. 92; Felix Grendon, "The Anglo-Saxon Charms," *Jour. Amer. Folklore* 22 (1909): p. 129; W. G. Wood-Martin, *Traces of the Elder Faiths of Ireland* (2 vols., London, 1902) 2: pp. 229–230; Jacob Grimm, *Deutsche Mythologie* (4th ed., Elard Hugo Meyer, 3 vols., Berlin, 1875–1878) 2: pp. 975–976; O. v. Hovorka and A. Kronfeld, *Vergleichende Volksmedizin* (2 vols., Stuttgart, 1908–1909) 2: p. 483 (crawling through trees to cure disease is of Indo-Germanic origin).

2. James George Frazer, *The Golden Bough* (3rd ed., 12 vols., London, 1911–1915) 2: pp. 7–96, *passim* (hereinafter cited *GB*); Paul Sébillot, *Le Folklore de France* (4 vols., Paris, 1904–1907) 1: pp. 253–299, *passim*; *HDA* 1: pp. 954–958, *passim*. One should also consult the basic writings of Wilhelm Mannhardt, particularly his *Wald- und Feldkulte* (2nd ed., W. Heuschkel, 2 vols., Berlin, 1904–1905).

3. *HDA* 9: pp. 971–978.

4. Gaidoz, *op. cit.*, p. 13.

5. *HDA* 9: pp. 971 ff.

6. *Cf.* H. F. Feilberg, "Zwieselbäume nebst verwandtem Aberglauben in Skandinavien," *Zs. d. Vereins f. Volkskunde* 7 (1897): pp. 42–53 (sketch of a *smöj-eka*, "holed-oak," on p. 47); Tillhagen, *op. cit.*, p. 297 (photograph of a *smöjtrā* at Nydala, Sweden), p. 293 (photograph of actual ceremony in progress).

7. Kristoffer Nyrop, "Kludertræet. En sammelignende Undersøgelse," *Dania* 1 (1900–1902): p. 3.

8. Valter W. Forsblom, *Magisk Folkmedicin* (Finlands Svenska Folkdiktning 7, Folktro och Trolldom no. 5, Helsingfors, 1927), p. 542.

9. *Mélusine* 10 (1900–1901): p. 255.

10. Antonio Castillo de Lucas, *Folkmedicina* (Madrid, 1958), p. 258; *Revista de Dialectología y Tradiciones Populares* 1 (1944): p. 314.

11. *Folk-lore* 9 (1898): pp. 333–335 (with an excellent photograph made in 1891 [facing p. 334]). *Cf.* Radford, *op. cit.,* p. 206.

12. Gaidoz, *op. cit.,* p. 14. I do not know of the existence of pictures of this celebrated tree. However, since writing this article, I have been informed by Professor Joseph D. Clark of the existence of a large holly tree in the Olympia community, Pamlico county, North Carolina, through which ruptured persons were once passed. The tree, pictured in the *Raleigh News and Observer,* June 9, 1968, stands 72 feet high, has a circumference of 11 feet, 1 inch at the trunk, and clearly shows the healed cleft. Since the appearance of this article Professor Clark was able to secure for me a photograph of this locally famous holly tree (fig. 3), and in his ongoing researches on the subject was successful in tracking down someone who had actually been "pulled through" a tree in a curative ritual. Pictured in 1974 (fig. 4) is Garvie Huffman of Purlear, North Carolina, who as an eight month old baby was passed through a split white oak sapling for the cure of a double rupture. Questioned at the time he was photographed beside the tree, Huffman, 58, said "as the tree growed up, I growed up too."

13. Tillhagen, *op. cit.,* p. 117. The weird windings and intertwinings did much to contribute to the notions that made the tree holy in the eyes of its worshippers. *Cf. HDA* 9: p. 972.

14. *Zs. d. Vereins f. Volkskunde* 12 (1902): p. 112; S. Seligmann, *Der böse Blick und Verwandtes* (2 vols., Berlin, 1910) 1: p. 327. *Cf. HDA* 9: p. 972. In some places these entanglements are called "witch's nests." (Frazer, *GB* 11: p. 185).

15. Frazer, *GB* 11: p. 185.

16. Elisabet Dillner, "Lisa of Finshult and Her *Smöjträ,*" *Arv.* 18–19 (1962–1963): pp. 274–289. Pictures of a portable *smöjträ* of Scotch pine dating from 1787, pp. 282–283. *Cf.* Feilberg, *op. cit.,* p. 49 (sketch). See aslo Tillhagen, *op. cit.,* p. 294, for a photograph of a portable *smöjträ* dating from 1696. Oval-shaped pieces of wood, fashioned for a child to pass through, were once kept in houses in Scandinavia, often being suspended between two chairs. Feilberg has associated the term *vålbundet,* etymologically, with household spirits in Sweden, and the Finnish term *luomarengas* is to the same purport (Feilberg, *op. cit.,* p. 49).

17. Harry Middleton Hyatt, *Folk-Lore from Adams County Illinois* (New York, 1935), p. 209, no. 4362.

18. Tillhagen, *op. cit.,* p. 291. *Cf.* Feilberg, *op. cit.,* p. 53 (a hunter who crawls under a tree blown down by the wind will lose his luck at hunting).

19. Mannhardt, for reasons that he does not explain, is of a contrary mind, believing that the use of natural clefts in trees was an outgrowth of the practice of artificial splitting (*op. cit.* 1: p. 33).

20. *Journal of American Folklore* 2 (1889): p. 293. *Cf. Popular Beliefs and Superstitions from North Carolina,* (= vols. 6–7 of the *Frank C. Brown Collection of North Carolina Folklore*), ed. Wayland D. Hand (2 vols., Durham, North Carolina, Duke University Press, 1961, 1964) 6: p. 52, no. 311 (hereinafter cited *Brown Collection*). For another New Hampshire attestation, this time from a medical doctor, see Harold D. Levine, "Folk Medicine in New Hampshire," *New*

England Jour. of Medicine 224, 12 (Mar. 20, 1941): p. 488: To cure a congenital "fissure," split an ash sapling near a brook so that the gap runs from north to south, and pass the baby through the tree.

21. Rodney Gallop, *Portugal. A Book of Folk-Ways* (Cambridge, 1936), p. 52.

22. *Revista de Dialectología y Tradiciones Populares* 3 (1947): p. 566.

23. Cited in T. F. Thiselton Dyer, *English Folklore* (London, 1878), pp. 24-25. *Cf.* John E. Raaf, "Hernia Healers," *Annals of Medical History,* n.s., 4 (1932): pp. 377-389; E. Sidney Hartland, "Cleft Ashes for Infantile Hernia," *Folk-Lore* 7 (1896): pp. 303-306 (three photographs: the one facing p. 306 is of a split ash in the Museum at Taunton). Further selective references include: Hovorka and Kronfeld, *op. cit.* 2: p. 694 (in the vicinity of Bergen a mountain ash in which subterranean spirits dwell is split open, and the child passed through on three successive Thursday nights amid strictest silence); Eveline Camilla Gurdon, *County Folk-Lore, Printed Extracts,* no. 2, *Suffolk* (Publ. Folk-Lore Soc. 37 [London, 1895]), pp. 26-27 (young child stripped naked and passed head foremost through the tree, for rickets as well as rupture); *ibid.*, p. 27 (tree must be split early in the spring, as near east and west as possible; child passed through naked, feet first, as the sun is rising); R. L. Tongue and K. M. Briggs, *Somerset Folklore* (Publ. Folk-Lore Soc. 114 [London, 1965]), p. 221 (child passed sunwise three times; tree bound up with a hay band).

24. *Folk-Lore* 16 (1905): p. 65. Further details on the "maiden ash" and the use of a female ash for male patients, and vice versa are to be found in John Symonds Udal, *Dorsetshire Folk-Lore* (Hertford, 1922), pp. 252-253; Tongue and Briggs, *op. cit.,* p. 42.

25. Ella Mary Leather, *The Folk-Lore of Herefordshire* (Hereford and London, 1912), p. 80.

26. Gaidoz, *op. cit.,* p. 17.

27. Frazer, *GB* 11: p. 170.

28. *Mélusine* 8 (1896-1897): p. 201.

29. Ignacio Maria Barriola, *La Medicina popular en el pais vasco* (San Sebastian, 1952), p. 98.

30. *Mélusine* 8 (1896-1897): p. 202.

31. *Revista de Dialectología y Tradiciones Populares* 1 (1944): p. 295.

32. Hovorka and Kronfeld, *op. cit.* 1: p. 57.

33. *Brown Collection* 6: p. 54, no. 321.

34. Helen Creighton, *Folklore of Lunenburg County, Nova Scotia* (National Museum of Canada, *Bulletin,* no. 117 [Ottawa, 1950]), p. 92, no. 40.

35. *Indiana History Bulletin* 35 (1958): p. 126, no. 144 (epileptic patient passed through three times; if parts of tree grow back together, etc.).

36. Fanny D. Bergen, *Animal and Plant Lore* (Mem. Am. Folklore Soc. 7 [Boston and New York, 1899]), pp. 101-102, no. 1166.

37. *Mélusine* 8 (1896-1897): p. 202.

38. *Rev. Dial. Trad. Pop.* 1 (1944): pp. 295-296 (Galicia, Spain); Feilberg, *op. cit.*, pp. 43-44 (Scandinavia).

39. *Notes and Queries*, 6th ser., 11 (Jan. 17, 1885): p. 46 (Limpfield, England). *Cf.* note 12, above, for the use of holly in America.

40. Paul Bartels, "Durchziehkur in Winkel am Rhein," *Zs. d. Vereins f. Volkskunde* 23 (1913): pp. 288-293. *Cf.* Hovorka and Kronfeld, *op. cit.* 1: p. 57 (cherry tree used in Central Germany around Magdeburg).

41. *Mélusine* 8 (1896-1897): p. 202.

42. *Mélusine* 8 (1896-1897): p. 170.

43. Tillhagen, *op. cit.*, pp. 116, 291; Forsblom, *op. cit.*, p. 542.

44. P. Kemp, *Healing Ritual. Studies in the Technique and Tradition of the Southern Slavs* (London, 1935), p. 148. Other details, including a sketch of the ritual (facing p. 148).

45. Frazer, *GB* 11: pp. 180–181.

46. Castillo de Lucas, *op. cit.*, p. 465 (oak tree); C. Seyfarth, *Aberglaube und Zauberei in der Volksmedizin Sachsens* (Leipzig, 1913), p. 207.

47. Sébillot, *op. cit.* 3: pp. 418–419.

48. William George Black, *Folk-Medicine: A Chapter in the History of Culture* (Publ. Folk-Lore Soc. 12 [London, 1883]): p. 70; de Cock, *op. cit.*, p. 71.

49. Samuel X. Radbill, "Whooping Cough in Fact and Fancy," *Bull. Hist. Med.* (1943) 13: p. 41.

50. *Folk-Lore* 54 (1943): p. 230 (citing Bonser from *Trans. and Proc. Birmingham Arch. Soc.* 56 (1932): p. 49).

51. Forsblom (*op. cit.*, pp. 542–543), however, reports the use of bushes in western Finland.

52. Radbill, *op. cit.*, p. 41; Gurdon, *op. cit.*, p. 14; Radford, *op. cit.*, pp. 19, 92; *Folk-Lore* 43 (1932): p. 105 (Buckinghamshire, *ca.* 1910). *Notes and Queries*, 1st ser., 1 (Apr. 20, 1850): p. 397; *ibid.* 7 (1853): p. 104.

53. Annie Weston Whitney and Caroline Canfield Bullock, *Folk-Lore from Maryland* (Mem. Am. Folklore Soc. 18 [New York, 1925]), p. 88, no. 1789.

54. Black, *op. cit.*, p. 70.

55. de Cock, *op. cit.*, p. 71.

56. Sébillot, *op. cit.*, 3: p. 418. *Cf.* Frazer, *GB* 11: p. 180.

57. Thiselton Dyer, *op. cit.*, pp. 171–172.

58. *Western Folklore* 15 (1956): p. 9, no. 197.

59. Black, *op. cit.*, p. 70; Radford, *op. cit.*, pp. 19, 200.

60. Thomas R. Brendle and Claude W. Unger, *Folk Medicine of the Pennsylvania Germans. The Non-Occult Cures* (Proc. Penna. German Soc. 45 [Norristown, Penna., 1935]), p. 195.

61. Udal, *op. cit.*, p. 231. We shall consider this notion of "escape" later in a discussion of Frazer's theory of an impassable barrier between the patient and a pursuing foe.

62. Gaidoz, *op. cit.*, p. 10; de Cock, *op. cit.*, p. 71.

63. Wood-Martin, *op. cit.*, 2: p. 235. Near to Button Oak, in the forest of Bewdly grows a thorn in the form of an arch, one end in the county of Salop, the other in Stafford. This was visited by numbers of people to make their children pass under it for the cure of whooping cough (*Notes and Queries*, 4th ser., 3 (Mar. 6, 1869): p. 216.

64. Leather, *op. cit.*, p. 82. *Cf.* Udal, *op. cit.*, p. 225, for a routine nine-time pass through a double-rooted briar.

65. *Brown Collection* 6: p. 352, no. 2722.

66. Edwin M. Fogel, *Beliefs and Superstitions of the Pennsylvania Germans* ([Americana Germanica 18, Philadelphia, 1915]), p. 294, no. 1555; Brendle and Unger, *op. cit.*, pp. 133, 196 (crawl toward the east).

67. Brendle and Unger, *op. cit.*, p. 131 (crawl through a double-rooted briar toward the east).

68. Brendle and Unger, *op. cit.*, p. 147.

69. Udal, *op. cit.*, p. 231 (for epilepsy; the evil spirit could not follow the child through the bush).

70. Radford, *op. cit.*, p. 113 (Slavic).

71. *Southern Folklore Quart.* 7 (1943): p. 84.

72. *HDA* 1: p. 1581 (Germany); *ibid.* (France, particularly in the Celtic areas); Wood-Martin, *op. cit.* 2: p. 234 (Ireland).

73. *Folk-Lore* 62 (1951): p. 260.

74. John George Hohman, *Long Lost Friend, or, Book of Pow-Wows,* ed. A. Monroe Aurand, Jr. (Harrisburg, Pennsylvania, 1930), p. 26 (thrust through three times from the same side).

75. *Brown Collection* 6: p. 352, no. 2721.

76. Whitney and Bullock, *op. cit.,* p. 88, no. 1787.

77. *HDA* 1: p. 1581.

78. Castillo de Lucas, *op. cit.,* p. 466 (croup); Hyatt, *op. cit.,* p. 209, no. 4340 (colic).

79. Grimm, *op. cit.* 2: p. 976; *HDA* 1: p. 1581 (on three successive Fridays).

80. Kemp, *op. cit.,* pp. 122–123. *Cf.* also p. 144.

81. *HDA* 1: p. 1581 (citing Cockayne, *Leechdoms* . . . 2: p. 291).

82. *HDA* 1: p. 1581.

83. *HDA* 1: p. 1581.

84. *HDA* 1: p. 1581.

85. de Cock, *op. cit.,* p. 71.

86. Whitney and Bullock, *op. cit.,* p. 88, no. 1788 (crawl under it three times); *Brown Collection* 6: p. 352, no. 2721 (three times); John W. Allen, *Legends and Lore of Southern Illinois* (Carbondale, Illinois, 1963), p. 84 (crawl toward the east).

87. Frazer, *GB* 11: p. 180.

88. Kemp, *op. cit.,* pp. 90–91.

89. *HDA* 9: p. 974 (*Schlingen,* so-called).

90. Seyfarth, *op. cit.,* p. 206; Kemp, *op. cit.,* p. 144, misshapen and freakish growths, or tangles, known in Germany as a *Hexenschlinge,* "witch's loop."

91. *HDA* 9: p. 972. Whether this loop is exactly the same as a "witch's nest," of which Frazer speaks (*GB* 11: p. 185), is not clear. At any rate, in Oldenburg, a cow giving little or no milk, because she is apparently bewitched, is milked through one of these boughs of a birch tree that have grown in a tangle.

92. Grimm, *op. cit.* 2: p. 976.

93. *Folk-Lore* 49 (1938): pp. 196–197; *Rev. Dial. Trad. Pop.* 1 (1944): p. 296; Kemp, *op. cit.,* p. 95.

94. Frazer, *GB* 11: pp. 184–185.

95. John Graham Dalyell, *The Darker Superstitions of Scotland* (Glasgow, 1835), p. 121.

96. Forsblom, *op. cit.,* p. 538.

97. Seligmann, *op. cit.* 1: p. 316.

98. Hovorka and Kronfeld, *op. cit.* 1: pp. 57–58; Frazer, *GB* 11: p. 186, *passim.*

99. In this regard, my views are at variance with those of de Cock, who concluded that the ritual of crawling through the earth probably grew out of the custom of being passed through trees (*op. cit.,* p. 72). In the same breath, I cannot agree with Mannhardt, as stated earlier, that passing through natural clefts of trees grew out of the custom of splitting trees for the purpose. Neither of these two eminent scholars gave reasons for judgments that, on the face of things, seem to run counter to what would have been an orderly development from primitive to advanced stages, and from a simple and natural state to one more

contrived. Even so, de Cock stands a better chance of being right in my estimation, than does Mannhardt.

100. Feilberg, *op. cit.*, p. 45.

101. Forsblom, *op. cit.*, p. 541.

102. Frazer, *GB* 11: p. 191; Gaidoz, *op. cit.*, p. 21.

103. Frazer, *GB* 11: p. 191; Gaidoz, *op. cit.*, p. 21.

104. Radford, *op. cit.*, p. 259; *cf.* Frazer, *GB* 11: p. 190 (proscription against driving sheep through holes in the earth as well as through holes in trees).

105. Grimm, *op. cit.* 2: pp. 975–976; Frazer, *GB* 11: p. 191; *HDA* 7: p. 504; 11: p. 974; Gaidoz, *op. cit.*, pp. 21 ff.; de Cock, *op. cit.*, p. 72.

106. Grendon, *op. cit.*, p. 130.

107. Thiselton Dyer, *op. cit.*, pp. 23–24.

108. Feilberg, *loc. cit.*; Forsblom, *loc. cit.*; Tillhagen, *loc. cit.* There is a fine photograph of *jorddragning* in Tillhagen, p. 295.

109. Tillhagen, *op. cit.*, p. 116; Hovorka and Kronfeld, *op. cit* 2: p. 695, Feilberg, *op. cit.*, p. 43.

110. Feilberg, *op. cit.*, p. 45 (where three paths cross).

111. Hovorka and Kronfeld, *op. cit.* 2: pp. 694–695; Tillhagen, *op. cit.*, p. 116.

112. Feilberg, *op. cit.*, p. 45.

113. Forsblom, *op. cit.*, p. 541.

114. Radbill, *op. cit.*, p. 48.

115. Feilberg, *op. cit.*, p. 44.

116. Hovorka and Kronfeld, *op. cit.* 2: pp. 694–695.

117. Feilberg, *op. cit.*, p. 53.

118. Feilberg, *op. cit.*, p. 44; *HDA* 7: p. 504; *cf.* also col. 503. One must resist the temptation, I believe, to think of the replacement of the sod as an example of "plugging." Even though the disease is perhaps symbolically buried in the hole, there is no actual *Zwischenträger* that is buried or "plugged" in. On this point see Wayland D. Hand, "Plugging, Nailing, Wedging, and Kindred Folk Medical Practices," in *Folklore and Society. Essays in Honor of Benj. A. Botkin,* ed. Bruce Jackson (Hatboro, Penna., 1966), pp. 65, 70–71.

119. Gaidoz, *op. cit.*, pp. 23–23.

120. Gaidoz, *op. cit.*, p. 25. Wood-Martin speaks of such magical stones as "holed stones," *op. cit.*, 2: pp. 226, ff. "Holey" stone is a term used in Yorkshire (*Folk-Lore* 54 [1943]: pp. 298–299).

121. Grimm, *op. cit.* 2: pp. 975–976; *HDA* 9: p. 974; de Cock, *op. cit.*, p. 73.

122. Wood-Martin, *op. cit.*, 2: p. 226.

123. Wood-Martin, *op. cit.* 2: pp. 226–250 (with numerous photographs of holed-stones, not only in Ireland, but elsewhere, particularly the Near East).

124. *Cf.* Gaidoz, *op. cit.*, pp. 25 ff.; Bérenger-Féraud, *op. cit.*, 1: pp. 529–532; Mélusine 8 (1896–1897): pp. 204–206 (excellent photographs).

125. Frazer, *GB* 11: pp. 187–188.

126. Hovorka and Kronfeld, *op. cit.* 2: p. 283. *Popular Superstitions,* ed. George Laurence Gomme, *Gentleman's Magazine Library,* Boston, n.d., p. 186 (hereinafter cited as Gomme); Black, *op. cit.*, p. 66.

127. Wood-Martin, *op. cit.* 2: pp. 233–234 (fig. 62, p. 233).

128. *Wiener Zs. f. Volkskunde* 43 (1938): p. 49.

129. Frazer, *GB* 11; pp 188–189.

130. Radford, *op. cit.*, p. 200 (Cornwall and Aberdeenshire): *ibid.*, p. 149 (Cornwall); Wood-Martin, *op. cit.* 2: p. 230 (County Carlow, Ireland); Mrs. [Eliza] Gutch, ed. *Examples of Printed Folk-Lore Concerning the North Riding of Yorkshire, York and the Ainsty* (Publ. Folk-Lore Soc. 45 [London, 1901]), p. 15.

131. *Folk-Lore* 54 (1943): pp. 298–299.

132. Frazer, *GB* 11: pp. 187–188; Black, *op. cit.*, p. 66.

133. Udal, *op. cit.*, p. 231.

134. *Folk-Lore* 29 (1918): p. 86.

135. G. F. Black and Northcote W. Thomas, *Examples of Printed Folklore Concerning Orkney and Shetland Islands* (Publ. Folk-Lore Soc. 49 [London, 1903]), p. 2.

136. Black, *op. cit.*, p. 66.

137. Grendon, *op. cit.*, p. 130; Wood-Martin, *op. cit.* 2: p. 232.

138. Wood-Martin, *op. cit.* 2: pp. 228–229 (fig. 59, p. 229).

139. Frazer, *GB* 11: p. 187.

140. Frazer, *GB* 11: pp. 186–187.

141. Wood-Martin, *op. cit.* 2: p. 231 (fig. 60, p. 231).

142. W. Branch Johnson, *Folktales of Normandy* (London, 1929), p. 188. (This is true also of the famous Men-a-Tol stones in Cornwall.)

143. Seligmann, *op. cit.* 1: p. 328.

144. *Zs. d. Vereins f. Volkskunde* 12 (1902): p. 112.

145. Eleanor Hull, *Folklore of the British Isles* (London, [1928]), p. 101 (Orkney Islands).

146. Wood-Martin, *op. cit.* 2: p. 247.

147. Wood-Martin, *op. cit.* 2: pp. 237–239 (fig. 63, p. 238 shows a typical one).

148. Wood-Martin, *op. cit.* 2: p. 239 (fig. 64, p. 239). *Cf.* also p. 226.

149. Wood-Martin, *op. cit.* 2: p. 226.

150. Wood-Martin, *op. cit.* 2: p. 227 (fig. 58).

151. Wood-Martin, *op. cit.* 2: pp. 226–227.

152. Wood-Martin, *op. cit.* 2: p. 249 (fig. 76).

153. Gaidoz, *op. cit.*, p. 33; Nyrop, *op. cit.*, pp. 23, 26.

154. Seligmann, *op. cit.* 1: p. 327.

155. de Cock, *op. cit.*, p. 75.

156. Sébillot, *op. cit.* 4: p. 59.

157. *Zs. d. Vereins f. Volkskunde* 12 (1902): p. 112.

158. *Zs. d. Vereins f. Volkskunde* 12 (1902): pp. 110–111.

159. *Mélusine* 8 (1896–1897): p. 284.

160. *Mélusine* 8 (1896–1897): p. 177.

161. Radbill, *op. cit.*, p. 42, *passim,* Radford, *op. cit.*, p. 257, *Folk-Lore* 22 (1911): p. 57 (Ireland): *Med. Hist.* 4 (1960): p. 350 (Scotland); Tongue and Briggs, *op. cit.*, p. 44.

162. Radford, *op. cit.*, p. 149; Black, *op. cit.*, p. 118; *Folk-Lore* 8 (1897): pp. 15–16 (she-ass); *ibid.* 15 (1904): p. 460 (Ireland).

163. *Mélusine* 8 (1896–1897): pp. 283–284.

164. Black, *op. cit.*, p. 118.

165. *Notes and Queries,* 7th ser., 4 (Aug. 27, 1887): p. 176.

166. Walter Gregor, *Notes on the Folk-Lore of the North-East of Scotland* (Publ. Folk-Lore Soc. 7 [London, 1881]), p. 132.

167. *Notes and Queries,* 5th ser., 10 (Aug. 17, 1878): p. 126; *Folk-Lore* 23 (1912): p. 478; Gutch, *op. cit.*, p. 179.

168. Bérenger-Féraud, *op. cit.* 1: p. 526.

169. Black, *op. cit.,* p. 118.

170. Radbill, *op. cit.,* pp. 43–44 (breadcrumbs which have fallen from a donkey's mouth are caught in aprons, and then fed to the child); *Folk-Lore,* 13 (1902): p. 57.

171. *Brown Collection* 6: p. 67, no. 421. *Cf.* Radbill, *op. cit., p. 42.*

172. *Notes and Queries,* 7th ser., 4 (July 2, 1887): p. 5; 8th ser., 11 (Mar. 13, 1897): p. 206.

173. *Notes and Queries,* 2nd ser., 11 (Mar. 30, 1861): p. 243 (a prayer to the Saviour and to the child's mother).

174. *Folk-Lore* 13 (1902): p. 57 (involving the eating of bread as well as the invocation of the Trinity).

175. See also, *Mélusine* 8 (1896–1897): p. 283.

176. Udal, *op. cit.,* p. 232; Wood-Martin, *op. cit.* 2: p. 189.

177. Radbill, *op. cit.,* p. 44.

178. M. C. Balfour and Northcote W. Thomas, *Examples of Printed Folk-Lore Concerning Northumberland* (Publ. Folk-Lore Soc. 53 [London, 1903]), p. 49.

179. Bergen, *op. cit.,* p. 20, no. 104.

180. Castillo de Lucas, *op. cit.,* p. 466; *Notes and Queries,* 10th ser., 10 (Oct. 24, 1908): p. 326 (measles).

181. *HDA* 2. p. 1005.

182. *Hoosier Folklore* 5 (1946): p. 70, no. 27.

183. Feilberg, *op. cit.*, p. 53.

184. Gregor, *op. cit.,* p. 46; Radford, *op. cit.,* p. 257 (where it is represented as being general).

185. Wood-Martin, *op. cit.* 2: pp. 232–233 (fig. 61, p. 232).

186. *HDA* 9: p. 974.

187. Whitney and Bullock, *op. cit.,* pp. 93–94, nos. 1880–1881. *Cf.* A. Monroe Aurand, *Popular Home Remedies and Superstitions of the Pennsylvania Germans* (Harrisburg, Pa., 1941), p. 8 (a spell).

188. Aurand, *op. cit.,* p. 8.

189. *West Virginia Folklore* 7 (1957): p. 36, no. 6c.

190. Allen, *op. cit.*, p. 84.

191. *Jour. Amer. Folklore* 10 (1897): p. 79.

192. Brendle and Unger, *op. cit.,* p. 195; Aurand, *op. cit.,* p. 8, *cf.* also the *Brown Collection* 6: pp. 53–54, no. 319, for additional references and other folkloric notions about this rare disease.

193. Brendle and Unger, *op. cit.,* p. 196.

194. *Mélusine* 8 (1896–1897): p. 176.

195. Feilberg, *op. cit.,* p. 46.

196. *Mélusine* 8 (1896–1897): p. 175.

197. *Notes and Queries,* 8th ser., 9 (May 23, 1896): p. 408.

198. Feilberg, *op. cit.,* p. 44 (ox harness); Tillhagen, *op. cit.,* p. 116 (hames standing on end; *ibid.,* p. 291).

199. Kemp, *op. cit.,* p. 142.

200. Forsblom, *op. cit.,* p. 539 (three times counter sunwise through the reins of a bridle).

201. Seligmann, *op. cit.* 1: p. 327.

202. Forsblom, *op. cit.,* p. 539.

203. *Zs. d. Vereins f. Volkskunde* 12 (1902): p. 112.

204. Theodor Zachariae, "Scheingeburt," *Zs. des Vereins f. Volkskunde* 20 (1910): p. 141 (hereinafter cited Zachariae, "Scheingeburt").

205. *HDA* 1: p. 1010; Zachariae, "Scheingeburt," p. 158.

206. Forsblom, *op. cit.*, p. 537.
207. *Rev. Dial. Trad. Pop.* 1 (1944): p. 264.
208. *Mélusine* 8 (1896–1897): p. 176.
209. Gaidoz, *op. cit.*, p. 58; Black, *op. cit.*, p. 69.
210. de Cock, *op. cit.*, p. 74.
211. Forsblom, *op. cit.*, p. 537 (other examples).
212. Arthur Palmer Hudson, *Specimens of Mississippi Folk-Lore* (Ann Arbor, Mich., 1928), p. 154.
213. Zachariae, "Scheingeburt," pp. 144–146.
214. Zachariae, *loc. cit.*
215. Bess Allen Donaldson, *The Wild Rue* (London, 1938), p. 28.
216. *Mélusine* 8 (1896–1897): p. 177.
217. Forsblom, *op. cit.*, p. 537.
218. Kemp, *op. cit.*, p. 227.
219. Forsblom, *op. cit.*, p. 537.
220. Forsblom, *op. cit.*, p. 538 (for rickets); Seligmann, *op. cit.* 1: pp. 327–328 (enchantment in Scotland).
221. Gregor, *op. cit.*, pp. 7–8; Finland: Forsblom, *op. cit.*, pp. 537–538 (pulled through mother's body linen at time of birth, for rickets).
222. Wood-Martin, *op. cit.* 2: p. 242.
223. Hovorka and Kronfeld, *op. cit.* 2: p. 694.
224. Gaidoz, *op. cit.*, pp. 35–54.
225. These essays are found in *Mélusine,* Supplements IV–VIII to his 1892 study, appearing in vols. 8–10 (1896–1901).
226. *Mélusine* 8 (1896–1897): pp. 175–176. *Cf.* Bérenger-Féraud, *op. cit.* 1: p. 525.
227. Wood-Martin, *op. cit.* 2: p. 227.
228. Wood-Martin, *op. cit.* 2: p. 228.
229. Radford, *op. cit.*, p. 123.
230. Gaidoz, *op. cit.*, pp. 35–54; de Cock, *op. cit.*, pp. 72–74 (including an item on p. 74 dealing with a custom in the Protestant north of Belgium, whereby sick children were pulled through the rungs of church chairs), *HDA* 9: p. 974; Feilberg, *op. cit.*, p. 43; *Rev. Dial. Trad. Pop.* 1 (1944): p. 255.
231. *L'Intermédiaire des Chercheurs et Curieux,* 30 Âout 1895, cols. 218–219.
232. Hovorka and Kronfeld, *op. cit.* 2: p. 694.
233. Joh. Th. Storaker, *Sygdom og Forgjørelse i den Norske Folketro* (Norsk Folkeminnelag, no. 28 [Oslo, 1932]), p. 70, no. 347.
234. Feilberg, *op. cit.*, pp. 46–47.
235. Hovorka and Kronfeld, *op. cit.*, 2: p. 694.
236. Radford, *op. cit.*, p. 259.
237. Forsblom, *op. cit.*, p. 539.
238. *HDA* 9: p. 974; Tillhagen, *op. cit.*, p. 116 (a chair with twelve rungs).
239. Feilberg, *op. cit.*, p. 44.
240. Brendle and Unger, *op. cit.*, pp. 133, 147, 195, respectively.
241. *Folk-Lore* 8 (1897): p. 187.
242. Brendle and Unger, *op. cit.*, p. 195; Fogel, *op. cit.*, p. 283, no. 1492.
243. Creighton, *op. cit.*, p. 85 (Nova Scotia); *Jour. Amer. Folklore* 2 (1889): p. 28.
244. Brendle and Unger, *op. cit.*, p. 147 (wasting sickness); Hyatt, *op. cit.*, p. 209, no. 4357 (colic).
245. Brendle and Unger, *op. cit.*, p. 133 (cough); *Keystone Folklore Quart.* 3 (1958): 66, no. 50 (hiccough).

246. Allen, *op. cit.*, pp. 85–86.
247. Kemp, *op. cit.*, pp. 88–90.
248. *HDA* 9: p. 974; Hovorka and Kronfeld, *op. cit.* 2: p. 695; Feilberg, *op. cit.*, pp. 52–53.
249. Thiselton Dyer, *op. cit.*, p. 177.
250. Dalyell, *op. cit.*, p. 394.
251. *Mélusine* 8 (1896–1897): p. 179.
252. Gaidoz, *op. cit.*, p. 67.
253. James Hastings, ed. *Encyclopaedia of Religion and Ethics* (13 vols., Edinburgh, 1908–1926) 4: pp. 846–852.
254. Sébillot, *op. cit.*, 3: pp. 416–417.
255. Tillhagen, *op. cit.*, p. 116; Forsblom, *op. cit.*, p. 540.
256. Forsblom, *op. cit.*, p. 539.
257. *Folk-Lore* 10 (1899): p. 181.
258. Hyatt, *op. cit.*, p. 280, no. 5655.
259. Frazer, *GB* 11: p. 185; *HDA* 9: 974; Feilberg, *op. cit.*, p. 44; Forsblom, *op. cit.*, p. 539; Tillhagen, *op. cit.*, p. 116.
260. Dalyell, *op. cit.*, pp. 121–122.
261. Seligmann, *op. cit.* 1: p. 327.
262. Seyfarth, *op. cit.*, p. 207.
263. Feilberg, *op. cit.*, p. 46; Forsblom, *op. cit.*, p. 538.
264. de Cock, *op. cit.*, p. 74; Gaidoz, *op. cit.*, pp. 57–58.
265. Zachariae, "Scheingeburt," p. 172.
266. *Zs. d. Vereins f. Volkskunde* 12 (1902): p. 112; *Mélusine* 8 (1896–1897): p. 179 (Poland).
267. Forsblom, *op. cit.*, p. 539.
268. Frazer, *GB* 11: p. 186.
269. Barriola, *op. cit.*, p. 115.
270. Seyfarth, *op. cit.*, p. 237.
271. Seyfarth, *op. cit.*, p. 238.
272. de Cock, *op. cit.*, p. 75, no. 1.
273. *HDA* 11: p. 974; *Mélusine* 8 (1896–1897): pp. 177–178 (Poland); Gaidoz, *op. cit.*, p. 63 (restlessness during the twelve days of Christmas).
274. Seligmann, *op. cit.* 1: p. 327.
275. Feilberg, *op. cit.*, p. 50.
276. *Folk-Lore* 32 (1921): p. 125.
277. Whitney and Bullock, *op. cit.*, p. 94, no. 1881.
278. *Brown Collection* 1: p. 667.
279. *HDA* 9: p. 974; Seyfarth, *op. cit.*, p. 206; Hovorka and Kronfeld, *op. cit.* 2: p. 695; Tillhagen, *op. cit.*, p. 116.
280. Tillhagen, *op. cit.*, p. 116.
281. Frazer, *GB* 11: p. 192, no. 2; de Cock, *op. cit.*, p. 74; Gaidoz, *op. cit.*, pp. 59–60.
282. *HDA* 11: p. 9, 4; *Zs. d. Vereins f. Volkskunde* 12 (1902): p. 112.
283. *Mélusine* 8 (1896–1897): p. 282.
284. Forsblom, *op. cit.*, p. 540.
285. *Rev. Dial. Trad. Pop.* 3 (1947): p. 567.
286. Wood-Martin, *op. cit.* 2: p. 233.
287. Moritz Busch, *Deutscher Volksglaube* (Leipzig, 1877), pp. 46, 190–191.
288. R. Hofschläger, "Über den Ursprung der Heilmethoden," *Festschrift zur Feier des 50jährigen Bestehens des Naturwissenschaftlichen Vereins zu Krefeld* (Krefeld, 1908), pp. 211, 215, *passim.* (I have not seen this). *Cf. HDA* 1: p.

121; Zachariae, "Scheingeburt," p. 158; Gaidoz, *op. cit.*, pp. 78 f.; Nyrop, *op. cit.*, p. 21.

289. *HDA* 1: p. 121.

290. Frazer, *GB* 11: p. 179.

291. Hovorka and Kronfeld, *op. cit.* 2: pp. 695, 694; Seligmann, *op. cit.* 1: p. 327; Radford, *op. cit.*, p. 229.

292. Tillhagen, *op. cit.*, p. 116.

293. Kemp, *op. cit.*, p. 91 *Cf.* also note 142, above, for passing through a menhir in France without one's back touching it, or the knees touching the ground.

294. Frazer, *GB* 11: p. 184.

295. Frazer, *GB* 11: p. 171, no. 1. Various examples on pp. 173–179.

296. Udal, *op. cit.*, p. 231. *Cf.* notes 61, 133, above, and the textual matter to which they refer. *Cf.* also note 50.

297. Wood-Martin, *op. cit.* 2: p. 247 (*Cf.* note 146, above.

298. For a general treatment of transference, see my article, "The Magical Transference of Disease," *North Carolina Folklore* 13 (1965): pp. 83–109. For the translocation of disease to trees and other objects by a special process of implantation and impregnation see my article, "Plugging, Nailing, Wedging and Kindred Folk Medical Practices," in *Folklore and Society. Essays in Honor of Benj. A. Botkin,* ed. Bruce Jackson (Hatboro, Pa., 1966), pp. 63–75.

299. Grimm, *op. cit.* 2: p. 976.

300. *Cf.* Nyrop, *op. cit.*, p. 20; Gaidoz, *op. cit.*, p. 78; Tillhagen, *op. cit.*, pp. 116–117; Brendle and Unger, *op. cit.*, p. 195. *Cf.* notes 50, 106, above, and the textual material to which they refer.

301. *Mélusine* 9 (1898–1899): p. 6.

302. *Mélusine* 8 (1896–1897): p. 284.

303. Tillhagen, *op. cit.*, p. 116.

304. Frazer, *GB* 11: p. 172. In this connection there are numerous instances in the literature of a person who has been cured by passing through, taking special pains to see that the tree through which he was passed as a youngster is cared for, and by no means cut down.

305. On this important point which I have raised, see *North Carolina Folklore* 13 (1965): pp. 83–84.

306. Des Gervasius von Tilbury Otia Imperialia, ed. Felix Liebrecht (Hannover, 1856), Anhang, pp. 170–171; "Die ursprüngliche Bedeutung dieses ganzen Verfahrens [des Durchkriechens] scheint mir nun aber in einer symbolischen Wiedergeburt des Kranken zu bestehen, wodurch er gleichsam aufs neue durch eine den weiblichen Geburtsteilen ähnliche "Öffnung in die Welt eintritt und seine frühere Krankheit hinter sich zurücklässt." Liebrecht makes the further point that the child is passed through headfirst and naked, as in natural birth. In seeking to explain the English custom of binding up the cleft in the tree, in order that it may heal and grow strong, Liebrecht speaks also of the recovery of the mother as her reproductive organs grow back in place. The time involved for both the tree and the mother to get back to a state of normalcy, he says, is sufficient for the child itself to become healthy and sound again.

307. Karl Weinhold, *Zur Geschichte des heidnischen Ritus,* Abhandlungen der königlichen Akademie der Wissenschaften zu Berlin (Berlin, 1896), p. 37.

308. Nyrop, *op. cit.*, p. 27; Gaidoz, Mélusine, 1898–1899, 9: 8; *cf.* also Gaidoz, *op. cit.*, pp. 24, 75–78.

309. Feilberg, *op. cit.,* pp. 42–43; Hovorka and Kronfeld, *op. cit.* 2: p. 694; Seyfarth, *op. cit.,* p. 248; Tillhagen, *op. cit.,* p. 116; *HDA* 1: p. 121.

310. Zachariae, "Scheingeburt," p. 172. See the full text as cited in connection with note 265, above.

311. Zachariae, "Scheingeburt," p. 155.

312. Brendle and Unger, *op. cit.,* p. 147.

313. Nyrop, *op. cit.,* pp. 23, 26; Zachariae, "Scheingeburt," p. 168; Gaidoz, *op. cit.,* p. 76.

314. Zachariae, "Scheingeburt," p. 169.

315. Wood-Martin, *op. cit.,* 2: p. 226. There is a picture of this ceremony at a shrine at Kollegor, India on page 227, fig. 58.

316. Frazer, *op. cit.,* 9: p. 195; *cf.* Theodor Zachariae, "Das kaudinische Joch," *Zs. d. Vereins f. Volkskunde,* 1914, 24: pp. 201–206.

317. Kemp, *op. cit.,* pp. 86, 90–91, 95, 104, 123, 137, 142–144, 148, 155, 227, *passim.*

318. Zachariae, "Scheingeburt," p. 172. *Cf.* note 265, above, and the text to which it refers.

319. Zachariae, "Scheingeburt," p. 172.

320. Wood-Martin, *op. cit.* 2: p. 228; Feilberg, *op. cit.,* p. 44; Tillhagen, *op. cit.,* p. 116.

321. Weinhold, *op. cit.,* pp. 37–38; Feilberg, *op. cit.,* p. 44; de Cock, *op. cit.,* p. 72; Tillhagen, *op. cit.,* p. 116.

12
Animal Sacrifice in American Folk Curative Practice*

Animal sacrifice has not yet outgrown its primitive roots in many parts of the world, but it will come as a surprise to many people interested in folk medicine that this inveterate practice should still be encountered in twentieth-century America. The term sacrifice as used throughout this paper generally does not refer to any religious act or ritual involving the propitiation of Gods and other divinities, nor does it denote measures to neutralize the hostility of demons or other powers thought to underlie impaired physical condition or disease.[1] Specifically, animals are killed so that the medical practitioner may gain medicinal products, or so that, among other things, the patient may benefit from the absorptive power of warm viscera or quivering flesh as an application to ailing parts. It is in the choice of animal to be dispatched, and the manner of killing, that ritualistic vestiges of sacrifice are to be seen in this country, rather than in religious or cultic acts of propitiation and worship. Altough it is nowhere hinted at in the literature, the forfeit of the animal's life may once have been construed, and still might be in the minds of some, as a miraculous means of restoring health to a disease-ridden body. Within the memory of man since the time of colonization, however, the taking of the animal's life was never likely thought of, except among the

*This article originally appeared in the *Bulletin of the History of Medicine,* 51 (1977), 232–244. Permission to reprint has been given by the editor and by the Johns Hopkins University Press.

aboriginal peoples, as a sacrificial act whereby sinful and diseased man could be rid of his malady as he was brought into harmony and favor with sacred powers specifically through the treasured offering of an animal's life. Since much is known about sacrificial practice among the North American Indians,[2] I am limiting my discussion of the subject to American customs deriving, in the main, from European tradition.

Treated in the present paper are only cases involving the actual killing of animals. The wide range of animal products, often called simples,[2] if they are not compounded with other ingredients, cannot be treated here. However, in passing, it must be noted that these medicaments are usually gained from the animal after it has been killed, either specifically for the purpose at hand, or as by-products of an animal slaughtered for meat, or birds and fish taken for the same purpose. In these cases the killing of the animal itself, or its death, if natural, is never mentioned. Products constituting the zoological materia medica range from all kinds of internal parts to hide and hair, hooves, horns, feathers, claws, beaks, scales, and the like, not to mention the excrement and other effluvia such as saliva and urine.

Blood, perhaps more than most of the animal products mentioned, is thought to possess special potency, and may, in the minds of many patients and healers, have a special magical efficacy as well. This special power is supposed to reside in the blood itself as the life principle, as well as the seat of human vitality and the physiological basis of life itself.[3] In some parts of the world the power of the soul is believed to be resident in the blood,[4] and in many religious systems blood figures importantly, if not centrally, in notions of sacrifice,[5] and in doctrines of sin and expiation.[6] Blood as a life token, of course, is well attested in folklore, where clear water, for example, may become bloody, or likewise a sword, when a friend or kinsman is in mortal danger or slain in a far distant place.[7]

The drinking of animal blood is not common in American folk medicine, and, where this practice is resorted to, it does not appear to have any special ritual significance. The consuming of blood in this way, most often for tuberculosis itself, takes place where animals are slaughtered.[8] I remember as a boy in Salt Lake accompanying my father with a consumptive who went to a slaughterhouse to imbibe the warm blood of a calf. The drinking of blood of creatures other than meat-producing animals would, in the ordinary scale of things, move into the realm of magical, if not sacrificial, healing. In the Rio Grande country, for example, a black cat was pressed into service for the cure of consumption. The cat was killed, the bones extracted, and the consumptive rubbed with the flesh from head to foot. Finally he was fed the cat's blood mixed with warm water.[9]

More ritualistic kinds of bloodletting, all resulting in the death of the animal in question, is seen in an account from Lunenberg County, Nova Scotia, where a child with asthma was made to stand in the hot blood of a slaughtered animal;[10] from Tennessee, where the gushing blood of a freshly killed pig was thought to help eczema;[11] and from Illinois where the warm blood from a freshly killed beef was made to drip on hands afflicted with eczema.[12] In their general outlines all three of these cures are not too unlike the *taurobolium* of antiquity,[13] where the blood of a slain bull was made to flow freely over communicants huddled beneath a sacrificial scaffold. To return to the point made earlier, even though sacramental regeneration did not figure in any of the American blood rituals listed above, physical renewal was at the basis of every single one. Once more I must emphasize the fact that this explanation is one which I myself have supplied. Never was the life of the animal itself thought of as effecting the cure; rather the cure was expected as a result of the special power of the blood as a medicine.

The use of the blood from a black cat for the cure of shingles is too well known for me to dwell upon it here. Whether the cat is killed outright,[14] or its blood is gained from an amputated tail,[15] there is a ritualistic and even magical character to the whole procedure. This aura is heightened when it is specified that the cat must be killed in the light of the moon,[16] or that the animal must be without a single white hair, as reported from the eastern and central parts of the United States.[17] An instructive item from western New York is worth giving in its entirety here for the light it sheds on the ritual aspects of the cure: "Shingles (Herpes zoster) is said to be cured by applying the skin of a black cat. The animal must be without a white hair; its throat must be cut, the blood collected in a cup and then poured into the freshly removed skin, which is to be applied to the diseased surface and will cure in a few hours. A correspondent says, 'This is no hearsay matter with the writer, for in his boyhood he was afflicted with the disease and passed a night with the blood of his favorite pussy covering his left side and the pit of his stomach.' "[18] As one further example of unadulterated quality sought in the animal, and also of the imbibing of blood from animals not used for food, a treatment for consumption from the Pennsylvania German country is cited. It dates from the early 1890s. "For curing consumption, catch a black cat without a single white hair; a teaspoonful of blood from the tail will surely cure."[19] More primitive in its impact on the average person, perhaps, is the following belief from Oklahoma: "Find an animal of absolute solid color, and bring it to the bedside of the patient. Kill the animal and quickly apply the hot blood to the affected place."[20] This practice, if indeed it was widespread enough to deserve the term, dates from the 1930s.

We have already seen examples of the cutting off of a cat's tail to combat shingles, so we can turn to other examples of a kind of ritual killing and torture. Ignoring cases of the use of the legs of various kinds of animals, once the animal has been dispatched, I cite only examples involving the severing of members while the animal is alive. In Illinois, within the last few years a cure for warts was prescribed which involves the cutting off of a frog's leg, and rubbing the leg to warts while the flesh still quivers.[21] Contact of the blood with the wart, though not stated, must be presumed. A related item from Indiana, collected only thirty years ago, does make clear the blood part of the office. "To facilitate the cutting of teeth, pull off the head of a black hen, and rub the child's gums with the blood neck."[22] The pulling out of the legs of insects is accomplished with less exertion, for which reason the ritual aspect of the dismemberment might be somewhat lessened. Among southern Negroes, the legs of live bedbugs and grasshoppers were pulled off, wrapped in dough, and swallowed alive to combat the chills.[23] The same process was followed in North Carolina, with the sacrifice of a "granddaddy."[24] This last ritual is rare because, as I suspect, the spider is an insect that enjoys immunity from pursuit in Anglo-Saxon countries, as attested by the old verse,

> If thou wouldst live and thrive,
> Let the spider run alive.

Since crickets enjoy the same favor and immunity, I am not surprised to find few examples of the mutilation of this fabled denizen of the hearth. An example from Texas, collected within the last five years, involves the killing of the cricket before its leg is cut off.[25]

The dry picking of birds and fowls, one of the lesser barbarities in killing and healing rituals, fortunately, is not widespread. The first of the following two examples, an item from

West Virginia, involves the plucking of the feathers from the breast of a live pigeon. The exposed part of the bird is placed on the stomach of a person suffering from convulsions, for the purpose of drawing off the seizure. The absorption of the malady definitely harms the bird, but apparently does not kill it.[26] The dry picking of a chicken in an Indiana folk medical prescription for scarlet fever, however, is only a prelude to flaying a strip of skin three inches wide from the breast bone and back while the chicken is warm. The skin is then placed around the patient's neck to draw out the poison. The reader is left to guess what finally betides the hapless fowl.[27]

Flaying alive is a brutality that even exceeds dismemberment. Widely known in animal sacrifice elsewhere,[28] this barbarity is little known in this country. Cases of freshly-skinned animals, however, are numerous in American folk medicine, but only flaying alive is adverted to here. In Newfoundland, lump cramp is treated by twisting an eel, skinned alive, around the affected muscles.[29] A Kentucky cure for warts involves the tearing off of a toad frog's skin, but one cannot tell clearly from the entry whether the creature is supposed to be alive or dead at the time the brutal flaying takes place.[30]

We have already learned of the consumption of animal blood and have considered cases of blood applied for maladies of the skin and for other external uses. We have also seen the animal's skin employed in various applications, with or without emphasis on the bloody component of the freshly skinned pelt. Now we come to what is perhaps one of the major uses of animals' parts freshly killed, namely, the application of the flesh and internal organs of animals applied to wounds of all kinds, swellings, and other conditions where the warmth and the supposed absorptive power of the animal flesh is thought to exert a sort of natural healing quality. The magical healing power of the flesh is never mentioned, if, indeed, there is any indication that such power is resident in the warm and bloody mass itself. The magical character of the ritual must be deduced from the nature of the animal, as seen in its total folkloric configuration. The details of the sacrificial ritual itself, the special actions of the officiant, if any, and other details may add up to enough information to distinguish these "ritualistic" killings from the ordinary slaughtering of animals, but there are no clear-cut criteria to follow.

In the case of larger animals, they are usually killed before any cutting open and evisceration can be undertaken. In the case of birds, barnyard fowls, and other small animals, however, the cutting open, the tearing apart, or the wringing of the neck is often the means of death itself. This ritual act is carried out in all parts of the country, and Foster assures us that this practice is also widespread throughout Spanish America.[31] In the United States, for example, the flesh of a chicken freshly cut open is applied not only to absorb the poison of various kinds of snakebites and insect stings and to reduce swellings and inflammations of all kinds, but it is used as a specific, among other things, for such assorted maladies as epilepsy, burns, shingles, pneumonia, and the like. Black chickens, magical animals widely used in witchcraft and conjury, are often preferable to ordinary ones. In North Carolina, for example, a black chicken is cut open while alive and bound to the foot of the patient to draw out the fever.[32] Erysipelas is treated in Louisiana by cutting open a black frizzly chicken and applying its warm parts to the inflamed area.[33] In the same state, special care is taken in the treatment of bites, that the black hen be applied while still jumping. When the chicken has stopped fluttering, the poison is supposed to have been withdrawn.[34] In Nebraska an option is given as to whether or not the hen should be placed on the bite after it has been killed, or while still alive.[35] This cure is specified for snakebite.

Frogs and toads, both highly magical animals, are cut open and bound to afflicted parts, for drawing out poison, inflammation, soreness, and the like, in parts of the country as far removed from each other as the eastern seaboard,[36] the Gulf states,[37] and the Rocky Mountain country.[38] An item from Texas specifies, for example, that the frog must be applied to a sore finger while the animal is still alive and kicking. In the Alleghenies, the bodies of living toads, successively applied to cancer, it is believed, will gradually remove the growth. At first the toads die very rapidly, but mortality is lessened with each application and finally ceases altogether. At this point, recovery is then complete.[39] The use of frogs, split open in the manner stated, dates from the time of Pliny the Elder, when it was noted as a cure for podagra.[40] The cutting open of household pets such as cats and dogs, known in Europe,[41] apparently is little encountered in America. A case of cutting off a cat's tail for use in curing shingles, however, was noted earlier in this paper, and we shall shortly see the sacrifice of a dog for the curing of erysipelas.

Cutting open is one thing. Tearing in half is quite another. This brutal business, perhaps more magical and ritualistic than cutting asunder, is certainly more primitive, and is to be found in different parts of the country. It must nevertheless be considered a rarity. In Texas, a jet black chicken is specified. Such a chicken is torn open, and the blood rubbed on chicken pox sores.[42] Although I have resisted citing European material in the body of this paper, a custom in Dorsetshire, still practiced in the early 1920s, shows what a firm hold the savage killing of animals still has on the minds of people in the modern civilized community. Udal writes: " 'Cunning men' used to hold an annual levée in the neighborhood of Stalbridge, and sold to the crowds legs torn from the bodies of living toads and placed them in a bag which was worn around the neck of a patient, and counted a sovereign remedy for scrofula and the 'overlooked.' It was called 'Toad Fair.' "[43]

An extension of the application of warm viscera to a wound is the placing of an ailing member into the body cavity of an animal killed for the purpose. Larger animals, mammals usually, are pressed into service. In the Ozarks a steer is killed, and the bare feet of a patient suffering from asthma are thrust into the warm bodily cavity until the entrails cool.[44] For snakebite, according to a Nebraska folk medical belief, an animal should be cut open, preferably a cow, and the bitten area should be buried in the middle of the animal until the poison is drawn out as the carcass becomes cold.[45] One must assume that the animal is killed specifically for this cure, as people would be unlikely to eat meat which is permeated by the poison of the snake. Among the Pennsylvania Germans the custom once prevailed of killing a dog, cutting it open, and then placing the feet of a patient suffering from erysipelas into the body cavity upon the entrails.[46] Dykstra mentions the use of cats as well as dogs for a similar office in Friesland.[47] Chickens, though smaller and little suited to this kind of a healing procedure, are nevertheless used in Illinois for the cure of rheumatic afflictions.[48] If both feet or legs are affected, two live chickens are cut open to encase one foot each.[49]

The rendering out of the fat of various kinds of worms, snails, spiders, and other kinds of insects, either by corking them up in a bottle to die of suffocation or starvation, and finally to be rendered out by the rays of the sun, or by other kinds of warmth, is a practice well known in all parts of the country.[50] Some of these cures derive, no doubt, from the so-called *Egyptian Secrets* of Albertus Magnus, cheap editions of which were once available in all parts of the country. In Indiana, oil was even tried out of toads in this conventional way, a little salt being placed into the sealed can with the animal.[51]

Akin to corking up a creature for the purpose of rendering out its fat, as treated above, is another form of sealing the animal up. In this latter instance, however, a magical cure, rather than one brought about by the use of an animal product, seems to be involved. Although the spider, caterpillar, woodlouse, or other kind of insect is placed in a thimble, a nutshell, or sewed up in a bag to be worn around the neck, its use as an amulet is contingent on the insect's death, for not until the creature dies is the cure effected. Cures of this kind, well known in Europe,[52] have been reported from the province of Ontario, throughout the South, and as far west as Illinois, Indiana, and Texas.[53] Not only are such diseases as whooping cough, thrush, and common coughs and colds involved in the cures, but these amulets are worn to aid dentition in children.[54]

Because of its affinity to rubbing and squeezing, mashing is taken up here rather than under mutilation, which was treated above. The mashing of sowbugs, angleworms, and spiders, often in one's own hands, is done either to alleviate pain magically through the act of crushing the creature to death,[55] or to provide a substance for salves, teas, or other medicaments destined for later use.[56] Holding a creature in one's hand until it dies, rubbing it to death; or squeezing the life out of it are all done to the same general effect. These magical practices are related to the ancient practice of squeezing a mole to death to obtain power as a healer. This whole subject deserves special treatment, but its salient features may be noted here. Before discussing moles as magical creatures in curative practices, we can briefly allude to the squeezing to death of a mouse in Alabama for curing of pain in general,[57] the throttling of weasels for the cure of felons and other maladies in Indiana,[58] use of frogs in North Carolina and Georgia for the cure of chills,[59] and bullfrogs in Georgia for the same malady.[60] A slower and more painful death comes to a toad used to cure warts in the Pennsylvania German country. Employed for this purpose is the first toad encountered in the spring. The creature is simply rubbed on the wart until the toad itself dies.[61] Contagious as well as symbolic magic, of course, is seen in this cure.

Perhaps the prototype of all rituals of rubbing to death and squeezing to death of small animals as a means of gaining healing power on the part of aspiring healers is the lowly mole. This idea, fathered on Paracelsus, but really centuries older, is known everywhere in Europe,[62] and it is also well known in many parts of America. Accounts of how the creature is killed vary from holding it until it finally dies,[63] rubbing it to death,[64] crushing it,[65] smothering it,[66] or dispatching it quickly.[67] In Louisiana it was believed, for example, that a live mole was caught and rubbed to death. If one succeeded in killing the mole in this manner without being bitten, he would gain the power of healing.[68] Healers who have acquired the magical gift perform the ordinary kind of ministrations for various ailments, or it is simply stated that they are able to cure such and such a disease, sometimes by the mere touch, at other times by squeezing such a growth as a felon, as in Maryland,[69] or rubbing pains out of the body, as in South Carolina, and elsewhere in the South.[70] In the Allegheny Mountains, sprains are cured by applying interrupted pressure to the affected area with the hand in which a mole has been squeezed to death.[71] The curing of warts is accomplished in the Ozark country by smothering a mole and then holding the animal above the head for a moment.[72] In addition to being credited with the ability to cure all manner of excrescences, including the allaying of common festerings and so-called risings,[73] a healer who has gained his curative power from a mole is supposed, in different parts of the country, to be able to cure such diverse ailments as rheumatism,[74] headache,[75] and milk leg.[76]

Ritual magic in connection with the sacrifice of moles is seen in the innocence of the healer receiving the highly prized gift of healing. In America, as well as in Europe,[77] this boon is thought best acquired by a child before his seventh year. In Pennsylvania and Kentucky, among other places, a youngster in this state of innocence, if he kills a mole with his own hands, is said to have the power to cure felons.[78] In Germany the gift of healing may be acquired, it is believed, even in the cradle.[79]

We have just considered the matter of innocence of the healer himself as a factor in the magical transmission of the gift of healing from the dying animal to the human recipient of the divine gift. There is not space to develop the whole notion of innocence, unadulterated quality, freedom from taint and blemish, and other states of perfection or acceptability that are often said to attend the healing office. This I have done in a recent paper,[80] but the emphasis in that effort was entirely on the healer. It is fitting in this present paper to call attention to certain of these qualities in the sacrificial animal. As we saw earlier in the discussion of shingles, they deal not so much with innocence as with unadulterated quality, solid color, and the like. In Alabama, a madstone gained from the stomach of a solid-colored cow that has never given birth, for instance, is used to combat hydrophobia.[81] The animal is not dispatched, of course, but in a cure for high fever, reported from Louisiana, a pigeon which has never flown from the cage (and hence is in the pristine state), is cut open and laid on the patient's head. The fresh blood is supposed to cure the fever.[82] The remaining examples deal with animals of solid color, in every instance of which store is laid by the fact that there is not a single white hair in the coat of the black cat in question, or the black dog, or the black hen. The blood of a black cat of this superb coating is credited, for example, with curing styes in Newfoundland,[83] fits in Nova Scotia,[84] and consumption and erysipelas in the German tradition of Pennsylvania.[85] In central Maine fat obtained from a black dog, without a single white hair, is cooked and eaten for consumption,[86] while in Maryland an entirely black chicken is cut in two and bound to the breast of a sufferer with fits.[87] Ritual magic is seen in all these cases of sacrifice.

Details of ritual often enhance the magical and sacrificial character of the killing of animals for curative purposes. Especially suited is nighttime, midnight itself, or times coinciding with different phases of the moon, as seen in examples from West Virginia and North Carolina.[88] The killing often takes place in such numinous places as a graveyard,[89] or at a crossroads.

That there is not more material in the corpus of American folk medical practice dealing with animal sacrifice may be due in part to the fundamental religious and philosophical cast of mind in this country. In the religious teaching of the New Testament, where the sacrifice of one's faith and the dedication of one's life to the Christian ideal counts far more than the sacrifice of animals,[90] as under the Old Covenant, even the word "sacrifice" itself is downplayed, if not taboo, being rarely mentioned except in the supreme sacrifice of Jesus himself, the one man without sin. Echoes of this perfection are seen in the few references I could muster to animals of solid color or virgin state. In the face of the American religious ethos, accommodations are made all along the line to the prevailing modes of thought, of course, and primitive expressions of all kinds, including ritual killing, have, as stated, been greatly played down. It is in the field of black magic, rather than in folk healing, a form of white magic, that sacrificial ritual is best seen. Animal sacrifice in witchcraft and conjury, unfortunately, cannot be taken up in this paper.

NOTES

1. James Hastings, ed., *Encyclopaedia of Religion and Ethics,* 13 vols. (Edinburgh: T. & T. Clark, 1908–1926), XI, 1–39, s.v. "Sacrifice," esp. pp. 1–7; Eduard von Hoffmann-Krayer and Hanns Bächtold-Stäubli, eds., *Handwörterbuch des deutschen Aberglaubens,* 10 vols. (Berlin and Leipzig: Walter de Gruyter, 1927–1942), IX, Nachtrag, 19 ff., s.v. "Opfer" (hereinafter abbreviated *HDA*); E. O. James, *Sacrifice and Sacrament* (London: Thames and Hudson, 1962); Northcote W. Thomas' entry on "sacrifice" in the 13th edition of the *Britannica* (1926), XXIII, 980–984, is exemplary.

2. Frederick Webb Hodge, ed., *Handbook of American Indians North of Mexico,* 2 vols. (Washington, D.C.: Smithsonian Institution, Bureau of American Ethnology, 1912), II, 402–407, s.v. "Sacrifice."

3. James, *op. cit.* (n. 1 above), pp. 60–63; Hastings, *op. cit.* (n. 1 above), II, 714 ff.; *HDA*, I, 1434, s.v. "Blut."

4. *HDA,* I, 1435, s.v. "Blut."

5. Hastings, *op. cit.* (n. 1 above), II, 719.

6. James, *op. cit.* (n. 1 above), pp. 104–114, esp. pp. 110–111.

7. Stith Thompson, *Motif-Index of Folk-Literature,* 2nd ed., 6 vols. (Bloomington, Ind.: Indiana University Press, 1955–1958), E761.1.

8. Pauline Monette Black, *Nebraska Folk Cures* (University of Nebraska Studies in Language, Literature, and Criticism, No. 15; Lincoln, 1935), p. 14, no. 81 (consumption); Joseph D. Clark, "North Carolina popular beliefs and superstitions." *North Carolina Folklore,* 1970, *18:* 17, No. 333 (consumption); Thomas R. Brendle and Claude W. Unger, *The Folk Medicine of the Pennsylvania Germans. The Non-Occult Cures* (Proceedings of the Pennsylvania German Society, XLV), Norristown, 1935, p. 106 (epilepsy). Negroes in the South drank the blood from the heart of a young heifer for bronchitis (Newbell Niles Puckett, *Folk Beliefs of the Southern Negro* [Chapel Hill, N. C.: University of North Carolina Press, 1926], p. 370).

9. John G. Bourke, "Popular medicine, customs, and superstitions of the Rio Grande," *Jour. Am. Folklore,* 1894, *7:* 123.

10. Helen Creighton, *Folklore of Lunenberg County, Nova Scotia* (National Museum of Canada, *Bulletin,* No. 117, Anthropological Series, No. 29), Ottawa, 1950, p. 86, No. 4.

11. Jerry S. Parr, "Folk cures of middle Tennessee," *Tenn. Folklore Soc. Bul.*, 1962, *28*: 10.

12. Harry Middleton Hyatt, *Folklore from Adams County, Illinois,* 2nd ed. ([New York]: Alma Egan Hyatt Foundation, 1965), p. 263, No. 5819.

13. James, *op. cit.* (n. 1 above), pp. 247–248.

14. Wayland D. Hand, ed., *Popular Beliefs and Superstitions from North Carolina* (constituting Vols. VI–VII of *The Frank C. Brown Collection of North Carolina Folklore*, 7 vols.: Durham, N.C.: Duke University Press, 1952–1964), VI, 271–272, No. 2096. (Hereinafter cited: *Brown Coll.*)

15. *Ibid.*, No. 2097

16. Daniel Lindsey Thomas and Lucy Blayney Thomas, *Kentucky Superstitions* (Princeton, N.J.: Princeton University Press, 1920), p. 123, No. 1443; Clark, *op. cit.* (n. 8 above), p. 33, No. 815.

17. Fanny D. Bergen, *Animal and Plant Lore Collected from the Oral Tradition of English Speaking Folk* (Mem. Amer. Folklore Soc., VII; Boston and New York, 1899), p. 68, No. 764.

18. *Ibid.*, p. 147, note to No. 764.

19. Frederick Starr, "Some Pennsylvania German lore," *Jour. Am. Folklore*, 1891, *4*: 322.

20. Oklahoma Writers' Project, unpub. MS, p. 51. (Copy in the author's possession through the courtesy of the Oklahoma Historical Society, Oklahoma City, Okla.)

21. John W. Allen, *Legends and Lore of Southern Illinois* (Carbondale, Ill.: Southern Illinois University Press, 1963), p. 61.

22. Paul G. Brewster, "Folk cures and preventives from southern Indiana," *Southern Folklore Quart.*, 1939, *3*: 39, No. 3.

23. Puckett, *op. cit.* (n. 8 above), p. 366.

24. *Brown Coll.*, VI, 144, No. 1047.

25. John Q. Anderson, *Texas Folk Medicine. 1,333 Cures, Remedies, Preventives, & Health Practices* (Austin, Tex.: The Encino Press, 1970), p. 81.

26. Ruth Ann Musick, "West Virginia Folklore," *Hoosier Folklore*, 1948, *7*: 7.

27. W. Edson Richmond and Elva Van Winkle, "Is there a doctor in the house?" *Indiana History Bull.*, 1958, *35*: 131, No. 231.

28. *HDA*, VII, 1076, s.v. "schinden."

29. Bergen, *op. cit.* (n. 1 above), p. 68, No. 770.

30. Genevieve Pope, "Superstitions and beliefs of Fleming County," *Kentucky Folklore Record*, 1965, *11*: 45.

31. George M. Foster, "Relationship between Spanish and Spanish-American folk medicine," *Jour. Am. Folklore*, 1953, *66*: 206.

32. *Brown Coll.*, VI, 187, No. 1415.

33. Hilda Roberts, "Louisiana superstitions," *Jour. Am. Folklore*, 1927, *40*: 167, No. 425.

34. Lyle Saxon, *Gumbo Ya-Ya* (Boston: Houghton Mifflin, 1945), p. 525.

35. Roger L. Welsch, *A Treasury of Nebraska Pioneer Folklore* (Lincoln: University of Nebraska Press, 1966), p. 357.

36. T. Horace Fitchett, "Superstition in North Carolina," *The Crisis*, 1936, *43*: 360.

37. Anderson, *op. cit.* (n. 25 above), p. 11.

38. Austin E. Fife, "Pioneer Mormon remedies," *Western Folklore*, 1957, *16*: 162.

39. J. Hampden Porter, "Notes on the folk-lore of the mountain Whites of the Alleghanies," *Jour. Am. Folklore*, 1894, *7*: 112.

40. Pliny, *Natural History*, XXXII, 36.

41. John Moncrief, *The Poor Man's Physician, etc.*, 2nd ed. (Edinburgh, 1716), p. 67; Ignacio Maria Barriola, *La medicina popular en el pais vasco*, (San Sebastian: Biblioteca Vascongada de los Amigos del Pais, 1952), p. 58.

42. George D. Hendricks, *Mirrors, Mice & Mustaches: A Sampling of Superstitions and Popular Beliefs in Texas* (Austin: University of Texas "Paisano Books," 1966), p. 37.

43. John Symonds Udal, *Dorsetshire Folk-Lore* (Hertford: S. Austin & Sons, 1922), pp. 215–216. For American examples of tearing apart see Ray B.

Browne, *Popular Beliefs and Practices from Alabama* (University of California Publications, Folklore Studies, IX; Berkeley and Los Angeles, 1958), p. 94, No. 1603: Frost Woodhull, "Ranch remedios," *Publ. Texas Folklore Soc.*, 1930, *8*: 64.

44. Vance Randolph, *Ozark Superstitions* (New York: Columbia University Press, 1947), p. 135.

45. Louise Pound, "Nebraska snake lore," *Southern Folklore Quart.*, 1946, *10*: 168.

46. Emma Gertrude White, "Folk-Medicine among Pennsylvania Germans," *Jour. Am. Folklore,* 1897, *10*: 79.

47. Waling Dykstra, *Uit Frieslands Volksleven van vroeger en later,* 2 vols. (Leeuwarden: Hugo Suringar, n.d.), II, 259.

48. Hyatt, *op. cit.* (n. 12 above; 1935 ed.), pp. 261–262, No. 5328.

49. Hyatt, *op. cit.* (n. 12 above; 1965 ed.), p. 256, No. 5691.

50. Bergen, *op. cit.* (n. 17 above), p. 73, No. 836; Musick, *op. cit.* (n. 26 above), p. 5; Edwin Miller Fogel, *Beliefs and Superstitions of the Pennsylvania Germans* (Americana Germanica, XVIII, Philadelphia, 1915), p. 336, No. 1781.

51. Brewster, *op. cit.* (n. 22 above), p. 35.

52. Sidney Oldall Addy, *Household Tales With Other Traditional Remains Collected in the Counties of York, Lincoln, Derby, and Nottingham* (London: David Nutt, 1895), p. 91; W. Branch Johnson, *Folktales of Normandy* (London: Chapman and Hall, 1929), p. 191.

53. W. J. Wintemberg, *Folk-Lore of Waterloo County, Ontario* (National Museum of Canada, *Bulletin,* 116, Anthropological Series, No. 28, Ottawa, 1950), p. 15; Brendle-Unger, *op. cit.* (n. 8 above), pp. 132–133; Richmond and Van Winkle, *op. cit.* (n. 27 above), p. 135, No. 311; Allen, *op. cit.* (n. 21 above), p. 83; Hendricks, *op. cit.* (n. 42 above), p. 54.

54. Collins Lee, "Some Negro lore from Baltimore," *Jour. Am. Folklore,* 1892, *5*: 111.

55. Fogel, *op. cit.* (n. 50 above), p. 302, No. 1598.

56. Saxon, *op. cit.* (n. 34 above), p. 536; Hyatt, *op. cit.* (n. 12 above; 1965 ed.), p. 325, No. 7031; Randolph, *op. cit.* (n. 44 above), p. 101.

57. Browne, *op. cit.* (n. 43 above), p. 123, No. 2149.

58. Richmond and Van Winkle, *op. cit.* (n. 27 above), p. 126, No. 147.

59. *Brown Coll.,* VI, 144, No. 1050; Saxon, *op. cit.* (n. 34 above), p. 527.

60. Marie Campbell, "Folk remedies from south Georgia," *Tenn. Folklore Soc. Bull.,* 1953, 10: 2.

61. Fogel, *op. cit.* (n. 50 above), p. 323, No. 1720).

62. HDA, III, 1393, s.v. "Hand"; VI, 20, s.v. "Maulwurf"; Paul Sébillot, *Le folk-lore de la France,* 4 vols. (Paris: Librairie Orientale & Américaine, 1904–1907), III, 48; *Revista de Dialectología y Tradiciones Populares*, 1947, *3*: 398; Johnson, *op. cit.* (n. 52 above), p. 195. Importance of the mole in matters pertaining to folk medicine, including a wide range of sacrificial customs and rituals, can be seen historically in a paper by Jaan Puhvel and Wayland D. Hand. "The mole in folk medicine: a survey from Indic antiquity to modern America," in Wayland D. Hand, ed., *American Folk Medicine: A Symposium* (Publications of the UCLA Center for the Study of Comparative Folklore and Mythology, 4; Berkeley and Los Angeles, 1976), pp. 31–48.

63. Lee, *op. cit.* (n. 54 above), p. 111. Cf. *Brown Coll.,* VI, 110, No. 750.

64. *Brown Coll.,* VI, 114, No. 778.

65. Browne, *op. cit.* (n. 43 above), p. 97, No. 1668.

66. *Brown Coll.*, VI, 110, No. 750.

67. Browne, *op. cit.* (n. 43 above), p. 123, No. 2148. Cf. *Rev. Dial. y Trad. Pop.*, 1947, *3:* 398.

68. Lyle Saxon, *Old Louisiana* (New York: Century Co., 1929), p. 352.

69. Annie Weston Whitney and Caroline Canfield Bullock, *Folk-Lore from Maryland* (Mem. Amer. Folklore Soc. XVIII; New York 1925), p. 83, No. 1707; Puckett, *op. cit.* (n. 8 above), pp. 378–379; Fogel, *op. cit.* (n. 50 above), p. 293, No. 1551.

70. Fitchett, *op. cit.* (n. 36 above), p. 360.

71. Porter, *op. cit.* (n. 39 above), p. 111; *Brown Coll.*, VI, 320, No. 2479.

72. Randolph, *op. cit.* (n. 44 above), p. 130.

73. *Brown Coll.*, VI, 299, No. 2314.

74. Puckett, *op. cit.* (n. 8 above), p. 362.

75. *Brown Coll.*, VI, 207, No. 1587.

76. Browne, *op. cit.* (n. 43 above), p. 80, No. 1351.

77. *HDA,* VI, 20, s.v. "Maulwurf"; Marcelle Bouteiller, *Médecine populaire d'hier et d'aujourd'hui* (Paris: Maisonneuve et Larose, 1966), p. 282.

78. E. Grumbine, *Folk-Lore and Superstitious Beliefs of Lebanon County* (Papers and Addresses of the Lebanon Co. Historical Soc., III, 1905–1906), p. 280; Thomas and Thomas, *op. cit.* (n. 16 above), p. 97, No. 1105.

79. *HDA,* VI, 20, s.v. "Maulwurf."

80. Wayland D. Hand, "The folk healer: calling and endowment," *J. Hist. Med.*, 1971, *26*: 263–275.

81. Browne, *op. cit.* (n. 43 above) p. 73, No. 1210.

82. Saxon, *op. cit.* (n. 34 above), p. 529.

83. Bergen, *op. cit.* (n. 17 above), p. 68, No. 761.

84. Arthur Huff Fauset, *Folklore from Nova Scotia* (Mem. Amer. Folklore Soc., XXIV, New York, 1931), p. 197, No. 334.

85. Starr, *op. cit.* (n. 19 above), p. 322; *Pennsylvania Dutchman,* Mar. 15, 1954, *5* (14): 6.

86. Bergen, *op. cit.* (n. 17 above), p. 72, No. 823.

87. *Jour. Am. Folklore,* 1907, *20:* 160.

88. *West Va. Folklore,* 1964, *14:* 47, No. 22; *Brown Coll.*, VI, 118, No. 812, Cf. *HDA,* VI, 20, s.v. "Maulwurf."

89. Elza E. Fentress, *Superstition of Grayson County* (Kentucky), unpubl. M.A. thesis, Western State Teachers College, Bowling Green, Ky., 1934, p. 58, No. 11.

90. Philippians 2:17.

13

The Mole in Folk Medicine: A Survey from Indic Antiquity to Modern America*

(PART II)

As anyone who has worked in the field of modern folklore knows, it is difficult to trace ongoing traditions back more than two or three hundred years and almost impossible to pursue leads all the way back to classical and Indic antiquity. In this folk medical study encompassing this tremendous time span, the two collaborators have been struck mainly by the general similarities in the way the mole has been associated with healing in the Indo-European continuum, seemingly from time immemorial. Details of the creature's healing office vary at different times in history and in different parts of the Western world, but the evidence, wherever encountered, points to the almost universal favor in which the mole was held as an agent of healing. With the skill of a classicist, and as a scholar trained in comparative Indo-European linguistics and mythology, Professor Puhvel has traced out the reverence shown the lowly rodent in earliest recorded history. In this portrayal the mole emerges almost as a divine being.

*This article originally appeared in *American Folk Medicine: A Symposium*. Ed. Wayland D. Hand. Berkeley and Los Angeles: University of California Press, 1976, pp. 37–48. Permission to reprint has been given by the editor and by the University of California Press. Part I, by Jaan Puhvel, is on pp. 31–35.

This vision of the mole has continued to modern times, though with a somewhat different emphasis. The divine attributes have been almost completely lost, but there has emerged from the time of Pliny the figure of a mysterious subterranean creature, almost a chthonic seer and divinity.[1] Because of its existence in the earth itself, the animal is connected in the folk mind with death and the realm of the dead[2] and likewise with the devil, witches, and magical powers.[3] In France the mole is thought to embody the powers of both good and evil.[4] The supposed blindness of the creature, a view established in classical times[5] and persisting to the present,[6] its sheltered and solitary life, and its acute sense of hearing[7] have invested the mole, in popular fancy at least, with divinatory powers,[8] but particularly with the power to predict death.[9]

The most striking attribute of the mole in modern as well as in classical times, however, is its supposed healing virtue. The blood, flesh, viscera, skin, teeth, feet, and claws are used for a whole range of diseases and ailments, as we shall see later. This is not unusual, of course, because many other creatures—animals, birds, reptiles, and even fish—figure in organotherapy, as Höfler and others have shown.[10] Yet over and above any other animal, the mole is so highly prized as a healer that people coveting the healer's art have seized upon the creature as a sacrificial animal.[11] The vital healing essence of the mole is secured either by suffocating or strangling the animal in one's hands, plunging one's finger into the live animal's body, biting off its head or its paw, or tearing the creature apart for the healing applications of its warm and quivering flesh.

Before we proceed further with an exploration of these matters, it is essential that we have before us the full text of what Pliny says about the mole in doctrines and false faiths spread westward from Persia into Greece and Rome by the magi. Pliny writes in his *Natural History,* Book XXX, chapter vii, sections 19 and 20, as follows:

> It should be unique evidence of fraud that they (the Magi) look upon the mole of all living creatures with the greatest awe, although it is cursed by Nature with so many defects, being permanently blind, sunk in other darkness also, and resembling the buried dead. In no entrails is placed such faith; to no creature do they attribute more supernatural properties; so that if anyone eats its heart, fresh and still beating, they promise powers of divination and of foretelling the issue of matters in hand. They declare that a tooth, extracted from a living mole and attached as an amulet, cures toothache. The rest of their beliefs about this animal I will relate in

the appropriate places. But of all they say nothing will be found more likely than that the mole is an antidote for the bite of the shrewmouse, seeing that an antidote for it, as I have said, is even earth that has been depressed by cart wheels.

The strongest European attestations of the throttling of moles to gain their healing virtue are to be found in the folklore of France, Germany, Czechoslovakia, and Lithuania, but this sacrificial act is also encountered in Transylvania, Austria, Switzerland, Spain, England, Scotland, Holland, Belgium, Sweden, and elsewhere[12]—that is to say, in countries that most immediately came under the sway of medical knowledge and lore that moved northward into Europe from the classical and Mediterranean lands in the early Christian centuries. The folklore of Czechoslovakia, France, Germany, and other European countries contains details on how the creature is killed, whether in both hands;[13] between one's fingers;[14] in the left hand;[15] with the left thumb, as in Czechoslovakia,[16] and the like. Often the process of smothering is very gentle, and it is prescribed that the creature simply be held until it dies, as in Scotland.[17] In French and German traditions where the healing hand is acquired in infancy, the creature is placed in the child's hand and gently done in, or it is left to smother in the infant's swaddling clothes.[18] In parts of Czechoslovakia the deed had to be performed by a posthumous child.[19] In the central part of France it was believed in the first decade of the present century that to acquire the healing gift, a youngster must have killed seven moles in his hand before being able to eat a rich soup,[20] and in other places the gift was acquired by a child under seven or an otherwise virtuous person.[21]

A bloody ritual act is often involved, particularly when the animal is strangled and crushed or impaled on the healer's finger; when it is cut open, torn apart for warm visceral applications to swellings, excrescences and the like; or when a paw is bitten off for medical or talismanic purposes while the creature is still alive.[22] The ritualistic transfer of power is clearest, of course, in cases where the healer's finger, the "murderous digit" (*le doigt meurtrier*) is left in the animal's body overnight.[23] Other ritualistic aspects involve carrying out the transfer of power at special phases of the moon, on various church holidays,[24] or at other times of the year.[25] A wide range of ailments is supposedly cured by what the French call *la main taupée,* "the mole-hand."[26] Included are sores, wounds, swellings, boils, abscesses, cancer, skin diseases, scrofulous conditions, and the like;[27] sore throat, fever, ague, colic in man and beast;[28] fits and convulsions;[29] felons, bone growths, goiter, toothache;[30] and even perspiring hands.[31] The use of the mole in curing scrofula in various parts of Slovakia, Moravia, and Bohemia amounted to a ritual. For example, the animal had to be taken before Saint George's Day, in some places after sunset,[32] and disposed of by strangulation or tearing off the right front leg;[33] sometimes the animal was even set free after its healing offices had been secured by a godfather.[34] As cures for this dread disease, baking the creature's heart and feeding it to the sufferer[35] and having the patient bathe in water in which a mole had been bathed were unusual in Czechoslovakia and not encountered elsewhere.[36] Another more or less ritualistic act involving the mole as an agent of healing is the drinking of the creature's blood, a treatment reported from Lithuania for the cure of epilepsy, itself a magically induced ailment,[37] and from France, where the blood was imbibed only three-quarters of a century ago to cure drunkenness.[38] Mole's blood, however, is applied to various maladies[39] and has been since the time of Pliny, apparently, when it was sprinkled on the delirious to restore them to their senses.[40] In France and England within the present century, the blood of a mole was applied to warts, wens, corns, and other excrescences.[41] It was also used against bed-wetting in France, where a thread soaked in the creature's blood was worn as a necklace.[42] In more recent times in Czechoslovakia, mole's blood was smeared on a patient to cure scrofula.[43] In the western part of France near Poitou, blood was instilled in the ear to cure deafness,[44] and in Puy de Dôme it served as a specific to restore lost virility in man.[45] The application of the warm viscera of a mole to cure felons, wens, and other growths is reported from Slovakia and England, where the animal was killed, cut in half, and applied to the ailing part.[46] In Lithuania the exposing of the viscera was accomplished in a more ritualistic and brutal way, namely, by tearing the creature in half. The warm parts were then applied to patients suffering from rheumatism.[47] The crushing of a mole's liver between the hands and its utilization in an ointment to cure scrofula, as reported in Pliny,[48] of course points to later sacrificial uses of the animal's vital parts. It is interesting to note that Höfler has devoted a whole section on the use of a mole's liver in modern organotherapy.[49] In Swabia early in the century the boiled flesh of a mole was rubbed on the scalp to cause hair to grow.[50] Just as the viscera, vital parts, and flesh of the mole were applied to the human body in various kinds of curative measures, so was the creature's skin. In France the skin was made into a skullcap or bonnet and worn against fits and convulsions, particularly those caused by dentition.[51] In England the skin was wrapped around the limbs and other parts to prevent cramp.[52]

The amuletic uses of moles' paws, claws, and teeth to aid dentition and cure toothache and other maladies is a subject so broad and involved that it deserves special treatment. Lack of time forbids more than a cursory treatment here. Once more, sacrificial elements are apparent in the way the feet and claws were gained. In Germany the paws were bitten off the living creature in an almost omophagous ritual;[53] in France, around Liège, they were torn out[54] or cut from the living creature,[55] a practice also noted from Moravia and England.[56] In most cases these appendages were sewn into a little sack and worn about the neck, or they were carried exposed, as in parts of Germany and Austria.[57] In England, not only were bags of moles' feet carried to prevent rheumatism and to avert toothache, but as late as 1910 they were also hanging on the mantlepiece as a cure for toothache, especially in Herefordshire.[58] I am unable to find modern cases in Europe of the extracting of teeth from a living mole for the cure of toothache, as described by Pliny,[59] but this hazardous act is reported from Kentucky, as I shall show later. In Swabia at the end of the century a mole's tooth worn on the chest in a sack was supposed to cure the gout.[60]

The mole also figured in veterinary medicine and in animal husbandry, especially in Lithuania, where horses were stroked with a live mole to keep them healthy and fat.[61] Moles were also killed in one's hand for the same purpose and were choked to death with the right hand to make the horses breed well.[62] In Bohemia one went into the fields before daybreak, caught a mole, opened it up, and rubbed the viscera on the stomach of the horse and on the manger, too, to make the animal thrive.[63] In Normandy a white mole taken into one's hand conferred the power to cure the colic in horses simply by touch.[64]

With European folk medical lore concerning moles before us, we can now look at these same manifestations in American folk medicine. Even though the traditions have been nowhere nearly so well preserved here as in Europe, one can nevertheless discover a considerable amount of related material—enough, at least, to warrant the title of this joint paper.

The smothering to death of a mole in one's hand is encountered in the Pennsylvania German tradition, among the southern whites, and also, sporadically, to be sure, and derivatively, in the American Negro tradition. These beliefs have been recorded from the early 1890s and continue through the first half of the present century. Bone felons, for example, were treated by those who had squeezed a mole to death or, as this act is often phrased, by those who had "allowed a mole to die in their hands."[65] This cure was practiced in the Pennsylvania German tradition, in Maryland,[66] and in Kentucky.[67] Risings—that is to say, swellings of any kind—receive a simple treatment in the white tradition of North Carolina and in the tradition of the southern Negro they are rubbed by someone who has smothered a mole.[68] Warts are cured the same way in North Carolina,[69] but in Taney County, Missouri, the sufferer smothers the mole and holds it above his head for a moment.[70] This act of holding the mole over the head, reminiscent of an Anglo-Saxon custom of waving the animal, is found in a curious Alabama cure, encountered nowhere else in the literature, so far as I know, European or American: "Catch a live mole, hold it between your hands above your head for an hour and you will gain the healing powers that will allow you to cure milk leg."[71] In the Alleghenies in the early 1890s, sprains were cured with the interrupted pressure of a hand that had squeezed a mole to death.[72] Headache, not encountered elsewhere in cures of this kind, is also cured by a hand in which a mole has been left to die, but only in North Carolina, so far as I can discover.[73] In the Negro tradition of Baltimore in the early 1890s, one could cure any pain if a mole were caught and allowed to die in one's hand.[74] From Europe the requirement of innocence in the healer has made its way to America. In Maryland around the 1920s, for example, it was believed that the mole must be killed by the hand of a child under two years of age. Another informant says that three moles must be killed by a child under seven.[75]

The folk medical use of the mole's bodily parts in America is scant, except for the creature's paws. For epilepsy, a magical disease, it is recommended in the Pennsylvania German country that the heart of the living mole be given to the patient.[76] Mole's blood for the cure of baldness in the mountain white tradition of North Carolina is reminiscent of a similar practice noted from Swabia earlier in this paper.[77] A curious belief about mole's flesh, rare and in the learned tradition, is found in Illinois: "If you boil a mole in an earthen pot and use this liquid when washing your hair, your hair will turn white."[78] This notion appears to have been handed down in the *Egyptian Secrets,* a nineteenth-century publisher's forgery purporting to derive from the writings of Albertus Magnus. That this magical quality of the mole's flesh is perhaps old is documented by a prescription in a sixteenth-century English redaction of the work, which claims that rubbing a black horse with a mole will turn its coat white.[79] The skin of a mole was worn in Illinois as recently as 1965 by those wishing relief from rheumatism.[80]

About the only part of a mole that is widely used in American folk medicine is the creature's paw. First of all, in different parts of the country it is worn as an amulet to ward off disease and to secure health and longevity.[81] It is most widely used, however, in childhood diseases, from cholera infantum and croup[82] to colds and whooping cough[83] and to teething and the convulsions that often accompany it. In the southern states, where the custom of placing a mole's foot around a child's neck is most prevalent, and as far west as Indiana, the foot is most generally suspended on a string, but it may also be enclosed in a bag or sack.[84] A mole's right front foot is prescribed in the Blue Ridge Mountain country, but in the neighboring state of Maryland it is the left hind foot, and the entry suggests the use of the foot itself as a teething instrument.[85] In Kentucky the tooth of a live mole was actually rubbed over an aching tooth to cure the pain as late as the 1930s.[86] Earlier in this paper I noted the use of teeth from a living mole for this purpose, as reported from the time of Pliny.

The only connection between the mole and deaf-mutes and other kinds of speechless humans is a measure reported from Illinois in the 1960s, wherein it is advised that a tongue-tied child wear a mole foot in a bag around its neck as a cure for the impediment.[87] The mole as a cure for deafness and speech defects is known in Europe, particularly in France.[88]

The comparisons that have been made between European and American folk medicine in modern times with regard to traditions involving the mole in curative practice accord pretty well with the transmission of other kinds of folk medical lore to these shores. Indeed, what has happened in the case of this one item of folk medicine is rather typical of what happens in folk belief and custom in general in the process of transmission across the Atlantic. For that matter, it mirrors what happens in folklore generally when a considerable time span, as well as changing patterns of culture, is involved. However, this is not really the problem before us. The more difficult part of this venture in a historical and comparative study is to trace the continuity of the tradition from ancient to modern times and from the classical lands to northern Europe.

This problem is made doubly difficult by the fact that folklore as such and folk medicine were not collected much before the eighteenth century. The principal exertions in this field of study actually did not come into full flower until the nineteenth century, and scholars of our own day are still trying assiduously to redress this neglect with last-minute efforts, as it were, to see that representative categories of material, at least, are turned up.

Through the courtesy of Professor Charles H. Talbot, the eminent historian of medieval medicine, I have been able to trace a continuing tradition of the mole as healer from the time of Pliny the Elder forward for some centuries, but the tradition is far from robust. Pliny's nephew, known as Pliny the Younger, transmitted at least three prescriptions involving moles that in their fundamental aspects were to live on until the present time. We read, for example, of the ashes of a mole mixed with honey and applied for boils and abscesses.[89] In a second cure for eruptions of the skin, the liver of a mole was ground between the hands, smeared on the neck, and left for three days without washing.[90] Finally, the heads of moles were cut off and ground up with earth thrown from the molehill and then fashioned into lozenges and kept ready in a box for all kinds of apostematic ailments.[91] In the fifth century Sextus Platonicus recommended that the entire mole be used to rub the neck for glandular swellings.[92]

In the first half of the fifth century, Marcellus of Bordeaux, drawing on the two Plinys and other sources, including contemporary local practitioners, repeated the first two prescriptions from Pliny the Younger cited above[93] and counseled the roasting of a mole for a head cold or catarrh. The roasted mole was supposed to be reduced to a powder and mixed with pepper and basil. This was given in wine in a bath in which the patient had never bathed before nor would ever be likely to bathe in again.[94] For glandular swellings a mole's liver was squeezed in the hands and applied to the throat.[95] I have not made much of the use of earth from a molehill, which is fairly common in modern European folk medical practice, but Marcellus prescribes an unusual remedy for nervous pains in the ligaments. "From three heaps of earth which moles throw up in their molehills," he writes, "one takes as much as one can grasp with the left hand three times, that is, nine handfuls, mixes this with vinegar, and kneads it up, applying it, where necessary, with healing efficacy."[96]

In the *Leech Book* of Bald, compiled about the middle of the tenth century in England, there is a prescription for pain in the fatty part of the belly which directs the sufferer to catch a dung beetle seen throwing up earth, wave it strongly in the hands, and then throw it over the shoulder without looking back after having thrice uttered the incantation "Remedium facio ad ventris dolorem." In a learned note, Cockayne has conjectured that the Anglo-Saxon author actually was talking about a mole rather than a dung beetle.[97]

At the end of this development before the Middle Ages, in which moles were variously squeezed, waved in the air, and the like, comes a purported cure for cancer, ascribed to Paracelsus, who flourished in the early sixteenth century. It has come down in a nineteenth-century chapbook known as the *Egyptian Secrets,* ascribed to Albertus Magnus, who, of course, predates Paracelsus by three centuries:

Secret Remedy of the Great Theophrastus Paracelsus
for Healing the Cancer

> This celebrated remedy is composed as follows: "When a human being takes hold with his right hand of a live mole, and keeps the mole so long with a tight grip until it dies, such a hand obtains by dint of this miraculous proceeding, such marvelous power that cancer boils, repeatedly rubbed, by moving up and down with this hand, will break open, cease to form again, and entirely vanish."[98]

It is difficult to say whether the above prescription is new in the long line of popular treatises connected with the famed Bishop of Ratisbon or whether it stems from some earlier folk or literary tradition. The fact that this specific cure is not found in the sixteenth-century *Boke of Secretes* published in London (1560) —that is to say, in Paracelsus's own time—makes one wonder about this nineteenth-century recipe. Since I do not have access to the long line of *grimoires* connected with Le Grand Albert nor to the prolific German treatises in this tradition, I am in no position to say whether this derelict nineteenth-century item was the sole influence on modern medical traditions concerning the mole as an agent of healing. At any event, in the give-and-take between folklore itself and folk literature, one must not foreclose the possibility that the throttling of the mole fed into the chapbook tradition from earlier oral sources. The general sacrificial and sacral use of the creature—evisceration, biting off of the appendages, and amuletic uses—all these things speak for an ongoing tradition of reverence for the creature as a healer.

As a working hypothesis, pending a closer look at old and

obscure literary sources, one must look at the rich corpus of folk medical items recovered in modern oral tradition, particularly in Europe. Folk medicine, I believe, constitutes a prime source of information for historical reconstructions such as the one we have undertaken today. That the published folklore record is rarely complete and never continuous need not deter us, really. This very lack of a precise line of descent of the various things we study should, on the contrary, only win us over with renewed dedication to the necessity of historical and comparative scholarship. Folklore, along with mythology, I need not remind you, has always stood in the forefront of disciplines committed to the study of cultural history—history in its broadest and most mysterious sweeps.

NOTES

1. Pliny, *Natural History,* ed. T. E. Page, E. Capps, W. H. D. Rouse, L. A. Post, E. H. Warmington, et al., 10 vols., Loeb Classical Library (Cambridge, Mass. and London, 1938–1962), XXX, vii, 19–20. (Hereafter *NH*; cited throughout by book, section, and lines.)

2. Max Höfler, *Die medizinische Organotherapie und ihr Verhältnis zum Kultopfer* (Stuttgart, Berlin, Leipzig, n.d.), p. 113. Cf. Pliny, *NH,* XXX, vii, 19. In France the expression *être taupé* means "dead and buried." See Eugène Rolland, *Faune populaire de la France*, 13 vols. (Paris, 1877–1911), VII, 25, no. 14.

3. Hanns Bächtold-Stäubli and Eduard von Hoffmann-Krayer, *Handwörterbuch des deutschen Aberglaubens,* 10 vols. (Berlin and Leipzig, 1927–1942), VI, 11–12. This is hereafter cited: *HDA*. See also H. F. Feilberg, *Bidrag til en Ordbog over Jyske Almuesmål,* 4 vols. (Copenhagen, 1886–1914), II, 620, s.v. *muldvarp*.

4. Robert Morel and Suzanne Walter, *Dictionnaire des superstitions* (Bibliothèque Marabout, n.d.), p. 225.

5. Pliny, *NH,* XI, ii, 139; XXX, vii, 19.

6. Rolland, VII, 28, no. 20; 29, no. 22; Paul Sébillot. *Le Folk-Lore de France,* 4 vols. (Paris, 1904–1907), III, 11; *HDA*, VI, 8–9.

7. Pliny, *NH*, X, lxxxviii, 191; Rolland, VI, 28, no. 21; *HDA*, VI, 9.

8. Pliny, *NH,* XXX, vii, 19.

9. Rolland, I, 14, no. 5; *HDA,* VI, 15–16; E. and M. A. Radford, *Encyclopaedia of Superstitions,* 2d rev. ed. Christina Hole, ed. (London, 1961), p. 235.

10. Höfler, *op. cit.* Höfler's work is organized according to the medical use of various animal parts, but there is an orderly survey of the different animals involved and an excellent index.

11. I have devoted considerable space to the mole as a sacrificial animal in my forthcoming article on "Animal Sacrifice in American Folk Curative Practice" in the *Bulletin of the History of Medicine.*

12. The true geographical spread of this phenomenon would no doubt show a much wider diffusion of this folk medical belief and custom than I have been able to trace out in this paper. That it is also known outside of Europe in

modern times would accord with the general presuppositions of the present study, particularly the broader Indo-European configurations charted by Professor Puhvel. I note, for example, that the strangling of a mole to cure swollen tonsils is reported from Syria; see Dr. O. v. Hovorka and Dr. A. Kronfeld, *Vergleichende Volksmedizin: Eine Darstellung volksmedizinischer Sitten und Gebräuche, Anschauungen und Heilfaktoren, des Aberglaubens und der Zaubermedizin,* 2 vols. (Stuttgart, 1908–1909), II, 13.

13. Rolland, I, 13–14, no. 3; William George Black, *Folk-Medicine: A Chapter in the History of Culture,* Publications of the Folk-Lore Society, XII (London, 1883), p. 16; *HDA,* VI, 20

14. Sébillot, III, 49.

15. *Ibid.,* pp. 48–49.

16. Josef Cizmar, *Lidové lékarství v Ceskoslovensku* [Folk medicine in Czechoslovakia] 2 vols. (Brno, 1946), I, 165, 219.

17. Black, p. 161.

18. Sébillot, III, 49.

19. Cizmar, I, 219.

20. Sébillot, III, 48–49.

21. Sébillot, III, 48.

22. J. Elisonas, "Musu krasto fauna lietuvių tautosakoje" [Our land's fauna in Lithuanian folklore], in *Musu Tatosaka* [Our folklore], V (Kaunas: Lithuanian Folklore Commission, 1932) p. 198; Sébillot, III, 48; Rolland, VII, 29, no. 23; Höfler, p. 113; Adolf Wuttke, *Der deutsche Volksaberglaube der Gegenwart* 3d ed., Elard Hugo Meyer, ed. (Berlin, 1900), p. 307, par. 451.

23. Sébillot, III, 48; Rolland, VII, 30, no. 23.

24. Sébillot, III, 48.

25. *Ibid.*

26. *HDA,* VI, 20.

27. Wuttke, p. 315, par. 466; Elisonas, p. 198; *HDA,* VI, 20; Hovorka and Kronfeld, II, 401; Sébillot, III, 49; Elisonas, p. 198; Cizmar, I, 165.

28. *HDA,* VI, 20; Roland, VII, 29–30, no. 23; Hovorka and Kronfeld, II, 13; Sébillot, III, 49; Cizmar, I, 219.

29. Rolland, I, 13–14, no. 3; VII, 31, no. 23; Cizmar, I, 219.

30. Wuttke, p. 315, par. 466; *HDA,* VI, 20; Sébillot, III, 48; Rolland, VII, 29, no. 23; Cizmar, I, 219.

31. Sébillot, III, 49; Rolland VII, 34, no. 25; *HDA,* VI, 20.

32. Cizmar, II, 133.

33. *Ibid.,* 134.

34. *Ibid.*

35. *Ibid.,* II, 133.

36. *Ibid.,* II, 132.

37. Elisonas, p. 198.

38. Rolland, VII, 34, no. 25.

39. *HDA,* VI, 19; Sébillot, III, 49.

40. Pliny, *NH,* XXX, xxiv, 84.

41. Sébillot, III, 49; Rolland, VII, 34, no. 25; Ella Mary Leather, *The Folk-Lore of Herefordshire* (Hereford and London, 1912), p. 84; Radford and Hole, p. 235.

42. Rolland, VII, 34, no. 25.

43. Cizmar, II, 133–134.

44. Rolland, VII, 34, no. 25; Sébillot, III, 49.

45. Rolland, VII, 35, no. 25.

46. Hovorka and Kronfeld, II, 501; Leather, p. 84; Radford and Hole, p. 235.

47. Elisonas, p. 198.

48. *NH,* XXX, xii, 38.

49. *Organotherapie,* pp. 180–181, no. 25.

50. Hovorka and Kronfeld, II, 762.

51. Rolland; VII, 31–32, no. 24.

52. Radford and Hole, p. 235.

53. Wuttke, pp. 124, par. 167; 393, par. 601; Höfler, p. 113. Höfler says that this is done against the elfin demons of disease.

54. Sébillot, III, 49; Rolland, VII, 29, no. 23.

55. Rolland, VII, 32–33, no. 24. In the Ardennes the claws were clipped and carried in a sack around the neck to aid in teething.

56. Hovorka and Kronfeld, II, 334; Cizmar, II, 134; Black, p. 161.

57. Hovorka and Kronfeld, I, 292–293, who reproduce a life-size likeness of the amulet. Paws in metal jewelry clasps are pictured in Liselotte Hansmann and Lenz Kriss-Rettenbeck, *Amulett und Talisman; Erscheinungsform und Geschichte* (München, 1966), pp. 87, figs. 187–188; p. 226, fig. 750.

58. Radford and Hole, p. 235; Leather, 82. In Denmark the teeth of a mole were placed in the child's drink to promote teething. Cf. Feilberg, I, 620.

59. *NH,* XXX, vii, 20.

60. Wuttke, p. 356, par. 534.

61. Elisonas, pp. 198–199.

62. *Ibid.,* p. 196.

63. Wuttke, p. 451, par. 711.

64. Rolland, VII, 30, no. 23.

65. Edwin Miller Fogel, *Beliefs and Superstitions of the Pennsylvania Germans,* Americana Germanica, no. 18 (Philadelphia, 1915), p. 293, no. 1551; E. Grumbine, *Folk-Lore and Superstitious Beliefs in Lebanon County* (Papers and Addresses of the Lebanon County Historical Society, III, 1905–1906), p. 280.

66. Annie Weston Whitney and Caroline Canfield Bullock, *Folk-Lore from Maryland,* Memoirs of the American Folklore Society, Vol. 18 (New York, 1925), p. 83, no. 1707.

67. Daniel Lindsey Thomas and Lucy Blaney Thomas, *Kentucky Superstitions* (Princeton, N.J., 1920), p. 97, no. 1105.

68. Wayland D. Hand, ed., *The Frank C. Brown Collection of North Carolina Folklore,* 7 vols. (Durham, N.C., 1952–1964), Vol. 6, *Popular Beliefs and Superstitions from North Carolina,* 299, no. 2314; Newbell Niles Puckett, *Folk Beliefs of the Southern Negro* (Chapel Hill, N.C., 1926), pp. 378–379.

69. Hand, VI, 320, no. 2479.

70. Vance Randolph, *Ozark Superstitions* (New York, 1946), p. 130.

71. Ray B. Browne, *Popular Beliefs and Practices from Alabama,* Folklore Studies, IX (Berkeley and Los Angeles, 1958), p. 80, no. 1351. Healing power gained in the same way is also applied for the healing of sore breasts. *Ibid.,* p. 42, no. 630. Cf. Walter Gregor, *Notes on the Folk-Lore of the North-East of Scotland,* Publications of the Folk-Lore Society, VII (London, 1881), p. 123.

72. *Journal of American Folklore,* 7 (1894), 111.

73. Hand, VI, 207, no. 1587.

74. *Journal of American Folklore,* 5 (1892), 111.

75. Whitney and Bullock, p. 83, no. 1708.

76. Thomas R. Brendle and Claude W. Unger, *Folk Medicine of the Pennsyl-*

vania Germans, Proceedings of the Pennsylvania German Society, vol. 45 (Norristown, Pa., 1935), p. 106.

77. Hand, VI, 122, no. 849; *North Carolina Folklore,* 18 (1970), 12, no. 184.

78. Harry Middleton Hyatt, *Folk-Lore from Adams County, Illinois* (Memoirs of the Alma Egan Hyatt Foundation, New York, 1935), p. 143, no. 295a.

79. *The boke / of secretes of Albartus Mag / nus, of the vertues of / Herbes, stones and / certaine beastes* (London, 1560), n.p. [78].

80. Harry Middleton Hyatt, *Folk-Lore from Adams County, Illinois,* 2d ed. (New York, 1965), p. 259, no. 5747.

81. Thomas and Thomas, p. 107, no. 1252; Hyatt, 2d ed., p. 195, no. 4551; Puckett, p. 316.

82. Hyatt, 1st ed., p. 208, no. 4338; Madge E. Pickard and R. Carlyle Buley, *The Midwest Pioneer: His Ills, Cures, and Doctors* (Crawfordsville, Ind., 1945), p. 77; John W. Allen, *Legends and Lore of Southern Illinois* (Carbondale, Ill., 1963), p. 83.

83. Hyatt, 2d ed., p. 277, no. 6087; "Oklahoma Writers' Project" (MS of the Oklahoma Historical Society, n.d.), pp. 44–45.

84. *West Virginia Folklore,* 12 (1962), 31; *Journal of American Folklore,* 12 (1899), 273 (Maryland); *North Carolina Folklore,* 18 (1970), 8, no. 58; Browne, p. 24, no. 327 (Alabama).

85. *Kentucky Folklore Record,* 9 (1964), 130 (Virginia); *Journal of American Folklore,* 12 (1899), 273 (Maryland).

86. Elza E. Fentress, *Superstition of Grayson County* (Kentucky) (M.A. thesis, Western State Teachers College, Bowling Green, Ky., 1934), p. 89, no. 151.

87. Hyatt, 2d ed., p. 334, no. 7194.

88. Rolland, VII, 30, no. 23.

89. *Plinii secundi iunioris,* edidit Alf. Önnerfors (Berlin: Corpus Medicorum Latinorum, III, 1964), p. 71, lines 8–9.

90. *Ibid.,* lines 9–10.

91. *Ibid.,* lines 10–12.

92. Höfler, p. 181.

93. Marcellus, *Über Heilmittel,* hrsg. Max Niedermann, 2d ed. Eduard Liechtenhan, trans. Jutta Kollesch und Diethard Nickel, 2 vols. (Berlin: Akademia-Verlag, 1968), I, Chap. XV, no. 81 [p. 260].

94. *Ibid.,* pp. 91–92, sec. 2, lines 29–[35].

95. *Ibid.,* Chap. XV, no. 81 [p. 260].

96. *Ibid.,* Vol. II, Ch. XXXV, no. 18 [p. 595].

97. The Rev. Oswald Cockayne, ed., *Leechdoms, Wortcunning and Starcraft of Early England,* 3 vols. (London, 1864–1866), II, 319, n. 2: "Our Saxon must have had Talpam or 'Ασπάλακα before him in this sentence; but he names the *Scarabaeus stercorarius.*"

98. Albertus Magnus, *Egyptian Secrets* (n.p., n.d.) p. 15.

14

Physical Harm, Sickness, and Death by Conjury

A Survey of the Sorcerer's Evil Art in America*

As a prelude to a companion study on witchcraft and disease in America, I propose in this paper to limit myself to a discussion of bodily harm and disease in all its forms, including mental ailments, in the United States and other parts of America, as induced by professional sorcerers and others skilled in the magic arts.[1] The term conjurer is more widely used and better understood in America than sorcerer, although, in matters having to do with bodily harm, disease, and death, the functions and skills of these practitioners often coincide. By whatever name,[2] whether root doctor, witch doctor, herb doctor, conjure man, herb man, or other terms discussed by Whitten,[3] these practitioners of magic are bent on the physical and mental harm of their victims, and often on their death as well. It is difficult to generalize about this more or less professional caste of workers of evil, and even more difficult to differentiate strictly between their office and function and those of witches. I have reserved an examination of this question for a later paper, contenting myself at the moment with noting one important distinction, even

*This article originally appeared in the *Acta Ethnographica Academiae Scientiarum Hungaricae*, 19 (1970), 169–177. Permission to reprint has been given by the editor and the publisher.

though this often breaks down in practice because of the existence of witchcraft and conjury side by side in America since its earliest settlement. It is this: whereas the witch often worked redressive magic on people for wrongs done her, real or fancied, or worked evil on people and their patrimony purely out of evil design, she seldom offered her black arts for sale. The conjurer, on the other hand, was a professional in the sense that he generally placed a price on his services, even though payment was often indirect or was regarded as a "love offering" or something of the sort.[4]

The practice of conjury, nowadays at least, has fallen largely into the hands of Negroes, although there are many white practitioners as well.[5] The "power doctors" of the Pennsylvania German country are almost exclusively white. It must be noted, however, that the range of magic between pow-pow doctors and "Brauchers" does not always coincide with that of conjure doctors. Bound up with the whole question of white and Negro practitioners in historical terms,[6] too, is the broader question of the relationship between witchcraft and conjury, as adumbrated above. As in other areas of folk medicine, one must also reckon with the possibility that the special knowledge of the conjurer may on occasion be retailed to people professing no special gifts either in causing or curing disease. In other words, certain rituals ultimately become so well known as to become a matter of common knowledge and practice.

As stated in the title, this paper is not a general treatise on conjury. It is a survey, essentially, of the physical harm wrought by conjurers, leaving out of account all other kinds of occult mischief, and ignoring, also, the practitioner's service in healing, restoring, righting wrongs, and in other kinds of positive service. Let us begin with a discussion of sickness and disease, and other categories of physical impairment, and then move to a consideration of the nature of the magic employed, and the various circumstances and conditions under which it is carried out. The way will then be clear for us to consider madness, and finally death itself. Material adduced comes in the main from the files of the Dictionary of American Popular Beliefs and Superstitions on which I have worked for over twenty-five years. Little of the material, unfortunately, could be included in my edition of the final two volumes in the Frank C. Brown Collection of North Carolina Folklore, which is a tributary study to the Dictionary.[7]

One of the more common manifestations of physical malady induced by the conjurer is sluggishness and malaise that result in wasting away. A common way, to cause harm, well known in the southern Negro tradition, is to sprinkle graveyard dirt about a person's yard or under his feet, so as to make him become sluggish and waste away.[8] Among Negroes in Adams County, Illinois, lizards' heads, dried and ground to dust, where sprinkled on a person's body, cause him, in the words of the informant, to "dribble away like consumption."[9] That fear and suggestibility are factors in bringing about an anxious state of mind is seen in a case reported among Virginia Negroes before the turn of the century. A bunch of hair or wool, a rabbit's paw, and a chicken gizzard were tied up in a cotton rag, and fastened in a bundle to some implement which the victim was accustomed to use. When the man saw this bundle, it was reported that his spirit left him, his eyes bulged out, and he broke out in a cold sweat. This conjure bag, or so-called "trick," often lasted long enough, the report stated, to cause him to waste away.[10] The wasting process, often referred to as "fading," frequently ends in death, as the following Negro attestation from Illinois shows: "If you can get someone's hair and bury it by a running stream, it will make them fade away and die."[11] Another symbolic act, one involving transference by "plugging," provides for a slow wasting and eventual death. To bring death to someone, take a lock of the person's hair, drill a hole in a tree and place the lock of hair within. When the tree dies, the person will die.[12] Puckett sums up the mental state into which the victim falls: "Sometimes the trick or spell will last so long that he (the victim) will grow weak and fall away to a mere shadow; of course he is then utterly unfit for work, and unless he is removed from the scene of his troubles, and his mind freed from the belief that he is conjured, he will soon die of pure fright."[13] A person wearing conjured shoes, for example, is thought among Virginia Negroes to grow weaker and thinner, suffering in a slow and painful way until he finally dies.[14]

Sometimes the pain induced is general, and sickness and disease are not more closely delineated. The following random examples show the various ways in which these generalized maladies may occur. In Missouri, for example, a witch (N. B.), can ruin a man's health by placing a photograph of him under the eaves of a house where the rain will fall upon it.[15] Among southern Negroes it is believed that "goofer dust," a powder representing the person hoodooed, when burned, even miles away, will cause a person to become sick.[16] In the same tradition a "tricken bag," made in cake form, tied with the ravelings from a shroud, and named for the enemy, will bring upon him disease.[17] Little bundles of sticks found in the kitchen where food is prepared are supposed in the traditions of Georgia Negroes to make people sick.[18] Among Negroes in Illinois it is said that "if you want to make a person sick, take a piece of their clothing and put sulphur on it, then bury the piece of cloth."[19]

Afflictions of various parts of the body, of course, are likewise detailed. In Illinois the dust of dried lizard heads, sprinkled on the head of the victim, will cause him to have headaches,[20] while a more elaborate ritual, recorded among Virginia Negroes, provides for the nailing of hair combings to a tree with the hair firmly entwined around the nail.[21] The feet are singled out for the sorcerer's spite; or the practitioner, working by principles of contagious magic, may achieve his purpose by concentrating on the victim's footprints. In the Bahamas, for example, graveyard dirt sprinkled at the front gate of an enemy, will cause his feet to swell.[22] In the traditions of slavery days, "hands," or conjure bags, were planted for every kind of ailment, including headache.[23] In Illinois, among Negroes, it was believed that if anyone drove a rusty nail into a person's footprint, the foot would burn him all the time.[24] Among Portuguese Negroes from the Cape Verde Islands living in Massachusetts and Rhode Island, it was believed that, if soil from a person's footprint were boiled and then thrown over a cliff, the person would himself fall over the cliff.[25] The conjurer can also blind a person or make him speechless. In the Blue Ridge country, for example, a toad in a bottle was thought to bring on blindness,[26] and in the same state of Virginia, snake's blood, mingled with that of a lizard, when administered to a person was thought to plunge him to the floor speechless within two minutes' time.[27] The inability to pass urine, a malady employed in the detection of witches, is a rare affliction visited on one's enemies in the tradition of Illinois Negroes: "If you fall out with someone, take a lock of their hair and a small photo and put it in a bottle, and wet in the bottle, and they will lose their life and they can't wet any more until they die."[28]

The inducing of sterility by casting knots is a practice introduced from Europe,[29] but was never so esoteric a ritual as to be limited to sorcerers, wise women, and cunning men. It is known in America, but is rarely reported in the literature.

Insanity is often regarded as one of the by-products of conjuration. Once afflicted with a magical ailment, many people are thought never fully to get over their harrowing experience, and are often believed to suffer more or less permanent mental impairment.[30] Puckett reports that some hoodoos burn a kind of powder, called "goopher dust," which represents the person being hoodooed. Even though the person may be miles away at the time, he may suffer loss of personality or go insane.[31] In some cases, as reported earlier, he may even die. Powdered snake dust put near the steps of an enemy will induce madness, according to Louisiana Negro tradition.[32] As recently as 1958 there was reported from this same state of Louisiana a "nailing" ritual whereby a person was driven out of his mind. A string of the victim's hair was secured, wrapped around a nail, and driven into a tree with a mallet.[33] "Mad water" was reported as being sold by New Orleans drugstores only a year earlier.[34] Salt, an important item in the magician's pharmacopoeia, was considered to have an important bearing on mental equilibrium. Withholding this vital commodity, for a space of three weeks, it was thought, could make a person lose his mental faculties.[35]

One of the most pathological of all ailments with which we are dealing in this paper is the notion that conjurers can insinuate animals into the victim's body. As early as 1890, in Maryland, a lame Negro claimed that a snake had been conjured into his leg,[36] and two years later a curious companion piece was noted from Arkansas. According to the account, a bottle in which a lizard was placed was put in the road in the thought that whoever stepped over the bottle would have the lizard hop into him and thus cause him to end his days in agony.[37] In more recent times, namely in the mid-nineteen-thirties, two extraordinary items from Illinois, both memorates, could be added to the scanty literature on the subject. "Squeeze a snake, a lizard, and a mole until they die. Dry the bones, grind them to powder and place them in a bag. If you do not like someone, throw this bag in front of him, and snake lizards and moles will enter his body."[38] Another account, too long to reproduce in its entirety, deals with a colored man who saw a person about to kill a puppy dog (salamander). The man begged for the creature, claiming that if he ground it to a powder, he could drop it on the sidewalk, the wind might blow it into someone's nostrils, and that this person would be "full of puppy dogs."[39] I have avoided mentioning cures for the magical ailments brought on by conjury, but I shall cite one instance of curing here as a validation of the notion of animals in the person's body. It was reported from Virginia in 1896 that a conjure doctor arrived with a bottle filled with herbs, roots, and leaves from which he made a tea that acted as an emetic, causing the patient to throw up a variety of reptiles.[40]

Many diseases inflicted by conjurers, as well as by those who share their secrets, may prove terminal. This is the case, for example, when one "wastes away until he dies," or in cases where he "fades and dies." In Georgia, as early as the turn of the century, it was believed that sprinkling graveyard dirt about the yard or house would make one sleepy, sluggish, and naturally waste away and perish.[41] In an item involving contagious magic, reported from Illinois in 1935, it was held that "if you can bury anyone's dirty clothes down by a stream of running water, when that cloth rots they will start to fade and die."[42] A more elaborate ritual from the same state, and one involving homeopathic magic, provided that if one had it in for someone, he should secure some of the person's hair, take a coconut and put a small hole in the end, and then place the hair in the coconut. This was then buried, hole downward, so that the milk of the coconut could drip out. It was claimed that, as the coconut dried up, the party would likewise dry up and fade away.[43] In Kentucky, it was believed in the 1920's that, if your photograph were buried by an enemy, your life would fade as the photograph faded.[44] Another item from the same state, likely in the white tradition, and definitely outside the professional caste of conjury, recommends that, to dispose of an enemy, one should bury a picture of the intended victim face down in the direction Jesus Christ was buried, that is, with his head to the west. As the picture faded, the enemy's life was supposed to fade.[45] Among the Germans of Adams County, Illinois, and presumably not within the conjurers' confraternity, the same end was achieved by simple invultuation. "Put a person's photograph on the wall and drive a tack into the heart and he will die."[46] The maltreating of a photograph or picture, either by burning or by placing in water (drowning), is also noted from Illinois.[47]

Death is brought on by a variety of magical acts, usually under the rubric of contagious magic, namely, by administrations that bring the victim into contact with noxious substances or expose him to processes by which he is figuratively done in, submerged, or consumed. We have already seen several of these magical principles at work in various connections; now we can consider the main ones in orderly fashion. The surest and most powerful way to involve a person in magical harm, short of direct physical assault or by the administration of poisonous or noxious substances that directly interrupt or affect the physiological processes is by resort to contagious magic. Rather than by overt intervention, the conjurer can work indirectly with items that represent an extension of the victim's person, either as excreta, effluvia, exuviae, items of clothing, or other objects once in close physical contact with the victim. Even tracks and footsteps qualify as imprints of what had once been an actual physical presence. A photograph or any other kind of pictorial representation, executed at a distance, is perhaps the closest representation of all. We have already considered cases of the burning, burial, and immersion in water of pictures; now we can consider one final kind of *envoûtement,* namely, shooting at the image. The Brown Collection contains two excellent examples of this phenomenon, with comparative notes from elsewhere.[48]

We have already noted the use of hair in conjure bags, in "nailing"; now we may consider a Maryland example of "plugging," in which a lock of a person's hair is plugged into a maple or hickory tree with salt and pepper, there to await rotting, as the person himself sickens and dies.[49] Hair is a principal ingredient, too, of waxen images and poppets which are melted down or otherwise abused. Notes to a North Carolina entry suggest the wide range of this vicarious torture.[50] Excrement is used in various ways. One of the more bizarre is in "plugging." As recently as the late 1950's it was customary in some parts of Alabama to bore a hole in a tree, fill it with the excrement of the victim, and then drive a peg into the hole. The tighter it was driven in, the more the person would suffer.[51] Puckett reports a variation on this, by first cooking the excreta in an old skillet, placing the residue in a tin snuff-box, and then placing the box in a hole in the tree. "Treated in this way," Puckett writes, "the victim dies an unusually hard and painful death."[52] Other bodily secretions used in the making of charms, not always alone, but in connection with other things, include such things as nail clippings, teeth, hair, saliva, tears, perspiration, dandruff, and even scabs of sores.[53] In addition to the victim's clothing, as mentioned above, which is often buried,[54] the employment of a woman's menstrual bandages is also noted.[55]

The extension of a man to the footprints he leaves is seen in the use of the dirt from his tracks in the fabrication of conjure bags or other objects meant to suggest a residual physical presence of the victim.[56] Just as pictures, poppets, and other kinds of figures representing the person singled out for torment and death are pierced with pins, needles, nails, and other piercing instruments, so also are a person's tracks and footprints pierced in the same way. The driving of nails into footprints is noted in states as distant from each other as Maryland and Illinois.[57] A curious twist, as brought out in an Illinois practice, is to drive a nail into the victim's footprint, and thus force him to walk himself to death.[58] The placing of harmful substances such as salt, red pepper, strychnine, and the like in a person's tracks accords with the practice,[59] of course, of placing conjure bags and other harmful gear in places where the victim is bound to come into contact with them. As the final part of the paper we can rapidly review these places of magical contact.

We have already seen instances of leaving the harmful token in the victim's yard.[60] Deposit is also made at such public places as roads and streets,[61] paths,[62] or some other more or less public place or one often traversed where the victim would likely come into contact with it. The well, particularly when it might have been shared by others, constituted a sort of public place, and it was therefore a favored spot for the deposit of noxious substances.[63] Affixing the conjure bag or ball to trees or bushes where it could be inadvertently touched is a method suggesting primitive origins.[64] The gate, of course, occupies a position midway between public thoroughfares and the privacy of one's own premises. In either case, it was a place that could not be avoided in the ordinary comings and goings and commerce of the day.[65]

Within the house itself, or around it, the doorstep was perhaps the most favored spot.[66] So was a corner of the room or the chimney.[67] Within the house itself, the surest contact with the evil token, and the most sustained contact, was the victim's bed.[68] It was for this reason that searches for evil "hands" and "tricks" often began with a search of the bedclothing. Even the baby's crib was not overlooked as a choice spot in which to deposit "tricken bags."[69]

This account has been more cursory than I should have liked, but limitations of space have precluded a more thorough examination of the evidence, particularly with regard to theoretical questions. I hope in subsequent papers to explore these interesting matters more fully.

NOTES

1. The evil eye is a special subject, and, even though the belief in this ancient occult art flourishes in parts of America, I can not enter into a discussion of the subject in this paper.

2. The term "medicine man" is applied largely to the American Indian medical practitioners and priestly functionaries, and the term "shaman" is little used in America, even though some conjurers indulge in rituals so elaborate as to remind one of shamanistic ordeals.

3. Norman E. Whitten, Jr. "Contemporary Patterns of Malign Occultism Among Negroes in North Carolina," *Journal of American Folklore,* LXXV (1962), 316.

4. *Cf.* Newbell Niles Puckett, *Folk Beliefs of the Southern Negro* (Chapel Hill, North Carolina, 1926), p. 206; Whitten, *op. cit.,* pp. 316–318; *Pennsylvania Folklife,* XII, No. 2 (Summer, 1961), 72. It is a general notion in white magic, of course, that the healer will lose his gift if he demands money for his services. *Cf. Handworterbuch des deutschen Aberglaubens* (10 vols., Berlin and Leipzig, 1927–1942), I, 1163, s.v. "besprechen."

5. The reader should read with care Whitten's discussion of Negro-White ratios in the parts of North Carolina surveyed, and also his theories on syncretism between the white and Negro races as it relates to magic and occult practices (pp. 320–322).

6. For a discussion of European elements in the Negro's cultural heritage in America, as over against his native African roots, see the brief bibliographical survey in Whitten (p. 323, note 2). Missing, unfortunatley, are the basic contributions to the subject by George Pullen Jackson.

7. *Frank C. Brown Collection of North Carolina Folklore* (7 vols., Durham, North Carolina, 1952–1964). Vols. VI–VII: *Popular Beliefs and Superstitions from North Carolina,* ed. Wayland D. Hand, 1961–1964.

8. Puckett, *op. cit.,* p. 247.

9. Harry Middleton Hyatt, *Folk-Lore from Adams County, Illinois* (Memoirs of the Alma Egan Hyatt Foundation, New York, 1935), No. 9179.

10. *Journal of American Folklore,* X (1897), 242.

11. Hyatt, *op. cit.,* No. 9154.

12. Yandell Collins, Jr., "Superstition and Belief Tales from Louisville," *Kentucky Folklore Record,* IV (1958), 76. On "plugging" in its medical uses, see Wayland D. Hand, "Plugging, Nailing, Wedging, and Kindred Folk Medical Practices," in *Folklore & Society: Essays in Honor of Benj. A. Botkin,* ed. Bruce Jackson (Hatboro, Pennsylvania, 1966), pp. 63–75.

13. Puckett, *op. cit.,* p. 223.

14. Miss Herron and Miss A. M. Bacon, "Conjuring and Conjure-Doctors in the Southern United States," *Journal of American Folklore,* IX (1896), 144.

15. Vance Randolph, *Ozark Superstitions* (New York, 1947), p. 279.

16. Puckett, *op. cit.,* p. 215.

17. *Ibid.,* p. 232.

18. Roland Steiner, "The Practice of Conjuring in Georgia," *Journal of American Folklore,* XIV (1901), 174. *Cf. JAF,* IX (1899), 299 (graveyard dirt placed in food will cause heavy sickness [Negro]).

19. Hyatt, *op. cit.,* No. 9117.

20. Hyatt, *op. cit.,* No. 9179; Cf. Clement Richardson, "Some Slave Superstitions," *The Southern Workman,* XLI (1912), 248.

21. Tom Pete Cross, "Folk-Lore from the Southern States," *Journal of American Folklore,* XXII (1909), 253.

22. Zora Hurston, "Hoodoo in America," *Journal of American Folklore,* XLIV (1931), 325.

23. Richardson, *op. cit.,* p. 248.

24. Hyatt, *op. cit.,* No. 9224.

25. Elsie Clews Parsons, "Folk-Lore of the Cape Verde Islanders," *Journal of American Folklore,* XXXIV (1921), 97.

26. Jean Thomas, *Blue Ridge Country* (New York, 1942), pp. 180–185.

27. Herron and Bacon, *op. cit.,* p. 143.

28. Hyatt, *op. cit.,* No. 9153.

29. In Germany it is known as *Nestelknüpfen* and in Holland as *nestelknoopen. Cf. Handwörterbuch des deutschen Aberglaubens,* VI, 1014–1016, s.v. "Nestelknüpfen"; K. ter Laan, *Folkloristisch Woordenboek* (s-Gravenhage, 1949), p. 256, s.v. "nestelknoopen"; *Folk-Lore,* XXXIII (1922), 391–392, in the discussion of "tying of the knot."

30. *Cf.* Herron and Bacon, *op. cit.,* pp. 146–147.

31. Puckett, *op. cit.*, p. 361.

32. Hurston, *op. cit.*, p. 361.

33. *Western Folklore*, XVII (1958), 277 (news item).

34. *Western Folklore,* XVI (1957), 60 (news report).

35. Hurston, *op. cit.,* p. 399.

36. Stewart Culin, "Negro Sorcery in the United States," *Journal of American Folklore,* III (1890), 285.

37. *Journal of American Folklore,* V. (1892), 123.

38. Hyatt, *op. cit.,* No. 9166.

39. Hyatt, *op. cit.,* No. 9177.

40. A. M. Bacon, "Conjuring and Conjure-Doctors in the Southern United States," *Journal of American Folklore,* IX (1896), 255. For a present-day instance, see Whitten, *op. cit.,* p. 311.

41. Steiner, *op. cit.,* p. 180.

42. Hyatt, *op. cit.,* No. 9116. *Cf.* Puckett, *op. cit.,* pp. 243, 272.

43. Hyatt, *op. cit., No. 9146.*

44. Daniel Lindsey Thomas and Lucy Blayney Thomas, *Kentucky Superstitions* (Princeton, New Jersey, 1920), No. 2176. *Cf.* Hyatt, *op. cit.,* No. 9209; Hurston, *op. cit.,* p. 378.

45. Thomas and Thomas, *op. cit.,* No. 2178.

46. Hyatt, *op. cit.,* No. 9212. *Cf.* No. 9210 (nails driven into image affixed to a white oak tree [Irish]). Additional helpful references include *Journal of American Folklore,* XXV (1912), 133 (Georgia); *New York Folklore Quarterly,* VI (1950), 252 (New York); *Kentucky Folklore Record,* I (1955), 68 (Kentucky).

47. Hyatt, *op. cit.,* Nos. 9208, 9211, respectively.

48. VII, 109–110, Nos. 5579–5580. Consult the notes for the wide range of examples.

49. Annie Weston Whitney and Caroline Canfield Bullock, *Folk-Lore from Maryland* (Memoirs for the American Folklore Society, XVIII, New York, 1925), No. 1684. *Cf.* Puckett, *op. cit.,* p. 272.

50. Brown Collection, VII 102, No. 5549.

51. Ray B. Browne, *Popular Beliefs and Practices from Alabama* (Folklore Studies, IX, Berkeley and Los Angeles, 1958), No. 3369.

52. *Op. cit.,* p. 255.

53. Puckett, *op. cit.*, p. 229.

54. Puckett, *op. cit.*, pp. 238, 297.

55. Puckett, *op. cit.*, 297; Hurston, *op. cit.*, 395; Hyatt, *op. cit.*, No. 9183.

56. Herron and Bacon, *op. cit.*, p. 145; Puckett, *op. cit.*, p. 237.

57. Whitney and Bullock, *op. cit.*, No. 1694; Hyatt, *op. cit.*, No. 9225 (rusty nail).

58. Hyatt, *op. cit.*, No. 9222.

59. Hyatt, *op. cit.*, No. 9248 (German tradition).

60. An additional excellent reference to the finding in one's yard of a hoodoo bag containing various substances is found in Hyatt, *op. cit.*, No. 9165. *Cf.* Brown Collection, VII, 1, No. 5542.

61. Herron and Bacon, *op. cit.*, p. 145 (Virginia); *Journal of American Folklore,* XIII (1900), 228 (Georgia); Hurston, *op. cit.*, p. 327 (Louisiana).

62. Brown Collection, VII, 101, No. 5543; Puckett, *op. cit.*, p. 237.

63. *Cf.* Brown Collection, VII, 105, No. 5558.

64. Puckett, *op. cit.*, p. 223; *Journal of American Folklore,* XIII (1900), 228 (Georgia).

65. Herron and Bacon, *op. cit.*, p. 145; Puckett, *op. cit.*, p. 291.

66. Culin, *op. cit.*, 285. (Georgia); Herron and Bacon; *op. cit.*, p. 145; Puckett, *op. cit.*, p. 230; Brown Collection, VII, 101–102, No. 5560 (comparative notes); *Journal of American Folklore,* LXXV (1962), 313.

67. Puckett, *op. cit.*, 297; Herron and Bacon, *op. cit.*, p. 144.

68. Puckett, *op. cit.*, p. 230; Herron and Bacon, *op. cit.*, p. 144.

69. Herron and Bacon, *op. cit.*, p. 144.

15

Witch-Riding and Other Demonic Assault in American Folk Legend*

As a field of scholarly investigation, witchcraft offers much to challenge the American worker who is interested in assessing American materials in the light of older European traditions. In this appraisal folk beliefs and customs connected with witchcraft are more meaningful if they are somehow held fast in the matrix of folk legend. Folk tales are useful, to be sure, in revealing the nature of witches and their doings, and folk beliefs and superstitions dealing with witches add scores of details about these creatures that are not contained in narrative accounts. It is to the folk legend, however, that we must turn for essential data in developing typologies of witches as well as for the range of their diabolical repertories.

In addressing myself to the theme of this conference, I have fastened upon one of the more spectacular kinds of *maleficia* wrought by witches, namely, the riding of animals and humans by witches. I am especially concerned here, however, with witch-riding as it relates to humans, and with physical oppression of any kind visited upon humans by demons or any of the creatures of lower mythology.

American legend scholars, unfortunately, are not endowed with the richness of source material for their researches as are

*This article originally appeared in *Probleme der Sagenforschung*. Verhandlungen der Tagung von der Kommission für Erzählforschung . . . vom 27. September bis 1. Oktober 1972. Freiburg, 1973, pp. 165–176. Permission to reprint has been given by the editor and publisher, Prof. Dr. Lutz Röhrich.

their European confrères, and in many areas of legend scholarship there are only the barest of outlines to follow and no encompassing resources to fall back upon. Witch-riding is tolerably well known in American folklore, but there are comparatively few accounts to be found in the corpus of American folk legend.[1] In the absence of any index of American folk legend I have searched through collections of legends available to me, as well as other sources. It is interesting, and perhaps ironic, to note that the best accounts are found, not in collections of legends, but rather in general works on folklore and particularly in collections of popular beliefs and superstitions. Many of the best items, in turn, have been encountered in specialized collections and articles in folklore journals.

The notion of witch-riding as a form of torture to victims of the witch's whim, rather than as a means of transport, seems to be known principally in the Anglo-American and the German-American tradition. The fact that it is not encountered in the Scandinavian-American tradition must be laid to the circumstance that there has been hardly any collecting of these materials in America. Witch-riding, of course, was known in the Scandinavian North in olden times, as well as in modern-day traditions, and systematic collecting among the American descendants of these North Europeans would no doubt turn up examples of this phenomenon of witchcraft, along with the usual run of witchcraft traditions.[2]

Witch-riding is also encountered in the Negro tradition in several parts of the country, but it is difficult to say whether these traditions stem from an African heritage or whether, like so much other "Negro" folklore, these beliefs were taken over from the stock-in-trade of witchcraft found among southern whites. In many other aspects of the black art, I have been able to show that in the complex of Negro witchcraft and conjury much black material stems from traditions brought to America from Europe by the white settlers. On the other hand, it is quite clear that certain aspects of the sorcery and magic of witchcraft, specifically Negro conjury, are part of the American Negro's African heritage.[3] In the South itself, Cross points out that witches in the white tradition and conjurers in the black often do the selfsame things.[4] Other writers have also addressed themselves to this confluence of traditions in the New World, notably Whitten.[5]

In his classic work on American Negro folk belief, Puckett frequently annotates Negro witchcraft beliefs with references from standard collections of folklore from the British Isles. His theory of the Negro as being "the custodian of former beliefs of the whites" has not been assailed, so far as I am aware.[6] As is well known, Puckett has also searched diligently for African, and particularly West African, antecedents of American Negro folk beliefs and customs and, in many categories of material, has demonstrated a dominant retension and borrowing of materials from the Negro's African past. In his treatment of witch-riding, however, it is significant to note that the only foreign analogues cited are from the British Isles.[7] The reason is easy to find, I think, but no one apparently has yet stated it; namely, travel on horseback was little known, if at all, in most parts of native Africa. Riding on other kinds of animals does not fit at all, of course, into the concept of saddling and bridling that is associated with horse travel wherever *Equus caballus* has been domesticated. For accounts of witch-riding among Negroes in other parts of the United States and Canada, one is obliged to consider the provenience of beliefs in terms of the flavor of the narrative accounts themselves and specific references to items in the classical witch's tradition of Europe. Most of the material from the central and northern states cited in this study predates the wholesale movement of Negroes from the agrarian South to the industrial North; so that, in effect, we are considering material possibly inherited by Negroes in the so-called "northern tradition" rather than in the Negro culture of the South where African retensions have always been more pronounced.

One of the most common features of legendary accounts of witch-riding is the saddling and bridling of the victim by the witch, much in the manner that a horse would be made ready to ride. The following illustrations come from widely different parts of the country and from different periods. One of the oldest is an account from Carroll County, Arkansas, dating from 1858 or 1859, as handed down in the Rea family:

> Sure, I'll tell you all I know about it. I got the Story from my grandfather, George W. Rea. Old Mrs. Inman was blind in one eye. She lived on Lick Branch, just east of Alpena, Arkansas. In 1858 or 1859 a young woman named Gaddy made a formal complaint to the church authorities, accusing Grandma Inman of witchcraft. A trial was held in the Primitive Baptist church at what is now called the Dunkard Community, south of Alpena. It was in Carroll County then, but is now part of Boone County. The testimony was that the accused had come to the complainant's house at night, saddled and bridled the complainant, and rode her for miles

over the hills and valleys of Carroll County. On at least one occasion the alleged witch rode Miss Gaddy into a neighbor's barn, and there bred her to a Spanish jack. The jury found Mrs. Inman guilty of witchcraft, and expelled her from the church. Grandfather always said that he was present at the trial, but took no part in it.
My father, George F. Rea, also told me about the case, as he heard it from his parents and others. The parties involved in the trial were still living when father was a boy. He saw many of them, including Grandma Inman and the Gaddy woman who testified against her.[8]

A nineteenth-century account from New England contains the essential features of saddling and bridling:

> There is a story of Captain Sylvanus Rich of Truro who, having taken on a cargo of corn for Boston in North Carolina, was held up by bad weather. Just before putting to sea, he had gone ashore and had bought a pail of milk from an old woman. This woman he blamed for the fearful gale he presently encountered off Cape Hatteras. . . . The captain suffered hallucinations and. . . . He solemnly informed his crew that every night the witch entered his cabin through the lazaret, and after bridling and saddling him, rode him over the sand dunes and through the woods of Truro and around Bound Brook Island.[9]

The next account is from the Province of Ontario in Canada at the time of the first World War:

> Again, an old man declared he was taken out every night by the witches and bridled and ridden like a horse; and he would show all the signs of being completely exhausted in the morning, and would exhibit the sores at the corners of his mouth where he had been unmercifully jerked by the bit. He so fully believed all this, that he walked fifty miles to consult a "witch-doctor," who delivered him from his tormentors.[10]

A more recent account, one collected in the white tradition on the Pennsylvania-West Virginia border during the late 1930's, stresses more than any other account in my possession the care and treatment of horses as extended to include humans metamorphosed into equine form:

> One frequently hears in this part of the country reference to the riding or chasing of cattle and horses by witches; less often a tale is told of witches riding men. Near Waynesburg (Greene County) there used to live a man who asserted that he had been the victim of such persecution; but the story he told of his experience is old and widespread. He had been saddled and bridled by a witch—being first rendered powerless to resist, of course, by her spell—and

ridden a great distance to the eastward, to a desert house where witches from various parts were having a "frolic." His rider tied him to a fence outside the house and went within to join in the mirth. While she was inside, he slipped his bridle; but she became aware of this and at once came outside to refasten him—which she did, treating him exactly like a horse, and slapping him to make him stand in a certain position. After the gathering broke up, the witch rode him home again.[11]

A legend in the Irish tradition of western Illinois, current in the 1930s, treats the debilitating effects of a witch ride by reversing the roles. In the following account, the victim is made to ride a witch, rather than himself being ridden by her:

> A man married a witch and he did not know it. He would sleep fine, but when he got up the next morning he was all in. One day he said to his neighbor, "I don't know what is wrong with me. I am so tired all the time." The neighbor said, "I spy a horse each night with you on its back. Tonight you act like you are asleep, and in the morning look in the bed and under it and see what you see." So that night after the man was sleeping, his wife turned herself into a horse and put this man on her back, and took him to the pasture and run around and around with him. In the morning he looked and found on the bottom of her feet the prints of the horse's shoe, and under the bed the horse's shoe. That was why this man was not resting. His wife was taking him riding every night through the pasture on her back.[12]

The previous account introduces the feature of horseshoes and serves as a point of departure to treat American accounts of the well-known German legend dealing with the shoeing of witches with horseshoes as a means of disenchantment. In the Schoharie Hills country of southern New York State there was a story current in the early part of the present century which, though shorn of details, one might well compare with the legend of "Die Trude und der Schmiedlehrjunge" found in Müller's collection of legends from Transylvania or Henderson's legend of "The Blacksmith's Wife of Yarrowfoot," in the North of England.[13] Here is the New York story as reported in the classic collection of Gardner:

> There was a man in our neighborhood who had a great time being rid by witches. One night it would be a girl who put a bridle on him; the next it would be a full-grown woman. After he had stood it as long as he thought he could, he fixed for whoever might come. He put a chair in the bed and covered it up, then got behind the door and waited. Pretty soon a girl came in with a bridle in her

hand. But he grabbed it out of her hand and put it on her. He rode her over hill and dale until near morning, then took her to a blacksmith shop and had her shod. When her folks got up in the morning they found the girl sitting in the kitchen with iron shoes on hands and feet. But the man kept the witch bridle, so she didn't trouble him again.[14]

In his collection of folk tales, *The Devil's Pretty Daughter,* Vance Randolph gives a version from the Ozarks of this legend under the title "The Blacksmith's Story."

One time there was a blacksmith that couldn't get no rest of a night, and he kept talking about how he was rode by a witch. Soon as he went to sleep a girl would put a hair bridle on him and ride him all over the country. That's why he was all tired out in the morning. He had scratches on his legs, too, and sometimes there was cockleburs in his hair. If a man was to tell such a tale nowadays folks would think he was crazy, but that was a long time ago, and everybody believed in witches then.

Finally the blacksmith made a dummy and put it in his bed, and then he hid behind the door. When the young witch come in he grabbed the bridle and put it on her. Sure enough, she turned into a fine mare. She bucked and kicked and tried to bite, but the blacksmith stayed right with her. They went a-flying up hills and through briar-patches, and he didn't spare the whip nor spur, neither. The mare didn't have no shoes on, so he went down to the shop. She carried on something terrible, but he tied her up like an ox and shod her all round. Then he snatched off the bridle, and away she run through the timber.

The blacksmith went home and slept fine, and the witch never bothered him no more. But about ten miles away a merchant's daughter showed up missing. Finally they found her, a-hiding in the barn. She was stark naked, with horseshoes nailed to her hands and feet.

There was a lot of talk, but nobody ever done anything about it. Her Pappy was a rich merchant and stood in with the county officers. So they just hushed the whole thing up and sent the girl off to a big hospital somewheres. Some of the town folks went so far as to claim it was just one of them old tales, and nothing like that ever did happen nohow.[15]

An Irish version from western Illinois, told in the more factual style of legends, does not employ the switch of roles, for the husband is the rider rather than the horse. The shoeing incident is a stable part of the legend.

A man worked in a foundry and was telling the men that he worked with that he was so tired every morning. And one of the men said, "Maybe your wife is a witch." He said, "No." Then he told them that every night he would be riding a beautiful horse. Then he would come back and tie the horse to a post out in front of the house. Then he would go to bed. His wife was always sleeping when he came to bed after tying the horse. The next morning when he woke up, his wife was too tired to get up. One of the men said, "The next time you are on this horse, take it to the blacksmith shop and have the horse shod." So that night when he was riding, he went to the blacksmith's house and the man said, "It is too late for me to shod your horse." The man said, "I will pay you well." So they started to shodding the horse. The horse kicked and kicked. They just had to tie the horse to be shod. He rode the horse home, tied it to the front porch. When he got in the house his wife was sleeping. The next morning when he got up, his wife would not get up and get his breakfast, said she was too sick, "I can't get up." Then he pulled the covers off her and the horse's shoes were on her hands and feet. So she was a witch and she was the horse he had been riding.[16]

Negro accounts of witch-riding are generally not as clearly conceived. Puckett remarks that, whereas in a Negro ballad an old woman is depicted as saddling, bridling, booting and spurring a person, and riding him for fox hunting, Negroes do not generally believe that the person is really changed into a horse.[17] The notion of riding is rarely well developed, even though the victim may be straddled, as in riding. Dorson gives an account of witch-riding in a Negro enclave at Calvin, Michigan, which was an early-day haven of Negroes in the North, well before the time of the Civil War.

I laid down one day at twelve o'clock. My husband was went to carry the mule to the lot an' I cooked dinner, and I said, "Well, I'll take me a little nap. I had a birthday-almanac—one of those birthday-almanacs you know—I was interested in readin'. I laid down, and I told Uncle Pete, well I wasn't 'sleep, it looked like a shadow come over my eyes. And I saw a woman come in the door. Both—all the doors were open—I lived in a little ol' two-room house, and I was layin' cross the bed. And she walked in an' she stepped straddle of me and she got on me, an' she just started doing' this a-way. "Runh-runh-runh, runh," an' she shook me till I said, "Well, Lord, I know I'm goin' to die" I give up to die, and I heard her when she hit the floor—*vlop*. She got offa me an' walked right out the door. . . . Rode me till I was drunk.[18]

In all of the legends that I know dealing with the transformation of a human to a horse at the moment the bridle is affixed to the head, there are no details. It is implied that the transformation takes place when this piece of harness is fitted on the victim—an action that accords well with magical transformations in folk tales. I do not know of a single account, however, where there is a detailed statement of how the bit is inserted into the mouth of the victim, although occasionally there is a mention of the bit's being in the horse's mouth. In the period when these stories were current, particularly in country areas and in small towns, most people would be presumed to know how horses were saddled and bridled; hence there would be no need to give details.

Oftentimes the Negro accounts remind one of nightmares and other creatures settling on a sleeping person and weighing him down. These stories are found in many parts of the country.[19] Although the notions are somewhat more primitive in conception, perhaps, than in witch-riding as depicted in the classical European tradition, they seem to accord more with European and American conceptions of nightmares and other oppressive forces.

The nightmare is rarely conceptualized as a creature in American folklore, and one is hard put to find accounts of its physical form, either in legend or in folk belief. In the Pennsylvania German country, however, there is a somewhat legendary account of how one can subdue a nightmare:

> Nightmare can sometimes be caught, as is illustrated by the following instance: A hostler in the service of the writer's father frequently suffered from nightmare, and to secure the intruder he procured a small phial which he placed within easy reach of his bed. After two or three nights the nightmare was caught and bottled and destroyed by burning. This was stated to have been the spirit of a black cat, under control of a witch with whom the hostler had had a previous misunderstanding.[20]

In the French tradition of Louisiana there is a belief in the *cauchemar.* In an account of an attack by this creature there is an association with a bad dream:

> During a bad dream I happened to roll over on my stomach. (*cauchemar* attacks) I could not shake her off my back. She rode me completely out of my bed onto the floor; then steering me toward the stairs, she proceeded to guide me to the very top. . . . By the time my mother found me I was almost ready to jump out the window.[21]

In Maine, nightmare is supposed to be caused by the nightmare man, a kind of evil spirit, struggling with one. It is prevented by placing a sharp knife under the pillow, and stuffing the keyhole with cotton.[22] For ancient Anglo-Saxon accounts of the nightmare fiend that rode humans to a point of exhaustion, or even to death, one should consult Grendon.[23] Modern legendary accounts, referable to the late 1960's are to be found in Virginia, among other places.[24] It is curious to note that even though nightmares are not often thought of as demonic creatures, most of the means to combat this nocturnal malady are the same as those used to combat witches and other evil creatures. The confusion of nightmare with witches also extends to ghosts. As early as 1889, W. J. Hoffman, a very knowledgeable scholar in the field of Pennsylvania German folklore, stated that "nightmares are often the direct doing of witches."[25]

Accounts of *Aufhocker* likely exist in American legend repertories, but no one has isolated a body of these stories and discussed them. If they exist at all, it is, perhaps, as a category of animal ghost stories. These tales should be brought together and studied to see if evil dogs and witch cats are among the creatures which pounce upon wayfarers or drag other mortals to the ground or otherwise immobilize them. Another fruitful line of inquiry, following the lead of Friedrich Ranke,[26] might be to investigate the part which the dead and ghosts play in weighing down travellers or those abroad at night or other uncanny times. American ghostlore does contain legends and other kinds of accounts of physical pressure exerted upon the living by those who have died. The following story from Illinois will serve to illustrate such ghostly assault:

> I used to work for a doctor in Fowler, Illinois, and he died. One night I was walking along the street, after the doctor was buried, and all at once I felt a warm hand take hold of my hand. I was not afraid because I knew when we got to the four corners of the street they would let loose, because spirits don't go across a road; and I knew it was the doctor. And his hand slipped right off when we got to the four corners.[27]

In Negro conjury, graveyard dirt thrown under the victim's house—a so-called "jack mulatta," has the same general effect as an *Aufhocker,* but functions more as an evil, tantalizing force than as a physical burden.

> . . . Well, dat's whut yo' call a jack mulatta an' it'll come in jes' lak a hag would—would ride yo' tuh death and tantalize (sic) yo' an' de person fo' who ah put it der couldn't even rest.
>
> But this doesn't ride you?
>
> It doesn't ride yo' but it jes somepin dat tantalize yo' tuh death —nobody couldn't "see" it bu chew.[28]

I hope that these representations will serve to stimulate my American colleagues in legend study to connect our American traditions up with European stocks and bodies of legend from elsewhere. America possesses greater legend treasures, really, than the record shows. This lack should be and will be corrected, I hope.

NOTES

1. The reader should note, for example, the material that I was able to bring together on belief in witch-riding by way of annotation for entries on the subject to be found in the North Carolina collection of the late Frank C. Brown/Wayland D. Hand, Popular Beliefs and Superstitions from North Carolina, vol. 6–7, 1961, 1964, of the Frank C. Brown, Collection of North Carolina Folklore. 7 vols. Durham/ North Carolina 1952–1964, vol. 7, 115–118, Nos. 5606–5608.

2. See Stith Thompson, Motif-Index of Folk-Literature, 6 vols. Copenhagen and Bloomington, Indiana, 1955–1958. vol. 3, 294 (G 241.2. Witch rides on person), where references are given to the standard works of Feilberg, Boberg, and MacCulloch.

3. See Melville J. Herskovits, The Myth of the Negro Past. New York and London 1941, 244–245. In numerous writings from the western part of Africa one can find prototypes of Negro practices of conjury in America, but there is no work, so far as I am aware, that takes up witchcraft and magic in a systematic way as they involve Negroes on both sides of the Atlantic. For a statement of possible European connections of American Negro magic see Herskovits, Life in a Haitian Valley. New York 1937, 237–239 et passim.

4. Tom Pete Cross, Witchcraft in Northern Carolina, in: Studies in Philology 16, No. 3, 1919, 267 et passim.

5. Norman E. Whitten, Jr., Contemporary Patterns of Malign Negro Occultism Among Negroes in North Carolina, in: Journal of American Folklore 75, 1962, 311–325.

6. Newbell Niles Puckett, Folk Beliefs of the Southern Negro. Chapel Hill, North Carolina 1926, 2.

7. Newbell Niles Puckett, l.c. 151–153 et passim.

8. Vance Randolph, A Witch Trial in Carroll County, in: Arkansas Historical Quarterly 16, 1957, 89-90. There are several accounts of witch-riding in the Brown Collection vol. 1, 649–650.

9. Edwin Valentine Mitchell, It's an Old Cape Cod Custom. New York 1949, 31.

10. F. W. Waugh, Canadian Folk-Lore from Ontario, in: Journal of American Folklore 31, 1918, 40, No. 589.

11. S. P. Bayard, Witchcraft Magic and Spirits on the Border of Pennsylvania and West Virginia, in: Journal of American Folklore 51, 1938, 53.

12. Harry Middleton Hyatt, Folk-Lore of Adams County. Illinois, New York 1935, 539, No. 9655.

13. Fr. Müller, Siebenbürgische Sagen, 144–146, No. 208. William Henderson, Notes on the Folk-Lore of the Northern Counties and the Borders. New. ed., in: Publications of the Folk-Lore Society 2, 1879, 190–192. Other accounts are also given.

14. Emelyn Elizabeth Gardner, Folklore from the Schoharie Hills New York, Ann Arbor, Michigan 1937, 65, No. 13.

15. Vance Randolph, The Devil's Pretty Daughter and Other Ozark Folk Tales. New York 1955, 153–154.

16. Harry Middleton Hyatt, Folk-Lore of Adams County. New York, 2d ed., 1965, 826, No. 16147.

17. Newbell Niles Puckett, Folk Beliefs of the Southern Negro 152.

18. Richard M. Dorson, Negro Witch Stories on Tape, in: Midwest Folklore 2, 1952, 236.

19. Cf. West Virginia Folklore 6, 1955, 10, No. 2. Fanny D. Bergen, Animal and Plant Lore, in: Memoirs of the American Folklore Society 7, 1899, 128, No. 62. Richard M. Dorson, Negro Witch Stories on Tape 235–236.

20. Thomas A. Brendle / Claude W. Unger, Folk Medicine of the Pennsylvania Germans. The Non-Occult Cures, in: Proceedings of the Pennsylvania German Society 45, 1935, 38.

21. Patricia Rickels, Some Accounts of Witch Riding, in: Louisiana Folklore Miscellany 2, 1961, 4–5.

22. Fanny D. Bergen, Current Superstitions, in: Memoirs of the American Folklore Society 4, 1896, 96, No. 827.

23. Felix Grendon, Anglo-Saxon Charms, in: Journal of American Folklore 22, 1909, 231. In this connection the reader should not fail to see the detailed typology compiled by Carl-Herman Tillhagen, The Conception of the Nightmare in Sweden, in: Humaniora, Essays in Literature, Folklore and Bibliography. Honoring Archer Taylor on his Seventieth Birthday, ed. Wayland D. Hand and Gustave O. Arlt. Locust Valley, New York 1960, 317–329.

24. Keystone Folklore Quarterly 14, 1969, 10, 37.

25. Journal of American Folklore 2, 1889, 31. For further illustrations of this confusion, see the Brown-Collection vol. 7, 136, No. 5704.

26. Handwörterbuch des deutschen Aberglaubens. 10 vols. Berlin-Leipzig 1927–1942. vol. 1, 675–677: "Aufhocker."

27. H. M. Hyatt, Folk-Lore of Adams County New York, 2d ed., 1965, 753, No. 15630.

28. H. M. Hyatt, Hoodoo-Conjuration-Witchcraft-Rootwork. 3 vols. New York 1970 ff., vol. 1, 40.

16

The Evil Eye in its Folk Medical Aspects: A Survey of North America*

Belief in the evil eye is as pervasive in many parts of the world as it is ancient. In compiling his classic two-volume work, *Der böse Blick und Verwandtes* in 1910, the well-known Hamburg ophthalmologist, S. Seligmann consulted over 2,100 bibliographical sources.[1] A sequel volume which was published a dozen years later and which dealt with the magic power of the eye and the phenomenon of fascination brought responses from scores of fellow practitioners all over the world,[2] including oculists and optometrists. In connection with the great work of Seligmann it is interesting to note that after the baneful power of the eye had been studied for centuries by scholars of anthropology, ethnology, and folklore, workers in literature and the arts, students of religion, geographers, travelers, and a host of other investigators, the evil eye finally claimed the attention of eye specialists themselves. A recent American writer on the subject, Dr. Edward S. Gifford, for example, is a Philadelphia ophthalmologist.[3]

In Europe, belief in the evil eye is most pronounced in the Mediterranean countries, an area that is part of the vast geographical continuum extending along a central axis from India westward through the Middle East and all the way to Spain and

*This article originally appeared in the *Actas del XLI Congreso Internacional de Americanistas, México 2 al 7 de septiembre de 1974.* 3 vols. Mexico City, 1975–1976, III, 183–189. Permission to reprint has been given by the editors and publisher.

Morocco. The spread of the belief in the evil eye to the New World, and particularly to Latin America, proceeded along an extension of this same central axis, as the New World was opened up to colonization and commerce after the fifteenth century.[4] A secondary route of transmission, and one more important for North America, came with the settlement of the St. Lawrence and lower Mississippi River basins by the French, and the colonization of the Spanish Southwest by explorers and colonists from Mexico. As an admixture to the basic Anglo-Saxon colonization of the eastern seaboard, which set in by the beginning of the seventeenth century, there came later—particularly during the nineteenth century—ethnic components from all parts of Europe, including strong representations of the Romance and Slavic, as well as of the Germanic, peoples. The interplay of these various cultures, as seen in the transmission of folk beliefs and superstitions concerning the evil eye, represents an historical development that is as intriguing as it is impossible to unravel.

The antiquity of beliefs in the power of the human eye is seen in the prevalence of fear of the evil eye in Old Testament times.[5] Besides being attested in the Bible, the evil eye is mentioned in the Apocrypha, in the Talmudic writings, and at a much later period, in the Koran.[6] References to the power of fascination go back to the seventh century B.C. in Assyrian and Akkadian documents,[7] and myths concerning it are to be found in Sumerian sources in Mesopotamia dating from the third millenium B.C.[8] Seligmann has traced the belief in the evil eye to all peoples of the Middle East, Southern Asia, and the Extreme Orient, as well as to inhabitants of most other parts of the world.[9] In this useful survey he has supplied a table of designations of the evil eye, by countries and language groups, together with the verb forms used to denote casting of the evil glance, the names of possessors of the harmful power, male and female, designations of the person harmed, a list of amulets and other apotropaic measures to deal with the malady, and the names of special healers invoked.[10]

Belief in the evil eye is attested in Northwest Europe in early times. The mythical Irish giant, Balor of the Evil Eye, for instance, was celebrated for his lethal gaze which could strike whole armies dead.[11] There is also mention of the "glance of eye" in Beowulf, Old English epic poem of about the year 1000 A.D., as one of the dark and evil forces to confront the warrior.[12] Feilberg has traced in convincing fashion the belief in the evil eye in Nordic tradition from early times to the present,[13] and

Vuorela has written a monograph on the prevalence of old beliefs and practices concerning the evil eye that are encountered in present-day Finland.[14] In the Anglo-Saxon countries the belief in the evil eye appears to have been better preserved in Scotland than elsewhere.[15]

From this brief historical and geographical survey it will be easy for the student of these matters to trace out North American manifestations of the evil eye and to connect them with their most immediate European sources and antecedents. In surveying so vast a field, however, the investigator, while recognizing local oikotypal differences in beliefs and traditions concerning the evil eye, will nevertheless be aware of certain basic notions encountered everywhere. Briefly summarized, these involve the possessor of the power of the eye, and the unusual nature of, or reasons for, his baneful gift, the manner in which the evil glance is cast on the victim, measures used to prevent, counteract, or repair the mischief, and special healers and functionaries who dispose over these magico-religious medical gifts.

Because it is impossible to deal with the manifold aspects of the evil eye, I have been obliged to confine myself in this paper to matters that come under the purview of folk medicine rather than entering upon the broader field of magic. Even though the magical component is not as rich and hardy as it is in the European homeland, there is nevertheless a reasonably representative body of folk beliefs and customs to be found in the United States and Canada. Despite the fact that I know the Latin American tradition much less well, I venture the guess that elements of the general European stock-in-trade, not found north of the border, are certain to be found somewhere in the Mexican tradition itself or elsewhere in Latin America.

Diagnosis of the evil eye involves not only the symptoms as observed in the victim but is also determined by some knowledge of the person causing the affliction. Admiration of a child by childless widows,[16] for example, or even a childless man,[17] particularly if the praise is fulsome, is a good indication of the jealous and designing person that is likely to possess the power of the evil eye. The case for suspicion of intended harm to the child is strengthened if the visitor is deformed in some way,[18] cross-eyed, possessed of eyes of a different color, or if his or her eyebrows should happen to meet.[19] Gypsies, Negroes, and other minorities are often singled out as bearers of the evil eye, as in Ohio, for example.[20] In some traditions persons born on Christmas day are thought to be bearers of the evil eye.[21] In the Mexican-American tradition one member of a set of twins is thought to have the power to harm people through his glance.[22] In New York State it is believed that persons are usually born with the evil eye.[23] Similarly, there is a notion in the northeast of Scotland, and elsewhere, that the evil eye is inherited, but I have not come upon this view in the United States.[24] In the Mexican-American tradition a person born with the *vista fuerte* may unwittingly bring harm to his fellows by a mere glance.[25] In the Jewish tradition it is believed that a child acquires the power of the evil eye by being suckled by a wet nurse.[26]

The symptoms of being "eye bitten," "blinked," "overlooked," or "forelooked," as this malady is variously described in vernacular terms,[27] generally involve the appearance of fatigue and discomfort, as in Pennsylvania,[28] or incessant crying on the part of the afflicted child, as in the Jewish tradition of Ohio and the Latin American tradition.[29] Even such a common ailment as colic, in which a child is costive and fretful, may be taken as a symptom of the evil eye.[30] Generally, however, the attack is associated with more sudden and violent onslaughts.[31] Chills and fever, coming on suddenly, are suspected to be magically induced,[32] particularly if the child vomits.[33] Cramps and convulsions fall into this same category of sudden and unexplained seizures.[34] Hiccups, with its jerking and uncontrolled spasms, is particularly singled out as an indication that the victim is suffering from the evil eye.[35] Perhaps the malady most often regarded as being caused by the evil eye is the common headache. This belief is encountered in the Italian, Jewish, and Russian traditions of New York State.[36] It is also found in Pennsylvania and Ohio,[37] among the Italians in West Virginia,[38] and in the Latin American tradition in Texas and New Mexico.[39] An unusual sign of being a victim of the evil eye is found in the Polish tradition of Ohio, where it is believed that a person with long, silky hair that becomes matted, has been smitten by the heated eye.[40]

Ritual diagnosis of the evil eye is a rarity. In the polyglot cities of Ohio, drops of olive oil are eased onto water in a flat container. If the oil mixes with the water it is generally believed that the person is under a spell. Some people believe, however, that if the drop of oil remains intact, the person being investigated is under the power of the evil eye.[41] In the Latin American tradition throughout the American Southwest there is a well-known European ritual involving the breaking of eggs on the body of the supposed victim, or placing the broken egg in a dish near the bed. In New Mexico, for example, if the child has *el mal de ojo,* the image of the eye will appear in the yolk.[42] There are various other indications, including a sure sign of possession when the raw egg yolk at the head of the bed is magically cooked, as it were, overnight.[43] Among American immigrants from various parts of Central and Northeast Europe bread is used in a ritual to detect the evil eye. The bread is broken and put into a glass of water. If the bread does not sink, this is taken as evidence that the patient has been eye-bitten.[44]

Ailments caused by the evil eye range from general malaise to wasting and decline, and other unspecified maladies;[45] also a whole range of diseases in addition to headache, fever, convulsions, cramps, and the like, mentioned above. Impairment of sexual capacity and function is also associated with the evil eye,[46] as are impotence and sterility in man,[47] and even nocturnal pollutions.[48] The evil eye also figures prominently in female complaints, menstrual disorders, and problems of pregnancy and childbirth.[49] In the Romance countries abortion is likewise associated with the evil eye.[50] Most heinous of all in connection with the birth cycle is the casting of the evil eye to dry up a mother's milk or to make a child refuse the breast.[51] I have not come upon these beliefs in the United States. In the light of this wide range of folk beliefs and superstitions it is not surprising that the evil eye should also be credited with causing mental and emotional disorders, all the way from nervous breakdowns[52] to imbecility and insanity.[53]

As in other magical diseases, the evil eye does not respond to the ministration of the usual medical practitioners.[54] Special healers are pressed into service[55]—powwow doctors, Jewish *Upsprechers* who know how to "talk off" the spell,[56] and the *felcher,* the doctor without a license.[57] Many women in South Philadelphia, for instance, know the proper prayers against fascination and are willing to remove the accursed evil eye without remuneration.[58] Among the Genoese of central California the secret words used by the healer of the evil eye can be divulged only on Christmas day.[59]

It is difficult, of course, to differentiate between natural and magical cures with regard to the evil eye because most cures, as befits the nature of the malady, often contain magical or religious aspects. In keeping with the principles of natural medicine, special herbs are pressed into service and are dried and held ready for use.[60] In 1905 Emil Berdau, writing on Mexican folk medicine along the Texas border, tells of the bathing of a child in a decoction of *Yerba de Cristo* as a preliminary to the disenchantment from the evil eye in an involved ritual employing eggs.[61] The use of garlic is principally apotropaic, although it is widely believed that the cloves possess absorptive power.[62]

The bathing of ailing children with herb baths was practiced,[63] but I find no mention of salt baths, for instance, which was used as an apotropaic ablution in Scotland, among other places.[64] In Maryland, however, salt was sprinkled in every corner of the room and on the threshold to disenchant a child stricken with the evil eye.[65] Licking a child with the tongue is encountered in curative procedures for the evil eye in New York State.[66] A most unusual ritual, met with only in the Latin American tradition in the Spanish Southwest, involves finding the culprit who had inflicted the evil spell, forcing him or her to drink a mouthful of water, and then making him empty it directly into the suffering child's mouth.[67] Berdau's account of the ritual specifies the use of water drawn in the moonlight outside one's yard.[68] A water ritual in New York City, formerly practiced by South Italians, involved placing a saucer of water on the victim's head preliminary to the mumbling of a verbal charm.[69] In New Mexico around 1910 the sweepings from the four corners of the sufferer's room were boiled in water, taken into the healer's mouth, and then spewed into the child's face. It was not specified as to whether the person performing the disenchantment had herself inflicted the spell.[70] The fiery element is resorted to in ritual cures just as is the use of water. Glowing coals, ashes, charcoal, and various fumigants are used to counteract the effects of the evil eye,[71] and the burning of a hole in the garment of the person communicating the evil will turn the harm upon the perpetrator himself.[72]

Time will not allow more than a listing of the usual kinds of preventive and curative agents employed against the evil eye in North America. In the main they are well known. Wherever excessive praise is heaped upon a child by a jealous or designing person, the child's mother, or anyone near, would customarily spit upon the child to prevent *el mal de ojo.*[73] Also, it was widely thought that touching the child after it had been unduly praised would somehow counteract the intended harm.[74] Sometimes the remark about a "beautiful child" is offset by the statement that "it's an ugly child," or some other disparaging remark, as in Ohio.[75] If, on the other hand, the admiration is sincere, the person must add "God bless," or some other religious remark to the same effect.[76] Because of the constant fear of enchantment, mothers carefully guard their children,[77] cover their faces, or even hide them.[78] In the New Mexican Spanish tradition, a mother taking a young child with *el mal de ojo* from the house must be sure not to cross rivers or ditches with it, in the fear that once she did so the child would become permanently afflicted.[79]

Preventive gestures of "the horns" or "the fig" are made with the hands,[80] and crosses are inscribed on the child's forehead.[81] In Brooklyn this is done with laundry bluing.[82] Perhaps the most common means to avert the evil eye, or to cure it, is the use of amulets. These range from bracelets and necklaces of various materials such as jet and coral,[83] to chains and crosses,[84] and beads of various kinds, including red and white beads as well as those of coral.[85] These latter were the favorites. Horns of various kinds, or amulets made of horn, are widely used.[86] Often they are mounted in silver, as in Toronto.[87] A favorite amulet is a miniature hunchback.[88] The familiar *gobbo* is often carved from mother of pearl or from stone of some kind, but this Italian charm is also made from almost any durable substance, including, of course, coral.[89] In a shop in South Philadelphia in the late 1950s Dr. Gifford was able to buy small gold figures and other kinds of amulets of hunchbacks, crescent moons, fish, and other votive pieces to counteract the evil eye.[90] Curio shops in almost every large American city carry trinkets of this kind. Horseshoes, common in witchcraft, are also used to protect the house from the evil eye.[91] They are nailed to the wall, or to doors, in the accustomed manner. Knives, scissors, and other bladed instruments employed in witchcraft are also pressed into service against the evil eye.[92] Finally, among several other kinds of objects employed, red ribbons were fastened to the child, often around the neck.[93]

It is difficult to summarize a paper as diffuse and wide-ranging as this. I hope, however, that these representations will convey some notion of the prevalence of folk beliefs and customs connected with the evil eye that are to be found in the United States and elsewhere in North America. More systematic work is needed, of course, to depict these interesting traditions in their variety and fullness, and even in their present-day vitality.

NOTES

1. S. Seligmann, *Der böse Blick und Verwandtes. Ein Beitrag zur Geschichte des Aberglaubens aller Zeiten und Völker* (2 vols., Berlin: Hermann Barsdorf Verlag, 1910). (Unless otherwise noted, all references are to this parent work.)

2. S. Seligmann, *Die Zauberkraft des Augens und das Berufen. Ein Kapitel aus der Geschichte des Aberglaubens* (Hamburg: L. Friederichsen & Co., 1922).

3. Edward S. Gifford, Jr., *The Evil Eye. Studies in the Folklore of Vision* (New York: The Macmillan Company, 1958). The reader should also know of the earlier standard work on the evil eye in English: Frederick Thomas Elworthy, *The Evil Eye, An Account of This Ancient and Widespread Superstition* (London: J. Murray, 1895).

4. George M. Foster's notions of the transmission of the evil eye to the New World from Mediterranean areas generally coincide with my own. See George M. Foster, "Relationships between Spanish and Spanish American Folk Medicine,"*Journal of American Folklore,* 66 (1953), 203, *passim.* (Hereinafter cited: Foster, Spanish Folk Medicine.)

5. J. D. Rolleston, "Ophthalmic Folk-Lore," *The British Journal of Ophthalmology,* 26 (1942), 484. Cf. Deuteronomy XV: 9; XXVIII: 54–56; Proverbs XXIII: 6.

6. Rolleston, p. 484.

7. *Ibid.,* Cf. Benjamin Lee Gordon, "The Evil Eye," *Hebrew Medical Journal,* 34 (1961), 292.

8. Edward S. Gifford, Jr., "The Evil Eye in Pennsylvania Medical History," *Keystone Folklore Quarterly,* 5, 3 (1960), 3. (Hereinafter cited: Gifford, Pennsylvania.)

9. Seligmann, I, 12–47.

10. *Ibid.,* I, 48–64. This appendix contains a bibliography of dictionaries and special glossaries.

11. Rolleston, p. 485; Alexander Haggerty Krappe, *Balor With The Evil Eye* (Institut des études françaises, Columbia University, New York, 1927).

12. Rolleston, p. 484.

13. H. F. Feilberg, "Der böse Blick in nordischer Überlieferung," *Zeitschrift des Vereins für Volkskunde,* 11 (1901), 304–330, 420–430.

14. Toivo Vuorela, *Der böse Blick im Lichte der finnischen Überlieferung* (Folklore Fellows Communications, No. 201, Helsinki, 1967).

15. John Graham Dalyell, *The Darker Superstitions of Scotland* (Glasgow: Richard Griffin & Co., 1835); Robert Craig Maclagan, *Evil Eye in the Western Highlands* (London: D. Nutt, 1902).

16. John R. Crosby, "Modern Witches of Pennsylvania," *Journal of American Folklore,* 40 (1927), 308.

17. Gifford, Pennsylvania, p. 6.

18. Crosby, p. 308.

19. Newbell Niles Puckett Collection of Ohio Popular Beliefs and Superstitions (unpublished; hereinafter cited: Puckett, Ohio); Foster, p. 207; E. and M. A. Radford, *Encyclopaedia of Superstitions* (ed. and rev., Christina Hole, London: Hutchinson & Co., 1961), pp. 155–156; Gordon, p. 267; Walton Brooks McDaniel, "The *pupula duplex* and Other Tokens of the Evil Eye in the Light of Ophthalmology," *Classical Philology,* 13 (1918), 336; Phyllis H. Williams, *South Italian Folkways in Europe and America. A Handbook for Social Workers, Visiting Nurses, School Teachers, and Physicians* (Institute of Human Relations, Yale University, New Haven: Yale University Press, 1938), p. 153.

20. Puckett, Ohio (unpub.); Radford and Hole, p. 156; Ella Mary Leather, *The Folk-Lore of Herefordshire, Collected from Oral and Printed Sources* (Hereford: Jakeman & Carver, 1912), p. 51.

21. Williams, pp. 142, 155.

22. William R. Holland, "Mexican-American Medical Beliefs: Science or Magic," *Arizona Medicine,* 20, 5 (May, 1963), 93.

23. Louis C. Jones, "The Evil Eye among European Americans," *Western Folklore,* 10 (1951), 11. Cf. Franz Boas, "Current Beliefs of the Kwakiutl Indians," *Journal of American Folklore,* 45 (1932), 224.

24. Dalyell, p. 22; Rolleston, p. 485.

25. Holland, p. 93.

26. Jones, pp. 11, 17.

27. Gifford, Pennsylvania, pp. 3, 7; Dalyell, p. 45.

28. Gifford, Pennsylvania, p. 7.

29. Puckett, Ohio (unpub.); Ozzie G. Simmons, "Popular and Modern Medicine in Mestizo Communities of Coastal Peru and Chile," *Journal of American Folklore,* 68 (1955), 62.

30. Jones, p. 17.

31. Benjamin S. Moya, *Superstition and Beliefs among the Spanish-Speaking People of New Mexico* (M.A. thesis, University of New Mexico, Albuquerque, 1940), p. 34.

32. Jones, pp. 17, 21; Gifford, Pennsylvania, p. 6; Moya, p. 36; Aurelio M. Espinosa, "New Mexican Spanish Folk-Lore," *Journal of American Folklore,* 23 (1910), 409.

33. Dorothy J. Baylor, "Folklore from Socorro, New Mexico," *Hoosier Folklore,* 6 (1947), 149; Simmons, p. 62.

34. Seligmann, I, 123 (USA); 200 (Germany, Ireland, Scotland); Jones, p. 17; George M. Foster, *Empire's Children: The People of Tzintzuntzan* (Smithsonian Institution. Institute of Social Anthropology, Publication No. 6, Washington, D.C., 1946), p. 267.

35. Jones, p. 17; Gifford, Pennsylvania, p. 4; Claudia de Lys, *A Treasury of American Superstitions* (New York: The Philosophical Library, 1948), pp. 312–313.

36. Jones, pp. 17, 19, 21; *New York Folklore Quarterly,* 21 (1965), 185.

37. Gifford, pp. 4, 7; Puckett, Ohio.

38. *West Virginia Folklore,* 12 (1962), 29.

39. Moya, p. 37; Florence Johnson Scott, "Customs and Superstitions among Texas Mexicans on the Rio Grande Border," *Publications of the Texas Folklore Society*, 2 (1923), 83.

40. Puckett, Ohio (unpub.).

41. Puckett, Ohio (numerous attestations), *West Virginia Folklore,* 12 (1962), 29; Foster, *Spanish Folk Medicine,* p. 208; Williams, p. 155; Antonio Castillo de Lucas, *Folkmedicina* (Madrid: Editorial Dossat, S. A., 1958), p. 56.

42. Moya, p. 37; Espinosa, p. 410; Foster, *Empire's Children*, p. 267, Foster, *Spanish Folk Medicine,* p. 209; Simmons, p. 65; Scott, p. 83; Josephine Elizabeth Baca, "Some Health Beliefs of the Spanish Speaking," *American Journal of Nursing*, 69 (1969), 2174; Servando Martínez and Henry W. Martin, "Folk Diseases among Urban Mexican Americans," *Journal of the American Medical Association,* 196 (1966), 162.

43. Ruth Dodson, "Folk Curing among the Mexicans," *Publications of the Texas Folklore Society,* 10 (1932), 84–85.

44. Jones, pp. 18, 21. Serbo-Croatians in eastern Nebraska still practice this test.

45. Rolleston, p. 484; Seligmann, I, 201; Jones, p. 17; George D. Hendricks, "Superstitions Collected in Denton, Texas," *Western Folklore,* 15 (1956),

9; Rodney Gallop, *Portugal: A Book of Folk-Ways* (Cambridge: Cambridge University Press, 1926), p. 59.

46. Rolleston, p. 484; Gifford, Pennsylvania, p. 4.
47. Seligmann, I, 197, 199; Leonard W. Moss and Stephen C. Cappannari, "Folklore and Medicine in an Italian Village," *Journal of American Folklore,* 73 (1960), 98.
48. Seligmann, I, 200.
49. Rolleston, p. 486.
50. Castillo de Lucas, p. 434; Moss and Cappannari, p. 98.
51. Seligmann, I, 93, 197, 200–201.
52. Jones, p. 17; Moss and Cappannari, p. 98.
53. *Anuario de la Sociedad Folklórica de México,* 3 (1942), 109; Seligmann, I, 200.
54. Seligmann, I, 200.
55. Jones, p. 19.
56. Jones, pp. 18–20.
57. James R. Foster, "Brooklyn Folklore," *New York Folklore Quarterly,* 13 (1957), 88.
58. Gifford, Pennsylvania, p. 7.
59. Jane Voiles, "Genoese Folkways in a California Mining Camp," *California Folklore Quarterly,* 3 (1944), 213.
60. Jones, p. 20; Foster, *Spanish Folk Medicine,* p. 209.
61. Emil Berdau, "Der Mond in Volksmedizin, Sitte und Gebräuchen der mexikanischen Grenzbewohnerschaft des südlichen Texas," *Globus,* 88 (1905), 384.
62. Puckett, Ohio (unpub.).
63. Jones, pp. 15–16.
64. James Napier, *Folk Lore, or Superstitious Beliefs in the West of Scotland within This Century* (Paisley: Alex. Gardner, 1879), p. 30.
65. Annie Weston Whitney and Caroline Canfield Bullock, *Folk-Lore from Maryland* (Memoirs of the American Folklore Society, Vol. 18, New York, 1925), p. 83, No. 1704.
66. Jones, p. 20.
67. Moya, p. 37; Espinosa, pp. 409–410; Baca, p. 2174; Martínez and Martin, p. 162; John G. Bourke, "Popular Medicine, Customs and Superstitions of the Rio Grande," *Journal of American Folklore,* 7 (1894), 126; Scott, p. 83.
68. Berdau, p. 384.
69. *New York Folklore Quarterly,* 21 (1965), 185–186.
70. Espinosa, p. 410.
71. Alixa Naff, "Belief in the Evil Eye among the Christian Syrian-Lebanese in America," *Journal of American Folklore,* 78 (1965), 50; Jones, pp. 20–21; Napier, p. 39.
72. Folk-Lore, 14 (1903), 83; Jones, pp. 20–21.
73. Moya, p. 35, Puckett, Ohio (unpub.); Eugene S. McCartney, *Folklore Heirlooms* (Michigan Academy of Science, Arts, and Letters, Vol. 16, 1931), p. 130. Because envy is a common cause of the evil eye, I have not done more than mention it here. The reader would be well advised, however, to consult the excellent article of George M. Foster, "The Anatomy of Envy: A Study in Symbolic Behavior," *Current Anthropology,* 13 (1972), 165–202, esp. p. 174, *passim.*

74. Dodson, p. 84; Hendricks, p. 4; Martínez and Martin, p. 42; Scott, p. 82; John Q. Anderson, *Texas Folk Medicine. 1,333 Cures, Remedies, Preventives & Health Practices* (Austin, Texas: The Encino Press, 1970), p. 30.

75. Puckett, Ohio (unpub.).

76. *Ibid.*

77. Helen M. McCadden, "Folklore in the Schools: Folk Beliefs, Current Report," *New York Folklore Quarterly,* 3 (1947), 337.

78. John H. Bushnel, "Medical Folklore from California, *Western Folklore,* 6 (1947), 273, No. 3; Charles Wagley, *The Social and Religious Life of a Guatemalan Village* (American Anthropological Association, Memoir Series, No. 71, Menasha, Wis., 1949), p. 26; Ruth Bunzel, *Chichicastenango, a Guatemalan Village* (Locust Valley, New York, 1952), p. 101.

79. Moya, p. 38.

80. Puckett, Ohio (unpub.); *Pennsylvania Folklife,* Vol. 14, No. 3 (Spring, 1965), 44; Williams, p. 95; *Keystone Folklore Quarterly,* 14 (1969), 113; Castillo de Lucas, p. 56.

81. Moya, p. 36.

82. James R. Foster, p. 89.

83. Moya, p. 35; Espinosa, p. 410; *Journal of American Folklore,* 4 (1891), 35 (Nicaragua); Puckett, Ohio (unpub.); Foster, Spanish Folk Medicine, p. 208.

84. Puckett, Ohio (unpub.).

85. O. H. Hauptmann, "Spanish Folklore from Tampa, Florida," *Southern Folklore Quarterly,* 2 (1938), 12; Puckett, Ohio (unpub.); Napier, p. 36.

86. Jones, pp. 13–14; *Pennsylvania Folklife,* 14, 3 (Spring, 1965), 44; Puckett, Ohio (unpub.).

87. *Journal of American Folklore*, 31 (1918), 134.

88. Jones, pp. 13, 17; *Pennsylvania Folklife,* 14, 3 (Spring, 1965), 44; Puckett, Ohio (unpub.).

89. Fanny D. Bergen, *Animal and Plant Lore* (Memoirs of the American Folklore Society, Vol. 7, Boston and New York, 1899), p. 131, no. 133.

90. Gifford, Pennsylvania, p. 8.

91. Jones, p. 14; Teresa Slamick *et al.*, "Sign of Spring," *West Virginia Folklore,* 10 (1960), 43; Puckett, Ohio (unpub.); Napier, p. 139.

92. Jones, pp. 13, 19; *Pennsylvania Folklife,* 14, 3 (Spring, 1965), 44; Moss and Cappannari, p. 98; Radford and Hole, p. 25.

93. Bushnel, p. 273, no. 3; Puckett, Ohio (unpub.); Anderson, p. 30; Foster, *Spanish Folk Medicine,* p. 208.

17

Animal Intrusion into the Human Body: A Primitive Aetiology of Disease*

As in other subject areas of folklore where conjunctures of data are encountered in both higher and lower cultures, the perceptive student of folk medicine occasionally has the opportunity to observe individual aspects of the causes and cures of disease that are to be found in the civilized as well as in the primitive community.

Clement's seminal paper on the causes of disease deals largely with ideas held within the primitive community in various parts of the world,[1] yet for almost all of his five main theories of the cause of disease (sorcery, breach of taboo, disease-object intrusion, spirit intrusion, soul loss) parallels can be adduced from medical and folk medical aetiologies that derive from peoples of high culture, modern as well as ancient. This circumstance might tempt one to hypothesize, perhaps, that these simple medical ideas found in many parts of the world—and in different segments of society—might be of such a basic and universal nature as to constitute a sort of *Elementargedanke* or *Völkergedanke* in accordance with the teachings of Adolf Bastian and later

*This paper first appeared in Spanish translation, "Intrusion animal en el organismo humano: una etiología primitiva de la enfermedad," *Logos: Revista de la Facultad de Filosofia y Letras,* Universidad de Buenos Aires, numeros 13-14, 1977-1978, pp. 321-330. Permission to reprint in English has been given by the editor and publishers.

advocates of polygenesis. Today there will be time to survey only one special facet of object intrusion, namely animals that get into the body, in one way or another, or are thought to do so, and thus induce pathogenic reactions.[2]

Because Clements is apparently more concerned with the spread of a primitive aetiology of disease among aboriginal peoples than in the documentation of primitive ideas as such, wherever found,[3] I am purposely drawing on material from America and Europe. This I do to establish the point that primitive beliefs and customs are often, if unexpectedly, encountered in traditions that have long maintained themselves with little or no contact with primitive cultures. An exception must be made, of course, with American Negro medical lore where the connections with the Negro's African past are immediate and clearly established.

There are basically two kinds of animal intrusion into the human body reported in the American and European literature on the subject. The first represents the insinuation of animal parts and even live animals into the body tissues from an external source. The second, which is much more common, involves the passage of animals into the bodily cavities by ingestion either through the mouth or by conduct through other body apertures. In the first instance, where animals move about under the skin or more deeply in the body tissues of the victim, a pattern of conjury and even shamanism is often discerned. This pathological condition is real enough in the mind of the victim, of course, even though the supposed animals in the body have nothing at all to do really with the patient's plight. Overwrought with fear and hysterical in the belief that a spell has been cast on him, the sufferer seeks magic help to counteract the spell. American examples of this kind of animal intrusion usually occur in the Negro tradition. Lizards, snakes, and other creeping animals are thought to find their way into the arms and legs or into parts of the trunk, particularly the back.[4] An account of the entry of a frog into a leg, and causing a lump, is found in a Louisiana collection of folk beliefs in the late 1920s. It is a simple and forthright statement but throws no light whatever on the mode of entry: "An old crippled Negro, who had a lump in her leg, claimed that it was a frog put there by a hoodoo. She died as a result of the trouble."[5] Shamanistic tricks to extricate living creatures from the body are frequently resorted to. In a typical case Puckett reports that a plantation Negro suffering from pains in his back was made to believe that a snake in his body was causing the trouble. Accordingly, the man was turned on his stomach so that he could not see how the conjuror's operation proceeded. After a small incision was made, and a little green snake produced by sleight of hand, he immediately recovered and went back to work, never knowing how the magical cure had been effected.[6]

Because manifestations of the sort discussed have no basis in fact, resulting as they do wholly from an overstimulated imagination or even an unstable mental state, there are naturally no plausible accounts as to how the animals penetrate the victims' body in the first place. The spells by which evil-designing persons cause the animals supposedly to invade the body of the host are equally vague. One can form some notion of how entry is effected by consulting Hyatt's detailed interviews with Negro conjure doctors, healers, and other kinds of practitioners of white as well as black magic.[7] Contagious magic, of course, figures prominently in these accounts. Whether one comes into contact with goofer dust and other animal parts, or whether the dust is simply wafted in the air, the victim suddenly comes to feel an animal in his body. Elf-shot in its various forms, and other kinds of missile intrusion, of course, do not figure in cases where live animals, whole animals, that is, are insinuated into the human body in some way. Magic projectiles involve only animal parts, and only those parts that are hard and resistant, namely, bits of bone, gristle, masses of dried blood, and the like. These are shot into the victim's body, being then somehow supposedly metamorphosed into animals in an almost inscrutable aspect of the magic of *pars pro toto.*[8] Wise women, cunning men, and various kinds of witches and sorcerers understand how to make and shoot these projectiles of disease; likewise mythical personages and even the dead, according to Honko.[9] Evilly disposed persons were also thought to possess this malefic power. As stated earlier, it is never clear just how the animal substances are made to penetrate the victim's body. Mexican brujos, for example, are reported to insinuate snakes and toads into the bodies of persons they wished to harm, but there is no explanation as to how the living creatures penetrated the body; however when the creatures were charmed out of the victim, egress was effected through the mouth and ears.[10] Because the casting of spells rests on the powers of suggestion and principles of magic rather than on actual physical forces and logical relationships, it is clear that the processes involved are veiled in mystery and are stated with calculated vagueness, if explained at all.

In addition to the shooting of animal substances into enemies or other intended victims by practitioners of evil, there are other magical ways of introducing foreign and harmful substances into the body, including animal parts. These intrusive objects are implanted superficially or deep. We have already considered ways in which animals are conjured under the skin and into the body by spells or other magical means, with or without contagious magic, at least without physical contact that is clearly expressed. A magic prescription from Chestertown, Maryland, Negroes before the turn of the century explains how salamanders get into the stomach:

> Get some ground puppies [i.e., salamanders, sometimes called ground-dogs]. Put them in a bottle and bury them under the threshold of the person you wish to conjure, making crosses with the four fingers on the earth above them. After a time the ground puppies will burst the bottle that holds them, and then they will get into the stomach of the person against whom the spell is directed, and will kill him.[11]

The exact manner of entry in this case, as in kinds of conjury discussed above, is not made clear.

Sorcerers and witches may introduce an animal into the body in some magical way, or conjure the food in such a way as to produce a creature within the victim. In the Carahua area of Chile, for example, a sorcerer brings on *mal impuesto* by means of a potion that introduces a lizard or a toad into a man's stomach.[12] Among the Cherokee in North Carolina a witch may even "change food" within a man's stomach so as to produce a lizard or a frog.[13] These instances are unusual. In most cases the creature is produced in accordance with the common principles of contagious magic. Any contact with an animal, even secondary contact, such as swallowing a pebble on the beach over which a snake has passed, for example, will cause a snake to grow in the stomach.[14] Kwakiutl Indians believe that if a person skins a snake that is with young, the young ones will crawl into his body and make him sick.[15] The most common indirect way to introduce snakes into the body is for the sorcerer or any other person bent on working harm on a person to kill a snake, dry it, and grind it into a powder. The powder is then either sprinkled onto the food or otherwise mixed with it, or it is placed in beverages such as coffee. When the foods and beverages are eaten or drunk, snakes are said to form in the stomach.[16]

Throwing snake-dust on a person, sprinkling it upon him

through cracks in the ceiling, or scattering the dust in his shoes will, according to a popular view, cause a snake to grow within the person. Because the stomach is not specifically mentioned in the cases cited,[17] one may assume, perhaps, that the snakes are lodged under the skin, or in the body tissues, and not necessarily in the stomach. The dust of spiders, lizards, and frogs, when consumed with food or drink, are likewise said to produce live creatures in the stomach of persons ingesting them.[18] In the same way scorpions dried and reduced to powder, when taken in drinks, are also supposed to produce fully developed creatures in the stomach.[19] Exceptional, and perhaps an erroneous account, is a belief in North Carolina that the dust of a dried lizard thrown on a person causes a snake (not a lizard) to come into him.[20] The blood of snakes coming into contact with a person in any way will cause snakes to grow within him, according to Puckett.[21] In Cumberland, England, a cat's hair, when swallowed, is thought to produce a kitten within the person who has swallowed the hair. This miracle takes place by the logic of *pars pro toto.*[22] As a counterpart to the widespread American notion that a hair will turn into a snake if placed in water and allowed to stay there awhile, there is a curious belief in Galicia (Spain) that if one swallows a hair, a snake will grow in his stomach.[23] Along the same illogical lines, it is believed in Kansas that a cat's hair will turn into a worm in a child's stomach.[24]

Far more common than the belief in animal parts being metamorphosed into fully developed creatures are the notions of animals, fully developed or embryonic, getting into a person's stomach or elsewhere in the body and actually living there. These ideas derive in part from a knowledge of tapeworms that are actually expelled from the bodies of persons suffering from intestinal worms, even though little thought is given as to how the worms got there in the first place. With other kinds of creatures that supposedly get into the body, there is a much easier explanation: They simply enter through the mouth when it is open, or they are swallowed while drinking, albeit as very minute creatures or as eggs, or they are ingested with food. Ingress through the mouth most often takes place while the victim is asleep, particularly if he sleeps on the ground or near places frequented by crawling or creeping creatures such as insects of all kinds, snakes, lizards, salamanders, and various kinds of worms. These creatures often lurk near wells, springs, and other places where drinking water is fetched, and may be swallowed as one drinks; or their eggs may be swallowed, only to develop into full-bodied creatures in the stomach.[25] The small animals and their eggs are also ingested with food, of course, and tenant the body in the same way. Flying insects, which are encountered everywhere, may easily get into the hair, the ears, or even the nostrils and the mouth. In all cases where entry into the body is by visible physical means, belief in the phenomenon is widely shared by all nationality groups, not merely by Negroes, Mexicans, and other ethnic groups that exhibit a belief in animals in the human body as a part of their traditions as expressed in folk beliefs, magic, and related fields.

Belief in a snake's entering a sleeping person's mouth is apparently a world-wide phenomenon, as entries in my possession from such widely separated parts of the world as Japan, Ireland, Spain, Hungary, and parts of the United States would indicate.[26] The belief in swallowing small creatures, most frequently snakes, lizards, crayfish, tadpoles, and the like, or swallowing their eggs or semen, is likewise widespread.[27] In the southern part of the United States people are warned not to drink from a spring at night, lest they swallow a "spring keeper," which is a crawfish or water lizard of some sort.[28] The drinking of a lizard or a crab in this fashion, and the developing of a monster within the man who had drunk it, was reported from Pennsylvania as early as 1809, and this same kind of experience was noted in a well-known case in Canada over a hundred years later.[29] In Ireland a batrachian creature, swallowed when drinking from a river, was known as a "man-keeper," and similar beliefs were encountered in Scotland during the latter part of the nineteenth century.[30] In Haute Bretagne there was a proverbial notion that if three people drank together from a fountain or a stream, one would drink a toad, the second a frog, and the third an adder.[31] Beliefs about swallowing these creatures while drinking is so common as to be listed in Thompson's *Motif-Index* (B784.1.1). Persons drinking from a brook swallows animal eggs (frog or newt).[32]

Presence of the animal in the body is the cause of physical discomfiture of all kinds, most usually felt as gnawing pains or the pangs of hunger. Among the southern Negroes it is reported that a youngster afflicted with reptiles inside of him had to eat incessantly to keep the snakes from devouring his vital organs.[33] Similar pathological states are noted from Scotland where a hungry snake in a child's stomach was said to have set its fangs in the child's heart and sucked it to death, and in the Basque country where hungry creatures were thought to gnaw at the victim's intestines to stay alive.[34]

Means used to rid the sufferer of his unwanted host that had entered the body by mouth usually involved luring the creature forth either for food or drink. The aroma of savory food was employed for the purpose in Massachusetts and Connecticut, according to nineteenth-century accounts,[35] but milk is most commonly noted elsewhere, as one can see from references to European and American sources.[36] The love of snakes for milk and groats is proverbial, and is depicted in the Grimm tale, "Märchen von der Unke" (No. 105) and traditions relating to it.

American Indians, believing themselves to harbor snakes and other creatures in their bodies were accustomed to lie beside a spring or a brook so that the creature would be lured forth to drink, and this same notion was also found among the white settlers of New York State in early days.[37] To heighten the thirst that would be transmitted to the creature, the sufferer was advised to eat salt itself, or salty food such as herring, and then lie down near a spring so that the lizard in his body would come out to drink.[38] Folk medical practitioners also resorted to emetics of various kinds, and to such special kinds of plant remedies as ipecac and John the Conquerer root.[39]

There are certain categories of animal entry into the human body, or tenancy there, that cannot be discussed in this paper. The worm-theory of disease, particularly as it related to the causes of tooth decay and toothache, is far too extensive, and deserves a discussion all its own. Much, of course, has already been written on this subject.[40] The entry of ticks and other parasites into the human body, and other kinds of animal infestation belong more to the realm of clinical medicine than they do to folk medicine and magic. So also do discussions having to do with the fabled earwig that enters a person's ear, penetrating deep enough to do damage and even induce deafness. Hudson, however, gives an account of the dread of this creature in Mississippi that clearly falls into the realm of folklore:

> Many folks believe that there is absolutely no hope for a person if an ear wig gets into the ear. The loathsome creature enters the ear and works its way all over the interior of the body, eating up all the tissues and leaving only a thin shell. Others hold out some hope and say that lard rendered from "Betsy" bugs will give relief if it is dropped into the ear soon enough.[41]

It is also feared in some parts of the United States that the common dragon fly—variously known as a darning needle, the devil's darning needle, Dickinson's mare, and the like—will enter the ears and even penetrate into the brain.[42] These fears are based more on considerations of the supposed natural habits of the creature than on notions having to do with magical intrusion of any kind.

Entry of animals into the vagina, particularly snakes and lizards, likewise is a special subject, being encountered more often in folk tales and other accounts than in disquisitions on folk medicine. Details ramify widely, from matters of purely erotic interest to considerations having to do with monsters engendered in the woman, animal possession, and the like.

I hope that this preliminary essay will throw light on a largely uncharted field of folk medicine. It is obvious that much work still remains to be done. Publication of the remaining volumes in Hyatt's monumental work on magic and medicine, *Hoodoo—Conjuration—Witchcraft—Rootwork,* and the vast index that must go with it, will help to open up and explain more fully many matters of animal entry into the body that are still very obscure. In this task it is clear that scholars must marshall data from conjury and witchcraft as well as from folk medicine itself to produce satisfactory answers to questions on this subject that have concerned medical scientists and practitioners from antiquity to the present time.

NOTES

1. Forrest E. Clements, *Primitive Concepts of Disease* (University of California Publications in American Archaeology and Ethnology, Vol. 32, No. 2, Berkeley, California, 1932).

2. Clements lists small animals last in a series of eight general categories of object-intrusion: "The most common intruders being small pebbles, bits of leather, sticks, little bones, hairs, coagulated blood, insects, and even small animals" (p. 211). See page 188.

3. I do not wish to infer that Clements is not aware of the presence of these primitive medical diagnostic ideas in high cultures; he is, but he does not pursue matters in any useful way.

4. Newell Niles Puckett, *Folk Beliefs of the Southern Negro* (Chapel Hill, North Carolina, 1926), pp. 253–254, 298; Miss Herron and Miss A. M. Bacon, "Conjuring and Conjure-Doctors in the Southern United States," *Journal of American Folklore,* 9 (1896), 146, 226; Fanny D. Bergen, *Animal and Plant Lore Collected from the Oral Tradition of English Speaking Folk* (Memoirs of the American Folklore Society, VII, Boston and New York, 1899), p. 14, No. 44; Myra Sanders, "Some Medical Lore," *Kentucky Folk-Lore and Poetry Magazine,* Vol. 5, No. 2 (October, 1930), 20–21.

5. Hilda Roberts, "Louisiana Superstitions," *Journal of American Folklore,* 40 (1927), 205, No. 1506.

6. Puckett, pp. 302–303. I have cited further examples in my article for the Festschrift for Gyula Ortutay, "Physical Harm, Sickness, and Death by Conjury: A Survey of the Sorcerer's Evil Art in America," *Acta Ethnographica Academiae Scientiarum Hungaricae,* Tomus 19, Budapest, 1970, pp. 173–174. (Included in this volume; see pp. 215–225.)

7. Harry Middleton Hyatt, *Hoodoo—Conjuration—Witchcraft—Rootwork* (5 vols., Hannibal, Missouri, 1970–1978), I, 227 ff., "Live Things in You."

8. The reader should consult the standard work on missile intrusion, Lauri Honko, *Krankheitsprojektile: Untersuchung Über eine Urtümliche Krankheitserklärung* (Folklore Fellows Communications, No. 178, Helsinki, 1959), pp. 231–232, who gives a whole list of animal, bird, and insect parts that are fashioned into arrows of one kind or another. Live animals, of course, could not be shot into a victim by means of a bow and arrow or similar weapon.

9. Honko, pp. 97–108.

10. S. Seligmann, *Der böse Blick und Verwandtes. Ein Beitrag zur Geschichte des Aberglaubens aller Zeiten und Völker* (2 vols., Berlin, 1910), I, 203–204.

11. Bergen, p. 14, No. 40.

12. Ramon A. Laval, *Contribucion al Folklore de Carahue* (Chile) [Madrid, 1916], p. 16, No. 165.

13. *Journal of American Folklore,* 3 (1890), 46.

14. Ernest W. Baughman, *Type and Motif-Index of the Folktales of England and North America* (Indiana University Folklore Series, No. 20, The Hague, 1966), B784.1.2.

15. Franz Boas, "Current Beliefs of the Kwakiutl Indians," *Journal of American Folklore,* 45 (1932), 222.

16. Bergen, p. 14, No. 43 (the snake will "breed" in you); Harry Middleton Hyatt, *Folk-Lore from Adams County, Illinois* (Memoirs of the Alma Egan Hyatt Foundation, New York, 1935), p. 467, No. 9167; Annie Weston Whitney and Caroline Canfield Bullock, *Folk-Lore from Maryland* (Memoirs of the American Folklore Society, No. 18, New York, 1925), p. 82, No. 1698; Puckett, p. 250.

17. Puckett, p. 251; Wayland D. Hand, ed., *Popular Beliefs and Superstitions from North Carolina,* Vols. VI and VII of the *Frank C. Brown Collection of North Carolina Folklore* (7 Vols., Durham, North Carolina, 1952–1964), VI, 107, No. 722 (cited as Brown Coll.).

18. Puckett, p. 250.

19. Whitney and Bullock, p. 82, No. 1697.

20. Brown Coll., VI, 106, No. 719.

21. Puckett, p. 251.

22. Bergen, p. 155, note 928.

23. *Revista de Dialectología y Tradiciones Populares*, 3 (1947), 178.

24. *Western Folklore*, 23 (1964), 22, No. 18.

25. Bergen, p. 74, No. 841.

26. *Journal of American Folklore,* 7 (1894), 30; *ibid.*, 4 (1891), 187; *Revista de Dialectología y Tradiciones Populares*, 3 (1947), 178; *Journal of American Folklore*, 75 (1962), 142; Thomas R. Brendle and Claude W. Unger, *Folk Medicine of the Pennsylvania Germans. The Non-Occult Cures* (Proceedings of the Pennsylvania German Society, Vol. 45, Norristown, Pennsylvania, 1945), p. 82; Clifton Johnson, *What They Say in New England. A Book of Signs, Sayings, and Superstitions* (Boston, 1896), p. 151.

27. Brendle and Unger, pp. 181–182; Hyatt, p. 71, No. 1581; John W. Allen, *Legends and Lore of Southern Illinois* (Carbondale, Illinois, 1963), p. 62; *Southern Workman,* 25 (1896), 16; Baughman, B784.1.3.

28. Puckett, pp. 434–435; *Publications of the Texas Folklore Society,* 5 (1926), 65; *Southern Workman,* 25 (1896), 15.

29. Virgil J. Vogel, *American Indian Medicine* (Norman, Oklahoma, 1970), p. 17; *Journal of American Folklore,* 31 (1918), 10, No. 85.

30. Bergen, p. 150, note to No. 839; James Napier, *Folk Lore: or, Superstitious Beliefs in the West of Scotland within This Century* (Paisley, 1879), p. 103.

31. Paul Sébillot, "Traditions et Superstitions de la Haute-Bretagne," *Les Littératures populaires des toutes les Nations,* Tome X (2 vols., Paris 1882), vol. 2, p. 218.

32. Stith Thompson, *Motif-Index of Folk-Literature. A Classification of Narrative Elements in Folktales, Ballads, Myths, Fables, Medieval Romances, Exempla, Fabliaux, Jest-Books, and Local Legends* (rev. ed. 6 vols., Bloomington, Indiana, 1955–1958).

33. Puckett, pp. 253, 303; *Journal of American Folklore,* 9 (1896), 146 (lizards).

34. Bergen, p. 150, note to No. 841; Ignacio Maria Barriola, *La Medicina popular en el pais vasco* (San Sebastian, 1952), p. 54. See also, Napier, p. 103; Thompson, *Motif-Index* G328.1. Serpent in man eats all his food.

35. Bergen, p. 74, No. 841.

36. *Journal of American Folklore,* 4 (1891), 187 (Ireland); *Southern Workman,* 25 (1896), 16; W. J. Wintemberg, *Folk-Lore of Waterloo County, Ontario* (National Museum of Canada, *Bulletin,* No. 115, Anthropological Series No. 28, Ottawa, 1950), p. 8 (from Alsace); Harry Middleton Hyatt, Folklore from Adams County, Illinois (2nd ed., New York, 1965), p. 335, No. 7204; Puckett, p. 254.

37. Bergen, p. 73, No. 838; Emelyn E. Gardner, *Folklore of the Schoharie Hills, New York* (Ann Arbor, Michigan, 1937), p. 268, No. 32. Gardner's notes show this belief to be world-wide.

38. John K. Strecker, "Reptiles of the South and Southwest in Folk-Lore," *Publications of the Texas Folklore Society,* 5 (1926), p. 62; Bergen, p. 74, No. 839. Cf. Thompson, *Motif-Index,* B784.2.1. (details).

39. Puckett, p. 304; Richard M. Dorson, *Negro Folktales in Michigan* (Cambridge, Mass., 1956), pp. 106–107.

40. Honko, p. 33.

41. Arthur Palmer Hudson, *Specimens of Mississippi Folk-Lore* (Ann Arbor, Michigan, 1928), p. 151.

42. W. J. Wintemberg, "German-Canadian Folklore," *Papers and Records, Ontario Historical Society* (Toronto, 1901), p. 90; Frank L. Rainey, "Animal and Plant Lore," *The Kentucky Folk-Lore and Poetry Magazine,* Vol. 4, No. 1 (April 1929), p. 11; Bergen, pp. 90–91, No. 1066.

18

Padepissers and *Wekschissers*: A Folk Medical Inquiry into the Cause of Styes*

Years ago when I began working in the field of popular beliefs and superstitions an item in a Dutch source caught my attention, and I have kept my eyes open for this folk belief and related items ever since. In what has since become a commonplace, Alfons de Cock, the noted Belgian folklorist, described how that urinating in a path or roadway would cause a sty, remarking on the side that such a person was known as a *Padepisser.*[1] Later on in working through the American corpus of folk beliefs and cures having to do with styes, I was able to add the term *Wekschisser* to the lexicon referring to an unpraiseworthy human species.[2] This came from the earthy Pennsylvania German tradition; and in other parts of the Pennsylvania German country, the sty itself is known as a *wekschisser,*[3] a term deriving from the High German *Wegscheisser,* as found in Franconia and elsewhere in Germany.[4] De Cock gives several examples for Holland and Belgium of the use of a vulgar term for excrement such as *strontje,* "excrement," *wegescheet,* "path-shit," and the like.[5] It is unusual, I think, that the point is nowhere made that the sty itself may resemble a speck of excrement.

*This article originally appeared in *Folklore Studies in Honour of Herbert Halpert: a Festschrift*, published by the Memorial University of Newfoundland, St. John's, Newfoundland, Canada, 1980, pp. 211–223 Permission to reprint has been given by the editor and publisher.

Even though this folk belief and this curious bit of scatological lore is known throughout the length and breadth of North America, one is not able to add comparable terms from English, the third West Germanic dialect covered in this paper. The culprit who defiles the thoroughfares apparently is not singled out with any special term of opprobrium, and the censurable act is usually depicted only in its most inoffensive way. This softening of a frank and unblushing earthiness is a feature of much American folklore that has been transplanted from Europe. This loss of openness in sexual matters, for instance, and in verbal vitality when dealing with sexual and eliminative functions, has been most frequently remarked upon in connection with ballad study, but the rationalization of suggestive matters, and even bowdlerization, seem to prevail throughout the whole body of adopted American folklore. Much more freedom is exercised, happily, in native American forms of folklore. From the formal terms, "urinating," found in all parts of the country, to the less-used words, "voiding" and "wetting," and to the more familiar juvenile locution "peeing,"[6] references to the act descend to the vulgarism, "pissing."[7] "Going to the bathroom" is a euphemism for both urination and defecation and is encountered in a variety of ungainly situations, such as "going to the bathroom in back of your car," as reported from Rigby, Idaho, in 1910; "going to the bathroom in the road," in such widely separated states as West Virginia and Kansas; "going to the bathroom outside,"[8] and the like.

"Defecate" seems less used than "urinate" in these forbidden acts, but the term is encountered widely in the literature in accordance with popular taste and breeding in referring to the natural bodily act.[9] A second reason for this predominance of "urinating" is the simple fact that this body function is mentioned in the literature much more often than defecating in discussions having to do with the causes of styes. The use of the term "going potty" is so infantine as to lead to the conclusion that very young children were warned about relieving themselves anywhere but in the appointed places. Among other parts of the country in which this term is heard is Pennsylvania,[10] Texas, as early as 1920, and a few other places. In Johnson Creek, Wisconsin, about 1930, for example, it was claimed that if you had a sty on your eye it was because you had "grunted" along the highway somewhere.[11] The Dutch explanation for a sty, namely for "pooping in the dike," is not equalled for earthiness in any other Western Germanic locution that I know.[12] Stepping in excrement as a cause of styes is reported from Saxony,[13] but I have not come upon this notion in American popular belief. In Germany it was especially bad if this misstep took place at a crossroads.[14]

Now that the terminology for referring to the two basic eliminative acts has been established, we can consider various details as they relate to both functions. Because more emphasis is laid on the place where the forbidden act occurs, than on the time and other attendant circumstances, let us begin with a survey of proscribed places. In keeping with the forbidden character of relieving oneself other than in the usual places provided for the bodily function—toilets, privies, chambers, "potties," and the like—the injunctions may be very general, such as one from Binghamton, New York: "A sty on a child's eye is an indication that he has been urinating someplace other than where he should." In Ohio in the late 1930s it was claimed that little boys would get styes if they urinated anywhere except in a toilet.[15] From the same state, in the English and German traditions of Cleveland, as recently as 1962, a sty indicated that one had urinated on public property.[16] An even more general location, simply "urinating outside" was collected in California in 1964, having been learned, however, from parents who came from New Orleans and Memphis.[17] Although the act of defiling public thoroughfares seems to apply most frequently to roads and paths, there is nevertheless a complete range of forbidden sites. In Indiana in the early 1940s urinating on a highway was believed to cause styes.[18] We have already noted the act of "grunting" along the highway somewhere, in a reference from Wisconsin. Like highways streets are a more modern form of the growing transportation system. In the Creole tradition of New Orleans at the end of World War I, urinating in the street was thought to cause a sty, and streets were likewise forbidden for "peain' " in the 1920s. In Denton, Texas, in the 1960s a bump was thought to form on the eye after such an act. Defecation on a public street was listed as causing a sty in Salt Lake City as late as 1925. From the childhood memories of an informant from a small Wyoming town in the 1930s, the prohibition against urinating on public thoroughfares included streets as well as roads and paths.

Urinating in the road, by various circumlocutions and all, is documented from the late 1890s from Ohio,[19] and Indiana, across Illinois,[20] Missouri, and Iowa, to Nebraska,[21] and Colorado,[22] to Utah and Oregon. In a lower tier of states, the belief is known from Missouri, and Oklahoma, to Texas,[23] and Arizona.[24] Urinating in the middle of the road is a detail that adds to the effrontery of the act. To the act of going "potty" in the middle of the road, in a Pennsylvania belief already alluded to, comes the more familiar belief about urinating in the middle of the road, also noted for the Keystone State.[25] The notion is recorded from Stillwell, Kansas, in the 1920s, and from Kansas City about the same time, with a verbal variation of "in the center of the road." From Arizona folk medical tradition "pissing in the middle of the road" was represented as being "as old as the hills," but that state can also boast a more modest way of stating the case, namely, "going to the bathroom in the middle of the road, etc."[26] "Peeing in the middle of the road" is noted for Utah,[27] and a more juvenile way of mentioning the act is found in Nevada, namely "wee-weeing" in the middle of the road. The center of the road is noted from two such widely separated parts of California as Sonoma and Costa Mesa over the eleven-year period, 1959–1970.[28]

Urinating or defecating on the side of the road as a cause of styes is known from Nova Scotia,[29] Pennsylvania,[30] and Ohio,[31] to Utah and California where people are warned not to void on the side of a country road,[32] nor to defecate on the roadside.[33] The German belief that urinating at the crossroads will bring on a sty,[34] is not known, apparently, in America, but this lack is more likely due to the fact that the item has not been collected. There is a Kentucky tradition, attested in three excellent entries, of ridding oneself of a sty by urinating at the crossroads after dark, the second involves urinating in the crossroads and then spitting in it; and the third advises that one wet at the fork of the road, so that the next person who comes along will get the sty and yours will leave.[35] An entry from Illinois, referable to the 1930s, simply advises wetting in the road, so that the next person who walks over it will catch the sty.[36] Akin to the Kentucky and Illinois rituals, but not involving a transfer to a second party, is a belief from Daly City, California, in 1971, that involves pissing in the middle of the road during a full moon as a way of getting rid of the sty.[37] Wetting in the alley is assigned as the cause of styes from Ohio,[38] and Michigan ("peeing" in the alley), to Illinois,[39] where also, by way of reversal, one could get rid of a sty by wetting in an alley.[40] The belief turned up in Los Angeles in 1960 where alleys are generally paved.[41]

In an earlier era of American life paths were to pedestrian

travel what roads were to vehicular traffic. Urinating in the path, or in someone's path, as a cause of styes were folk beliefs known in Virginia and Tennessee. An Ohio admonition puts the matter in a somewhat less genteel way: "If you piss, get out of the path, or else you will get a sty on your eye."[42] Even less-frequented paths should be avoided, as in an Illinois belief: "The person who stops in a path to urinate while crossing a field will get a sty."[43] From the area around the town of Liberal, Kansas, in the late 1920s children were told that if they "peed" in the path they would get a sty. The informant said that because there were very few inside toilets in the area, this was a good way to carry out "rural toilet training." Going "bathroom" in the path is noted from Tucson, Arizona, in 1965.[44] The taboo is heightened in the Netherlands where the church path is specified.[45] That these beliefs are not entirely rural in inspiration and setting is seen in the substitution of sidewalk for path in cities and small towns. Attestations of sidewalk, however, come only from New Orleans, about 1900, from Lorain, Ohio, in 1959,[46] and the small town of Bear River City, Utah, in 1957,[47] all three cases referring to urinating. Unusual places and ways of relieving oneself are rare. Urinating over a fence is mentioned from Ohio in the English and German traditions of Cleveland at the end of the 1950s.[48] German taboos include urinating between two houses, against the sun, and the like.[49] Taboos of time were apparently not important, at least as compared with the place where the forbidden act was carried out. In Missouri at the end of the 1920s, however, people were warned against urinating in the open road at night. This likely comes in the same southern tradition that says, in a Kentucky entry, you'll get a sty if you piss in the middle of the road at nighttime. Urinating in a squatting position, presumably referring to males, is said to cause a sty, according to an entry from Toronto, Ohio, in the late 1950s.[50]

Because many of these beliefs were of a hortatory and cautionary kind, helping to train the young in good toilet habits, it is not surprising that a sty became a badge for all to see of one who had either wetted the bed, as in Ohio and Utah,[51] or who had wetted his pants, as in Ohio.[52]

Next to outraging the sense of public decency with regard to the choice of improper places for relieving oneself, witnessing these scandalous acts on the part of others was also believed to be the cause of styes. Because this involves "looking" and voyeurism in a general way, we should be aware at the outset of this discussion of the taboo against looking at forbidden things. The taboo against seeing naked women, for example, goes back to classical mythology in the well-known story of Tiresias's beholding Athena in her bath.[53] Even better known to the modern reader is the celebrated case of Peeping Tom's not turning his head when Lady Godiva rode naked through the streets of Coventry on a white horse, shielding her nakedness only with her tresses.[54] This old taboo is encountered only sparingly in American folk belief,[55] nor is the notion widespread that seeing a naked person will cause a sty. Two California entries, however, are worth noting: "If you see a person of the opposite sex unclothed (other than your husband or wife), you'll get a sty on the eyelid." This is from Los Angeles in the mid-1950s. A young Stanford biologist reported in 1965 that peeking at someone nude would induce a sty.[56] In Silesia seeing a person's bare backside was sufficient to bring on the dread eye affliction.[57] In Utah, however, the taboo against "looking" was much broader, for it was believed that styes came from witnessing something that should not be seen.[58] These taboos naturally run to watching someone pass water or evacuate. In Holland de Cock reported that whoever watched a man urinate would get a sty,[59] but Bakker says that the punishment would be visited upon someone for watching an old woman pass water.[60] A California belief collected in 1973 says that the only way you can get a sty is to watch someone use the bathroom.[61] A curious California twist, in the 1940s, a reversal actually, was that the person urinating outdoors would get the sty himself if someone were watching.[62]

Watching dogs defecate is an offense punishable by the development of a sty,[63] but documentation comes only from Texas, Arizona,[64] and California.[65] An item from Camarillo, California, claims that you will get a sty unless your little fingers are crossed and tugged.[66] Even if you laugh when a dog farts, according to a belief collected in Berkeley in 1968,[67] you will have to endure a sty Finally, watching dogs fornicate will bring a sty to the eye of the beholder.[68] In a city of dog lovers, San Francisco, this sight is all but commonplace. In another reversal, reported from Yuma, Arizona, in 1964,[69] you will get a sty if a dog pees on your leg.

With the exception of references to viewing nude persons and to watching dogs fornicate, the whole discussion of the cause of styes thus far has centered around eliminative functions and scatological beliefs and practices. Now we shall consider styes in connection with sexual and procreative matters. The corpus of available information in these areas is admittedly far lighter, but the outline of folk beliefs is nevertheless broad enough to show that sexual and procreative functions figure importantly enough in the purported causes of styes to warrant much more intensive study than has been hitherto devoted to this aspect of the subject. In two provocative papers in British medical publications and journals in the field of psychology and psychiatry in the 1940s, W. S. Inman connected styes with the onset of menstruation in adolescence and with sexual repression and the emotional stress and conflict growing out of socially imposed customs of behavior at this critical period of a young person's life.[70] Acne, of course, is another physical bodily manifestation of this period of turmoil, being associated with sexual repression, with masturbation, and the feelings of guilt that arise from sexual longing and solitary vice. The use of wedding rings to cure styes, a practice that is widely known in folk tradition, according to Inman, draws its special sanction and validity from the fact that the wedding ring confers upon a woman the legal and moral right to bear a child.[71] In an earlier paper dealing with the couvade,[72] Inman connects styes with the whole interest that men have in the procreative process. These tarsal cysts on the eyelids also occur in people of all ages who have thoughts and fantasies about birth,[73] including women who have never borne children. A talking out of one's feelings and repressions and a general airing of these thoughts about the whole procreative process are often sufficient to relieve the mental stress causing the sty.[74] In Basque folk medicine merely dreaming of the birth of a child was thought to bring on a sty.[75] In America the only belief that I have come across that fits into Inman's general thesis is an item from Ohio stating that if a woman develops a sty it is because she is longing to have a baby.[76] Inman's representation makes clear why people stood in awe of pregnant women and often feared them. In Spain, for example, pregnant women with the evil eye were thought to inflict styes on people by a mere glance.[77] Elsewhere in Europe and America the belief took on a more subjective aspect, for styes were thought to come as a punishment for one's failure to meet the request of a woman with child.[78] In Ohio, for example, it is believed that if you refuse a pregnant woman something you will get a sty.[79] In the Italian traditions of California such incivility is thought to be punished when the unfeeling person breaks out with a sty.[80] The Dutch notion that a pregnant woman should be offered any kind of food she craves[81] finds a reasonable parallel in California, where it was believed in Berkeley in the 1960s that if you were eating, and failed to offer a pregnant woman some of the food,[82] you would get a sty. This has a European analogue from Asturias, Spain.[83] Closely connected with the beliefs concerning styes and pregnant women are notions having to do with nursing women and lactation. These notions are found in Europe and America and involve the use of breast milk in the treatment of styes.[84] In this general connection it should be noted that breast milk, often squirted from the nipples, is widely used in all kinds of eye ailments.

In the Latin tradition love affairs were often connected with styes. In the Basque country, for example, a sty was believed to form on a woman when she was proposed to by a widower.[85] Erotic overtones are discernible in the use, in Chile, of the tail of a shirt owned by someone of the opposite sex in a curative ritual. Such a shirt was simply drawn over the sty of the one afflicted.[86] In a highly erotic ritual, reported from Los Angeles in the late 1950s, it was believed that a sty could be cured by making the sign of the fig with one's right hand three times. This was done by pressing the thumb between the index finger and the infamous digit, as in a penis penetrating the vaginal labia.[87] In the light of these loosely assorted bits of information, it will come as no surprise that kissing a redhead, presumably a red-headed woman, will cure a sty, as reported from both Ohio and California.[88]

Because the sun, moon, stars, and other heavenly bodies are sacred, one should not urinate in their presence on pain of getting a sty.[89] "Pissing at the moon" was particularly proscribed in Holland,[90] as was relieving oneself amid lightning and thunder.[91] Pointing at the stars, a somewhat softened display in the presence of stellar light, was a taboo known in the Negro tradition of Louisiana in the 1950s,[92] as well as in Arkansas, Texas, and elsewhere in the South. It is also encountered in Ohio.[93] Simply counting stars will bring on styes, as Negro entries from Alabama,[94] Maryland, and elsewhere in the South attest.[95]

Other kinds of censurable conduct are believed to cause styes. Badness and moral turpitude may be responsible, with some connections, perhaps, to the notions put forward by Inman,[96] or they may be due to lesser categories of moral failings, such as avarice,[97] selfishness, and stinginess.[98] Lying, in particular, has been singled out, with interdictions, on pain of developing styes, in accounts coming from Europe[99] and from many parts of the United States.[100] There are many verbal charms involving styes and lying but they cannot be treated here. This budget of sins, moral failures, and irregularities in one's eliminative functions and sex life must be brought to an end. Perhaps this can be done by mentioning a category of behavioral excess not yet noted, namely, drunkenness. In France it is claimed that if you drink at a crossroads at night, you will have a sty on your eye in the morning.[101]

NOTES

1. A. de Cock, *Spreekwoorden, Zegswijzen en Uitdrukkingen op Volkgeloof Berustend.* 2 vols. (Antwerpen: De Sikkel, 1920–1922), II, 36, No. 281, s.v. "Gerstekorrel."

2. Thomas R. Brendle and Claude W. Unger, *Folk Medicine of the Pennsylvania Germans. The Non-Occult Cures* (Proceedings of the Pennsylvania German Society, XLV, Norristown, Pennsylvania, 1935), p. 121.

3. Edwin Miller Fogel, *Beliefs and Superstitions of the Pennsylvania Germans* (Americana Germanica, No. 18, Philadelphia, 1915), p. 295, No. 1560.

4. *Handwörterbuch des Deutschen Aberglaubens,* ed. Hanns Bächtold-Stäubli und Eduard von Hoffmann-Krayer. 10 vols. (Berlin and Leipzig, 1927–1942), I, 715, s.v. "Augenkrankheiten." (Hereinafter cited as *HDA.*)

5. de Cock, II, 35 ff., No. 281.

6. Documentation of entries is for published items only and for major state collections of popular beliefs and superstitions being edited at UCLA, namely, the Ohio, Kentucky, Utah, and California collections. Material from other states, running into many thousands of items, is not specially identified other than in the selected texts. For the present entry: Utah Coll. (unpub.), No. 4087; Kentucky Coll. (unpub.).

7. Ohio Coll. (unpub.), No. 11603.

8. Utah Coll. (unpub.), No. 4087; Calif. Coll. (unpub.).

9. Harry Middleton Hyatt, *Folklore from Adams County, Illinois,* 2nd ed. (Memoirs of the Alma Egan Hyatt Foundation [New York], 1965), p. 243, No. 5461; John H. Bushnell, "Medical Folklore from California," *Western Folklore,* 6 (1947), 274, No. 8.

10. Wayland D. Hand, "More Popular Beliefs and Superstitions from Pennsylvania," in *Two Penny Ballads and Four Dollar Whiskey,* ed. Robert H. Byington and Kenneth S. Goldstein (Hatboro Pennsylvania: Folklore Associates, 1965), p. 145, No. 94.

11. UCLA Coll. (unpub.).

12. C. Bakker, *Volksgeneeskunde in Waterland: een Vergelijkende Studie met de Geneeskunde der Grieken en Romeinen* (Amsterdam: H. J. Paris, 1928), p. 196. Bakker gives two or three other scatological terms (ibid.).

13. *HDA,* I, 715, s.v. "Augenkrankheiten."

14. *HDA,* V, 335, s.v. "Kot."

15. UCLA Coll. (unpub.).

16. Ohio Coll. (unpub.), No. 11602.

17. UCLA Coll. (unpub.).

18. Paul G. Brewster, "Folk Beliefs and Practices from Indiana," *Hoosier Folklore Bulletin,* 2 (1943), No. 180.

19. Ohio Coll. (unpub.), No. 11601; UCLA Coll. (unpub.).

20. Hyatt, 2 ed., p. 243, No. 5458, p. 243, No. 5461 (defecation).

21. Eston Everett Ericson, "Nebraska Folklore and Popular Sayings," *Folk-Lore,* 49 (1933), 150, No. 9; Wayland D. Hand, "A Miscellany of Nebraska Folk Beliefs, *Western Folklore,* 21 (1962), 261, No. 41; Roger Welsch, *A Treasury of Nebraska Pioneer Folklore* (Lincoln, Neb.: University of Nebraska Press, 1966), p. 336.

22. Marjorie M. Kimmerle and Mark Gelber, "Popular Beliefs and Superstitions from Colorado" (unpub.), No. 442.

23. John Q. Anderson, *1, 333 Cures, Remedies, Preventives, & Health Practices* (Austin, Texas: Encino Press, 1970), p. 72 (2 other entries).

24. Ariz. Coll. (unpub.).

25. Wayland D. Hand, "Popular Beliefs and Superstitions from Pennsylvania," *Keystone Folklore Quarterly,* 3 (1958), 67, No. 56: idem., "More Pennsylvania," p. 145, No. 94.

26. Ariz. Coll. (unpub.).

27. Utah Coll. (unpub.), No. 4087.

28. Calif. Coll. (unpub.).

29. Richard S. Tallman, ed., "Belief and Legend from Northern King's County, Nova Scotia," mimeographed (Canning, King's County, N.S., 1969), p. 37.

30. Fogel, p. 295, No. 1560.

31. Ohio Coll. (unpub.), No. 11605 (next to the road).

32. Calif. Coll. (unpub.).

33. Bushnell, p. 274, No. 8.

34. *HDA,* I, 715, s.v. "Augenkrankheiten"; V, 526, s.v. "Kreuzgang."

35. Kentucky Coll. (unpub.).

36. Hyatt, p. 243, No. 5460. (No. 5078 in the first edition of 1935.)

37. Calif. Coll. (unpub.).

38. Ohio Coll. (unpub.), No. 11601.

39. Hyatt, 2nd ed., p. 243, No. 5437; Bushnell, p. 274, No. 8.

40. Hyatt, 2nd ed., p. 243, No. 5459.

41. Calif. Coll. (unpub.).

42. Ohio Coll. (unpub.), No. 11603.

43. Hyatt, 2nd ed., p. 243, No. 5456.

44. Ariz. Coll. (unpub.).

45. de Cock, p. 36, No. 281.

46. Ohio Coll. (unpub.), No. 11600.

47. Utah Coll. (unpub.), No. 4087.

48. Ohio Coll. (unpub.), No. 11599.

49. *HDA,* III, 698.

50. Ohio Coll. (unpub.), No. 11596.

51. Ohio Coll. (unpub.), No. 11598; Utah Coll. (unpub.), No. 4089.

52. Ohio Coll. (unpub.), No. 11597.

53. H. J. Rose, *Handbook of Greek Mythology* (New York: E. P. Dutton & Co., 1959), p. 195.

54. E. Sidney Hartland, "Peeping Tom and Lady Godiva," *Folk-Lore,* 1 (1890), 207–226.

55. Fogel, p. 212, No. 1965; *Southern Folklore Quarterly,* 11 (1947), 211.

56. Calif. Coll. (unpub.).

57. *HDA,* I, 715, s.v. "Augenkrankheiten."

58. Utah Coll. (unpub.), No. 4085.

59. de Cock, II, 37, No. 281.

60. Bakker, p. 196.

61. Calif. Coll. (unpub.).

62. Bushnell, p. 274, No. 8.

63. George D. Hendricks, "Superstitions Collected in Denton, Texas," *Western Folklore,* 15 (1956), 9, No. 183. (There is one other unpublished item.)

64. Ariz. Coll. (unpub., 3 items).

65. Calif. Coll. (unpub., 4 entries).

66. *Ibid.*

67. *Ibid.*

68. *Ibid.*

69. Ariz. Coll. (unpub.).

70. W. S. Inman, "Styes, Barley, and Wedding Rings," *The British Journal of Medical Psychology,* 20 (1946), 331–338, esp. p. 332.

71. *Ibid.*, p. 332. On the use of gold rings and wedding rings to cure styes in America, see my edition of *Popular Beliefs and Superstitions from North Carolina* in *The Frank C. Brown Collection of North Carolina Folklore.* 7 vols. (Durham, North Carolina: Duke University Press, 1952–1964), VI, 294 f., Nos. 2283–2287. Comparative references to other countries are also given.

72. W. S. Inman, "The Couvade in Modern England," *The British Journal of Medical Psychology,* 19 (1941), 37–55. (I am indebted to Frances M. Tally for calling this important paper to my attention.)

73. *Ibid.,* p. 38.

74. *Ibid.,* p. 41. Inman writes: "In the cure of styes the laying bare of the emotional factor usually has more effect than any remedy with which I am acquainted. I have known it to succeed when years of 'scientific' treatment, including an autogenous vaccine, have failed."

75. Ignacio Maria Barriola, *La Medicina popular en el pais vasco* (San Sebastian: Biblioteca Vascongada de los Amigos del Pais, 1952), p. 42.

76. Ohio Coll. (unpub.), No. 11584.

77. *HDA,* I, 714, s.v. "Augenkrankheiten."

78. *Ibid.,*; S. Seligmann, *Der böse Blick und Verwandtes: Ein Beitrag zur Geschichte des Aberglaubens aller Zeiten und Völker.* 2 vols. (Berlin: Hermann Barsdorf Verlag, 1910), I, 93; Raffaele Lombardi Satriani, *Credenze Popolari Calabresi* (Naples: Fratelli de Simone, Editori, 1951), p. 35; *Biblioteca de las Tradiciones Populares Española* (Madrid, 1886), VIII, 263, No. 120.

79. Ohio Coll. (unpub.), No. 11585.

80. Calif. Coll. (unpub.).

81. Bakker, p. 47.

82. Calif. Coll. (unpub.).

83. L. Giner Arivau, "Folk-Lore de Proaza. Notas y Apuntes Recogidos y Ordenados," *Biblioteca de las Tradiciones Populares Española* (Madrid, 1886), VIII, 263, No. 120.

84. O. v. Hovorka und A. Kronfeld, *Vergleichende Volksmedizin: Eine Darstellung volksmedizinischer Sitten und Gebräuche, Anschauungen und Heilfaktoren, des Aberglaubens und der Zaubermedizin.* 2 vols. (Stuttgart: Verlag von Strecker & Schröder, 1908–1909), II, 795; Barriola, p. 42, Brown Coll., VI, 294, No. 2276; Calif. Coll. (unpub.).

85. Barriola, p. 42.

86. Julio Vicuña Cifuentes, *Mitos y Supersticiones: Estudios del Folklore Recogidos de la Tradición Oral.* 3rd ed. (Santiago de Chile: Editorial Nascimento, 1947), p. 317.

87. Calif. Coll. (unpub.).

88. Ohio Coll. (unpub.), No. 11586; Calif. Coll. (unpub.).

89. de Cock, I, 37, No. 281.

90. *Ibid.*, p. 36, No. 281; also p. 37.

91. *Ibid.*, p. 37, No. 281.

92. *Western Folklore,* 17 (1958), 278, No. 20.

93. Ohio Coll. (unpub.), No. 11665.

94. Ray B. Browne, *Folk Beliefs and Practices from Alabama* (Folklore Studies, No. 9, Berkeley and Los Angeles: University of California Press, 1958), p. 105, No. 1824.

95. Newbell Niles Puckett, *Folk Beliefs of the Southern Negro* (Chapel Hill: University of North Carolina Press, 1926), p. 434.

96. Ohio Coll. (unpub.), 11609.

97. Barriola, p. 42.

98. Ohio Coll. (unpub.), Nos. 11610–11611.

99. Barriola, p. 42.

100. Puckett, p. 382; Daniel Lindsey Thomas and Lucy Blaney Thomas, *Kentucky Superstitions* (Princeton, N.J.: Princeton University Press, 1920), p. 116, No. 1358; Anderson, pp. 71–72; Utah Coll. (unpub.), No. 4086.

101. Robert Morel et Suzanne Walter, *Dictionnaire des Superstitions* (Paris: Bibliotheque Marabout, n.d.), p. 244.

19

Folk Medical Inhalants in Respiratory Disorders*

Several years ago as I began to work through my voluminous files on American folk medicine, I became interested in some of the unusual remedies that have been employed to combat respiratory ailments in the United States and Canada. This interest was considerably heightened in 1964 when two Virginia scholars called attention to the use of grist mills in the treatment of whooping-cough in their own state and in the neighbouring state of West Virginia.[1] Their search was prompted by a Pennsylvania Dutch custom, dating from the 1880s, or before, of placing a child with whooping-cough in a hopper of grain in a grist mill until the grain was ground out. In the same year my research assistant and I made a preliminary survey of American folk medical prescriptions for the cure of respiratory ailments.[2] On the basis of further study, I am now able to make a fuller statement. The survey is now being broadened to include material that has come to hand from the British Isles and from several countries of Europe.

An eighteenth-century Scottish physician, William Buchan, writing on chin-cough, or whooping-cough, in 1772, said that 'the most effective remedy in this disease is a change of air. This often removes the malady even when the change seems to be from a purer to a less wholesome air. . . .'[3] Part of this prescription was the recommendation that the patient should be

*This article originally appeared in *Medical History,* 12 (1968), 153–163. Permission to reprint has been given by the editors and by the Wellcome Institute for the History of Medicine.

removed some distance from the place where he contracted the disease. These views on a change of air were widely accepted and became, or were already a part of the folk medical treatment of whooping-cough in the British Isles.[4] A change of air has not been reported for the treatment of whooping-coughs or hiccoughs in the folklore literature from Scandinavia, Germany, the Low Countries, and France, but this may be due to the failure to collect and report this popular folk medical custom. In Spain, for example, croup, a malady of the throat which affects breathing in children, is treated by sending the patient into the mountains for a change of air.[5] Likewise, children were carried to Gowk Craig in Forgan Parish in Fife so they could recover from whooping-cough by remaining for two hours where the 'seven airs' blow, and in the North Riding of Yorkshire patients ordered to go to the country for a change of air were told to seek a spot 'where three roads meet.'[6] Another famous high place to which people with respiratory disorders went was the viaduct, Archway Road, Highgate, in the northern part of London. Nurses formerly took children to this spot, and people are reported to have come to the bridge from far and wide with their children.[7] Tan-Hill was a north country place to which people in Lancashire and Westmorland also took their children for relief from whooping-cough.[8] That faith in high ground and a change of air was generally believed as being efficacious for the treatment of whooping-cough is seen in a cure performed in the 1880s in the West Riding of Yorkshire whereby the young patient was pulled under the stomach of a donkey three times in a passing-through ritual. The correspondent to *Notes and Queries* believed, however, that the cure was due in part to the fact that the ceremony was performed on a high hill where a change of air was an important factor in the cure.[9] The taking of children with whooping-cough atop the Blackpool tower in Lancashire for a change of air,[10] in very recent times is further evidence of the faith which people have in the beneficial effect of rarified atmosphere in the treatment of this disease. Even more striking are the so-called 'Nursery Flights' of the Royal Air Force station in Austria in 1955, in which the children of R.A.F. members suffering from whooping-cough were taken aloft to expose them to the low barometric pressure in aeroplanes flying at high altitudes.[11]

Mothers of Hull are reported to have taken their suffering youngsters across the Humber to New Holland and back again for the change of air this trip afforded. Such a mission was called 'crossing strange water.'[12] Like the mountains, the seaside afforded a welcome change of air, and the sea air was sought by Lancashiremen and Westmorlanders for the treatment of whooping-cough.[13] In the light of the examples cited, one might wonder if the prescription for whooping-cough, namely, to carry a child fasting into three parishes on a Sunday morning, as reported from Devonshire in the 1850s, might not somehow have involved, whatever other virtues, the change of air that such a lengthy journey might have entailed.[14]

Just as a change of air brought relief to sufferers from whooping-cough and other respiratory ailments, whether by trips to high places or to the seaside, so also were the natural earth fumes and gases thought to be beneficial. Making the whooping-cough patient follow the plough and inhale the smell of the newly turned land was widely reported in Essex,[15] and no doubt regarded as beneficial elsewhere. In County Fife, likewise, the smell of freshly-dug earth was held to be beneficial for whooping-cough. Accordingly, a hole was dug in the earth and the patient made to breathe the emanations.[16] In Norfolk and Suffolk a hole was dug in a meadow, and the child's head held in it until a cough was heard.[17] Transference of the disease to the earth seems to have been involved in an Essex cure for the same disease. After the child's head had been held in the hole until he coughed, the hole was filled again and the cough left there with it.[18] Sometime during the second half of the nineteenth century a group of sufferers from pulmonary tuberculosis were reported to have taken up residence in the Mammoth Cave in Kentucky for what benefits the air of the cave would bring, but the whole venture was a failure. Several died and the remainder returned to daylight with the chance of life sadly impaired.[19]

By way of analogy to natural caves in the earth, man-made holes such as mines and charcoal pits were used in the treatment of whooping-cough.[20] The patients were either held over the opening of the pit so as to breathe the escaping air, or they were actually taken into the mines on the advice of a physician, as in Scotland.[21] In County Fife bread was taken into the pits, impregnated with the air of the mine, and then given to the patient for 'a change of air'.[22] A beneficial change of air was likewise associated with lime kilns, where not only whooping-cough was treated,[23] but also pulmonary tuberculosis. Patients suffering from this disease were encouraged to sleep near the old-fashioned open lime kilns, as in the Lake District.[24] Apparently, belief in the so-called 'harmonious air' of lime kilns,[25] also lay at the base of an Alabama belief in the efficacy of croup patients inhaling the fumes of unslaked lime to keep them from strangling.[26]

The custom of taking children suffering from whooping-cough to the gas-works has been reported from different parts of England and the United States, and the breathing of such air was likewise recommended as a cure for croup in Spain.[27] Writing in 1879, William Henderson reports that a girl suffering from whooping-cough in one of the northern counties was taken several days successively to the gas-works to breathe what her mother called the 'harmonious air'.[28] Children of Glasgow suffering from whooping-cough were taken to the gas-works for relief,[29] as were those of Westmorland and Lancashire,[30] while afflicted youngsters in Norfolk were encouraged to 'sit in the lee of the local gas works'.[31] This strange folk medical custom was also observed elsewhere in Scotland besides Glasgow. When an outbreak of whooping-cough occurred in County Fife in 1891, it was observed that the keeper of the gas-works did not take the complaint. This was explained as being due to the fact that the air near a gas-works contains pyradin, which is supposed to act as an antiseptic and a germicide.[32] This is the only attempt at an explanation of the practice which I have encountered in the folklore literature, and may or may not have a basis in fact. The supposed cure of whooping-cough by the inhalation of ammoniacal fumes at a gas-works, turns up in one of the earliest American folklore publications, a small brochure dealing with beliefs and customs in and around Philadelphia in the late 1880s. There are no details, simply the reporting of the fact that children could be cured by inhaling the ammoniacal fumes at the gas-works.[33] In Adams County, Illinois, young sufferers from whooping-cough were taken to a gas-house and carried through the building several times.[34] Related to breathing the vapours of gas-works is the breathing not only of fumes from chemical plants, as recommended in Scotland,[35] but the vapours of distilleries also, as in Glasgow.[36]

More widely known geographically than any treatment involving mines, kilns, factories, or other industrial works is the curious custom, alluded to at the beginning of this article, of taking a child into a grist mill and holding it over the hopper. This practice is reported from the British Isles and Spain, and from several parts of the United States. In England and Scotland, inhalation of the dust from the mill is not specifically stated, as the child is pulled in and out of the hopper, often as many as nine times.[37] In Ireland, likewise, the child was lifted rapidly into a mill hopper and out again three times in succession.[38] In his three-volume medical dictionary of 1743–1745, in an entry under 'pertussis', Robert James explained the placing of a child in a grist mill as being done to induce fright, with the grinding of the wheels, the noise, etc.[39] Credence is lent to this view by the practice in Galicia, Spain, of carrying a child nineteen times around the cogwheel of a mill, with no reference to placing the child near the hopper, nor even the intimation that it was specifically a grist mill, even though the word 'mill' generally connotes some sort of flour or grist mill.[40] The theory of inducing sudden fright, as in the case of hiccoughs, is unknown to me, and does not occur in my files containing some five hundred entries on 'whooping-cough'. However, elements of fright to the child are seen in a folk medical ritual from the Ozarks where a child is taken to the grist mill to be 'ground in the hopper' for the cure of paralysis.[41] American examples, apparently, never specifically mention inhalation of the air and dust from the mill hopper. In the twenty careful interviews made by Smith and Stewart in Virginia, West Virginia, and the Pennsylvania German country, breathing the emanations from the mill does not come up. Also, there is no lifting in and out of the hopper, as in the British Isles. Usually the child is placed in the mill 'until the grist is ground', as in Pennsylvania,[42] 'until the mill grinds a half a bushel of corn', as in North Carolina, where the practice is carried out by Negroes as well as whites,[43] or the child is made to sit in the hopper of a mill 'until the grain has run out', as in Illinois.[44] It should be noted that children in the United States were also taken to grist mills as a preventive measure.[45] The only place where the breathing of the dust from the freshly-ground flour and meal is specifically mentioned is from two different parts of Spain. In both cases the treatment is for whooping-cough.[46]

Other kinds of polluted air caused by industrial works, or products or waste products of their manufacture, together with emanations of smoke from other sources, can now be taken up as they relate to the curing of whooping-cough and other diseases, including the plague. The breathing of smoke from a railroad tunnel by patients while on a train,[47] or their specifically entering a tunnel to inhale the smoke left in the tunnel after a train has passed through, is a custom reported from Spain as late as the 1940s.[48] This latter practice also applied to the treatment of croup.[49] In America resort to railroad tunnels for the cure of whooping-cough is reported only from the Pennsylvania

German country.[50] Miners in Pennsylvania and adjoining states where coal is mined believed that powder smoke was the only cure for whooping-cough, and fathers, accordingly, would carry their ailing youngsters into the mines to be exposed to the sulphurous fumes.[51]

Early in the nineteenth century, T. W. Wansbrough, a surgeon in Fulham, used tar vapour successfully in treating whooping-cough. He simply produced the vapour by sticking a hot poker into Barbadoes tar and then letting the child breathe the fumes.[52] Since relegated to the realm of folk medicine, this practice has continued in use until our own time.[53] In *Moby Dick* (1851) Herman Melville tells how sailors, thinking they would catch the plague, would dip oakum into coal tar and hold it to their nostrils (ch. 91). Pine resin put into a pot of boiling water is used much the same way for the cure of croup in Alabama as the patient inhales the fumes.[54] Breathing the smoke from pine knots taken from lumber was a method of treating croup in Texas.[55]

Among the kinds of 'less wholesome air', which William Buchan alluded to as being beneficial for the treatment of chincough in the eighteenth century, the following can be mentioned. Apart from gases and vapours of the kind we have just considered, there are human and animal odours of various kinds that are recommended in folk medicine. The holding of a child over a privy or commode for example is reported from both the British Isles and the United States.[56] More widely known as a cure for respiratory ailments and throat infections was the air of the stable. In the Slavic countries and Germany tuberculars were taken into animal stalls,[57] while asthma was treated in Holland in the same way.[58] A cowstall is specifically mentioned. In Scotland patients suffering from whooping-cough were taken to a byre. If, during the process, the child gave a *kink,* or cough, it was considered a good sign.[59] In Virginia, children with whooping-cough were allowed to play in the stable all day.[60] A manure-pile ritual, wherein a child with thrush was held over a steaming manure pile, as a verbal charm was said over him in the three highest names, was reported from Indiana as late as the early 1960s.[61]

The breath and smell of a cow were considered good for consumption in Scotland,[62] while the smell of sheep, particularly in the sheepfold, was recommended not only for whooping-cough pretty much throughout England and Scotland, but for other diseases as well, including bronchitis, consumption, and tuberculosis. In Somerset, for example, it is thought that one may still cure bronchitis simply by passing through a flock of sheep.[63] In the shires of Dorset, Somerset, and Oxford, consumption was treated by having the patient enter a sheep-fold, or walk around a sheepfold, very early in the morning, early enough in Dorsetshire, for example, to see the sun rise.[64] Treatment in the sheepfold for whooping-cough is reported from Devonshire and Essex.[65] In an earlier day it was sufficient for the patient simply to roll around on the spot where a sheep had bedded down for the night, the only stipulation being that the dew must still be on the field.[66]

Less well-known cures relating to animal odours and offensive emanations involve the breathing of the unpleasant smell of a goat or a fox for a week,[67] and the taking of children to pigstyes before dawn and forcing them to bite into the hog trough.[68] In the Bradford-Shipley district the smell of a maggot farm was thought to be beneficial for tuberculosis, and during World War I soldiers were marched through it to strengthen their resistance to tuberculosis.[69] In Oklahoma the smell of the warm viscera of a slaughtered hog was recommended as a cure for a common cold and sore throat.[70]

The inhalation of the breath of horses, mules, and donkeys, or oral contact with these creatures, is well known in the British Isles, but perhaps even more widely so in the United States. In Suffolk, for example, the custom is known as 'taking the horse's breath',[71] and is reported from the early 1850s.[72] The breath of a stallion was prescribed in Suffolk,[73] and that of a piebald horse in Herefordshire.[74] In 1882, a correspondent to *Notes and Queries,* area unstated, wrote that a cart-horse is supposed to snort into the face of a child suffering from whooping-cough,[75] while across the Atlantic, in states as widely separated as Georgia, Tennessee, Kentucky, and Illinois, a stallion or a horse is made to snort or blow into a child's face for thrush (thrash) or tonsilitis.[76] Running a horse or racing one until it froths at the mouth, and then holding a child with whooping-cough to its mouth is reported from both Maryland and Louisiana from the mid-1920s.[77] Ten years later this custom was reported for the same disease from Illinois, but the case discussed was referable to about 1860. It is specified that after racing a horse until it is almost out of breath, the child should breathe 'what little breath is left' in the horse's mouth.[78] A stallion breathing into the throat of a child suffering from whooping-cough was recommended in North Carolina after World War I,[79] while a white horse was specified for this special office in Mississippi as late as 1923.[80]

Contact with the mouth of animals involves an exchange of air, so the kissing of mules and donkeys deserves to be mentioned in connection with inhalation of the breath of animals. A sore throat in Ireland, for example, was cured by inhaling and swallowing the breath of a donkey three times in succession for three consecutive mornings.[81] A Scottish curative ritual for whooping-cough involved inhaling the breath of an ass and then passing the patient under its belly and over its back.[82] The only instance of a mule or donkey-kissing ritual for the cure of a respiratory ailment that I can turn up comes from Illinois, where it was known over twenty years ago. Kissing the nostrils of a mule, according to the belief, would cure catarrh.[83]

Close oral contact with other animals, including kissing, is seen in a Georgia cure for hiccoughs whereby the victim kisses a dog in the mouth,[84] and an Irish and American treatment for sore throat, thrush, and whooping cough, which involves making a gander hiss or spit down the victim's throat. Details, unfortunately, are lacking.[85]

Fish were also pressed into service for the curing of whooping-cough. They were either held against the child's mouth so as to breathe down it, or the process was reversed, whereby the patient breathed down the fish's mouth, thus communicating the disease to the fish. Finally, live fish, usually minnows, were swallowed. Interesting though these two last-named categories are, I cannot treat them here.[86] The breathing of fish down the throat of a sufferer from whooping-cough was known in the British Isles during the nineteenth century,[87] and this old practice has lived on in twentieth-century America. An interesting account of a young mother begging a fish from a fisherman along the banks of the Schuykill River in the neighbourhood of Philadelphia around 1875, indicates that perhaps this custom is of long standing in America.[88] Other cases of this custom have been reported from Pennsylvania.[89]

Frogs and toads were likewise held in the mouth or up to the mouth of a child, but it is not always clear whether the frog or toad blew into the child's mouth, or whether it sucked the child's breath and thus absorbed the disease. The reference given here for Shropshire may involve the same kinds of cures we have been discussing in connection with animals and fish,[90] but in all of the rest of the cases cited from the British Isles, transference of the disease to the frog is either clearly indicated, or to be implied.[91] The German and Dutch examples likewise emphasize transference of the disease to the frog.[92] An American example from New York State also clearly deals with the transfer of the child's sore throat to the frog, which absorbs the poison and spits forth green froth.[93] The holding of toads to a child's mouth in Cheshire for the cure of whooping-cough apparently involves a passage of air from the toad to the child, in the regular way,[94] as does a case cited in the *English Dialect Dictionary,* wherein it is reported that a child could not 'get shut of the chin-cough, though he had sucked two toads to death.'[95]

Though the drinking of a child from a bucket or from a drinking trough immediately after a horse had drunk has elements that are related to the practices under discussion, there is not space to enter upon a discussion of this matter here. Nor is there space to consider the drinking of milk by a child for various respiratory conditions after a cat, ferret, or fox has lapped milk from a saucer or other receptacle. At best these would represent only secondary contacts, for the exhalations of the animals over the milk would long since have been dissipated by the time the child could be brought to the vessel to drink.

Finally, we come to a discussion of the use of the human breath in the curing of respiratory and throat ailments. Claiming our interest in this connection is the qualification of the person himself as a healer, whether he be a posthumous child, a child born with a caul, a seventh son, a seventh son of a seventh son, a third son of a third son, a daughter who has never known her father, or a woman whose last name remains unchanged after marriage. Once more, references from the British Isles and America predominate. In the North Riding of Yorkshire, for example, a female who never knew her father blew in the mouth of a child suffering from whooping-cough nine mornings in succession, this with fasting breath.[96] Posthumous sons are credited with curing victims of whooping-cough in Georgia, Maryland, Illinois,[97] and among the southern Negroes,[98] and a child born with a caul was believed in Indiana to possess this same gift of curing whooping-cough.[99] In Ireland a seventh son could cure thrush, so it was believed, by breathing into the mouth of a child,[100] as could a posthumous son.[101] A posthumous son, likewise, or the seventh son in a family, were believed in Indiana to have the gift of curing thrush in the aforesaid manner.[102] In Kentucky a third son of a third son was thought to be thus endowed,[103] while in Tennessee the healing power rested with a woman who had married without changing her name.[104] Posthumous children, when grown, are also credited with being able to cure croup, as cases reported from Maryland and the Ozark country show.[105]

Finally, among the Pennsylvania Germans there is a belief that if a child kisses a Negro full in the mouth, he will be free of whooping-cough.[106] Some say a lifelong immunity is built up by such a kiss if the act takes place while the child is under one year of age.[107]

Fumigation of all kinds, including the burning of animal and plant products and mineral compounds cannot be taken up here for lack of space, nor can the inhalation of water vapour, and the fumes of such common household remedies as vinegar (hot vinegar), turpentine, kerosene, creosote, sulphur, and the like. Many of these household remedies and treatments are so common as not to be of great concern in a paper devoted mainly to the more unusual kinds of inhalants.

The preponderance of data from the British Isles and America does not, it seems to me, invalidate the notion that the use of inhalants for respiratory ailments was once widespread throughout Europe, and perhaps still is known in many countries; it simply points out the need for more and better collecting, and for the researching of scattered materials that have not always found their way into the standard compilations of folk medicine, country by country.

NOTES

1. Smith, Elmer L., and Stewart, John, 'The mill as a preventive and cure of whooping-cough', *J. Am. Folklore,* 1964, 77, 76–77.

2. Hand, Wayland D., and Griffin, Marjorie, 'Inhalants in respiratory disorders', *J. Am. Folklore*, 1964, 77, 258–61.

3. Buchan, William, *Domestic Medicine, or The Family Physician,* Philadelphia, R. Aitken, 1772, p. 199.

4. Black, William George, *Folk-Medicine: A Chapter in the History of Culture*, Publications of the Folk-Lore Society, XII, London, 1883, p. 183; Simpkins, John Ewart, *Examples of the Printed Folk-Lore Concerning Fife, With Some Notes on Clackmannan and Kinross-Shires,* Publications of the Folk-Lore Society, LXXI, London, 1914, p. 408; *Folk-Lore,* 1943, 54, 305.

5. Castillo de Lucas, Antonio, *Folkmedicina,* Madrid, Editorial Dossat, 1958, p. 467.

6. Simpkins, op. cit., p. 134; Gutch, [Eliza], *Examples of Printed Folk-Lore Concerning the North Riding of Yorkshire, York, and the Ainsty,* Publications of the Folk-Lore Society, XLV, London, 1901, p. 180.

7. *Folk-Lore,* 1926, 37, 367.

8. *Folk-Lore,* 1951, 62, 259, Moorland air recommended (ibid., no. 1).

9. *Notes and Queries,* 7th ser., vol. 4, 27 August, 1887, p. 176.

10. Mckelvie, Donald, 'Some Aspects of Oral, Social and Material Tradition in an Industrial Urban Area', unpublished, Ph.D. diss., Leeds, 1963, p. 279, no. 138.

11. Shrewsbury, John Findlay Drew, *The Plague of the Philistines and other Medical-Historical Essays,* London, Victor Gollancz, 1964, p. 43.

12. Radbill, Samuel X., 'Whooping-cough in fact and fancy', *Bull. Hist. Med.,* 1943, 13, 49.

13. *Folk-Lore,* 1951, 62, 260, no. 11.

14. *Notes and Queries,* 1st ser., vol. 11, 31 March 1855, p. 239; Black, op. cit., p. 89; Radford, E., and Radford, M. A., *Encyclopaedia of Superstitions,* London, Rider and Company, [1947], p. 231.

15. *Folk-Lore,* 1951, 62, 260.

16. Simpkins, op. cit., p. 408.

17. *Folk-Lore,* 1943, 54, 305.

18. *Folk-Lore,* 1951, 62, 260.

19. *Western Folklore,* 1961, 20, 276.

20. *Folk-Lore,* 1943, 54, 305 (mines); 1951, 62, 260 (charcoal pits).

21. [Moir, David Macbeth], *Mansie Wauch, Tailor of Dalkieth,* New York, J. & J. Harper, 1828, ch. XIII, 'The chincough pilgrimage'; Simpkins, op. cit., p. 134 (for kingkost, local dialect name in County Fife for whooping-cough).

22. Simpkins, op. cit., p. 408.

23. Balfour, M. C., and Thomas, Northcote W., *Examples of Printed Folk-Lore Concerning Northumberland,* Publications of the Folk-Lore Society, LIII, London, 1903, p. 49; Simpkins, op. cit., p. 409; *Folk-Lore,* 1951, 62, 262.

24. *Folk-Lore,* 1951, 62, 256.

25. Radford, op. cit., p. 259.

26. Browne, Ray B., *Popular Beliefs and Practices from Alabama,* Folklore Studies, IX, Berkeley and Los Angeles, University of California Press, 1958, p. 19, no. 222.

27. Castillo de Lucas, op. cit., p. 467.

28. Henderson, William, *Notes on the Folk-Lore of the Northern Counties and the Borders,* Publications of the Folk-Lore Society, II, London, 1879, p. 142.

29. Black, op. cit., p. 183; Radbill, op. cit., p. 49; cf. p. 42, also.

30. *Folk-Lore,* 1951, 62, 260.

31. *Folk-Lore,* 1929, 40, 117.

32. Simpkins, op. cit., p. 409.

33. Phillips, Henry, Jr., 'First contribution to the folk-lore of Philadelphia and its vicinity', *Proc. Amer. philos. Soc.,* XXV, no. 128, March 1888, p. 163, no. 11; cf. Radbill, op. cit., p. 49.

34. Hyatt, Harry Middleton, *Folk-Lore from Adams County Illinois,* New York, Alma Egan Hyatt Foundation, 1935, p. 212, no. 4413; Hand, Wayland D. (ed.). *Frank C. Brown Collection of North Carolina Folklore,* vols. 6–7, Durham, North Carolina, Duke University Press, 1961–1964, vol. 6, p. 68, no. 423.

35. Napier, James, *Folk-Lore: or, Superstitious Beliefs in the West of Scotland within this Century,* Paisley, Alex. Gardner, 1879, p. 96.

36. Black, op. cit., p. 183; Radbill, op. cit., p. 49.

37. Radbill, op. cit., p. 42; Dalyell, John Graham, *The Darker Superstitions of Scotland,* Glasgow, Richard Griffin, 1835; p. 117; Black, op. cit., p. 119.

38. Wood-Martin, W. G., *Traces of the Elder Faiths of Ireland. A Folklore Sketch,* 2 vols., London, Longman, Green, 1902, vol. 2, p. 189.

39. James, R., *A Medicinal Dictionary, Including Physic, Surgery, Anatomy, Chymistry and Botany,* etc., 3 vols., fol. London, 1743–1745, vol. 3, s.v. 'pertussis' [no pagination]: 'Another empirical Method of curing the Chin-cough, when Medicines prove ineffectual, is, to fright the Child, by putting it in the Hopper of a Mill, which makes a terrible Noise, and the Aspect of whose Wheels is dreadful; and by this Method of Chin-cough is sometimes suddenly cured; the Reason of which undoubtedly confits in this, not only that the animal Spirits, being, by the Fright, forced into new Distractions, leave their former inordinate Motions, but also, that the matter producing the Spasms is, by such Perturbation, either dissipated, or forced into other Nerves, where it proves less troublesome.'

40. *Revista de Dialectología y Tradiciones Populares,* 1947, 3, 567. (Hereinafter abbreviated: *Rev. Dial. Trad. Pop.*)

41. Randolph, Vance, *Ozark Superstitions,* New York, Columbia University Press, 1947, p. 149.

42. *J. Am. Folklore,* 1891, 4, 125.

43. Hand, op. cit., VI, 67, no. 422.

44. Allen, John W., *Legends and Lore of Southern Illinois,* Carbondale, Illinois, Southern Illinois University, 1963, p. 84.

45. On this phase of the treatment, and for other details, cf. the two articles in the *J. Am. Folklore,* refs. 1 and 2.

46. *Rev. Dial. Trad. Pop.,* 1944, 1, 161 (Coruna); ibid., 1947, 3, 567 (Galicia).

47. *Rev. Dial. Trad. Pop.,* 1949, 5, 505.

48. *Rev. Dial. Trad. Pop.,* 1944, 1, 321.

49. Castillo de Lucas, op. cit., p. 467.

50. Fogel, Edwin M., 'Beliefs and superstitions of the Pennsylvania Germans', *Americana Germanica,* XVIII, Philadelphia, 1915, p. 339, no. 1806; Radbill, op. cit., p. 42.

51. Korson, George, *Minstrels of the Mine Patch. Songs and Stories of the Anthracite Industry,* Hatboro, Pa., Folklore Associates, 1964, pp. 146–47.

52. *Lancet,* 1828–1829, ii, 523–24.

53. Black, op. cit., p. 183; *Folk-Lore,* 1932, 43, 256 (Halifax); ibid., 1951, 62, 259, no. 2 (Essex, Westmorland, Lancashire); McKelvie, op. cit., pp. 278–79.

54. Browne, op. cit., no. 1704.

55. Publications of the Texas Folklore Soc., 1938, 14, 268.

56. *Folk-Lore,* 1929, 40, 117; Puckett, Newbell Niles, *Folk Beliefs of the Southern Negro,* Chapel Hill, N. C., University of North Carolina Press, 1926, pp. 371–72.

57. V. Hovorka, O., and Kronfeld, A., *Vergleichende Volksmedizin,* 2 vols., Stuttgart, Verlag von Strecker und Schröder, 1908–1909, vol. 2, 49.

58. Van Andel, M. A., *Volksgeneeskunst en Nederland,* Utrecht, Boekhoven, 1909, p. 224.

59. Napier, op. cit., p. 96; cf. Simpkins, op. cit., p. 408 (smell of the byre good for invalids generally).

60. Puckett, op. cit., p. 371.

61. *Midwest Folklore,* 1961, 11, 47 no. 151; cf. *Southern Folklore Quarterly,* 1939, 3, 40, s.v. 'thrush', no. 4.

62. Black, op. cit., p. 161; Simpkins, op. cit., 21, 133.

63. Tongue, R. L., and Briggs, K. M., *Somerset Folklore,* Publications of the Folk-Lore Society, CXIV, London, 1965, p. 34.

64. Udal, John Symonds, *Dorsetshire Folk-Lore,* Hertford, 1922, p. 224; Black, op. cit., p. 157 (Somerset); *Folk-Lore,* 1909, 20, 218 (Oxfordshire); Radford, op. cit., p. 86 (Surrey).

65. *Folk-Lore,* 1943, 54, 304 (Devon); ibid., 1951, 62, 260 (Essex).

66. *Folk-Lore,* 1908, 19, 345.

67. Sticker, Georg, *Der Keuchhusten,* Wien, 1896, p. 65 (citing an unidentified man by the name of Morris who prescribed this cure in the nineteenth century).

68. Wuttke, Adolf, *Der deutsche Volksaberglaube der Gegenwart,* 3rd ed., Meyer, Elard Hugo, Berlin, Verlag Wiegandt & Grieben, 1900, p. 361.

69. McKelvie, op. cit., p. 279, no. 138.

70. Publications of the Texas Folklore Society, 1930, 8, 82.

71. *Folk-Lore,* 1924, 35, 356.

72. *Notes and Queries,* 1st ser., vol. 5, 6 March 1852, p. 223.

73. *Folk-Lore,* 1945, 56, 270.

74. Leather, Ella M., *The Folk Lore of Herefordshire,* Hereford, Jakeman & Carver, 1912, p. 82; cf. *Notes and Queries,* 1st ser., vol. 5, 6 March 1852, p. 223 (where the mere sight of a piebald horse was held to effect the cure).

75. *Notes and Queries,* 6th ser., vol. 6, 18 November 1882, p. 407.

76. Campbell, Marie, *Folks Do Get Born,* New York, Reinhart & Company, 1946, p. 35 (Georgia: thrush); *J. Am. Folklore,* 1939, 52, 114, no. 62 (Tennessee: thrush); Thomas, Daniel Lindsey, and Thomas, Lucy Blayney, *Kentucky Superstitions,* Princeton, N.J., Princeton University Press, 1920, p. 118, no. 1380 (thrush); *Hoosier Folklore,* 1946, 5, 70, no. 25 (Illinois: tonsilitis).

77. Whitney, Annie Weston, and Bullock, Caroline Canfield, *Folk-Lore from Maryland,* Mem. Am. Folklore Soc., XVIII, New York, 1925, p. 87, no. 1774; *J. Am. Folklore,* 1927, 40, 166, no. 388 (Louisiana).

78. Hyatt, op. cit., p. 212, no. 4415; cf. also no. 4414.

79. Hand, op. cit., VI, 352, no. 2717.

80. Hudson, Arthur Palmer, *Specimens of Mississippi Folk-Lore,* Ann Arbor, Mich., 1928, p. 154, no. 2.

81. *J. Am. Folklore,* 1894, 7, 226.

82. Gregor, Walter, *Notes on the Folk-Lore of the North-East of Scotland,* Publications of the Folk-Lore Society, VII, London, 1881, p. 132.

83. *Hoosier Folklore,* 1946, 5, 68, no. 3.

84. *Tennessee Folklore Soc. Bull.,* 1953, 19, 2.

85. *J. Am. Folklore,* 1894, 7, 226; *Folk-Lore,* 1897, 8, 180 (both thrush: Ireland); *New York Folklore Q.,* 1947, 3, 169 (whooping-cough).

86. Cf. Hand, op. cit., VI, 351, no. 2712 for the swallowing of live fish for whooping-cough.

87. Black, op. cit., p. 36; Henderson, op. cit., pp. 140–41; (a trout); Balfour and Thomas, op. cit., p. 49 (a trout).

88. *Notes and Queries,* 5th ser., vol. 3, 1 June 1875, pp. 345–46.

89. *J. Am. Folklore,* 1891, 4, 125; Fogel, op. cit., p. 339, no. 1805; *Pennsylvania Dutchman,* vol. 2, no. 11, 1 November 1950, p. 7.

90. *Folk-Lore,* 1943, 54, 303–4.

91. Black, op. cit., p. 35; *Folk-Lore,* 1911, 22, 455 (County Clare); ibid., 1929, 40, 117 (hold a small frog in the mouth of a child for awhile, and 'it will

soon be heard whooping and wheezing all over the garden'); Leather, op. cit., p. 82 (thrush).

92. *Handwörterbuch des deutschen Aberglaubens,* 10: vols., Berlin and Leipzig, Walter de Gruyter, 1927–1942, vol. 3, p. 136; Andel, op. cit., p. 205.

93. *New York Folklore Q.,* 1945, 1, 180.

94. *Notes and Queries,* 1st ser., vol. 3, 5 April 1851, 258.

95. Wright, Joseph (ed.), *English Dialect Dictionary,* 6 vols., reissue, Oxford, Oxford University Press, 1923, vol. 1, p. 586.

96. Gutch, op. cit., p. 180.

97. *J. Am. Folklore,* 1892, 5, 62; Whitney and Bullock, op. cit., p. 83, no. 1710; *Illinois Folklore,* 1948, 2, 7.

98. Puckett, op. cit., p. 371.

99. *Indiana History Bull.,* 1958, 35, 134, no. 307.

100. *Folk-Lore,* 1908, 19, 316.

101. *Western Folklore,* 1957, 16, 57 (news report from *Dublin Irish Times,* 21 July 1956.)

102. *Midwest Folklore,* 1961, 11, 47, nos. 150, 149, respectively; cf. no. 148.

103. *Kentucky Folklore Record,* 1955, 1, 70.

104. *J. Am. Folklore,* 1935, 48, p. 327, no. 40; ibid., 1939, 52, p. 114, no. 67.

105. Whitney and Bullock, op. cit., p. 83, no. 1710; Randolph, op. cit., p. 136.

106. Brendle, Thomas R., and Unger, Claude W., 'Folk Medicine of the Pennsylvania Germans. The Non-Occult Cures', *Proc. Pennsylvania German Soc.,* XLV, Norristown, Pa., 1935, p. 132 (for a child suffering from the 'blue cough'); *Papers and Addresses of The Lebanon Co. Hist. Soc.,* 1905–1906, 3, 276; Fogel, op. cit., p. 337, no. 1791.

107. Brendle and Unger, op. cit., p. 132; Fogel, op. cit., p. 337, no. 1792; Allen, op. cit., p. 84 (Illinois, and not noted as being of German origin).

20
Curative Practice in Folk Tales*

Conflict and disappointment are prime requisites of the folk tale, for they place upon the hero the burden of overcoming difficulties placed in his path, and winning through to great ends. This is often accomplished at enormous cost, and by ordeals frightful to contemplate. The means by which the hero overcomes his handicaps or accomplishes his difficult and often impossible tasks are the ingredients from which a good tale are made. They are anticipated eagerly by those listening to the tales in person, or by the reader who has become accustomed to the wide range of problems confronting the hero, and the equally broad array of means for their solution.

Physical malady and disease fit naturally into the troubled world of the hero and of other characters in the tales, and often involve natural impediments that in their own way are as serious as the difficulties which result from irrational or supernatural causes, or from other developments which arise at the whim of the storyteller. It must be noted at the outset, however, that, like all other narrative elements or devices used in the tales, physical impairment or disease may result quite as much from supernatural as from natural causes. Thus, in the matter of disease and curative practice, as in other kinds of elements making up the tales, the student of folk tales must be aware of conditions and developments at two levels. 1. the level of reality and human experience in terms of the natural world, and 2. the

*This article originally appeared in *Fabula: Zeitschrift für Erzählforschung,* 9 (1967), 264–269. Permission to reprint has been given by the editor and by Walter de Gruyter & Co.

supernatural level—the level of magic and marvel, where natural law is held in abeyance.

In putting this paper together, therefore, I have constantly been faced with the problem of seeing how folk medical beliefs and practices are adapted to the needs of the tales in which they are used, and noting the results. These results are of two kinds. The first observation is that folk curative practice, with its rich detail, and with a medical magic of its own, is not really drawn upon in an empirical folk medical sense. The second feature noted grows perhaps out of the first, namely, folk medicine itself is often replaced by curative practice that is outwardly magical to meet the needs of the folk tale, but at the same time is lacking in the internal magic of folk medicine proper. Perhaps this fine distinction can be made clearer in terms of actual examples. The first, illustrating what, for want of a better term, I shall call the external or superficial and is a variant of Grimm 31, "The Girl without Hands" (Das Mädchen ohne Hände), Aarne-Thompson 706. Here the innkeeper's daughter has her hands restored magically by St. Joseph. There are no details; the hands are simply healed. In a Hungarian variant of the tale, however, the girl's hands grow back together only after she has bathed them in a lake full of magic water which has the power of reviving and making whole the limbs of any cripple. This last example, of course, accords with the folk notion of healing wells and healing waters that is still encountered in many parts of Europe, particularly in the Latin countries, but also, vigorously enough, in the British Isles as well.

At the outset, it will be discovered that there is no full range of diseases or physical ills in the tales, nor, as a matter of fact, can there be found even a representative budget of them. Maladies, where mentioned, are either vague, such as the hero's being sick, or love sick; or, they deal with more drastic ailments such as his being blind, maimed, or snake bitten. It is apparently not within the economy of the folk tale, with its sharp outlines, its swift-moving narrative, and its black-white literary technique, to mention the hero's or the heroine's having something so trivial, say, as a headache or a sore throat. By the same token, since great handicaps are involved, the hero might be far more likely to suffer from leprosy, or the falling sickness than from asthma, measles, or the toothache.

This paper does not purport to constitute a complete list of diseases and unusual physical states of being encountered in folk tales, together with cures and prescribed measures for their alleviation or removal. Rather, as a sampling, it will attempt to show how medical problems are dealt with when they do occur. Perhaps the crucial point of the paper will be to show, as I have indicated above, how folk medical belief and practice are adapted, by and large, to the needs of the tale. In every assessment of folk medicine in a tale one is faced with the essential dilemma that has already been stated, namely, the problem of deciding whether the item in question accords with folk medical practice, or whether the cure is effected by external folk tale magic. This task would hardly repay the doing if it were to serve no larger end. At issue here, as I see it, are notions put forward by Kahlo, Röhrich, and others, having to do with the essential truth and reality that are to be found in folk tales, on the one hand, and the views of Lüthi and his confrères, on the other, as they relate to folk narrative and fiction in basically literary terms, where facts and realism are often sacrificed for the demands of narrative. In terms of the underlying motive force that makes a story a story, it is the magic of the tale, and particularly the marvel, that steer the tale in the direction of fancy, and even of caprice—into the area of folk literature, fiction, and romance, more than into the more earthy reaches of folklore proper. Folk medical practice itself is of this more prosaic and practical realm.

In singling out medical matters for discussion, I have naturally avoided maladies and unusual physical states, including death itself, which clearly fall outside conventional folk medical practice. The raising of the dead by water fetched from a magic fountain at the end of the world, for example, would not come within our purview. Nor would the curing of a love-sick princess by the coming of a destined suitor, or, for that matter, the rescue of Little Red Riding Hood from the belly of the wolf. Likewise, in the case of "Faithful John" ("Der treue Johannes"), the sacrifice of the royal couple's two sons to restore to life the faithful servant from a state of petrification, is not within the compass of folk medicine. It is clearly a folk tale fiction, even though there may be a very distant kinship between petrification and what is medically known, nowadays, as muscular distrophy. On the other hand, the closely related curing of leprosy by blood sacrifice has a long tradition in the Mediterranean world, and is a fit subject for folk medical discussion, whether for leprosy or for other ailments. The use of human blood, gained in every conceivable way, including the sacrificial blood of persons brought to the headman's axe, has continued to our own time.

In the absence of a well-rounded body of ailments and cures

from folk medicine proper, the temptation is great to treat magical cures involving maladies induced, among other ways, by the creatures of lower mythology. Folk medicine, however, is one thing, fairy disenchantment and release from evil power, quite another. The difference between the two can be clearly seen in an English folk tale communicated to me by Katharine Mary Briggs. In this tale, "Princess Flora," a changeling is disenchanted by being dowsed with boiling water in which elder twigs, onions, and blackthorn berries have been steeped. The ingredients, including hot water, to be sure, are familiar in the folk pharmacopeia, but the violence of the treatment, and a peculiar external magic bring about the miracle of restoration, not the gradual natural healing and betterment that one would expect in a folk medical regimen.

Madness is a category of illness somewhere between common sickness and fairy enchantment, but I have not found ready examples in collections of tales available to me while away from my home base. I shall leave this interesting field of enquiry to psychiatrists interested in folk tales, and hope that they may fruitfully extend upon the work of Laistner, Friedrich Ranke, Peuckert, and others.

Let us look now at some specific examples of curing and curative practice in folk tales. The consuming of foods to promote health, virility, and long life is an area of folk belief that falls into the realm of folk medicine. The old proverb, "An apple a day keeps the doctor away," finds embodiment in a prophecy in "The Griffin Bird" ("Der Vogel Greif"), that a girl will eat herself well on apples. There is, however, no discussion of apples themselves as a health-promoting food. Aarne-Thompson tale-type No. 708 involves an apple, albeit a magic apple, in conception. The association of the apple with love and fertility is as old as Eden. In this same general connection there is, in an Armenian folktale, "The Magic Horse" (Hoogasian-Villa, No. 14), a fine example of the use of apples in rejuvenation.

Jungbauer, following Seyfarth and other writers, has called attention to areas of folk medicine where man has patterned after animals in caring for himself, licking or sucking his wounds, rolling or passing through brush to rid himself of vermin, and the like. Dr. C. L. Jarvis, American country doctor who has written a best seller on folk medicine, and other writers, too, assert, for example, that animals somehow maintain a balanced regimen, and that nature has endowed them with an instinctive sense of remedies through diet—a harmonious balance of grasses, berries, herbs, etc., as it were. Dogs, for example, are known instinctively to eat grass when sick, and this observation has become a commonplace in veterinary medicine as well as in the folk mind. A fanciful extension upon this doctrine would be the proposition that animals could seek out, pluck, and administer useful healing plants to other animals, whether as food, drink, or by external application. This last named faculty, marvellous in conception as it is, constitutes the main point of Grimm 16, "The Snake's Three Leaves" ("Die drei Schlangenblätter"), where an observant spouse, watching over his dead mate, adapts a procedure employed by a snake to cure a fellow reptile. Just as the snake applies healing herbs to the severed parts of his comrade, the man restores his wife to life by placing these selfsame sanative plants on her mouth and on her two eyes. In an Italian version of this same tale the secret is learned from a dragon who uses an herb on its neck to rejoin its severed head.

The application of animal cures and curative practices to the human sphere is a branch of folk medicine in need of further study. Insight into this fascinating relationship can be gained by a study of the Armenian folk tale of "Lochman Hehkeem, the Great Healer" (Hoogasian-Villa, No. 98), whose knowledge of herbs was conferred by the king of the snakes. That this tale, and related folk tales involving snakes as purveyors of herbal and other medical wisdom owes much to the early association of the snake with the healer's art, and medical lore generally must certainly be assumed. The real problem is how early in human thought and history these ideas took shape and how widely, and by what means, they spread. Involved are not merely matters of health and medicine, but notions of fertility, rejuvenation, and eternal life itself.

A genuine folk medical item dealing with animals as causative agents of disease is found in Grimm 165, "The Griffin Bird" ("Der Vogel Greif"), where a common toad, using a girl's hair to make its nest, causes her to fall ill. This is, of course, a variation on the widely known folk belief that birds using one's hair combings to make a nest bring on headache in the person whose hair has been thus used. Yet another folk medical prescription involving a toad is found in Zaunert's collection of tales from the Danubian country. Here, in the tale, "The Lie and the Truth" ("Die Lüge und die Wahrheit"), the sick princess is fed pulverized toad, which has been a staple among animal simples in western Europe from early times to the present.

As we return now to points raised earlier in the talk, there is in the folk tale of "Sleeping Beauty" an excellent illustration of a magical cure of an unnatural bodily state. Be it noted, too, that the hundred year's sleep was also brought on by supernatural means. Instead of resorting to the materia medica of the folk to rouse the sleeping princess, and then claim her as a lover, the hero restores her from her magic sleep by a kiss and accomplishes both purposes at once. Within the spirit of the tale it would have been incongruous, to say the least, and out of all taste in a highly romantic tale, to have applied some of the cures prescribed for the so-called "drousie diseases called coma and lethargy," as contained, say, in John Moncrief's *The Poor Man's Physician*, Edinburgh, 1716. "1. The fume of Brimstone doth raise from sleep. 2. The hairs of a Goat burnt; or, the horn of a Deer or Goat burnt, are most strong for raising up of him, who is in a deep sleep." Even a more romantic sounding cure, and one less offensive than the three treatments suggested, namely, "the fume or smoak *(sic)* of white Amber is excellent," would still lack greatly in the romantic and magical quality necessary to sustain the mood of the tale. Under the circumstances one is wont to think that even though the teller of tale had known these folk medical prescriptions for deep sleep and a comatose condition, or any treatments like them, he would as an artist in folk narrative inevitably have rejected them. He would have done so on grounds of the complete unsuitability of the treatment. If for any reason he could not have used the familiar motif of the disenchanting kiss, he would have devised something in general keeping with the spirit of the tale such as whispering sweetly into the sleeper's ears, touching her eyes gently, or something of the sort.

Having used one of the best known of all the Grimm tales to illustrate the subordination of folk medical lore to the artistic needs of the folk tale, I can now take an equally well-known tale to illustrate a very prosaic and practical course of treatment where a more elaborate and engaging means might have easily been chosen. In "Snow White" the poison apple is not charmed away, rendered harmless, or neutralized by special herbs brought by some wise old granny woman—it is simply jarred loose from Snow White's throat when the coffin bearers stumble over a shrub.

Here then in these last two famous tales we have seen both tendencies at work, the elaborate and the fanciful, on the one hand, and the prosaic and practical on the other. In summary, however, I must reiterate the point that magical and fanciful kinds of curative practice seem to predominate in the folk tale, not measures born of a rudimentary kind of medical science based on the long practice and enriching experience of folk medical practitioners.

If one could hope for some degree of realism in folk tales, and were still unwilling to see the artistic values and the essential fantasy of the tales suffer, one might reasonably expect, I think, to see occasional touches of folk medical realism introduced where appropriate.

Instead of saying that the wise old woman took herbs and placed them on the patient's wound, or upon his blind eyes, one might expect, with reason, an occasional reference to herbs plucked at midnight, or herbs with the morning dew still upon them. Other cogent observations from popular botany and herb-gathering practice would suggest themselves region by region where the tales are told. On the other hand, anyone interested in the essentially horizontal movement of the tale, and its rapid sweep, would certainly not countenance the impeding of the narrative flow by a recitation of other details of herb gathering, such as "gathered on a fasting stomach by a blameless youth of seven at dawn on St. Jutta's Day," or other equally interesting information and lore that is firmly believed and practiced by herb gatherers and those who patronize them.

I hope in the foregoing remarks to have sharpened for one small area of human activity and folklore our focus on how the folk tale utilizes, or fails to utilize, the essential materials of folklore itself. At the very least, I trust that these adumbrations will have thrown light on the relationship of folk literature to those branches of the discipline of folklore which are concerned with the more prosaic and common areas of human thought and action. I do not suggest a basic dichotomy in method and purpose between the folk tale and other branches of folklore, notably folk belief and custom, but rather a different emphasis in the handling of the same or similar human materials.

21
The Curing of Blindness In Folk Tales*

The treatment and cure of disease in folk tales, as I have pointed out in a recent paper,[1] rests essentially on two different kinds of medical principles: (1) on accepted folk medical therapeutic measures, and (2) on magical remedies that accord with the general spirit of folk tales and the world of magic and marvel in which they move. Resort to magical cures is far more common than the utilization of procedures well established in folk medicine. The situation generally prevailing in curing of disease in folk tales is not radically different with regard to the cure of blindness, but in this latter case the reasons for magical cures and magical intervention are more compelling, the cure of blindness itself being almost always regarded as one of the miracles of medicine, and often a miracle wrought by God himself, or by the Virgin Mary.[2] In honoring a man, who, in addition to being one of our greatest folk tale scholars, is also an expert in the field of folk medicine, I shall try to show in this brief essay that in addition to the curing of blindness by religious miracles and outright medical magic, there is some resort to what might be regarded as usual curative procedures for blindness, however limited in scope. As we shall see, cures are usually achieved by the application of plant and animal simples,

*This article originally appeared in *Volksüberlieferung. Festschrift für Kurt Ranke zur Vollendung des 60. Lebensjahres.* Ed. Fritz Harkort. Göttingen: Verlag Otto Schwartz & Co., 1968, pp. 81–87. Permission to reprint has been given by the publishers.

saliva, magical water and dew, and other substances of the folk pharmocopeia. As one would suspect, internal build-up of the neural system serving the eyes is completely missing, so is modern manipulative therapy, apart from healing by touch and rubbing. Verbal adjuration is not widely employed, but there are some excellent examples from Israel,[3] reported by Noy. Taking all of these kinds of cures into account, one must still conclude that the range of cures for blindness found in folk tales, and in curing practice, is rather limited as compared with curative practice in folk medicine itself.

In the following representations I shall not attempt to differentiate the causes of blindness, except as these reasons may indicate the kind of a cure needed, as for example in cases where the eyes have been removed and thus must be replaced. Apart from natural blindness in the tales, accidental blindness is noted, as in the piercing of the eyes by thorns;[4] also, blindness is brought on by overmuch weeping.[5] Likewise, in legends, but also in tales, blindness is magically induced in the sense of a person's being stricken blind. This drastic punishment is most often inflicted as a curse for viewing such forbidden things as the deity or holy of holies,[6] the beauties of heaven or some earthly paradise, or various kinds of sacred and magical objects not exposed to profane gaze. Furthermore, the curse extends to seeing ghosts, to spying on fairy folk and their kin at work and at play,[7] and to gazing on nude women.[8]

Blinding inflicted as a physical punishment involves the piercing or searing of eyeballs, the introduction of injurious substances to the eyes, or the outright removal of the eyes from their sockets, whether by cutting or gouging. The pecking out of one's eyes by birds is done either as a punishment, or it may be held out, albeit humorously, as a threat or fate hanging over those who do not pay proper attention to the tale teller, or who are loathe to believe the tale itself. Blinding by moonlight is a folk belief, and if it occurs in folk narrative at all, it would be more likely to appear in legends.[9] The borrowing and stealing of eyes is beyond the range of the present discussion.

Starting with plant cures, which by and large constitute the principal therapeutic agents employed in folk medicine, we may consider the use of trees, leaves, barks, flowers, moss, and other vegetable products in the curing of blindness.[10] In one folk tale of considerable antiquity, known as "Truth and Falsehood," or "The Two Travelers," and dealing with blinding and blindness, vegetable products of all kinds constitute prominent secret cures for blindness which the victim overhears from birds, animals, robbers, the devil, fairy folk, and other creatures of lower mythology who have expert knowledge in medical matters.[11] In a French text from Haute-Bretagne, for example, the victim overhears a tiger telling a bear and a monkey that the bark of an oak tree nearby, rubbed on the eyes, will cure blindness. After two applications sight is restored better than before.[12] In a mediaeval tale the devil himself reveals that an herb under a tree near where the hapless victim finds himself, will, if placed on the pierced and bleeding eyes, draw away the blood and restore the sight.[13] In a Chilean tale a blind king who has taken refuge in a cave for the night, hears from robbers who have come to the cave to divide their booty that a decoction made from a shrub hanging from the roof of a cave by boiling it in water will cure him.[14] In a Danish variant of the same tale, the victim of blinding in exchange for food simply applies the leaves of a tree located at a crossroads where the fox, the bear, and the lion have met on Walpurgis Eve to discuss matters of importance.[15] The use of trees themselves, as distinct from bark, leaves, and the like, is seen in a Siberian tale in which two aspen trees, capable of restoring hearing and sight, are rubbed against the empty eye sockets.[16] Striking one's head against a tree to cure blindness is seen in an Indic tale, in which a tiger whose eyes have been pecked out by a crane, strikes its head against an akauna tree, the juice of the tree itself not having been fully efficacious.[17]

In a Lithuanian tale, moss found between the rocks is used to restore the sight of a victim blinded by his friend. The victim, following the instruction overheard from the wolf as told to a mouse, rubs the moss on his eyes and is cured.[18] In Ceylon blindness is cured by rubbing the eyes with a flower.[19] The placing of the Apple of Life upon the eyes, in a Greek tale, falls more into the realm of magical cures, and is to be likened with the use of the Water of Life,[20] a curative agent which will be taken up later.

Blinding of humans by the dung of bats, birds, and other animals,[21] by the effluvia of skunks, and the venom of serpents is encountered more in folklore than in folk tales proper; likewise the blinding of people by the dust and pollens of puffballs and other kinds of plants.[22] Curing by animal products goes back, in legend, to Old Testament times, and the tale of Tobit in the Apocrypha, where the gall of a fish was used to cure the just man's eyes.[23] In a version of the "Two Travelers" from the

Near East, the hide of a blue goat is used to cure blindness.[24] Farther east, in India, the warm dung of the chicks of a bihangama bird, retrieved from a land beyond seven oceans and thirteen rivers, is applied to the eyeballs of the blind king.[25] The use of a griffin feather, but without details as to how it is employed, is reported from Italy.[26] Shock therapy, almost in the sense of disenchantment, is seen in a German tale, whereby a live toad is struck with such force against the eyes three times, that a cure is promised when the toad bursts.[27]

Water as a natural cleansing and curing agent is fairly widespread in tales where the curing of the blind is involved. For this purpose water is applied to the eyes from springs, brooks and streams, wells, and fountains, including fountains and sources where the fabled Water of Life is to be found.[28] As we shall see later, dew is also thought to possess healing properties, and folktale tellers often mention the curative properties of the night dew in connection with the curing of the blind. From the Eastern Mediterranean there is a Greek tale of a man blinded by sticks and a princess who has been blinded by a needle, who are cured by washing in the water of a certain ditch. As in most tales of the Aa-Th 613 cycle, the stream is near the place where the information is overheard, in this particular case, from the devil himself.[29] Similar information gained from fairies brings about the healing of a blind queen with water from a running brook in a tale from Quebec.[30] Blind animals plunging into streams to cure themselves serve to commend these healing waters to blind humans in tales from Germany.[31] In variants of "The Two Travelers," wells or sources found at the foot of trees, or close by, where the message is overheard, cure the blind, as the following representative tales show.[32] Among the Wendic peoples of Lusatia the healing water comes from a fountain or well under the gallows.[33] In an unrelated Gypsy tale, blindness is cured by the application of healing water to the eyes by means of a goose feather.[34] A more fanciful kind of water, namely the Water of Life,[35] is used by fairies to restore sight,[36] while an Armenian tale collected in Detroit speaks of a special pool of water in which the sun rises and sets as being efficacious for the treatment of blindness.[37]

Although oil and other unguents are well-known palliative agents, little mention is made of them in folk tales in the curing of eye disorders.[38] In the familiar pattern of overheard medical wisdom, a blind brother, abandoned in the woods, climbs a tree and overhears a witch proclaim the virtues of a certain kind of oil beneath the tree for the curing of blindness.[39] Furthermore, in Transylvania a salve is applied to the eyes, but its contents are not divulged.[40]

In the "Two Travelers" cycle, as well as in other tales, magic dew effects a cure of blindness. This well-known and highly efficacious folk remedy may be found under trees following the night on which the secret is made known,[41] or it may be found on a gallows,[42] or a wayside cross.[43] Other details assuring the potency of the dew are seen in the following references to propitious times for the recovery of dew: Norway: St. John's Eve;[44] Hungary: night of a new moon cripples roll in the dew and the blind wash their eyes in it;[45] Mexico: the first week of April.[46]

By the laws of sympathetic magic tears are also used to heal blindness. The best known example is found in Grimm 12, "Rapunzel," where the heroine's tears, falling into the blinded eyes of her lover, restore his sight.[47] In the *Vetalapancavimsati* the tears of a mare are said to restore sight.[48] The tears of a serpent restore a girl's gouged out eyes to their sockets in a tale from Chile involving a child that was on friendly terms with the snake by virtue of having cared for it while the creature was young. The precise nature of the miracle is difficult to follow, but contagious magic is involved, since the girl has hold of the serpent's eyes with her hands as his tears shower over her to restore her own lost eyes.[49] Saliva, a kindred substance, is also known, going back to antiquity, where saliva was spit into the eyes of the blind. This practice, and the use of saliva generally, are widely known in folk medicine, but not often encountered in folk tales. In an unusual case recorded in a Russian folk tale, however, eyes that have been gouged out, are replaced after having been spat upon.[50] In an African folk tale a snake licks the eyes of a blind king to restore his sight.[51] In a Neapolitan tale, a child begotten by a snake that crawled into her mother's womb is blinded out of jealousy when she is chosen to wife by the king of Naples. Wandering in the woods in despair, and about to commit suicide, the girl comes upon the snake who places wondrous healing herbs on her eyes and cures her.[52]

In addition to the human secretions mentioned, namely tears and saliva, human blood is used in the curing of blindness. In the *Vetalapancavimsati* a son is able to cure his father's blindness, brought on by overmuch weeping, by stroking his father's eyes with blood from his own finger.[53] Mother's milk, widely used as a cleansing and healing agent for the eyes of infants, is also used for eye maladies generally,[54] but is not encountered in folk tale accounts of the treatment and cure of the blind. The use of earth or clay, mixed either with water to make an ointment, or with spittle itself, is little encountered in folk tales dealing with the curing of the blind. This treatment, made famous by Jesus himself,[55] is followed in a folk tale from Hungary.[56] Various kinds of stones are used for the treatment of blindness and other eye disorders, but this folk medical usage is not reflected in folk tales so far as I have been able to determine. Worth noting here, however, is a French legend having to do with the swallow, a bird noted for its connection with blindness. According to the legend, the swallow is able to find on the beach a pebble that has the power to cure blindness. In order to gain such a stone for their own use, peasants put out the eyes of fledgling swallows so that the mother will go in search of the magical stone to cure her brood. After having applied the stone to the eyes of her offspring, she will drop the stone onto a red cloth placed beneath the tree, mistaking the cloth for fire.[57] Among other kinds of objects placed on the eyes, or in the eyes, as a treatment for blindness, one finds the so-called Necklace of Life,[58] sand,[59] and ashes.[60] In areas as far removed from each other as Ireland and the Caucasus, magical pieces of cloth, including gold cloth, are either placed over the eyes, or the eyes are rubbed with them.[61]

Healing by touch, which has religious overtones, and the rubbing of the eyes of the blind, involve well-known folk curative measures.[62] In an Armenian tale collected in Detroit, for instance, a princess in bird form needs only to place her hands on the eyes of the blind king to heal him.[63] In the Caucasus a blind king is cured merely by the stroking of his eyes on the part of the Virgin Queen.[64]

NOTES

1. "Curative Practice in Folk Tales" (in: Fabula, Zeitschrift für Erzählforschung, Bd. 9, Berlin 1967, p. 264–269), delivered before a special meeting of the International Society for Folk-Narrative Research (Liblice, Czechoslovakia, Sept. 3, 1966). For help in preparing this present paper I am indebted to my colleagues Frederic C. Tubach and Yolando Pino-Saavedra. I also wish to thank Reba Bass and Marina Bokelman.

2. Joseph Klapper, *Erzählungen des Mittelalters,* Breslau 1914, p. 96, Nr. 82. (= Wort und Brauch, Bd. 12.)

3. Repeating the words, "Dieu d'Abraham, Dieu d'Isaac et Dieu de Jacob," the victim is cured of his blindness. Dov Noy, *Contes populaires racontés par des Juifs du Maroc,* Jerusalem 1965, p. 73. —A related cure involves the saying of these same words and the plunging of the head of the victim into healing waters (p. 72). In a third example, a blind pigeon is cured by placing a

leaf from a tree on its eyes, and a blind youth is healed by doing likewise, aiding the process by repeating three times, "Dieu est dans le ciel!" (p. 70–71). Cf. *Handwörterbuch des deutschen Aberglaubens*, hrsg. von Hanns Bächtold-Stäubli und Eduard von Hoffmann-Krayer, 10 vols., Berlin und Leipzig 1927–1942, vol. 1 p. 717, s.v. "Augensegen." [Hereinafter cited HDA.]

4. An example of this is seen in the prince in "Rapunzel," who, after jumping from the tower, falls among thorns and briars, thus blinding himself. Jacob und Wilhelm Grimm, Kinder- und Hausmärchen, Bd. 1, Nr. 12. (Hereinafter cited Grimm, KHM).

5. Grimm, KHM, No. 44, "Der Gevatter Tod."

6. HDA, I p. 711.

7. HDA, I p. 711.

8. E. Sidney Hartland, Peeping Tom and Lady Godiva; in: Folk-Lore, a quarterly review of myth, tradition, institution, and custom, vol. I (London 1890), p. 207–226.—HDA, VI, p. 839, *passim*.

9. For detailed information on blinding and blindness in folk tales the reader is directed to the excellent article on "Blendung" and "Blindheit, blind" in: Lutz Mackensen und Joh. Bolte, *Handworterbuch des deutschen Märchens*, 2 Bde., Berlin 1930–1940, I, p. 270–277 (Hereinafter cited HDM.) Further insight, particularly throughout folklore generally, may be gained from the entries under "blenden" and "blind" in HDA, I, p. 1392 ff. ("blenden"), I, p. 708 ff. ("Augenkrankheiten: blind").

10. HDM, I, p. 274.

11. See Grimm, KHM, Nr. 107, and the notes in Bolte-Polívka, II, p. 468–482.—Cf. AT 613.

12. Ariane de Félice, *Contes de Haute-Bretagne*, Paris 1954, No. 8 "La belle Kévale." For other French texts and those from the French-speaking world, see Paul Delarue and Marie-Louise Tenèze, *Le Conte Populaire Français,* vol. 2, Paris 1963, No. 515, with reference to AT 613.

13. Albert Wesselski, *Märchen des Mittelalters,* Berlin 1925. p. 44–45. With sight restored, the hero later heals a blind princess. Wesselski contains excellent notes on the early history of this story.

14. Yolando Pino-Saavedra, *Chilenische Volksmärchen* (= Märchen der Weltliterature), Düsseldorf-Köln, 1964, p. 104–105, Nr. 18 "Der reiche und der arme Gevatter."

15. Laurits Bodker, *Dänische Volksmärchen* (= Märchen der Weltliteratur), Düsseldorf-Köln, 1964, p. 278. Cf. J. Rivière, *Contes Populaires de la Kabylie*, Paris 1882, as cited in W. A. Clouston, *Popular Tales and Fictions,* 2 vols., Edinburgh and London 1887, I, p. 252. The blind person is directed by a bird to apply a leaf to his eyes.

16. C. Fillingham Coxwell, *Siberian and Other Folk-Tales,* London 1925, p. 356–357.

17. A. Campbell, *Santal Folk Tales,* transl. by Pokhuria, London 1892, p. 95. Cf. Thompson-Balys, F952.4.

18. Edmund Veckenstedt, *Die Mythen, Sagen und Legenden der Zamaiten* [*Litauer*], 2 vols., Heidelberg 1883, I, 163 Nr. 23 "Die Wahrheit und die Ungerechtigkeit." At the level of legend, and hence somewhat nearer actual folk medical practice, a French legend tells of the use of moss growing on an oak to cure the blind. Paul Sébillot, *Le Folk-Lore de France,* 4 vols., Paris 1904–1907, III p. 530.

19. Henry Parker, *Village Folk-Tales of Ceylon,* 3 vols., London 1910–1914, II, p. 358–359.

20. R. M. Dawkins, *Modern Greek Folk Tales,* Oxford, 1953, p. 155.

21. Cf. HDA, I, p. 708.

22. Cf. HDA, I, p. 708.

23. Bible, O. T., Tobit VI:9 and XI:2–13. For a treatment of these materials in folk tale, see Sven Liljeblad, *Die Tobiasgeschichte und andere Märchen mit toten Helfern,* Lund 1927.

24. Wilhelm Geiger und Ernst Kuhn, *Grundriß der iranischen Philologie,* I Abt. 2, Straßburg 1895, p. 333.

25. Lal Bahari Day, *Folk-Tales of Bengal,* London 1883, p. 219. Belief in bird dung for the curing of blindness is also found among the Eskimo. *Cf. Journal of American Folklore,* III (Boston and New York 1890), p. 8.

26. Thomas F. Crane, *Italian Popular Tales,* New York 1889, p. 40–41.

27. Paul Zaunert, *Deutsche Märchen seit Grimm* (= Märchen der Weltliteratur), 2 vols., Jena 1922–1923, I, p. 336.

28. HDM, I, p. 274.

29. Georgios A. Megas, *Griechische Volksmärchen* (= Märchen der Weltliteratur), Düsseldorf und Köln 1965, p. 241–242.

30. Soeur Marie-Ursule, "Civilisation traditionnelle des Lavalois"; in: *Les Archives de Folklore,* V–VII (Quebec 1951), p. 226–227.

31. Kurt Ranke, *Schleswig-Holsteinische Volksmärchen,* Bd. 2, Kiel 1958, p. 339–340; Zaunert, Seit Grimm, Bd. 1, p. 255. Cf. HDM, I, p. 274.

32. Wuk Stephanowitsch Karadschitsch, *Volksmärchen der Serben,* Berlin 1854, p. 129 (victim overhears a Vila); Anders Allardt, *Sagor i Urval* (= Finlands Svenska Folkdigtning), 2 vols., Helsingfors 1917–1920, I, p. 447–448; Juan B. Rael, *Cuentos Españoles de Colorado* y de *Nuevo Méjico,* 2 vols., Stanford / Cal., II, p. 206–207; Joseph Médard Carrière, *Tales from the French Folk-Lore of Missouri,* Evanston and Chicago 1937, p. 208–212.

33. Leopold Haupt und Johann Ernst Schmaler, *Volkslieder der Wenden in der Ober- und Niederlausitz,* Grimma 1841–1843, p. 183.

34. Dora E. Yates, *A Book of Gypsy Folk-Tales,* London 1948, p. 62.

35. HDA, V, p. 972 ff., s.v. "Lebenswasser." Cf. also IV, p. 1349 ff.; HDM, I, p. 275.

36. R. M. Dawkins, *Modern Greek in Asia Minor,* London 1916, p. 45. Cf. B. Schmidt, *Griechische Märchen, Sagen und Volkslieder,* Leipzig 1877, No. 18 (not verified).

37. Susie Hoogasian-Villa, *100 Armenian Tales and Their Folkloristic Relevance,* Detroit 1966, p. 533 (unpublished version).

38. Cf. HDM, I, p. 276.

39. Christian Schneller, *Märchen und Sagen aus Wälschtirol, ein Beitrag zur deutschen Sagenkunde,* Innsbruck 1867, p. 18–19.

40. Heinrich von Wlislocki, *Märchen und Sagen der Bukowinaer und die Siebenbürger Armenier,* Hamburg 1891, p. 128.

41. Johannes Wilhelm Wolf, *Deutsche Märchen und Sagen,* Leipzig 1845, p. 26; Wilhelm Wisser, *Wat Grotmoder vertellt, ostholsteinische Volksmärchen,* Jena 1909, II, p. 29–30; J. Jegerlehner, *Sagen und Märchen aus Oberwallis* (= Schriften der Schweizerischen Gesellschaft für Volkskunde, IX), Basel, 1913, p. 125; A. J. Witteryck, *Oude Westvlaamsche Volkvertelsels,* Brugge-Brussel 1946, p. 37–38; *Journal of American Folklore,* vol. 34 (1921), p. 76 (Antigua, British West Indies). Cf. HDM, I, p. 274 + 276.

42. Grimm, KHM, Nr. 107 "The Two Travelers."

43. Gyula Ortutay, *Ungarische Volksmärchen,* Berlin 1957, p. 421–422.

44. George Webbe Dasent, *Popular Tales from the Norse,* Edinburgh 1881, p. 5.

45. William Henry Jones and Lewis L. Kropf, *The Folk-Tales of the Magyars* (= Publications of the Folk-Lore Society, XIII), London, 1889, p. 37.

46. Gabriel Córdova, *Magic Tales of Mexiko,* El Paso 1951, p. 10–12.

47. Grimm, KHM Nr. 12. Cf. HDM, I, p. 276. In Nebraska it is said that a baby's first tear will cure a man of blindness. Pauline Monette Black, *Nebraska Folk Cures* (= University of Nebraska Studies in Language Literature and Criticism, XV), Lincoln 1935, 16 No. 27.

48. Walter Ruben, *Ozean der Märchenströme,* I. *Die 25 Erzählungen des Dämons* (Vetalapancavimsati) [= FF Communications, No. 133], Helsinki 1944, p. 214, No. 22b.

49. Yolando Pino-Saavedra, *Cuentos folklóricos de Chile,* 3 vols., Santiago 1960–1963, III, p. 230–232.

50. Norbert Guterman, *Russian Fairy Tales,* New York 1945, p. 329. For historical examples of physicians using spittle, see William George Black, *Folk-Medicine, a Chapter in the History of Culture* (= Publications of the Folk-Lore Society, XII), London 1883, p. 181.

51. Harold von Sicard, *Ngano dze Cikaranga, Karangamärchen* (= Studia Ethnographica Upsaliensia, XXIII), Uppsala 1965, p. 10. For other African examples of the use of snakes in curing blindness see *Journal of American Folklore,* LXVIII (1955), p. 309.

52. *The Facetious Nights of Giovanni Francesco Straparola,* transl. by W. G. Waters, 4 vols., London 1891, Night the Third, The Third Fable.

53. Ruben, Märchenströme, 214 No. 22a. Cf. HDM, I, 276.

54. HDA, VI, p. 277 ff. Cf. Pliny, *Natural History,* Book 28, 72; *Frank C. Brown Collection of North Carolina Folklore,* 7 vols., Durham, North Carolina, (1952–1964), VI, No. 885.

55. Bible, N. T., John IX: 6. Cf. HDM, I, p. 274.

56. Jones and Kropf, Magyars, p. 152–153.

57. W. Branch Johnson, *Folktales of Normandy,* London 1929, p. 110.

58. Hoogasian-Villa, 100 Armenian Tales, p.95.

59. James Drummond Anderson, *A Collection of Kachári Folk-Tales and Rhymes,* Shillong 1895, pp. 49–50.

60. [Veckenstedts] *Zeitschrift für Volkskunde,* II (1889), p. 264–265 (Albania).

61. Adeline Rittershaus, *Die neuisländischen Volksmärchen,* Halle 1902, p. 254; Adolf Dirr, *Caucasian Folk-Tales,* transl. by Lucy Menzies, New York 1925, p. 146 (a fox's gold cloth).

62. Cf. HDM, I, p. 276.

63. Hoogasian-Villa, 100 Armenian Tales, p. 465.

64. Dirr, Kaukasische Märchen, p. 91. For hoodoo curing of the blind by rubbing, see Harry Middleton Hyatt, *Folk-Lore from Adams County Illinois,* New York 1935, No. 9105.

22
Folk Medical Magic and Symbolism in the West*

The collecting of folk medicine in the West has not been under way long enough to permit anything approaching a full survey of the causes and cures of disease and matters having to do with the medical aspects of the life cycle, particularly with birth and death. Even so, there is at hand a sufficiently representative body of medical folklore to constitute at least an adumbration of the kinds of material that still await the hand of the collector in the sprawling country beyond the Mississippi.[1] It is my purpose here to concentrate on the more neglected areas of folk medical study in the West, namely magical medicine and folk medical symbolism as it derives from elementary forms of magic.

In putting this paper together, I have drawn on archival material for California and other western states that has been accumulating from student collectanea for the past fifteen or twenty years in the Archive of California and Western Folklore at the University of California at Los Angeles. Systematic collecting in Utah, also through students, has been undertaken by my colleague at the University of Utah, Professor Anthon S. Cannon, who is collaborating with me in the preparation of the Utah volume tributary to the Dictionary of American Popular Beliefs and Superstitions. The extensive Austin and Alta Fife

*This article originally appeared in *Forms upon the Frontier.* Ed. Austin and Alta Fife and Henry H. Glassie, Utah State University, Monograph Series, XVI, No. 2, April 1969, pp. 103–118. Permission to reprint has been given by the editors and by the Utah State University Press.

collections, made in Moab, Utah, in 1953, have also been at my disposal. To the heavy unpublished material from California and Utah have been added much lighter samplings from other western states, but the footnotes to this paper contain a backup of published material from older parts of the country, particularly from the eastern seaboard and the South. (In the main, these references are found in the notes to the entries from the Brown Collection.) For the purposes of defining the West, I am including all states west of the Mississippi, including Minnesota, when it has served my purposes to do so. In taking only unpublished material to illustrate magical folk medicine I have sought to show field collectors that it is still possible to collect magical medical lore in the West in addition to turning up accounts of the use of plant and animal simples, the preparation and administration of various kinds of medicines, teas, and tonics, the application of different sorts of dressings and poultices, and resort to manipulative therapy of one kind and another.

Homeopathic principles of medicine are well known,[2] and are based on analogic magic,[3] wherein it is assumed that external similarity rests on what would seem to be an apparent internal connection and a basic inner unity and dependence. Under this premise, cures are undertaken on the theory that similar things are cured by similar means, as set forth in the celebrated Latin phrase, *similia similibus curantur.*[4]

Though these notions were known in antiquity, it remained for later medical practitioners such as the Italian physician Jean Baptiste Porta to state these principles of unity in more specific terms. Porta, among other things, enunciated the "doctrine of signatures," whereby the efficacy of a plant for the cure of a certain malady could be assessed in terms of its shape, its color, its appendages, and the essences secreted as they related to the diseased part or the impeded function.[5] These simple preliminary observations on magic and symbolism, then, will prepare us for assorted folk medical notions that involve homeopathy which are still to be found in the West.

Similarity of shape is seen in a Utah belief, supported by seven texts from different parts of Salt Lake County, that walnuts are good for diseases of the brain, one informant declaring that the efficacy rested in the fact that "the meat of the nut looks like the brain, and the shell resembles the skull."[6] Also from Salt Lake County comes a variation on the doctrine of signatures affecting shape and relative position, namely, the belief that the tops of plants should be used to cure diseases of the head, while the roots of plants should be utilized for maladies of the legs.[7] Kissing a pain better is an age-old custom of the nursery employed by mothers to assure children that the pain will go away. The kissing of a person's thumb when he stubs his toe, rests on an extension of the principles of analogy stated above, and is made necessary by the fact that a person is actually unable to kiss his own toe. Examples of this whimsical notion come from California, one entry being possibly of ultimate Polish provenience. The other allusion comes from Helena, Montana.

The use of appropriate colors to combat disease is seen in the following examples from western states: in Missouri, South Dakota, Washington, and Utah, a nosebleed is stanched by wearing either a red string,[8] red yarn,[9] a red handkerchief, or a red necklace about the neck. Two additional items from Utah prescribe carrying the red yarn or red string in one's pocket.

A Salt Lake doctor reports having heard many times in his practice that yellow jaundice should be treated with yellow drugs, on the theory that "yellow rids yellow."[10] A variation on this general prescription, also from Salt Lake, is the hanging of a carrot in the basement, which is supposed to absorb the jaundice as the carrot dries up.[11] Scarlet fever was treated in Utah by wrapping the patients up in scarlet blankets, and doctoring them with medicine scarlet or red in color.[12]

The curing of frostbite and other conditions brought on by cold are treated in their own terms in Minnesota, where frozen members are treated with snow, in Kansas, where frostbitten ears are likewise rubbed with snow.[13] and in Utah, where chilblains are combatted by the same agent that caused them, namely, snow.[14] In Los Angeles, for example, it is recommended that one swim in the ocean to combat a cold. In heat therapy, on the contrary, an old lady in Moab, Utah, reported to be a witch, cured burns by holding the wound over heat until it supposedly drew the heat out of the burn.[15] In Ogden, Utah, in an entry dating back to 1885, it was recommended that a hot stone be placed on the head of a person suffering from fever. This application supposedly caused the fever to leave.

The almost classical cure of a disease by the agent causing it, is seen in the well-known example of curing the bite of a mad dog by "the hair of the dog that bit you."[16] Three recent California examples and one from Oregon dating from 1915, attest to this old folk medical belief and practice, as do a spate of examples from Utah, including a prescription from Park City

(1930) to the effect that the mad dog be killed immediately so that the person bitten would not go insane. Two other Utah items employ this same primitive logic, one recommending the eating of a snake that has inflicted a bite, and the other, from Provo about 1900, merely dictating that the snake's head should be bitten off.[17]

The taking of children to chicken coops to let the chickens fly over them is reported from Arkansas and Oklahoma and is found also in two entries from California, one of which indicates that "when the chickens fly over the kids, they take the pox away."[18] In parts of California as widely separated as San Luis Obispo, Ojai, and Los Angeles, the eating of poison oak is supposed to convey a lasting immunity against skin poisoning by this plant.

Space precludes a treatment of the sympathetic principles related to the marking of unborn children, a situation, or course, in which contagious magic as well as homeopathic principles come into play.[19] I shall cite but a single example from the unpublished Fife collection. ". . . during the pregnancy the father or some close relative had an accident . . . and the child was born with a mark resembling the injury the father had." Here, you see, the child's most immediate connection, namely, the mother, is not mentioned at all. One might think of this as a secondary situation on which the analogy rests. Even so, a purely external event is magically communicated to the child by its mother.

The following four items—none related to each other—have in common only the sympathetic enlistment of a similar response, or the avoidance of an act that will induce a similar reaction. In Moab, Utah, for example, in order to get a child to fall asleep, it was prescribed that the person holding the child must herself yawn. In a California belief that probably came from Russia before 1900 it was feared that if a person swallowed string he would tie up his intestines. Another Utah example, and one involving contagious magic also, indicates that if a person carries the crutches of someone with a broken arm or leg, he or she too will be the next to break a limb. A New Mexico belief that if one has boils, and a menstruating woman comes into the room, the boils will get worse, rests on the notion that one ailing person can influence another adversely. It does not matter that the respective maladies have nothing whatsoever in common.

The ancient notion of treating the weapon that has inflicted a wound,[20] raised to a doctrine and widely advertised by Sir Kenelm Digby in 17th-century England, is seen in the West by the fact that lard or turpentine is put on a rusty nail after it has inflicted a puncture wound. Treatments of this kind are reported from Missouri and Oklahoma, and from three different parts of Utah.[21] The Salt Lake version is summed up in a neat prescription: "Treat the weapon that made the wound."[22]

Contrary measures, or a sort of reverse magic, are seen in the notion, for example, that playing with fire or matches will induce bed-wetting. Reports of this folk belief come from Utah, North Dakota, and New Mexico, the last-named instance stemming from the Latin-American tradition.[23] It must be noted that the principle of reversal, or *contraria contrariis*[24] as seen here, represents the cause of this noisome frailty in young children. Cures are seen in the combatting of a cold with hot drinks of various kinds, sweating, etc., etc. These are so common that I have not listed them. An unusual cure for sore throat—perhaps a bit of whimsy—involves reverse magic so extraordinary that one is tempted hardly to take it seriously. This cure from New Mexico prescribes rubbing Vicks Vaporub into the rectum to cure a sore throat.

Contagious magic opens up an even wider range of unusual folk medical beliefs and practices than those we have considered under homeopathic magic. All of these rest on the fundamental assumption that things once conjoined remain magically connected, even though dissevered.[25] In folk medicine the law of contact, and of contagion, almost invariably has to do with the magical divestment of disease, whereby the malady is passed off wholly, or in a part which still represents the whole. This is a corollary of contagious magic known under the Latin formulation *pars pro toto*.[26] In the ensuing discussions we shall see various manifestations of contagious magic. Intermingled will also be some symbolic cures not resting on actual contact. In handling material of this kind, one must bear in mind that contagious magic, as well as homeopathic magic, are part of the broader category of sympathetic magic.

Let us begin with the transference of disease.[27] The cure of venereal diseases by transmitting the malady to a virgin, as found elsewhere in the United States, but not widely,[28] is reported from Oakland and Hanford, California, for gonorrhea. A less sensational kind of transference is recommended from Montana for the cure of a cold, simply by passing it on to another person, and making a scapegoat of him. The transference of warts either to a willing or an unwary host is one of the commonplaces of magical transference of disease.[29] This is usually done outright by "sale." In various examples from Iowa, Nebraska, New Mexico, Utah, and California, the buyer usually pays a small sum of money, for instance, a penny, for each wart, or a dime. Contagious principles are not at work here,[30] except where the owner of the wart himself makes the sale, and pays out his own money to be freed of the wart. Under these circumstances the buyer, as in a California example, must bury the money to avoid getting the wart himself. Equally common with an outright sale is the use of a penny as a so-called *Zwischenträger,* or an intermediate agent.[31] Once rubbed on the wart, and hence impregnated with part of it, the coin may be thrown away, buried, or sold, as is seen in various practices from Iowa, North Dakota, Washington, Idaho, Utah, and California.[32] A common way of wishing the wart onto others is to cast it off in such a way that it will be picked up by another person, who is thus sure to contract the wart.[33] This traffic is seen in a riddance cure from Salt Lake.[34] A unique cure from Iowa, dating from 1902, and involving a reversal, is seen in the following prescription: "Pick out a special dime and rub it over the wart, and give it to the person with the wart. As soon as the dime is spent the wart will disappear. The dime is kept with the patient's other money so it cannot be distinguished." Warts may be transferred to another person merely by his counting them,[35] or by placing as many pebbles in a candy bag, or other kind of container, as there are warts. The bag is then left in some likely place to be picked up by an inquisitive person.[36] Utah, Idaho, and California examples do not involve rubbing the wart to impregnate the pebbles, but an instance from Vernal, Utah, runs true to the more traditional form, wherein stones, peas, and beans are rubbed on the warts and then disposed of in a roadway. Even so, the picking up of the new host objects is not recorded in this last-named instance. The use of a transient in the ritual of divestment is seen in a California prescription from Hollywood, wherein the itinerant person counts the warts, writes them (the number ?) on the inside of his hatband, and then magically takes the warts with him when he leaves town.

Aid of the dead in disposing of warts and other excrescences, and maladies of all kinds, is known in the United States, but this practice is no longer as common as it once was. From the western area of the country under survey, however, I have only two or three good examples, and two of these are from California. A friend of mine in Canoga Park, California, who had a goiter was once waiting for a green light at an intersection, when an unknown woman walked up and said: "Lady, if you place your hand on a dead person's throat, your goiter will go away."[37] The other item is a less striking variant of this well-known cure for goiter. As late as 1960 there is a report from Salt Lake City that a dead hand touched to a cancer will cure it.[38] In another Utah cure involving the dead, or objects connected with the dead, it was believed in Helper years ago that the cutting of a wart with a razor used to shave a dead person would cause the wart to disappear. Two other wart cures, both reported from California, involve traffic with the corpse. "When a corpse (in a funeral procession) goes by," the entry reads, "flick your wart, and say, 'Corpse take my wart with you.' Then forget about it, and the wart will soon be gone."[39] The other instance reveals the common practice of rubbing the wart with a rag, but instead of burying the rag in the usual way, it is placed in the coffin with the dead person. When the rag rots, the wart will be gone.

Communicating disease to animals and thus ridding oneself of the malady is a prominent form of magical divestment of sickness.[40] This transfer is accomplished by contact with the animal, usually a dog or a cat, in sleeping or in other kinds of contact. In the classical sense of magical transference, however, as I have discussed it elsewhere,[41] the animal manifestly contracts the disease, and often dies as a result. Three Utah examples, the earliest from Grantsville, about 1880, display this cardinal feature. The Grantsville item reads: "Three hairs taken from the cross of an ass will cure whooping cough, but the ass will die." A cure for this same disease is reported from Salt Lake in 1928: "Tie a hairy caterpillar in a bag around a child's neck. As the insect dies, the whooping cough will vanish."[42] The sacrificial role of the caterpillar, of course, is envisioned as part of the cure, and actually is thought to insure its success. The final Utah example, which was recorded in Salt Lake in 1953, is equally illuminating, and bears out the traditional pattern of eventual death to the creature to whom the disease has been communicated. "To cure warts, impale a frog on a stick and rub the warts on the frog. They will disappear as the frog dies."[43] In less drastic kinds of transference to animals, rheumatic diseases are cured by contact with the animal, usually a dog or a cat, in sleeping or in other kinds of contact.[44] Sleeping with a cat at the foot of the bed is recommended in

Nebraska, and a dog is thought to accomplish the same purpose in California. It is claimed in this same California entry that a cat sleeping with you will result in your contracting arthritis from the cat. The wearing of a cat's fur on one's skin is recommended in Utah for the cure of pneumonia and consumption.[45] In California and Nebraska the fur of both cats and dogs is recommended for rheumatism.[46] Merely keeping a Mexican Chihuahua dog in the house will ward off asthma, it is claimed in two entries from the Los Angeles area.[47] In an item from Murray, Utah, it is believed that sleeping on a bear rug will cure backache. In a very rare item from California, but possibly referable to Michigan, the cure of tuberculosis by sleeping in the hay with horses is recommended. Riddance of stone bruises by contact with a frog according to Oklahoma belief, and the loss of a wart in California by touching a frog are reported,[48] while in Utah it is recommended to let a horny toad crawl on the victim's bare skin so he can carry off the rheumatism.[49] In the same way, a snake wrapped around the neck will take the goiter with it when it disengages itself and crawls away, according to a Colorado belief.[50]

Chickens are used to consume grains of barley after the barley has been rubbed on the wart. In this way, both by symbolic and contagious principles, the fowl takes the wart as it ingests the kernel of barley. This belief and practice is reported from Oklahoma, but the observance is widely reported wherever standard collections of folk medicine have been made.[51] Another item from Oklahoma, far more inscrutable than the first, recommends a cure for night blindness wherein a chicken is made to jump over the sleeping victim. No explanation is given, nor can I offer one.

In folk medicine swallows figure importantly in maladies of the eye, and there is an interesting Utah belief in the ability of this bird to help in restoring sight. The first time you hear the swallow in the spring, it is said, if you go to a stream or fountain and wash your eyes, at the same time making a silent prayer, the swallows will carry away all your eye troubles. A brutal ritual in contagious magic is reported from California, wherein a congenitally blind person must secure a frog, gouge its eyes out, return the frog to the water alive, and then place the animal's eyeballs on his own neck, in order to regain his eyesight.

Oral contact with animals, or breathing their expired breath, is a category of folk medical therapy found in the area under survey, even though the tradition is not well known.[52] Kissing a donkey for the relief of toothache is reported from California and Utah, and having a full-bred stallion blow its breath in the face of the victim of whooping cough, is also reported from California,[53] although this cure ultimately comes from West Virginia. Spitting into the mouth of a frog is supposed to cure one of asthma, as reported in an instance from California. From the same state a recommended cure of whooping cough is to have the child cough into the mouth of a live fish.[54] In Utah, as three Salt Lake entries attest, toads are credited with being able to suck the poison of cancer from the system. One other magical cure involving the passage of air into the respiratory tract of the patient is the well-known cure of thrush by having a posthumous child breathe into the mouth of a baby with thrush, as is reported in a case from Bakersfield, California.[55]

A curious connection between headache and discarded hair combings that eventually are used in birds' nests is found in some California items, two of which stem from Louisiana and Georgia before the turn of the century.[56] Loss of hair is also reported from the misappropriation of a person's hair for nest building, as is seen in two Los Angeles county entries. Here, of course, harm to the hair, even though it is no longer connected with the person, results in harm to the person himself.

Transference of diseases to trees, generally rare in America, is found in only two reports. In Utah, around 1918, warts were transferred to an aspen tree by means of a piece of bacon. According to the classical requirements of such a transfer, the warts were thought to "grow on the tree and vanish from you," as the report states. Transference of diseases to trees by "plugging," "nailing," "wedging," and kindred means is more common in my sampling than communication to trees by means of strings, rubbing against the tree, and the like,[57] but, once more, it must be remembered that records of the practice in the western part of the country are scanty. In Missouri before the turn of the century, the victim probed a wart with a pin until it bled, and then stuck the pin into the tree.[58] Instead of the tree's getting the wart, as in normal procedures of this kind, it was supposed to be passed on to the first person who touched the pin. A more typical example of this general kind of transference, and one which I have called "wedging," is seen in a Utah example collected in Salt Lake as late as 1959: "Rub your warts with a piece of bacon, and then put the bacon in the slit of a tree. The warts will grow on the tree as knobs." To cure chills and fever in California, an "X" mark was cut in a persimmon tree, but details are lacking as to how the magical transfer took place. The incisions were made on different sides of the tree according to the seasons, as follows: summer: south; fall: west; winter: north; spring: east. In a wart cure reported from Los Angeles, a lock of the victim's hair is placed in the natural cleft of a tree, and he is supposed never to return to it. At best this is a secondary contagion, since the hair apparently was not brought into contact with the wart. Another California account of plugging runs truer to form: "To cure asthma cut a square from the door facing where the person gasped for breath. Take out a chunk of wood, cut a lock of hair off the person, and place it back in the hole; then cover it up with a chunk of wood.[59]

Magical "plugging" of diseases is frequently confused with magically outgrowing a disease by a procedure of "measuring." A good example of this confusion is contained in a curative ritual reported as a memorat from Tarzana, California. "To cure a child of asthma, stand he or she (sic) against a door-jamb and drill a hole just above the head. Put a hank of hair in the hole and plug. After the child has grown above the hole he or she will never have asthma again." In another cure for asthma, a prescription recorded in North Hollywood, a lock of the child's hair is cut and placed in the window sill. When the child grows as high as where the hair was placed, he will have outgrown the disease. Measuring a wart with a pine needle in Spanish Fork, Utah, and then burying it, seems to emphasize the magic of burial and decay more than that of measurement.[60] This would be true, too, of course, for all counting rituals having to do with warts, in which the string or thread is ultimately buried, there to await rotting and the magical disappearance of the warts.

The accounts at my disposal of "notching" as a magical folk medical practice are inadequate to convey this complicated ritual, which involves, in its various manifestations, not only notching as a measurement,[61] but also as a means of counting warts, and the like, and in some cases it also involves elements of plugging. A South Dakota entry, dating from World War I, simply involved notching a piece of wood and throwing it away to get rid of a wart. A more detailed procedure is indicated in a practice reported from Moab, Utah, in 1953, but referable to a much earlier date, wherein a notch was cut in a stick for every wart, and then some other person made to bury the stick. When the stick decayed, it was thought that the warts would be gone.

"Passing through," or "pulling through," as this symbolic curing ritual is known, is little reported from the western part of the United States, and it is also rapidly becoming a thing of the past elsewhere in America. A good example that fits the usual description of this healing ritual is an item from San Diego, California. If a child gets a rupture, to heal it one has to find a young living willow, or any other young suitable tree, cut it lengthwise at the time of the full moon, and then pass the child through the willow. Tie the two parts together, and as the tree grows together, so will the rupture heal together.[62] The Utah examples fill out the picture a bit. In southern Utah about 1920, for example, a person suffering from blackheads was made to creep on hands and knees under a bramble bush three times with the sun (clockwise) in order to be cured. In Logan, it was claimed as recently as 1938 that a child's cough could be cured by passing him three times underneath the belly of a horse. In enquiring for old medical practices of this sort, including such additional practices as pulling people through water-worn holes in stones, through rungs of ladders, and the like, one should not fail to mention the ailments for which these passing-through rituals are most often employed, namely, rupture, fits, whooping cough, rheumatism, rickets, epilepsy, and even boils. Blackheads, mentioned above, I should regard as being exceptional.

The circumscribing of an area within which the disease must remain, or an area within which the cure will be carried out, is one of the rarities of magical medicine. For this purpose rings or other ring-shaped objects are used, or string and thread are also pressed into service. In Moab, Utah, for example, some people wear lead around their necks, tied with buckskin, to keep mumps from "going down." For this same purpose a sock was tied around the neck in Centerville, Utah, in 1920, and a plain string as late as 1955 in Morgan County of the same state.[63] A Utah physician had encountered in his practice the custom of tying string around an infected area to confine the malady to that spot. It was stated that this was to "keep the spirit from going deeper into the body." Los Angeles public health nurses, for example, frequently find ribbons or string around the abdomens of pregnant Mexican women who wear them to protect the unborn child from harm and fairy influences of all kinds. Ringworm is circumscribed in New Mexico by placing a gold ring on it, drawing a circle around the ring, and then wearing the ring until the rash disappears.[64] In Los Angeles, for the same malady, one should spit on a golden thimble, place it on the affected spot, and turn it three times. This should be done by the light of the moon.[65]

Spitting as a means of divestment is seen in California and Utah cures for sideache, wherein the sufferer spits on a rock and either throws it away, or he spits under a stone, which he then replaces.[66] This is an aspect of burial of disease, it would seem. A more magical cure involves going to a crossroads at night and spitting to rid oneself of a sty,[67] as reported in a Utah item a few years ago. According to the belief, the sty will be gone by morning.

I am sorry that lack of space precludes my doing more with such relatively common magical practices as getting rid of warts by burial, measurement, notching, floating away, and the like. Likewise, curing rheumatism by various kinds of absorptive measures has had short shrift, and I have said nothing at all about the supposed magnetic and galvanic cures of this dread disease. These are subjects for independent treatment,[68] as is also the widespread use of various kinds of amulets in folk medical practice, including the still popular buckeye and the whole nutmeg pierced and suspended on a string around the throat. Verbal magic, finally, is also widely used in folk medicine, but this subject, too, must await a later discussion.

NOTES

1. By way of a start, John Q. Anderson has done a fine article on "The Magical Transfer of Disease in Texas Folk Medicine," *Western Folklore,* XXVII (1968), 191–199, and has completed a general book on folk medicine in Texas. Other articles of folk medicine in western states include the following: Austin E. Fife, "Pioneer Mormon Remedies," *Western Folklore,* XVI (1957), 153–162; Amy Lathrop, "Pioneer Remedies from Western Kansas," *ibid.,* XX (1961), 1–22. My own articles have treated the West only incidentally, except for a short essay on "The Common Cold in Utah Folk Medicine," in *Lore of Faith and Folly,* ed. Thomas E. Cheney, Austin E. Fife, and Juanita Brooks (Salt Lake City: University of Utah Press, 1971), pp. 243–250. (See this present volume, pp. 321–329.)

2. *Dictionnaire encyclopédique des sciences médicales,* 4ème sér, tome 14 (Paris, 1888), 239–255, s.v. "Homéopathie." Cf. Gerard Bakker, *Positive Homöopathie* (Ulm, 1960). The practice of homeopathic medicine continues in many countries even today. For example, there are twenty-one drug stores in Santiago de Chile alone that handle homeopathic preparations of various kinds, and the licensed sale of these medicaments throughout this South American republic amounts to big business. For a discussion of homeopathic principles and analogic magic in general, see *Handwörterbuch des deutschen Aberglaubens* (10 vols., Berlin, 1927–1942), I, 385–395, s.v. "Analogiezauber." (Cited: HDA.)

3. Gustav Jungbauer, *Deutsche Volksmedizin. Ein Grundriss* (Berlin und Leipzig, 1934), 79–84; Adolf Wuttke, *Der deutsche Volksaberglaube der Gegenwart* (3rd ed., Elard Hugo Meyer, Berlin 1900), 321–322, Section 477.

4. Pliny and the ancients seem to have known in a general way of homeopathic principles. Cf. Wilfrid Bonser, *The Medical Background of Anglo-Saxon England. A Study in History, Psychology, and Folklore* (London, 1963), ch. 15 "Sympathetic Magic." These rudimentary notions concerning the nature of organic materials were also known in Germanic antiquity. Cf. Eugen Mogk, *Germanische Mythologie* (Sammlung Göschen, Bd. 15, Leipzig, 1906), 98.

5. *Dictionnaire encyclopédique des sciences médicales,* 3ème sér., 6. 9 (Paris, 1881), 615–618, s.v. "signatures mystiques."

6. This item is traceable to the informant's grandfather who came from Denmark before 1910, although one informant claimed to have heard it at a medical convention.

7. The ages of the three informants contributing the four items on the subject are: 16, 25, 54.

8. *Frank C. Brown Collection of North Carolina Folklore* (7 vols., Durham, North Carolina, 1952–1964; vols. VI–VII *Popular Beliefs and Superstitions from North Carolina,* ed., Wayland D. Hand, 1961–1964), VI, 241, No. 1874 (notes only). (Hereinafter cited: Brown, No. . . . Unless otherwise stated, all references are to Vol. VI.)

9. Brown, No. 1875; Austin E. Fife, "Pioneer Mormon Remedies," *WF,* XVI (1957), 157, 160; Janice C. Neal, "Grandad—Pioneer Medicine Man," *New York Folklore Quarterly,* XI (1955), 291.

10. *Journal of American Folklore,* LVII (1944), 41, 46 (yellow root [Catawba Indians, South Carolina]). (Hereinafter cited: JAF.)

11. Cf. Neal, p. 289 (use of carrots recommended, but not in the way specified in the second Utah item.)

12. Reported by a physician from his own medical practice in Salt Lake in 1959.

13. Brown, No. 1532 (notes); Amy Lathrop, "Pioneer Remedies from Western Kansas," *WF,* XX (1961), 9.

14. Brown, No. 1040.

15. Brown, No. 991; Fife, WF, XVI (1957), 160.

16. Brown, No. 1293; George D. Hendricks, *Mirrors, Mice & Mustaches: A Sampling of Superstitions and Popular Beliefs in Texas* (Austin, Texas: University of Texas Press, "Paisano Books," No. 1, 1966), 33; JAF, LXVIII (1955), 131 (Mexican Indian).

17. Cf. Brown, Nos. 2141–2143; WF, X (1951), 78 (New Mexico: Indian).

18. Brown, Nos. 1019–1024; Hendricks, p. 36.

19. The reader will find numerous examples in the Brown Collection, Nos. 85–113.

20. HDA, I, 902, s.v. "Bär" (bear fat as weapon salve).

21. Cf. Brown, Nos. 1403, 1781–1790, 2756–2757.

22. Brown, VI, xxviii.

23. Brown, No. 278; WF, XXVIII (1964), 76 (Kansas: playing with matches).

24. Jungbauer, 85; HDA, VII, 845–846, s.v. "rückwarts."

25. The classic statement on contagious magic, as well as for his treatment of all other forms of sympathetic magic, was made by James George Frazer in the *Golden Bough* (3rd ed., 12 vols., London, 1911–1915), I, ch. III (52–219).

26. Jungbauer, 89–91.

27. See Wayland D. Hand, "The Magical Transference of Disease," *North Carolina Folklore,* XIII (1965), 83–109. (Hereinafter cited: Hand, Transference.)

28. Hand, Transference, 84 (and notes).

29. The transference of warts is a subject of great complexity; so the reader is advised to familiarize himself with the section devoted to warts in the Brown Collection (VI, 309–350). Random items of interest: Nos. 2428, 2439, 2446, 2452, 2468, 2484, 2497, 2540, 2586, 2610, 2627, 2645, 2660, etc., etc. Western examples not cited in Brown include Fife, WF, XVI (1957), 159; Earl J. Stout, *Folklore from Iowa* (Memoirs of the American Folklore Society, XXIX, 1936), No. 761.

30. Brown, Nos. 2675–2683; Ida Mae McKinney, "Superstitions of the Missouri Ozarks," *Tennessee Folklore Society Bulletin,* XVIII (1952), 107; Stout, No. 761.

31. Hand, Transference, 84–85, *passim.*

32. Brown, Nos. 2684–2686.

33. Brown, No. 2685.

34. Western wart cures of this kind are not as clear with regard to the manner of transmittal of the warts to others as elsewhere in the United States. Cf. Hand, Transference, 89.

35. Brown, No. 2417.

36. Brown, No. 2639.

37. Cf. Wayland D. Hand, "Hangmen, the Gallows, and the Dead Man's Hand in American Folk Medicine" (forthcoming). (See pp. 69–80 of this volume.)

38. Pauline Monette Black, *Nebraska Folk Cures* (University of Nebraska Studies in Language, Literature, and Criticism, No. 15, Lincoln, 1935), 38, No. 93.

39. This item may stem from Germany.

40. Hand, Transference, 91–98.

41. On this subject I have elsewhere written that "To claim our attention here the disease must be communicated to second parties or things, and it must be expressly stated, or clearly implied, that the disease is received by a new victim, or a new receiving agent that is itself affected by the transfer. Neither does communication to an intermediate agent, a *Zwischenträger,* suffice for this discussion. Ideally for the argument of this study, it should be shown that when the disease is communicated from the victim to other persons, or to animals, it will continue its ravages or induce disease or death in the new victim." (Hand, Transference, 83–84.)

42. Although there are several references in my files from the British Isles and elsewhere, I have accumulated only one American example, namely, a reference to Quebec (*Folk-Lore,* XXIV [1913], 360–361). Cf. *Notes and Queries,* 9th Series, Vol. 12 (Aug. 15, 1903), 26; William George Black, *Folk-Medicine. A Chapter in the History of Culture* (Publications of the Folk-Lore Society, XII, London, 1883), 61.

43. Cf. Brown, No. 2453; also No. 2454.

44. Brown, Nos. 1973, 1975.

45. Brown, No. 1188.

46. Brown, Nos. 1973, 1975; Hendricks, *Mirrors,* 51.

47. Cf. Hendricks, *Mirrors,* 32, 51 (rheumatism); *Kentucky Folklore Record,* II (1956), 134–136. This last reference contains basic material.

48. This would seem to be by some kind of reverse magic, for usually one acquires warts by touching or handling frogs. Cf. Brown, No. 2410.

49. Cf. Brown, No. 1993 (toad).

50. Black, *Nebraska,* 35, No. 40; *Southern Folklore Quarterly* X (1946), 166.

51. Cf. Brown, Nos. 2502–2507 (corn rather than barley).

52. See Wayland D. Hand, "Folk Medical Inhalants in Respiratory Disorders," *Medical History,* XII (1968), 153–163.

53. Hand, Inhalants, 157; Brown, No. 2717.

54. Hand, Inhalants, 158; cf. Brown, No. 2712.

55. Hand, Inhalants, 159; Brown, No. 413.

56. Brown, No. 1578.

57. Cf. Wayland D. Hand, "Plugging, Nailing, Wedging, and Kindred Folk Medical Practices," in Bruce Jackson, ed., *Folklore & Society, Essays in Honor of Benj. A. Botkin* (Hatboro, Pennsylvania, 1966), 63–75. Cf. HDA, index, s.v. "verbohren," "vernageln," "verpflöcken." (Hereinafter cited: Hand, Plugging.)

58. Cf. Brown, Nos. 2662–2664.

59. Cf. Hand, Plugging, 66–67.

60. For the "measuring" of warts, see Brown, Nos. 2613–2615.

61. For examples of the "notching" of warts, see Brown, Nos. 2616–2620.

62. For a fuller discussion of this subject, see Wayland D. Hand, " 'Passing Through': Folk Medical Magic and Symbolism," *Proceedings of the American Philosophical Society,* Vol. 112, No. 6 (1968), 379–402. Cf. HDA, index, s.v. "durchkriechen," "durchlaufen," "durchziehen."

63. Brown, No. 1832.

64. Cf. Brown, No. 2087.

65. Cf. Brown, Nos. 2085–2086.

66. Cf. Brown, Nos. 2104, 2107.

67. Cf. Daniel Lindsey Thomas and Lucy Blayney Thomas, *Kentucky Superstitions* (Princeton, N.J., 1920), No. 1363.

68. Cf. Brown, Nos. 2051–2068.

23

The Common Cold in Utah Folk Medicine*

The common cold, still as baffling to modern medical men as it was to their confrères of an earlier generation, claims more attention in Utah folk medical practice than any other single malady. What was once largely the concern of granny women and other folk medical practitioners in the diagnosis and arrest of the disease has lived on in families and in individuals in the form of individual folk notions and curative practices. Taken as a whole, these beliefs and customs concerning colds, and folk medical lore generally, constitute a body of traditional lore from early times that is only now being slowly discarded with the advance of medical science. It is one of the ironies of this scientific advance, and of cultural history generally, that some of the practices now falling into desuetude themselves derived from the medical learning of an earlier day.

Folk medical beliefs presented in this paper constitute only a sampling of Utah material, but they accord in a general way with folk medical lore found elsewhere in America.[1] In making no apology for a limited survey of only one small subject field of folk medicine, the author can only hope that this article will stimulate further study in a broader field of inquiry that is only beginning. Much folk medical material can still be collected in

*This article originally appeared in *Lore of Faith and Folly*. Ed. Thomas E. Cheney, Austin E. Fife, and Juanita Brooks. Salt Lake City: University of Utah Press, 1971, pp. 243–250. Permission to reprint has been given by the editors and by the University of Utah Press.

oral tradition, especially from older people, but to give historical perspective whole treasures must be unearthed from old diaries and daybooks, books of recipes, and special treatises on the part played by early-day practitioners of folk medicine, if such records can still be found.[2]

There are very few beliefs about colds and sore throats in Utah that involve ominal or causative magic. In fact, there is very little lore that deals with catching a cold. Perhaps the common ways of catching a cold are too well known for informants to have enumerated them. However, in Vernal one person at least in a family is said to come down with a cold if a cat sneezes or coughs (ominal). An informant from Salt Lake claims that the wearing of overshoes in the house brings on a cold (causative), a belief deriving from his English forebears.

Preventive measures against colds fall into magical as well as regular prophylactic treatments. We shall consider the items of pure folklore first. In 1961 a ninth-grader in a Salt Lake school reported that if you catch a falling autumn leaf you will not have a cold all winter. The wearing of necklaces, strings, and even hosiery and socks around the neck, as elsewhere, has been noted for Utah.[3] A necklace of amber beads is noted in two items from Salt Lake, both recent.[4] The keeping of a black silk cord as a protection against a cold is noted from Kearns in the 1930's, while any string around the neck is prescribed for the same purpose in an unplaced entry from 1961 designated as "an old American belief." A silk-stitched chain worn around the neck to prevent sore throat is another Salt Lake item noted in 1957, but also known in Sandy. The well-known prescription of a dirty sock worn around the neck against sore throat is recorded from Delta in 1930. This same procedure, widely used in cures, is treated below.

The wearing of asafetida around the neck, either in a chunk or in the more common asafetida bags is apparently common in Utah.[5] The theory is that by its strong smell, asafetida wards off disease. Another notion is that this noisome plant substance absorbs disease and miasmas. This practice is prescribed in five items of fairly recent date from Salt Lake, one of which represents an importation from Georgia through a Negro woman, ca. 1920. That the practice was widely known and tolerably old as such material goes is seen from entries from Ogden (ca. 1900), Bountiful (ca. 1910), Richfield (1915), Heber City (1916), Roy (1920), Layton (1934). The same preventive is noted for sore throat: Magna (1920), Salt Lake (1961), but referable to Georgia, ca. 1920 (Negro).

Garlic was worn around the neck much for the same reason as asafetida, although notions of it as a general purifactory agent are widespread, particularly in Europe. Moreover, its use in magically induced ailments (witchcraft and the evil eye), places it in the category of a general apotropaic agent. Although the practice is very old, whether the garlic is worn in a bag or in cloves, attestations in the UCLA collection are relatively recent: Midvale (1950), Vernal (1951; also 1956 from an Indian), Ogden (1957).[6] Items from Salt Lake (clove) and Magna (bag), both collected in 1963, show how both practices have persisted side by side. The wearing of the garlic in a dirty sock around the neck is noted from Midvale for 1948, and from Magna in 1963.

The therapeutic uses of onion parallel those of garlic in many ways; also here in the prevention of colds. An onion hung around the neck was prescribed in Bountiful, 1958, and this belief was noted in Salt Lake the same year. The placing of an onion under the pillow to ward off colds was noted from Bountiful in 1933, but is traceable to kinfolk coming from upper New York state. The eating of onions to prevent colds, as well as the far more prevalent use of them once a cold has been contracted, is a prescription learned from a sixty-seven-year-old woman in Salt Lake in 1964.[7]

Miscellaneous preventives include the dousing of boys' heads in water after haircuts to keep them from taking cold (1957, no place mentioned; probably Salt Lake) and the wetting of one's feet daily in salt water (Salt Lake?, ca. 1900). An item from Provo, dating from around 1900, and not entirely clear, states that no child ever catches cold from its own spit or its own "pea." One more matter-of-fact view, remembered in Salt Lake from the year 1913, holds that if you got a cold or the flu, it was always due to something you had done, such as becoming chilled or otherwise neglecting yourself during cold or rainy weather. Unexplained in any way is a "rose cold," represented as being a dangerous kind of cold (Salt Lake, 1961).

In the cure of colds and sore throat, magical therapeutic agents, as in the case of preventive measures, will be discussed first. Protective and heat applications, ointments, plasters, gargles, foods, and teas and decoctions will then be taken up, in that order.

From the field of magical folk medicine, then: To cure a cold you are supposed to plant a rusty nail six feet from the east side of your house, and in two or three days your cold will go away (Salt Lake, ca. 1915). A more important item, since it ties in to the folk medical concepts of "measuring," and perhaps also to "plugging," is an item from Salt Lake dating from 1950: If you tie a lock of your hair to a stick, it will cure a cold. This item is unusual in the sense that sticks are used in "measuring," generally, and hair in "plugging."[8] The hanging of nutmegs around the throat to cure colds (Salt Lake, 1958; Bountiful, 1959) and sore throat (Ogden, 1959) implies magical connections in view of the wide use of nutmeg as an amulet.[9] The binding of asafetida on a rag around the neck to cure a sore throat (Bear River City, 1957),[10] and the hanging of an onion around the throat (Salt Lake, 1964) and on a wet string for the same purpose (Salt Lake, 1963), are perhaps somewhat less magical in character. Nondescript is the following: For sore throat tie a piece of unwashed lamb's hair dunked in brandy around your neck (Salt Lake, 1932). Other items, partly magical, but perhaps better to be explained in terms of the warding off and absorption of disease and corruption, deal with crushing onions underfoot and leaving them in the room. Four items, all from Salt Lake (1955–1963) attest to this practice, one of them specifying the treading of the onions with bare feet (1954). One of these items contains a possible clue to this rather curious usage, namely, the inhalation of the odor (1963). Onions quartered and placed in each window of the house is a kindred practice, but is not further explained (Salt Lake, 1964). The placing of a cut potato under the bed, cut side up, for the purpose of drying up a cold, is a related notion (Bountiful, 1960), although absorption rather than an exuded odor or inhalant properties would seem to explain this practice.

The binding of stockings around the neck, which appears to have been applied with some intended magical efficacy in the prevention of cold and sore throat, becomes a regular therapeutic device in their treatment, namely, as applications of warmth and protection.[11] This is especially true in the case of sore throat, which will be taken up first. Of eight items collected in Salt Lake between 1900 and 1964, four recommend the wearing of a "dirty sock" around the neck and one a sock "worn that day." A stocking worn on the left foot is prescribed in two items (1957, 1958), a detail which reveals lingering magical aspects of the practice.[12] A woolen sock is indicated in an entry from 1900. Elsewhere in the state the "dirty sock" treatment is reported from Randolph (1910), Murray (1935), Bingham (1944), and Bountiful (1960). Variations include a "stocking you have been wearing" (Honeyville, 1902), and "a soiled wool sock" (Bear River City, 1957, but referable to the early 1930's).

Red flannel cloths, widely known elsewhere in the United States, apparently are little prescribed for sore throat.[13] The UCLA files contain only one entry, an item from Salt Lake (1957). Important also for its magical connections is the following item from Salt Lake (1928): When you wrap a wet rag around your neck when you have a sore throat, the evil spirits are chased away. Magical rather than therapeutic also, apparently, is the application of a rubber band around the arm (N.B.!).

The binding of a dirty sock around the neck to cure colds is reported in eight texts from Salt Lake, and from Salt Lake County (Hunter), but the time span is very recent (1958 to date). Whether "a clean silk stocking" is prescribed (three entries), "a worn stocking," or "a dirty woolen sock," the practice is all to the same end. Two entries specify that the sock should be kept around the neck overnight. A related cure recommended in Hooper about 1890 is clearly magical rather than curative: If a person has a summer cold, tie a string around his neck and the cold will go away.

Applications of heat for the cure of colds, over and above the protection and warmth afforded by the proverbial "dirty sock," involve the placing of a heated brick to the neck. This may be done by putting the brick in a sack and placing it on the neck as one reclines (Salt Lake, 1962, but referable to 1920). An ice pack on one's head and a hot brick in a sack on one's neck is a variation involving the contrast of heat and cold therapy (Salt Lake, 1955). The application of bricks to the head, with no mention of heat in connection with the bricks (Salt Lake, 1955), must be regarded as exceptional. So far as the author knows, bricks are used magically only in love divinations.

The use of salves, whether those of a single ingredient or compounds, is still tolerably widespread, as is the application of plasters, a practice that will be taken up later. Rubbing oneself with goose grease (presumably the neck?) is a cure dating from the 1890's or before (Salt Lake?).[14] Even though goose grease is not as easily available as it once was, this cure is noted from the same area as recently as 1945. The greasing of the neck and chest with hot skunk oil is noted from Provo in 1945 and from Salt Lake somewhat before that. A third Utah entry, stemming from the Ozarks, was collected in Salt Lake in 1964, but goes back twenty years. Goat tallow applied to the neck and chest (1945; no place), camphor and lard (1945; no place),[15] and plain grease rubbed on the soles of the feet (Salt Lake, 1964), are other ointments involving animal fat. Raw sliced onions in kerosene, made into an ointment, was used in the informant's (Salt Lake, 1963) family "for generations."

Plasters of various kinds, widely used in an earlier day, still linger on in the curing of colds, sore throats, and kindred maladies. Plasters were made by covering brown paper, or pieces of cloth, with various curative agents. Sometimes brown paper alone was used, especially for cold in the lungs (Salt Lake, 1890's; 1944). Plasters made of animal fat include a bacon rind hung around the neck (Salt Lake, 1957),[16] a strip of fresh bacon held in place around the throat by a dirty sock (Lehi, 1957), black pepper on a strip of bacon, with the pepper next to the neck (Tooele, 1957). All three plasters are prescribed for a sore throat, the last one for sore throat in a child. Other sore throat plasters made of pork involve a slice of pork fat under a flannel cloth (1943; no place),[17] a strip of salt pork bacon with drops of turpentine applied to the neck with a woolen sock (Salt Lake, 1906), and a piece of "salted pork on your throat" (Ogden, 1919). A scatological poultice of chicken droppings placed in a cloth and tied around the neck (Salt Lake, 1915), must be regarded as a curiosity, even though the use of animal excrements, particularly sheep droppings, has lingered on into our own time in American folk medicine. Among the varieties of plasters made of vegetable products, one can note only the use of mustard plasters on the chest and back for colds (and also pneumonia) (Salt Lake, 1930, but traceable to 1888 within the informant's family)[18] and an onion plaster on the chest, also for a cold (1945; no place); and likewise on the neck (Salt Lake, 1945). Carrots in a cloth around the neck are said to relieve sore throat (Salt Lake, 1940).

Gargles prescribed include the following: Gargle with salt water every two hours—the water being as hot as you can take—to cure sore throat (Salt Lake, 1961), salt and vinegar for colds (Salt Lake, ca. 1910; 1945, no place), and gunpowder and glycerin mixed (Salt Lake, 1941; 1944, no place). Boil the inner bark from an oak tree until you obtain a dark brown fluid; cool and gargle with it three times a day for sore throat (Vernal, ca. 1910).[19]

Eating a large amount of food is a good cure for a cold (Salt Lake, 1963).[20] This theory is expressed in an old proverb, "Feed (stuff) a cold and starve a fever," which appears to be fairly well known in Utah even on the basis of a limited sampling (Salt Lake, 1961, 1963).[21] The variant reading, "Starve a fever and feed a cold," is likewise known (Payson, 1900; Salt

Lake, 1928).[22] Laxatives for colds "to clean out the system," as everyone knows, are widely prescribed, but the files contain only one entry (Woods Cross, 1891).

The eating of special foods, as well as the drinking of teas and the taking of tonics, should be noted. Onions are taken in a variety of ways: Onions cure a cold (Salt Lake, 1960); eat a whole onion, go straight to bed, and keep covered up (Salt Lake, 1961); onion juice, made by putting sugar on sliced onions and putting them in a warm oven so the sugar would draw the juice out (Bear River City, 1957);[23] cooked onions (Salt Lake, 1964);[24] fried onions (Salt Lake, 1910, 1942; Provo, 1943). Raisins likewise are prescribed for sore throat (Salt Lake, ca. 1880, 1910, 1943; 1942, no place). Other foods, or combinations of foods, include yeast sprinkled on food (Hunter, 1950), and molasses and soy beans mixed together (Salt Lake, 1950), both items being prescribed for colds. Ginger is said to cure a sore throat (1930's, no place), but no details are given (See ginger tea in the next paragraph). Cinnamon and sugar mixed well, but apparently taken dry, were swabbed around the tonsils to cure sore throat (Salt Lake, 1932).

A variety of teas and other decoctions were also used in combating colds. Among the teas were hog ginger tea (Salt Lake 1910),[25] horehound tea (1942, 1945, places not mentioned),[26] a tea made of sage and catnip (Salt Lake, 1910; 1943, no place).[27] Brigham tea goes back to an earlier period.[28] Vinegar and honey (Salt Lake, 1963), lemon juice and honey (Salt Lake, 1920), and a syrup made of vinegar, butter, and molasses (Salt Lake, 1942) were taken more in the manner of medicines than of teas. Tabasco sauce was taken as a medicine as colds were coming on (Salt Lake, 1954). A drink made of three parts mustard and two parts cornstarch water was administered for colds (Salt Lake, 1950 [Irish]). Two or three drops of kerosene in a teaspoonful of sugar was known in Provo around 1900. Kerosene on a feather heals sore throat (Salt Lake, ca. 1915), but the entry lacks details as to how the treatment was carried out.

The favorite American nostrum for colds, whiskey, did not lack adherents in Utah.[29] Taken straight—often hot (Helper, 1930)—qualified by rock candy (Salt Lake, ca. 1910; 1945 [two items]; 1950), or taken with aspirin (Salt Lake, ca. 1920), whiskey was a specific against the common cold in the homes of any save the most devout Mormons.

There is very little on the duration of colds or on their recurrence. The following two items may serve as an aid to collectors in bringing in further items in a subject field that must have endless variety: If a person catches a cold on an even day of the month, he will get over it soon, but if he gets one on an odd day, he shall have "phenomena" soon (Salt Lake, 1957). If you take a bath while you have a cold in winter time, you'll surely not recover (Salt Lake, 1964; heard originally in Mexico).

After the foregoing, it will perhaps come as no surprise that even dried rats' tails will cure a cold (Murray, 1963), but the reader must forego specific information on this engaging entry. In normal folk medical practices, as we have seen, treatment for colds is undertaken in two main ways, internal dosing or external applications. Take your pick.

NOTES

1. There has been very little published on folk medicine in Utah. Austin E. Fife's fine article, "Pioneer Morman Remedies," *Western Folklore* 16 (1957): 153–62 (hereafter cited as Fife), is about the only general survey to which the reader may be referred. The present study rests on the author's field collecting in Utah in 1957 and before, and on material collected from Utahns and former Utahns in his folklore classes over the years at UCLA. Mainly, however, the article rests on the extensive folklore collectanea of Anthon S. Cannon at the University of Utah during the past several years. Entries are naturally weighted heavily in favor of Salt Lake and environs, but material stemming from elsewhere in the state shows that there was once a representative body of folk medicine known throughout the Utah territory. If nothing more, this study bears out the strong need to launch folklore collecting projects at several strategic spots throughout the Beehive State.

2. These rare personal documents may still occasionally be encountered in private hands, but many kinds of useful information of this sort are on deposit in public archives such as those of the Utah State Historical Society and the Daughters of the Utah Pioneers.

3. Readings from North Carolina, with comparative notes from elsewhere in the country, are to be found in my edition of *Popular Beliefs and Superstitions from North Carolina* (*Frank. C. Brown Collection of North Carolina Folklore,* vol. 6 [Durham, North Carolina: 1961]: 76–357, hereafter cited as Brown); cf. nos. 1141, 1144, 2208, *passim.*

4. Brown, no. 2218.

5. Brown, no. 1099; Fife, p. 161.

6. General items in the field of popular beliefs and superstitions, published and unpublished, are being collected from all over America at the Center for the Study of Comparative Folklore and Mythology, University of California at Los Angeles. The Utah material, including a special monograph on the human body, folk medicine, and the life cycle, will be edited by Wayland D. Hand and A. S. Cannon within the next five years. (The Utah Collection, edited by Wayland D. Hand and Jeannine E. Talley, will be published by the University of Utah Press in 1981.)

7. Brown, no. 1112.

8. Brown, nos. 828 (notes), 829 for "measuring" and 1923f for "plugging."

9. Brown, no. 2106. For a more general application see no. 757.
10. Cf. Brown, no. 1099.
11. Brown, nos. 2209ff.
12. Brown, no. 2211.
13. Brown, nos. 1140, 2208.
14. Cf. Brown, nos. 1127, 2192.
15. Brown, no. 1129.
16. Brown, no. 2188; Fife, p. 156.
17. Cf. Brown, no. 2190.
18. Brown, no. 1132; Fife, p. 161.
19. Cf. Brown, no. 2200.
20. Brown, no. 1100.
21. Brown, no. 1102, where reference is given to Stuart A. Gallacher's treatment of this old medical proverb, "Stuff a Cold and Starve a Fever," *Bulletin of the History of Medicine* 11 (1942): 576–81.
22. Brown, no. 1410.
23. Brown, no. 1113.
24. Cf. Brown, no. 1112; Fife, p. 161.
25. Brown, no. 1107.
26. Brown, no. 1110; Fife, p. 161.
27. Brown, no. 1106, 1120.
28. Fife, p. 154.
29. Cf. Brown, no. 1117; Fife, p. 154.

Index

Compositor: Freedmen's Organization
Text: Baskerville, Compugraphic
Printer: Thomson-Shore
Paper: 50lb P&S Offset Vellum, acid-free
Glatfelter Paper Mill